The **DIGIT**

Revolut

The DIGITAL Revolution

ASIS Mid-Year 1996

Proceedings of the ASIS Mid-Year Meeting

San Diego, California
May 18-22, 1996

Editor and Contributed Papers Chair
Gretchen Whitney
The University of Tennessee

Technical Program Chair
José-Marie Griffiths
The University of Tennessee

SIG Sessions Chair
Carol Hert
Indiana University

Published for the
American Society for Information Science
by
Information Today, Inc.
Medford, New Jersey
1996

ISBN: 1-57387-028-5

The opinions expressed by contributors to this publication do not necessarily reflect the position or official policy of the American Society for Information Science.

Cover Design: Jeanne Wachter
            Bette Tumasz

Printed in the United States of America

CONTENTS

Part 1: Contributed Papers

Part 2: SIG Sessions

Preface to the Proceedings

The original call for participation in the Conference read, in part:

"As the Industrial Revolution radically altered the means of production and transformed in the process the way people viewed their work, their societies, and each other, so too the Digital Revolution has the potential to profoundly alter the way that societies function at the global, local and personal level.

The Digital Revolution, simply put, involves both subtle as well as radical changes in the way that information is created (by anyone, for example, with a home page or e-mail account as a soapbox), stored (in media, as yet unknown in archival quality), and transmitted (more and more of it, faster and faster in numbers we struggle to comprehend).

We would like to think that the effects will be felt by everyone: and in terms of population groups this is true: young as well as old, men as well as women, any ethnic or national group you can name. No employment category (nor the unemployed) will be left out: academics, clergy, police, architects, sales clerks. But parts of these groups will be left out: and the distance between those included and those not included is widening.

Any discussion of information demands the consideration of many paradoxes. Perhaps the most important paradox for this conference is that of information's economic nature: it is an important economic good, but also it is an essential component of all political and social interaction, especially in open, democratic societies. It is a social good that contributes to THE social good: exacerbating the distance between those that have and those that do not.

The conference is an exploration of the issues of and the effects that this Revolution is having - or will have - on the ways we conduct business, the ways that we teach, and the ways that we interact to build a social structure that forms our society. The conference seeks to identify and understand the dynamics of these changes, and to develop and debate methodologies for this assessment."

These ideas have been expanded and enhanced in the proceedings, both in the Contributed Papers and in the SIG sessions. Perhaps most striking in the collection, though, is the emphasis by the participants on various user groups, and this is most evident in the index to the Proceedings. It is clear that while the authors and contributors are concerned about new techniques, or of providing faster and more effective ways of doing things, in the end it is the affect on users in different groupings that is of deep concern. And these concerns span the Conference themes of business, education, and societal changes.

The Proceedings are divided into two parts. The Contributed Papers are presented in the themes that organized the conference. These themes also organized the presentation of papers themselves. The SIG Sessions, which follow, also are in the order that they were presented at the conference.

The Author Index and Subject Index follow. The Author Index includes names of Contributed Paper authors and SIG session contributors, panelists, and participants.

The plenary sessions, continuing education sessions, tours, and special sessions are detailed on the printout of the home page of the program, as of the date this document went to press. Updates to these are included on the Conference program home page accessible through the ASIS web site at http://www.asis.org. Also, any updates to papers received after the final printing of this document are linked there.

Impact on Business I: Changes in Direction

An Integrated Approach to Creating the Information-Enabled Organization: Actions in Support of Change

Michael O. Luke
Atomic Energy of Canada Limited
Whiteshell Laboratories
Pinawa, Manitoba

In this presentation the opportunity for organizations to develop comprehensive and well-integrated approaches to the use of information is briefly outlined. This opportunity arises as a result of dramatic changes in the information environment. It is not a simple matter to exploit the opportunity because of several significant impediments to change including an overemphasis on information technology, human resistance to change, unrealistic expectations, and limitations of conventional cost/benefit analyses. Some suggestions are provided about how to develop appropriate action agendas for developing information-enabled organizations based on various methods of getting organized, promoting awareness and taking action. Action programs include information and knowledge mapping, formation of interdisciplinary teams, a focus on users and creative project rationales. The usefulness of action agendas is two-fold: first as a means of improving the effectiveness of the business functions and processes within organizations and second to assist in formulating and reinforcing research objectives aimed at enlarging and improving the set of methods and tools from which those wishing to work towards the information-enabled organization can draw.

1. Introduction

A year and a half ago, Peter Drucker [1] wrote, boldly, "the corporation that is now emerging is being designed around a skeleton: information", but went on to point out that "the majority of enterprises have yet to start the job..... of building systems to gather and organize .... information." Since then there have been many signs of vigorous interest in information. For example development of intranets is now proceeding rapidly [2] and many organizations have found ways to improve their effectiveness through the systematic capture and analysis of information, both internal and external. However, Drucker's words still remain largely true. Many organizations are applying at least some of the results of the on-going information revolution to their business or function, but few if any have yet devised integrated, coherent and comprehensive programs to do so. Indeed, most organizations are like consumers in a large and very noisy supermarket that is being reorganized radically even as they shop, a supermarket in which advertisers have entered the premises in force and pitch their wares from the isles, that is they are confused, incoherent and stressed out.

How can we assist organizations to adopt an information-centric approach to managing change? And how can we help them leap the hurdles that confront them in moving towards an improved information environment? As information scientists and specialists, we have a special obligation to help pose such questions and to try to answer them. This presentation provides a generic, integrated approach towards the use of information as a central focus for improving organizational effectiveness and becoming what I call information-enabled.

2. Forces Driving the Information Revolution

When we consider the forces at work in the business and economic environment and in the world of organizations of all kinds, what do we find? Most of us already have seen this theater - the sets, the actors, how the lights work and so on - but let's just step back and review it briefly together with fresh eyes before we turn to the new play we are about to put on.

Some of the drivers of change in the information environment are show in Table 1 and described in more detail in the text that follows..

TABLE 1.   Change Drivers

1) Downsizing and restructuring
2) Leverage of data, information and knowledge
3) The move to "wired" science and "wired"

place
5) The evolution of the extended enterprise

2.1 Downsizing and delayering in organizations

Stirred by competitive pressures and the development of global markets, the far from exhausted force for downsizing creates a need for systems that give employees (contract and permanent), prompt, direct access to the information they require to do their jobs and to help them cope with increased work loads and fewer support staff. The rise of the mercenary workforce and piece-work managers has also created the need for better methods of providing context and background information to employees and contract staff.

2.2 Leverage of data, information and knowledge

The effective capture and use of internal and external information is rapidly becoming a precondition for business success. Organizations such as Canadian Imperial Bank of Commerce [3], Dow Chemical [3], Hughes Aircraft [3], Zenaca Pharmaceuticals [4], several large health care organizations [5], the RCMP [6], and a great many others have identified specific ways to become more effective and productive by leveraging their internal information. Data mining allows organizations to focus their services and marketing sharply [7].

2.3 The move to "wired science" and "wired business"

Business activity of all kinds increasingly is based on a rapid flow of electronic information and data. There has been an explosive growth in the Internet and a concomitant move to replace conventional methods of communicating and distributing information of all kinds. Banks, hospitals, government, insurance companies, libraries, universities, are all affected . Online authoring, the rise of hypermedia online journals [8] and the establishment of digital libraries [9] provide increasingly potent information interconnectedness.

2.4 A dramatic increase in the information intensity of work and knowledge work in particular

In many areas of science and technology, the ability to capture and manipulate large amounts of information has become a key factor in the development of understanding, new products, new levels of service and improved efficiency. This trend is clear in health care, the retail trade, banking, aerospace, the automotive industry and in fact in most sectors of the economy. Scientific collaboratories demonstrate how this functions in the scientific community. In general terms, the amount of information needed to make effective decisions is on the increase as the pace of business accelerates.

2.5 The move towards the extended enterprise

Leading organizations are laying the foundations for what they believe will be future success by establishing strong information links between the organization and its customers, stakeholders and suppliers. Electronic commerce breaks the normal physical and geographical bounds between organizations. This increasingly intimate electronic interconnectedness poses complex challenges and opportunities.

These trends are emerging against a background of rapid change on a global basis. The world of a hundred years ago was one third the size of today's world in terms of population [10], one fortieth speaking in terms of manufacturing output [11] and one hundredth on the basis of information [12]. The basic, fundamental human experience and the difficult questions may not have changed much over time, but the trappings and methods of our lives and our work have been altered and continue to change with unsettling rapidity.

3. Visions of the Future But Obstacles on the Way

In our information oriented profession we have all been exposed to ideas about what the future holds and may even have developed such visions ourselves [13]. We are animated by such ideas, and perhaps feel that we are somehow part of a high-value endeavour that is future oriented, pointing aggressively at the next millennium. But if the information revolution is so potent, if the visions of change we see are so dramatic, if the opportunities of using information to transform our organizations and our work are so immense, why is progress seemingly so slow? One reason, of course, is that there are a number of real obstacles in the path of change that act as anchors. As the digital revolution continues it is creating a shock wave that profoundly affects the information environment through which the wave front is travelling. The need to take action is urgent, either defensively to protect and preserve or opportunistically to exploit the new possibilities that appear. Yet applying the fruits of the information revolution to an organization is not simply a question of taking the developments and clicking them into place in the opportunity wells that are scattered about. Some of the impediments to doing this are listed in Table 2. Understanding them is critical if we are to be successful in coping with the rapid transitions and unpredictability of this revolution.

TABLE 2. Possible Impediments to the Information-enabling Agenda

1) What Actions To Take?
2) Operating in the Shadow of IT
3) Business Case Challenge
4) Unrealistic Expectations
5) Resistance to Change: The Inertia of Human Behaviour

3.1 What Actions To Take?

At times there's a feeling of being overwhelmed. So much to do! Where to start? The best term I've come across to describe this is the "insurmountable opportunity". Sometimes we also shoulder the burden of being bearers of the torch - we know there is a revolution taking place around us, but many managers and decision makers seem unaware, perhaps not particularly of the changes that are occurring, so much as of the rapidity with which events now are moving and of how profoundly different the environment into which they carry us will be.

3.2 Operating in the Shadow of IT

Although Drucker has made it very clear that IT is the servant of information - the enabler, or perhaps still often the disabler - at times we (I mean information science) operate in IT's shadow. In my view, this is a major blunder that limits our inventiveness and clouds our judgement. Information technology and the computing and communications architecture dominate the agenda of CIO conferences which seem to have only secondary interest in information, how to organize it for effective use or how to invigorate the operation of the organization by ensuring facts-based decisions and operation. There is still much talk about transforming the organization through IT and

much less about the work needed to arrive at revitalization through the development of the information-enabled organization, an effort which requires many tools in addition to those which IT can offer. As we well know, in the end it is content that matters and the meaning users derive from that content. A preoccupation with technology also deflects us from matters such as information management and human resource management, which interact with information technology but which are of critical importance in their own right.

3.3 Business Case Challenge

Cost driven managers and organizations may demand exacting business case analyses before endorsing programs aimed at exploiting the digital revolution. In such turbulent times, however, insisting on precisely quantifiable outcomes is unrealistic. Indeed conventional cost/benefit analyses may force a focus that deflects the action towards counterproductive goals. Fundamentally, the case for the development of information-enabled organizations is that organizations that do not get it right simply will not be around. In short it is a strategic issue and should be accepted as such. Projects should be judged on the basis of how well they assist in projecting that strategy and how well they balance risks and opportunities. Payoffs often are intangible or defensive (everyone else is doing it, so....) or if quantified are lacking in rigour (time saved by simplifying procedures times number of employees times labour cost per hour). Sometimes significant, quantifiable value may come only towards the end of a series of changes that eventually reach critical mass. An approval environment that does not understand these realities and that is overly rigid will ensure that appropriate projects have immense difficulty in getting approved.

3.4 Unrealistic Expectations

Managers and executives often have unrealistic expectations about what the digital revolution can deliver and simplistic views about cost, difficulty and time required for project implementation. This creates a double pressure on project champions who must navigate between this set of challenges and the business case challenge without jeopardizing their chances of gaining approval.

3.5 Resistance to Change: The Inertia of Human Behaviour

Anyone who has had to lead major change in any organization knows how challenging it can be to gain user co-operation and enthusiasm. The old order dies hard! Any change, no matter how well thought out and planned will bring, inevitably, some criticism and argument. Change that has hard-to-quantify outcomes and based on judgement that is not widely shared is particularly difficult to bring about. Special efforts and clever management are necessary to overcome this challenge

4. Actions in Support of Change

All revolutions involve turbulence and uncertainty. However, knowledge of the forces at work and impediments to dealing with them can suggest ways of capitalizing on the changes underway. What can be done to take the opportunities that the digital world presents and apply them, navigating successfully through the challenges that have been identified? In my opinion the best method of institutionalizing the information revolution is to develop an integrated approach to its application. By integrated, I mean:

- across disciplines,
- across information sources,
- throughout the organization,
- across the industry,
- into all work functions and activities.

There is, in short, a multi-dimensional set of integration requirements.

Now lets be clear what we are about here. The concept of the information-enabled organization is one of an organization transformed through the collection, organization, generation and use of information. It is transformed through its staff, who create and use its information infrastructure, and through its stakeholders, customers and suppliers, who are influenced by and who enrich this infrastructure. And this infrastructure is the product of an intense focus on information plus contributions and essential support from four other infrastructures: information management, information technology, human resources and the organizational structure itself. It is thus a complex product of a complex set of interactions, a product that will have a long genesis and a long evolution.

Doing this is not the work of an afternoon, or something that can be worked out in detail in a half hour presentation. So what follows is intended to be suggestive, rather than exhaustive. It is not for me to determine what each of us should do within our own organizations. But these are some of the kinds of things that make sense in most organizations. I make no claim of originality here: these are simply obvious ideas put together into a coherent program and imbued with a single focus - the use of information within the organization. I hope we will discover more ways of doing this as time goes by and that we will develop or discover more advanced methodologies, a fuller literature of success stories and even failures, for as George Gilder said, "successful people and organizations have more failures than failures do". But it is impossible even to have failures unless you can get to the starting gate!

An overview of suggested actions is provided in Table 3 and more details are given in the material that follows.

TABLE 3. Action Programs for the Information-Centric Approach

Organize for Action	• Enlist colleagues • Form ad-hoc, informal teams, legitimize them later • Influence others
Promote Awareness	• Write position papers, literature reviews, etc. • Give or host seminars • Promote via newsletters, newsheets • Target special audiences for e-mail
Take Action	• Information mapping • Knowledge mapping • Establish action teams

Few of us will have the opportunity to introduce such a program as a top-down process. Most of us will have to work at a somewhat lower level as infectious agents, not pathogenic but benign, injecting, like a virus, material into our organizations that will then be replicated and released.

Of course the three stages shown in Table 3 do not have to be sequential. More typically, they may be carried out in parallel, at least to some degree, and there is considerable interconnectivity between them. Within each of these three main stages are a host of possible actions, only some of which are described here.

4.1 Getting Organized

The first stage involves finding out who else in the organization now believes or can be persuaded to embrace the view that the effective deployment of information is of central importance in the organization. Forming a network of fellow sympathizers is an obvious and effective way of gaining internal encouragement, defining and developing action agendas that are practical and implementable within the organization and helping to work out how to enlist even broader support as a prelude to more concrete actions later. Forming informal and unofficial teams is one way of developing action agendas and determining how to proceed in more detail. It helps establish a consensus among influential staff about the desired direction and methods to be used to get there.

4.2 Promoting Awareness

Once there is some level of organization, it is important to move into a program designed to bring the subject to the attention of other employees and managers. Again there are many possible ways of implementing this kind of awareness program. The basic idea is to sensitize employees about the need to use information as a focus for change and for running the business. Staff who understand the background are more likely themselves to adopt new approaches and to co-operate with those who wish to implement them. They are also more likely to contribute to the design of new programs helping to ensure that they will be focused on real needs and real users. Multiple means of communication should be used to get the message out, to teach by the use of examples from the literature, to increase the level of understanding within the organization, and to win over new converts to the cause.

4.3 Taking Action

The action program itself may take many forms. Some considerations and items that may be of value are given here.

4.3.1 Develop an information map. This is intended to show what kinds of information are kept by the organization, where they are, the size of each collection, how they are maintained, how access is provided, if there are electronic metadata about them and so on. In most organizations the surveying and auditing need to do this is likely to reveal an information environment that is chaotic and heterogeneous. The results are to be used not to criticize past action or inaction but to indicate what needs to be done. Information maps can be developed at several levels of detail. Logically the first pass should be a rough one intended to give an overall picture of the internal information resources and to suggest where further examination may be warranted. This kind of information coupled with the objectives of the organization may suggest areas where providing better management of the information resource such as by digitization might be most profitable. In some cases, this kind of information could lead to organizational redesign to take better advantage of "natural" information flows and to provide enhancement, reinforcement, augmentation, multiplication, leverage, and focus for these flows.

4.3.2 Develop a knowledge map. This differs from the previous item in being intended to identify the sources of expert knowledge about core subjects within the organization or industry. It might for example consist of lists of topics with references to the departments or individuals to consult about such topics. Alternatively it could consist of a network of intranet postings where subject experts provide information about recommended sources of information, including external internet sources that involve their areas of expertise. Both the information map and the knowledge maps should be works in progress that are refined and developed over time. The spread of cohesiveness and comprehensiveness in these maps could be markers of progress.

4.3.3 Establish an inter-disciplinary action team. To tackle the challenge of the digital revolution requires a multitude of skills including experts in information technology, information management, information systems and information science as well as traditional librarian, records management and other related skills. Pretexts should be found for creating interdisciplinary teams involving all of these skills. A particular project might be the initial stimulus for forming such a group but ideally the group or some part of it should survive this initial project and move on to take a systematic look at information leverage in the whole organization or major parts of it. Such an approach might also be useful for tackling the opportunity for co-operative programs of information integration across an industry.

4.3.4 Focus on users. Without users with problems and needs there is little point to any of the work suggested here. Commonly, however, user communities include a wide diversity of interests, knowledge, skills and sensitivity to the need for change. Since the information revolution will buffet experts and users alike, the aim should be to establish a collaborative working environment in which everything is geared to the level of understanding of the user. Activities that promote awareness but which are sensitive to the range of opinions and behaviours of staff are essential. Where it is necessary to introduce concepts that are unfamiliar, this should be done in the context of a mutual learning environment, perhaps on a small scale at first to increase the comfort level and to work as a spark or seed for further development. Focusing on users means not just on work needs but also on the psychology of users, as has been exposed for example by the development of scientific collaboratories. A project such as the development of a digital library could be an excellent way of bringing into being both an inter-disciplinary team and a mutual learning environment with users.

4.3.5 Shift the focus of cost analyses. It is important to avoid having a proposed digital information project forced into a narrowly focused justification environment because some of the most important outcomes will be hard to quantify and their exact impact hard to predict. One way of doing this is to strive to broaden the decision horizon. Questions such as what are we really trying to do here? and if we wanted to look at break-through changes or ones that support boundaryless (or some such term currently in favour in the executive suite in your organization) how would we proceed? may help. In the end, any project you propose must be focused on the business needs of your organization but it is critical to escape the inhibitory influence of traditional cost justifications which are much better suited to incremental changes from a traditional platform than to situations involving step changes with considerable uncertainty.

The basic idea of developing an understanding of forces for change, the resistance that they meet, and

the development of an action agenda that takes these into account, leading to the information-enabled organization is shown in Fig. 1

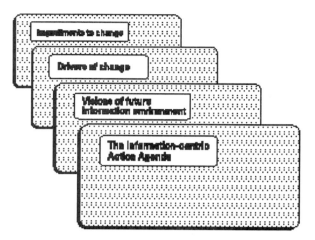

FIG. 1. Creating the Information-Centric Organization

5. Developing a Better Human Resources Model

Earlier I said that one of the impediments to a successful program of change involving information was the all-to-prevalent preoccupation with IT. IT is a necessary component of our program indeed a critically important one but it is only one of several. The human side of change is at least as important as technology, perhaps more so. In an age of disposable employees, the mercenary workforce, and piece-work managers it is discouraging to read, as far too often we do, of successful change programs within organizations that have little footnotes about how the entire such and such department had to be replaced, as if they were like old PC XTs that could no longer cut it. Staff operating under the wrong paradigm suddenly become sacrifices. Yesterday's hero-of-the-week is now dragged off in chains! This is the face of change as destroyer, brutal cleanser. Personally, I much prefer a model that resembles metamorphosis, in which the beautiful butterfly emerges from the ugly chrysalis through a transformation and I have the hope at least that using information as the focus of change programs has the potential to allow organizations to retool people rather than replace them.

I suggest that as organizations become information enabled they will avoid the waste of human resources that replacement involves. Such organizations may do so in one of two ways. First, they will manage the future somewhat better than most organizations have done in the past. A more information intensive type of operation ought to be able to navigate the shoals of change somewhat better than previous navigators who have relied more on hunch and experience. Second, the development of new models for education and new learning technologies should make it more practical and more feasible to retrain staff both technically and attitudinally, rather than to replace them as our organizations lurch through the filters that the competitive environment creates.

6. Conclusion

Analysis of the drivers affecting the digital revolution and identification of obstacles to implementing changes that will take advantage of the revolution are necessary preliminaries to designing effective action plans aimed at developing the information-enabled organization. Ways of at enhancing access to information and of increasing its use and usefulness should be based on an integrated approach involving interdisciplinary teams, a strong customer focus, imaginative project justifications, and a new style of human resource management. These specific ideas for developing an action plan are merely starting points for a great journey of exploration and discovery within our own organizations. Further work is warranted to develop further techniques and procedures that work well and to organize an experience base.

References

(1). Drucker, Peter F. (1995). The Information Executives Truly Need. *Harvard Business Review*, *73,* 54-62.

(2)a Enter the Intranet. *The Economist*. January 13 1996, 64-65.
b. Here Comes the Intranet, *Business Week*, February 26, 1996, 76-84.

(3). Data mining literature is copious. CWI, Data Mining, The search for knowledge in databases, URL: http://www.cwi,nl/~marcel/papers.html provides a useful definition and references to some papers. Contents and abstracts of papers presented at the First International Conference on Knowledge

Discovery and Data Mining can be found at URL: http://www-aig.jpl.nasa.gov:80/kdd95/. A useful site with pointers to numerous sources of information about data mining is URL: http://www.cs.bham.ac.uk/~anp/sites.html

(4). Stewart, Thomas A. (1994). Your Company's Most Valuable Asset: Intellectual Capital. *Fortune*, October 3, 68-74.

(5). Loftus, Frank (1993). Controlling Your Information Haystack. *CHEMTECH*, August, 12-15.

(6). HMOs: Medicine's New Weapon: Data. *Business Week*, March 27, 1995.

(7). Clark, Doug (1995). In Pursuit of Human Predators (describing ViCLAS, the Violent Crime Linkage Analysis System), *The Financial Post Magazine*, May, 18-22.

(8). See for example: Seitter, Keith L. (1995). An All-electronic, Peer-reviewed, Scientific Journal Published as a Collaboration of Five Societies and Delivered via the Internet. Presented at 58th. Annual Meeting of the American Society for Information Science, Chicago, October 9-12. Information about Internet Archaeology, a journal with similar aims (but different subject matter), which is in the planning stages, is at http://www.intarch.york.ac.uk

(9). Excellent single links to information about digital libraries are the Digital Libraries Resource Page at http://coulomb.uwaterloo.ca/~ktrgovac/digital/digital.html, and Digital Libraries Resources and Projects (International Federation of Library Associations and Institutions) at http://www.nlc-bnc.ca/ifla/II/diglib.htm

(10). (1989). *The New Encyclopaedia Britannica.* Encyclopaedia Britannica, 1045-1046.

(11). Kennedy, Paul (1993). Preparing for the 21st. Century. Random House, New York.

(12). de Solla Price, Derek J. (1962). Science Since Babylon, Yale University Press.

(13). Luke, Michael O. (1996). The Information Future. *ONLINE, 20,* 65-68.

Web Usage by American Fortune 500 Business Organizations

Yin Zhang and Hong Xu
Graduate School of Library and Information, University of Illinois at Urbana-Champaign
Champaign, Illinois

With the Internet opening its door to the commercial world, especially with the powerful Graphical User Interface (GUI) WWW browsers (e.g. Mosaic and Netscape) being introduced, more and more business organizations realize the strategic importance of the Internet for business, especially the business use of the World Wide Web (Web). According to Open Market's Commercial Sites Index Weekly Summary, as of February 16, 1996, there are more than 23,000 organizations with a presence on the Web, and commercial sites have been increasing at the rate of several hundred per week recently.

The Web usage by large business organizations, to some degree, could represent the tendency and current status of commercial use of the Web. Thus this research seeks to analyze the Web usage of the largest American business organizations -- Fortune 500 (F500) companies through online investigations of their Web sites.

I. Literature Review

Beginning in the late 1970s and early 1980s, a major change occurred in business computing. The traditional hierarchical structure of computers, shared computing in the 1970s and personal computing in the 1980s, has been replaced by nonhierarchical networked computing. In this distributed approach based on communication technologies, computers could be seamlessly networked. This change represented a fundamental upheaval in the way organizations share and assimilate information (Bergquist, Betwee & Meuel 1995; Verity & Hof, 1995). In parallel with this change, companies in this decade around the world have faced a tremendous increase in competitive pressures. Safe markets have been transformed into fluid and complex business environments (Smithson, Baskerville & Ngwenyama, 1994).

Given this background, the power of information has been recognized by business organizations (Davidow & Malone, 1992). Information is thought of as one of the weapons used for competitive advantage and as a major component of added value in today's business environment (Donovan, 1994). It can help firms develop new products and services, target specific market niches, discourage customers and suppliers from switching to competitors, provide products and services at lower cost than competitors, and create new relationships with customers (Laudon & Laudon, 1994; Cronin, 1994, 1995).

With the Clinton administration's emphasis on technological development for U.S. economic growth and the implementation of the National Information Infrastructure (NII), especially with the Internet being commercialized, businesses are recognizing that a high-speed information infrastructure can play a big part in speeding the pace of operation and cutting costs.

They see the potential to save costs and boost responsiveness if they can take advantage of the Internet to conduct business (Verity, 1994).

The information-rich Web page, which is the most popular information resource being visited via the Internet, can be well used for business purposes. The multimedia capability of the Web, which can present images, sound and video as well as well-formatted hypertext, has a great potential ability to distribute various kinds of business information widely , quickly and effectively.

There has been a good deal of research on Web usage by companies (Verity & Hof, 1994; Vaughan-Nichols, 1994; Singleton, 1995; Hoffman, Novak & Chatterjee, 1995). There are also some comprehensive books on how to do business on the Internet (Resnick & Taylor, 1994; Ellsworth & Ellsworth, 1994; Cronin 1994,1995; Angell & Heslop, 1995), in which there are chapters on how to do business on the Web.

The Web is being used by business organizations in various ways. Verity & Hof (1994) gave a good summary of Web usage by business organizations:

- Publishing
- Shopping
- Commerce
- Broadcasting
- Advertising

Singleton (1995) summarized the usage as:

- Publishing Medium
- Marketing
- Background Information, and News
- Online Ordering
- After Sale Support

Hoffman, Novak & Chatterjee(1995) gave a thorough examination of the commercial development of the Web and developed a new classification of commercialization efforts that categorizes commercial Web sites into six distinct types which include the following:

- Online Storefront
- Internet Presence
- Content
- Mall
- Incentive Site
- Search Agent

11

Cronin (1995) explained the effectiveness of the Web for business. The ability to link and connect to multiple information files from a single screen facilitates the interaction of all corporate information, products, and services in one readily accessible, interactive location. Popular home pages serve the equivalent of thousands of pages of information directly to Internet users each day, bypassing traditional print, fax, and telephone channels. In particular, it can eliminate barriers of geography and time accompanying traditional communication tools. However previous research did not provide information on the popularity of each usage category or examine the connection of different business organizations and usage categories.

Web100, which is produced by Internet Marketing, is a monthly updated list on which the largest U.S. corporations on the Web today are listed and hyperlinked to their sites. It is the first large scale research based on a real investigation of Web sites. It reveals "which companies are taking advantage of this new mode of communication, and what industries are taking the lead". But in this research, there was no information available on how many usage categories were being used by the companies. All companies were classified into three sectors: Computing Technology, Services and Industrial, with each sector further divided into several industries. This research emphasized the usage character of each industry sector, but it was not clear which companies were in which industry group since no information was available on what classification standard was applied in this research.

II. Data Collection

This paper examines how the Web is being used as a business tool by F500 companies, and asks whether there are any differences in usage among industries. The Fortune 500 companies refer to top 500 American companies ranked by company's sales/revenue. Fortune 500 list is available both online and in print format. For search convenience, the online source provided by Pathfinder (see Bibliography for URL) was chosen.

A Fortune 500 company with a Web page is defined as in Web100: a company in the Fortune 500 list with its own public Web site. Since the data collection was done initially during the period August 19 to 27, 1995, and later from December 23, 1995 to January 3, 1996, the time limit should also be considered as part of the definition.

When doing statistical analysis, the following invalid cases were omitted even though they were included in the overall count: 1) companies with Web pages which had no information available; 2) companies whose Web servers were down during the investigation periods. For example, in August 1995, the Web site of McDonnell Douglas was undergoing a major renovation; the sites of Whirlpool and McGraw-Hill were under construction; and the sites of Quaker Oats and Merisel were not available. In December 1995 and early 1996, Delta Air Lines only had an activated image in its site, and the sites of Whirlpool again and Quaker Oats were under construction. All such companies were counted, but they were omitted as invalid cases when statistical analysis was done.

By using Internet search engines (Infoseek, Yahoo, and Lycos), F500 companies having Web sites could be found. Two comprehensive lists of companies with Web pages were developed for the two time periods when searching was conducted. The lists can not be guaranteed to be complete, but if a Web site could not be found by these major Internet search engines, the ordinary user would have difficulty locating it as well.

In order to analyze the usage difference among industries, it is necessary to classify the companies. The four-digit Standard Industrial Classification (SIC) (Dun & Bradstreet Information Resources, 1989) system, which is widely used by the U.S. government and researchers to identify the industrial categories of companies, was used. The first two digits of SIC, which range from 01 to 97 and represent 82 basic industrial categories, divide all business organizations into the following ten divisions:

- Division A: Agriculture, Forestry and Fishing;
- Division B: Mining;
- Division C: Construction;
- Division D: Manufacturing;
- Division E: Transportation, Communication, Electric, Gas & Sanitary Services;
- Division F: Wholesale trade;
- Division G: Retail trade;
- Division H: Finance, Insurance & Real Estate;
- Division I: Services;
- Division J: Public Administration.

The unique 4-digit SIC code of most F500 companies can be searched from the Compustat PC Plus database. For those twelve cases whose SIC codes could not be found in this source, volumes of both U.S. Public Companies and U.S. Private Companies of the 1995 Directory of Corporate Affiliations by National Register Publishing were used. Since several companies were listed under several SIC codes in the latter sources, the one which represented its Fortune 500 industry membership was chosen for data inputting. For example, LDDS Communications is listed uniquely under 4813 in the 1995 Directory of Corporate Affiliations, so 4813 was chosen as its SIC code; Metropolitan Life Insurance is listed under 6311, 6321, 6324, 6371, 6411, 6512 and 6531, but in the Fortune 500 industry listing, it is under the Insurance Category, which could be well represented by 6311. Therefore, 6311 was chosen. Five companies required such a choice of code.

Based on a literature review on commercial use of Web pages, and a trial visit to more than 50 sites, a list of Web usage categories was developed for recording in the process of the investigation:

- Career opportunities (CarOpp);
- Community affairs & social responsibility (ComAff): e.g. arts, sports, educational, and other events;
- Customer support (CusSup): e.g. technical support, services guide, training program;
- Customers survey (CusSur);
- Industry related information (InRInfo): e.g. new technologies, important events;

- Marketing (<u>Market</u>): e.g. catalog of products or services,   location assisted information;
- Publishing (<u>Publish</u>): e.g. company information, news releases, financial information for investors;
- Sales (<u>Sales</u>): e.g. on-line ordering.

III. Hypotheses

There are several questions of interest in this study.   Does one usage category occur more frequently than others on the Web pages? Are there any differences in Web usage for companies in different industrial divisions? Are some usage categories more likely included on the Web by companies in one particular industrial division? Based on these research questions, the following null hypotheses are formulated:

H1: There is no significant difference in Web usage across usage categories.
H2: There is no significant difference in Web usage among industrial divisions.
H3: The differences in Web usage do not significantly depend on industrial divisions.
The null hypotheses were tested in both investigation periods.

Since the extent of commercial use of WWW is increasing, it is also important to compare data collected at two different time periods to see whether there are any changes in the number of Web sites available and the frequencies of WWW usage categories in the different industry groups.

IV. Data Analysis

Two investigations -- one in late August, 1995 and another one in late December, 1995-- were performed in order to trace the development of Web usage of these F500 companies. In addition to exploring the important descriptive statistics, two way ANOVA with repeated measures design on one factor was applied to further test the null hypotheses.

1. General statistics

The general statistics of the two investigations are summarized in Table 1. One may find that among F500 companies, 25% (127) of them have Web sites in August, 1995, and the percentage has increased to 37% (187) after 4 months. Most F500 companies belong to Division D (Manufacturing), H (Finance, Insurance & Real Estate), E (Transportation, Communication, Electric, Gas & Sanitary Services), and G (Retail Trade). There is no one in Division J (Public Administration) and few of them are in Division A (Agriculture, Forestry and Fishing), B (Mining), and C (Construction). Thus most F500 companies with Web pages are in Divisions D, H, E, and G and the percentage of Web sites for these divisions is also relatively high. However, the On Web Rate of each division is not consistent with their proportions in F500: since Division A only has two F500 companies, it has the highest On Web Rate (50%) with only one Web site; in the first investigation period, Division D has the second highest On Web Rate (32%)

whereas Division E becomes the second (46%) in December; although there are only 4% of Division I (Services) companies in F500, it's On Web Rates in two periods are 19% (the fifth) and 38% (the fourth) respectively. Division G and F (Wholesale Trade) are the fourth and fifth biggest categories in F500, but Division G's On Web Rates rank sixth in two periods, and Division F's rank seventh and eighth respectively .

Table 1 Industrial Distribution of F500 Companies and Those with Web Pages
(August, 1995 : December, 1995)

Divisio	A	B	C	D	E	F	G	H	I	J	Total
F500	2	2	6	207	78	27	60	97	21	0	500
Web	1 : 1	0 : 0	0 : 1	66:85	24:36	3 : 4	7:17	22:35	4 : 8	-	127:187
Web%	.8:.5	0 : 0	0 : .5	52:46	19:19	2 : 2	6: 9	17:19	3 : 4	-	100:100
On%	50:50	0 : 0	0 :17	32:41	31:46	11:15	12:28	23:36	19:38	-	25: 37
Valid	1 : 1	0 : 0	0 : 1	61:78	23:32	2 : 4	7 : 16	20:32	4 : 8	-	118:172
Valid%	.9:.6	0 : 0	0 : .6	52:45	20:19	2 : 2	6 : 9	17:19	3 : 5	-	100:100

Note:
- ":" : Separates data collected in August, 1995 from data collected in December, 1995. Same in Table 2 and 7.
- F500: Number of F500 companies in each division.
- Web: Number of F500 companies with Web sites.
- Web%: Percentage of Web sites = number of Web sites in a division / number of F500 companies with Web sites.
- On%: On Web Site Rate (%) = number of Web sites in a division / number of companies belonging to F500.
- Valid: Valid Web Site--information on the Web sites was available during the investigation periods.
- Valid%: Percentage of Valid Web Sites = number of valid Web sites in a division / total number of valid Web sites.

Since nine Web sites in August and fifteen sites in December were either no information available (mainly under construction) or unable to connect, the number of valid Web sites was reduced to 118 and 172 respectively. Statistical tests were based on the data from the valid Web sites.

2. Usage category analysis

Table 2 reflects how the eight usage categories are related to the different divisions. Among all the usage categories, the major emphases of the Web pages are on Marketing (Market.

86% of companies in August and 91% in December) and Publishing (Publish. 82% in August and 93% in December). Customer Support, Career Opportunities posting, Community Affairs and Industry Related Information come next. On-line sales is the least used among the eight usage categories. Since August, Publishing has been received more attention than Marketing. Customer Support is also an important field, and more companies are interested in posting job openings on the Web.

Table 2   Usage Category Analysis Summary I (August : December)

Division\Usage	CarOp p	ComA ff	CusSu p	CusSu r	InRInf o	Market	Publis h	Sales
A	0 : 0	1 : 1	1 : 1	0 : 0	0 : 0	1 : 1	1 : 1	1 : 1
C	0 : 1	0 : 0	0 : 0	0 : 0	0 : 1	0 : 1	0 : 1	0 : 0
D	17 : 30	19 : 32	28 : 41	14 : 15	15 : 18	53 : 70	51 : 73	6 : 8
E	4 : 12	8 : 16	11 : 23	1 : 2	6 : 8	19 : 30	19 : 31	0 : 4
F	0 : 0	0 : 0	1 : 1	0 : 0	1 : 1	1 : 3	1 : 3	0 : 0
G	3 : 7	0 : 4	3 : 9	1 : 4	2 : 2	7 : 14	6 : 14	0 : 4
H	6 : 13	4 : 9	10 : 24	1 : 3	4 : 10	17 : 30	17 : 30	5 : 6
I	3 : 4	1 : 2	2 : 5	1 : 1	0 : 2	4 : 7	2 : 7	0 : 0
Total	33: 67	33 : 64	56 : 104	18 : 25	28 : 42	102: 156	97:160	12 : 23
% of the usage	28:39	28 : 37	48 : 61	15 : 15	24 : 24	86: 91	82: 93	10:13

Note:
- Data in the table refer to the number of companies with that usage category.
- % of the usage = number of companies in each usage category / number of valid Web sites (118: 172).

Tables 3 and 4 summarize the statistical test results of the above data sets. In both August and December, there are significant differences for Web usage categories (at $p \leq 0.0001$ level). That means Hypothesis 1 was rejected. Some usage categories tend to be used more than others across the industrial divisions.

Table 3   Summary Table of Two Way ANOVA (August, 1995)

Source	DF	SS	MS	F
Division	6	1.1	0.18	0.55
Usage	7	14.45	2.06	14.53*
Division x Usage	42	6.15	0.15	1.03

$p \leq 0.0001$

Table 4 Summary Table of Two Way ANOVA (December, 1995)

Source	DF	SS	MS	F
Division	7	2.10	0.30	0.99
Usage	7	16.95	2.42	17.25*
Division x Usage	49	7.8	0.16	1.14

$p \leq 0.0001$

Pairwise contrasts allow us to examine whether a particular usage category is significantly different from each of the other categories.   Tables 5 and 6 reflect that Marketing and Publishing are two major categories which are significantly different from other usage categories across the industrial divisions. Customer Support is somewhere in the middle. It is significantly different from two heavily used categories (i.e., Marketing and Publishing) and also from other less used categories (i.e., Customer Survey and Sales). Customer Survey has never received much attention from these companies. On-line Sales is still a concern.

Table 5 Significant Differences Among Usage Categories (August, 1995)

Usage Category	CarOpp	ComAff	CusSup	CusSur	InRInfo	Market	Publish	Sales
CarOpp		--	+	--	--	+	+	--
ComAff			--	--	--	+	+	--
CusSup				+	+	+	+	+
CusSur					--	+	+	--
InRInfo						+	+	--
Market							--	+
Publish								+
Sales								

Note:
For Table 5 & 6, "+" means two usage categories are significantly different at $\alpha = .05$ level whereas "--" mean they are not significantly different at $\alpha = .05$ level.

Table 6 Significant Differences Among Usage Categories (December, 1995)

Usage Category	CarOpp	ComAff	CusSup	CusSur	InRInfo	Market	Publish	Sales
CarOpp		--	--	+	--	+	+	--
ComAff			--	+	--	+	+	--
CusSup				+	+	+	+	+
CusSur					+	+	+	--
InRInfo						+	+	--
Market							--	+
Publish								+
Sales								

Tables 3 and 4 also show that there are no significant differences (even at α = .10 level) in the emphasis of usage categories for different industrial divisions. Significant differences were not found for the interaction factor of Division and Usage either. Thus, Hypotheses 2 and 3 were retained. However, if we examine the descriptive statistics, we can still find trends of some particular usage associated with certain divisions. Since the number of companies which have Web pages is too small in Division A, C, and F to show the significance, they are not considered in the usage category analysis in Table 7.

Table 7 Usage Category Summary II (August : December) *

Division\Usage	CarOpp	ComAf	CusSup	CusSur	InRInfo	Market	Publish	Sales
D	28:39	31:41	43:53	23:19	25:23	87:90	84:94	10:10
E	17:38	35:50	48:72	4:6	26:25	83:94	83:97	0:13
G	43:44	0:25	43:56	14:25	29:13	100:88	86:88	0:25
H	30:41	20:28	50:75	5:9	20:31	85:94	85:94	25:19
I	75:50	25:25	50:63	25:13	0:25	100:88	50:88	0:0

Note:
- Data in the table represent the percentage of each usage in each division (i.e. number of companies with that usage category / number of valid Web sites in a division) .

The Career Opportunity was very common in the Services profession (Division I). It is least common in Transportation, Communication, Electric, Gas & Sanitary Services (Division E.) although more sites have posted advertisements since August 1995. Division E had the most emphasis on community affairs and social responsibility. Finance, Insurance & Real Estate (Division H) and Division E paid more attention to Customer Support while other divisions put almost the same weight on it. Interestingly, Customer Survey was very infrequent in sites for companies in Division E and H. Industrial Related Information provided by Division G companies is the highest in August, but declined sharply since then; in contrast, this usage category was not presented in Division I in August (0%) but appeared in December (25%). Marketing and Publishing were emphasized by all companies. There was a slight change in the rank of the divisions in the two usage categories: in August, all companies in Division G and I used the Web page for Marketing, while Division G had more companies in Publishing. However, in December, Companies in Division E and H have more marketing activities than Division G and I; Division E has the highest percentage of usage for Publishing. Only a few companies have sales available on the Web. Division I has no Sales via the Web, while the highest proportion on Web sales belongs to Division G.

V. Discussion and Implications

This study shows that the eight Web usage categories do occur with significantly different frequencies on Web pages. There are no significant differences in Web usage for companies in different industrial divisions. The differences in Web usage do not significantly depend on the nature of industrial divisions although some differences are observable. According to Hoffman, Novak, and Chatterjee (1995), fifty to one hundred Web servers come online daily and the size and growth of commercial Web sites have jumped tremendously since 1994. However, based on this investigation, there are still fewer than half of the F500 companies with Web sites. Usage categories did not change although the emphases might not be the same in the two investigation periods.

The reason for the overall similarity of the business use of the WWW may be that the commercial development of the Web has not yet taken into account industrial differences. Companies may copy from each other on Web page content design. How to establish a customized Web page which can best reflect the picture of the company and attract customers to the sites deserves to be considered by companies.

It is necessary to point out that companies with the same usage category for their Web pages may have differences in terms of the amount of information that category carries. Some companies have paid closer attention to enriching contents, updating information on the Web page, and maintaining the Web sites than other companies. For example, both Wal-Mart Stores and J. C. Penney in Division G (Retail Trade) had information on Marketing and Publishing. However, Wal-Mart only had location assisted information under Marketing and general company news and financial information under Publishing whereas J. C. Penney had a catalog of products and services as well as a locator under Marketing and company information, news releases, annual / quarterly reports, and detailed financial information under Publishing. BellSouth's Web page included information on Community affairs & social responsibility, Marketing, and Publishing in both investigation periods. However, during the first period, the content in Publishing covered only information and current news about the company while the content extended to financial information and annual reports or quarterly reports in December.

Several researchers suggest that Web-based commercial efforts are more efficient and possibly even more effective than efforts mounted in traditional channels. Verity and Hof (1994) point out that marketing through conventional channels is four times more expensive than marketing over the Internet. Web-marketing results in "ten times as many units sold with one-tenth the advertising budget." (Potter, 1994). Therefore, it is very natural that Marketing is one of the most important usage categories on the commercial Web page. Company news and financial information are also very important indicators of business success and are of interest to investors. Customer service and support could be very efficient and effective by using the Web. According to a report, SunSolve Online has saved Sun Microsystems over $4 million in FAQs alone since they "re-engineered information processes around the WWW" (Neece, 1995).

It is surprising that Customer Survey is the second least used category while Web site survey is popularly used by almost all sites for feedback on the sites' quality. The potential use of the Web for collecting information about products or services may be strengthened later.

Although the potential for online sales has been a hot topic in commercial use of the Internet, sales is used the least among all the usage categories according to findings from this study. The most frustrating problem in online sales is the security concern by both companies and customers. We may not expect this usage category to increase much in the near future. Seymour Merrin, head of a technical research firm, even estimates that online shopping ultimately could represent 6% to 8% of all mail-order sales (1996) because "the buying population on the Net is essentially social misfits. People who are comfortable in public will go to a store". The existing habits of purchasing are still affecting sales on the Web.

Web sites are also used to serve as information centers by companies to provide some unrelated information as well as company or industry related information. For example, Texas Instruments has its own Virtual Library on the Web, where Papers/Articles and Company periodicals are available. Reebok has an information center on sports news. James River Corp. of Va.--which is a company producing forest and paper products, provides information on business, government, travel, and weather. This reflects that companies are not only making the Web sites as an image of themselves but also are interested in the potential power of the Web page as an information provider.

The Web presents a fundamentally different environment for business. As a commercial medium, it has the potential ability to provide a more efficient and effective channel for advertising, marketing, customer service and support, and direct online ordering as well as releasing company-related information. However, there is as yet little concrete evidence of benefits from using this new Internet tool. It is very clear that, at the current stage, the Web site only serves as an additional channel for business development. The conventional business strategies and systems are still playing important roles.

References:

Angell, David, Brent Heslop. *The Internet Business Companion.* Reading, Mass.: Addison-Wesley, 1995.

Bergquist, William, Juli Betwee, David Meuel. *Building Strategic Alliances.* San Francisco: Jossey-Bass Publishers, 1995.

Cronin, Mary J..*Doing Business on the Internet: How the Electronic Highway Is Transforming American Companies.* New York: Van Nostrand Reinhold, 1994.

Cronin, Mary J.. *Doing More Business on the Internet: How the Electronic Highway Is Transforming American Companies.* New York: Van Nostrand Reinhold, 1995.

Davidow, William H., Michael S. Malone. *Structuring and Revitalizing the Corporation For the 21st Century: The Virtual Corporation.* New York: HarperCollins Publishers, 1992.

Donovan, John J..*Business Re-engineering with Information Technology.* Englewood Cliffs, NJ: PTR Prentice Hall, 1994.

Dun & Bradstreet Information Resources. *Standard Industrial Classification Manual*. Murray Hill, NJ: Dun & Bradstreet Information Resources, 1989.

Ellsworth, Jill H., Matthew V. Ellsworth. *The Internet Business Book*. New York: John Wiley & Sons, Inc., 1994.

Hoffman, Donna L., Thomas P. Novak., & Patrali Chatterjee. "Commercial Scenarios for the Web: Opportunities & Challenges. " Journal of Computer-Mediated Communication, December 1995. *Special Issue on Electronic Commerce.*
URL: http://shum.huji.ac.il/jcmc/vol1/issue3/hoffman.html

Infoseek: http://www.infoseek.com/

Internet Marketing: http://fox.nstn.ca/~at_info/w100_table2.html

Laudon, Kenneth C., Jane P. Laudon. *Management Information Systems: Organization and Technology*. 3rd ed. New York: Macmillan College Publishing Company, Inc. 1994.

Lycos: http://lycos.cs.cmu.edu/

Merrin Seymour. "Online Shopper Demographics." *Investor's Business Daily*, Jan.8, 1996, A10.

National Register Publishing. *1995 Directory of Corprate Affiliations*. New Providence, NJ: National Register Publishing, 1995.

Neece, Jerry. "Caught in a net of Support," *Sunday Times*, June 11, 1995.

Open Market's Commercial Sites Index Weekly Summary:
http://www.directory.net/dir/statistics.html

Pathfinder Fortune 500 listing:
http://pathfinder.com/@@@Y9xO8GAgwIAQKlQ/fortune/magazine/specials/fortune500/results/salesrank.html

Pathfinder Fortune 500 by industry :
http://pathfinder.com/@@yQjOOaGyGgEAQGSU/fortune/magazine/specials/fortune500/industry.html

Potter, Edward. WELL Topic "Commercialization of the World Wide Web" in the Internet conference on the WELL. November 16, 1994.

Resnick, Rosalind, Dave Taylor. *The Internet Business Guide : riding the information superhighway to profit*. Indianapolis: Sams Publishing, 1994.

Singleton, Andrew. "The Virtual Storefront." *Byte*, Jan. 1995, 125-132.

Smithson, Steve, Richard Baskerville & Ojelanki Ngwenyama. "Perspectives on information technology and new emergent forms of organizations." In R. Baskerville, S. Smithson, O. Ngwenyama and J. I. DeGross (eds), *Transforming Organizations with Information Technologies*. Amsterdam: North-Holland, 1994, PP.3-13.

Standard & Poor's Compustat. *Compustat PC Plus: Corporate Text Status Report (CD-ROM)*. Englewood, Colorado: Standard & Poor's Compustat , 1995.

Vaughan-Nichols, Steven J.. "The Web means business." *Byte*, Nov. 1994, 26-27.

Verity, John. "Truck lanes for the info highway." *Business Week*, Apr. 18, 1994, 112-114.

Verity, John W., Robert D. Hof. "Planet Internet: How the center of the computing universe has shifted." *Business Week*, Apr. 3, 1995, 118-124.

Verity, John W., Robert D. Hof. "The Internet: How it will change the way you do business." *Business Week*: Nov.14, 1994, 80-88.

Yahoo: http://www.yahoo.com/

Information Markets and the Information Highway: Building New Bridges, Not New Roads

Rosalie Liccardo Pacula and Gary P. Schneider
School of Business Administration, University of San Diego
San Diego, California

ABSTRACT

The dramatic growth of the Internet raises some interesting questions regarding the economic role these entities play in business. Although many individuals and firms have made extensive information available on the Internet, economic theory asserts that individuals and firms have no incentive to disclose private information. Economic theory predicts that any information individuals or firms make available on the Internet would be already publicly available. Individuals or firms that disclose private information on the Internet would provide an interesting exception to established theory that explains economic behavior in other communications media rather well.

This paper addresses the question of why firms disclose information on the Internet and the Web despite accepted economic theory that predicts they would not disclose information. The paper identifies two significant conditions under which firms might have an incentive to disclose private information: when firms are not profit-maximizers and when significant barriers to entry do not exist. The paper also examines consumers' incentives to obtain information via the Internet and discusses the costs that consumers face when accessing the Internet.

Finally, the paper discussed the nature of information markets and concluded that the Internet and the Web serve as bridges across geographically disjunct markets. In essence, the Internet provides a gathering place for the exchange of information that reduces physical distance and reduces a number of transaction costs. The Internet and the Web provide bridges across space, time, and cultures to join markets in efficient and effective ways that were not possible with slower and less powerful forms of information dissemination. The Internet offers a low cost and enough advantages to attract investment by sellers, buyers, and consumers of information about products and services.

INTRODUCTION

The dramatic growth of the Internet and the World Wide Web (the Web) (Berghel, 1996; Berners-Lee, et al., 1994) raises some interesting questions regarding the economic role these entities play in business. Although many individuals and firms have made extensive information available on the Internet, economic theory asserts that individuals and firms have no incentive to disclose private information (Tirole, 1988). Therefore, economic theory predicts that any information individuals or firms make available on the Internet would be information that is already publicly available. Individuals or firms that disclose private information on the Internet would provide an interesting exception to established theory that explains economic behavior in other communications media rather well. However, an alternative view of the Internet as a vehicle for disseminating information that is already publicly available to a broader set of information consumers is consistent with economic theory. As a bridge across formerly disjunct markets, rather than a medium for disclosure of private information, the Internet's existence provides enormous opportunity for firms to improve their overall economic efficiency by reducing both producer and consumer information costs.

This paper begins with an outline of the economic incentives that would prevent individuals from disclosing private information on the Internet. If entities do disclose formerly private information on the Internet, special circumstances must exist to induce this behavior. The paper presents a brief discussion of these special circumstances. Then the paper analyzes the economic factors that information consumers consider when they choose to use the Internet as an information acquisition tool. This analysis focuses on the characteristics of consumers that have access to the Web and why those characteristics might induce specific information-producing individuals or firms to disclose information. Finally, the paper discusses how the Internet can reduce information market inefficiencies by bridging existing markets. In its analysis of the economic incentives to both information suppliers and information consumers, the paper shows that the Internet and the Web serve as clearing houses for existing information rather than as a source of new information.

INFORMATION SUPPLIER DISINCENTIVES TO REVEAL INFORMATION

The amount of information available on the Internet—and the number of products that are being offered or promoted—has grown at an exponential rate over the last five years (Kambil, 1995; Semich, 1995). What began as an efficient method for researchers to share data across the country and around the world has transformed itself into a major information source and marketplace for selling a variety of goods ranging from airline tickets to software. Services, such as the courses offered by major universities, have also become widely available on the Internet.

Today, firms use the Internet to lower communication costs, improve customer service and foster innovation (Erkes, et al. 1996; Kendall, 1995; Perlman, 1995; Strom, 1995). As more businesses sell and support their products on-line, consumers have developed a growing misperception that they have access to new information about these companies and their products. Although the Internet provides a new and inexpensive medium for selling products (*Business Week*, 1996), it does not provide firms with an incentive to reveal any private information about themselves or their products. Indeed, firms have strong incentives—among them, eager competitors and a desire to maintain higher profits—to keep certain information from public disclosure.

The Role of Information in Producer Competition

Beginning with Adam Smith, economists have maintained a basic assumption that firms are profit-maximizers (Smith, 1776; Coase, 1937). That is, firms are in business to make money. A firm that is in a competitive market has two ways to earn positive profits. First, the firm may have exclusive information about—or exclusive access to—cost-saving production or distribution processes. In this case, the firm's ability to continue generating positive profits depends on its ability to keep this exclusive information out of competitors' hands. Second, information asymmetries may exist which allow firms to extract higher profits from uninformed buyers. *Asymmetry* is a term economists use to describe market situations in which the seller has more or better information about the product than a potential buyer (Akerlof, 1970). When a selling firm has asymmetric information, that firm's ability to continue generating profits depends on its ability to keep information about its production processes, distribution processes, or product quality from becoming widely available.

Price Competition

To begin the analysis, we will assume that the firm's customers are purely price-takers; that is, buyers cannot influence the price at which they purchase specific products no matter what information they have. The selling firm knows that any information it makes available to potential buyers will also be available to the firm's competitors. Firms generally cannot selectively reveal information because firms generally cannot distinguish potential buyers from competitors. Therefore, firms will not release sensitive information about product features, product quality, production techniques, or distribution techniques for fear that their competitors will obtain and use this information to achieve competitive advantage. If the industry does not have significant barriers to entry, new firms will also enter and use this information, further increasing competition.

Disclosure of private information can increase competition and lower a firm's profits in two ways. First, when competitor firms learn new cost-efficient methods of production or distribution, they can reduce the price they charge on their own products. Faced with lower prices from competing firms, the original firm must lower its price or lose market share. When the original firm lowers its price, it lowers its revenues which, assuming constant costs, decreases profits.[1] Second, new firms that are eager to earn some of the positive profits obtained by the original firm can enter the market since they now have better information about how to produce a similar product. As these new producers enter the market, the total supply of the product increases and the market price falls.

A good example of how increased competition lowers the market price for specific products is the personal computer (PC) market. IBM was the leader in developing PCs for work and home. However, in a relatively short time the technical knowledge needed to produce low-cost PCs became available throughout the high-technology world. Soon, new PC manufacturers emerged.

---

[1] The profits of a firm are equal to the difference between the firm's total revenues and its total costs, or:

$$\text{Profits} = P(q) - TC$$

where: P = the market price of the firm's output.
    q = the quantity of output produced by the firm.
    $P(q)$ = the firm's total revenues.
    TC = the total costs of the firm

Apple developed its own variety of PC while other companies simply cloned IBM's machine. As each new firm entered the market, the supply of personal computers began to grow and the market price fell as shown in Figure 1.

Figure 1
The Market for Personal Computers

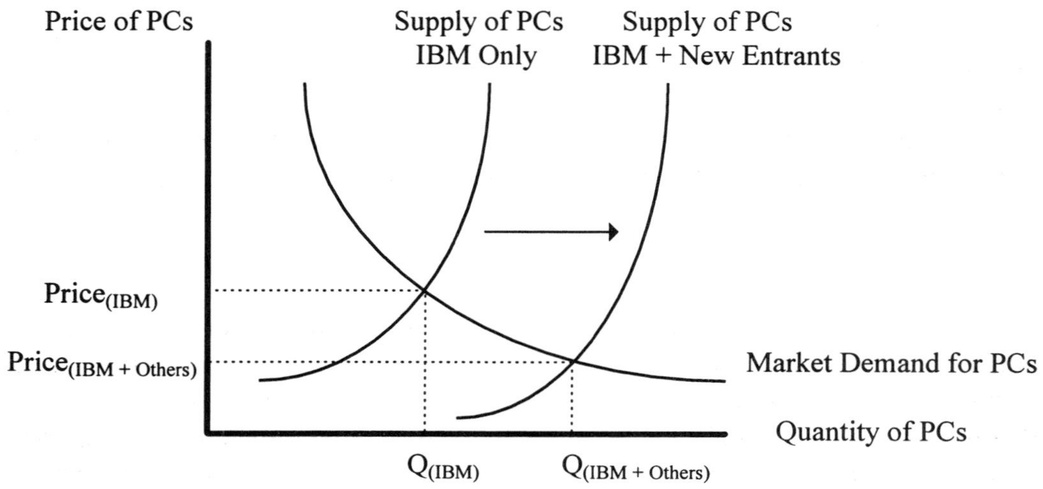

As the market price for individual machines fell, the industry supply curve shifted to the right. IBM's revenues and profits fell along with the revenues and profits of the entire PC industry. You can see in Figure 1 that the value of $Q_{(IBM + Others)}$ increased, so unit sales in the industry increased. however, these sales were at such a lower average price per unit ($Price_{(IBM + Others)}$) that total revenue for the industry decreased.

Information Asymmetry and Well-Informed Buyers

Market competition is not the only factor that may reduce the profits of a particular firm. Well-informed buyers may also reduce profits. Typically firms know more about the product they sell than potential buyers know. The existence of asymmetric information regarding the product and its quality can generate profits for a firm. The classic case of asymmetric information is the market for used cars (Akerlof, 1970). Only the seller knows the true quality of the car—i.e., how many accidents it has been in, how well it has been maintained, if the odometer reading is correct. In most cases, a buyer only knows what the seller reveals about the car's condition. Car buyers' only other source of information is what they can physically observe. For example, a car mechanic will probably have a more informed opinion of a car's value after physically examining the car than would an untrained buyer. The car mechanic might demand a lower price for the car based on this higher level of information. An economist would note that the mechanic's higher level of knowledge has reduced the information asymmetry in the situation and forced the seller to offer a price closer to the car's true value. An untrained buyer—in a condition of higher information asymmetry—would not know how close the asking price is to the car's true value so would be more likely to pay what the seller asked.

Conditions of information asymmetry between buyers and sellers exist in all markets, not just the market for used cars. Certain buyers, because of their background or willingness to search for additional information, will know more about the products than other buyers and will use this information to bargain with the seller. Buyers will be more successful in price bargaining with sellers in markets that do not have a large number of uninformed buyers. If a market includes a large number of uninformed buyers, then sellers can choose not to sell to informed buyers and wait for the next uninformed buyer to come along. Every time a seller lowers the asking price for an informed buyer, it reduces the seller's profit on that transaction. Therefore, firms have an incentive to ensure that certain product information remains unknown or difficult for buyers to obtain. If the number of informed buyers remains low, profits will remain high.

Summary

To summarize, economic theory argues, *ceteris paribus*, that a firm will not willingly reveal any information to its buyers that it does not want to reveal to its competitors. Further, a firm will not willingly reveal any information that would enable a buyer to demand a lower price. Since the release of some information could reduce a firm's profits, the firm will choose to keep much information private. Therefore, we can predict that the Internet and the Web will only contain information that is already publicly available. However, the Internet may serve as an easier way for buyers and competitors to obtain already-available information.

VIOLATIONS OF ASSUMPTIONS

The results presented in the above analysis depend on two key assumptions. First, we assumed that all firms are profit-maximizers. Second, we assumed that the firms were participating in a perfectly competitive industry, so there were no barriers to entry. Violations of either of these assumptions may yield different behavior.

The Goal of Profit Maximization

Not all firms are profit maximizers. Many hospitals, foundations, public interest groups and other organizations are non-profit organizations. Since these firms have different incentives, they may be more willing to disclose private information. In fact, it may actually be beneficial for these firms to disclose private information if that information can increase contributions made to the organization or improve the credibility of their organization.

Absence of Barriers to Entry

If barriers to entry exist in a market, then firms may have some incentive to disclose private information when existing competitors in the industry cannot use the information. For example, a company that has information protected by a patent or exclusive contract would actually benefit by disclosing how its product or production process differs from its competitors (Tirole, 1988). Alternatively, a company may try to gain market share by building a reputation of quality, which would require them to deal honestly with problems surrounding their product or production process. By disclosing negative information about its products, a company may be able to gain the trust of current and future buyers. However, a firm can only disclose negative information advantageously when there are not a large number of competing firms offering similar products.

Internal Information Transfers

The above discussion does not imply that there is no private information transmitted via the Internet. Many firms have found the Internet to be a useful way to cut down on production and communication costs. Large companies with worldwide offices can share information over the Internet by creating their own electronic offices or internal networks. This information, however, is protected by firewalls, proxy servers, and other security devices so that the general public cannot access it.

INFORMATION CONSUMERS' INCENTIVES TO ACCESS THE INTERNET

Even if no new information exists on the Internet, information consumers may still have incentives to use the Internet or the Web. Information consumers may find that the Internet is the most efficient way for them to obtain information (Brooks and Sutherland, 1995; Cohen, 1995). For those individuals who already have access to the Internet at home or at work, it is a low cost way of accessing detailed information regarding a product and the firm that produces it. By accessing a company's home page, they can obtain detailed data in minutes (Garcia, 1995).

The prevalence of search engines such as Lycos, Yahoo, and Alta Vista allows consumers to collect related Web information sources and sort through them fairly easily (Verity, 1996). Consumers can access bulletin boards and newsgroups to get instant feedback from current users about goods and services purchasing them. Some companies even have developed on-line demonstrations of their products. For example, Digital Equipment Corporation allows its potential customers to test drive a workstation, including its software and applications, on the Internet (Kalil, 1995). The time and energy that consumers save by obtaining information through the Internet or the Web is a real economic savings for them.

Enhancing the Quality of Existing Available Information

This breadth of data available in a single location increases the overall quality of information obtained by most consumers. Through the Web, information consumers can gain insight into issues and facts about companies and products about which they might not have otherwise inquired about. This does not mean that the information was not already publicly available. It simply means that some consumers may have been unaware of the information's existence or importance.

Costs to Information Consumers

Although access to the Web can improve information flows and reduce the search costs of obtaining information, it does cost money for most consumers to go on-line. Typical access costs currently run $20 to $30 per month. Some consumers, however, can access the Internet at no personal monetary cost because their employer pays a general fee for all of its employees. Of course, even these individuals incur the opportunity cost of time spent using the Internet. This cost will vary among consumers, depending on their experience with computers, using the Internet, and using specific search engines.

The costs of using the Internet for information gathering purposes means that only certain types of consumers will choose to use it as an information acquisition tool. Research that evaluated the demographics of Internet and Web users as of November, 1995, revealed that two-thirds of the 18 million Canadian and U.S. users are male and 53% are between the ages of 16-34 years old (*Online Business Today*, 1995). Furthermore, 64% of the current users have at least some college education and 25% earn over $80,000 a year (*Online Business Today*, 1995). Given the young age of this population, the high educational and income backgrounds are particularly surprising. Clearly, the users of the Internet are a sophisticated group.

NATURE OF INFORMATION MARKETS

Although economists generally assume perfect information, few markets today actually function with all players having identical information about a good or service. Some buyers and sellers always have more information than other buyers and sellers in the same market. Information rarely flows freely and ubiquitously. A number of different factors influence the quantity and quality of information that individual buyers and sellers possess about a product. These factors include geographic location, transaction costs, and personal experience. The existence of the Internet and the Web, however, has reduced the importance of these factors in determining the amount of information available to players in the market.

Geographic Location

Geographic location has always played an important role in determining the amount and type of information a customer had about a vendor and its product (Tirole, 1988). There are at least two practical reasons why geographic location is so important. First, the jobs available in a local area are determined by the companies in that area. A great deal of information about a company and its products can be obtained when one either works for a company or knows someone that does. Having access to people who have first-hand information about the company can significantly influence the amount and quality of information one can obtain in a short amount of time. Second, local newspapers often run in-depth stories about local companies and their products, so it is possible to get detailed information just by reading the local news.

Today, geographic location can still influence the amount of information individuals have access to. It is not as large a factor, however, because of the Internet and the Web. Through the Internet, information consumers can scan a variety of local newspapers to obtain detailed information about a particular company and its products at very little cost. Furthermore, by using electronic mail and bulletin boards, information consumers can obtain first-hand information about a product from people who either produce the product or use the product on a regular basis. Thus, the Internet has become an extremely useful tool for bridging disjunct markets. The Internet provides a way in which individuals from different geographic locations can communicate cheaply.

Transaction Costs

There are a number of different costs involved in every market transaction. Costs incurred by producers include the costs of: finding a buyer, arranging and carrying out the exchange, ensuring that payment is received on time, and verifying that the customer is satisfied with the quality of the product. Buyers include such costs as those of finding a seller, shopping for the best price and verifying the quality of the product to be purchased. All of these costs are referred to as transaction costs. Depending on the type of transaction, these costs can be substantial. In the past, the existence of these costs may have prohibited some buyers and sellers from participating in the market.

Today the Internet is reducing many of these transaction costs. For example, software applications like Netbill and Digital Cash let customers purchase products over the Internet using a credit card or electronic check (Kambil, 1995). Programs such as these dramatically reduce firms' time, effort, and cost of processing payments. Electronic browsers or software agents, such as Lycos and Yahoo, let consumers quickly search the Internet for information about a product and its competitors. Sellers can create home pages to advertise their products on the Internet. These possibilities reduce search costs for both buyers and sellers. Many companies even offer on-line help pages that provide solutions for customer questions and problems (Erkes, et al., 1996). All of these services provided through the Internet help reduce costs associated with market transactions.

Extant Knowledge and Expertise

There is no better way to obtain information about a product than through first-hand experience with that product. Information consumers can use their extant knowledge about an industry or specific firms in that industry to improve their information search efficiency and effectiveness. Individuals can gain first-hand information through their work experiences and their recreational experiences. Individuals who work with technology firms, for example, will understand the benefits and shortcomings of particular software or hardware products better than, say, individuals who teach elementary school.

Since people have different life experiences, they are bound to have different information sets when they come to the market. Access to the Internet can help reduce the variation across individuals' information sets. The Internet provides a forum in which different individuals can share their expertise about particular products. This activity can take place on bulletin boards, chat lines, and newsgroups. By making inquiries in any of these forms on the Internet, individuals can obtain a virtual cornucopia of information about almost any company or product in which they are interested. By becoming aware of what others know about a product, the information gap between buyers and sellers narrows.

SUMMARY AND CONCLUSIONS

This paper addressed the interesting question of why firms disclose information on the Internet and the Web despite accepted economic theory that predicts they would not disclose information. The paper identified two significant conditions under which firms might have an incentive to disclose private information. The first condition occurs when firms are not profit-maximizers. The second condition occurs when significant barriers to entry do not exist—either by legal constraint, such as a patent, or by market structure, such as highly capital-intensive industries. The capital barriers may be a result of either financial capital or intellectual capital requirements.

The paper also examined consumers' incentives to obtain information via the Internet and discussed the costs that consumers face when accessing the Internet. Consumer incentives included search efficiency, search effectiveness, and reduction of consumer-borne transaction costs. Costs included the out-of-pocket costs that some must pay for Internet access and the opportunity costs of the time invested. Consumers invest time in acquiring Internet search skills and they invest time in the search activity itself.

Frequently, consumers become information providers by voluntarily posting information and knowledge they have gathered during their Internet searches or from other sources. This information-providing behavior is costly. Consumers engage in this costly behavior with the expectation, either explicit or implicit, that other information consumers will reciprocate. Therefore, the time and expense of posting information in expectation of *quid pro quo* is an additional access cost for information consumers.

Finally, the paper discussed the nature of information markets and concluded that the Internet and the Web serve as bridges across geographically disjunct markets. In essence, the Internet provides an information age equivalent of the corner grocery store, neighborhood barbershop, and town commons—a gathering place for the exchange of information that reduces physical distance and reduces a number of transaction costs.

The Internet and the Web provide bridges across space, time, and cultures to join markets in efficient and effective ways that were not possible with slower and less powerful forms of information dissemination. The Internet offers a low cost and enough advantages to attract investment by sellers, buyers, and consumers of information about products and services.

REFERENCES

Akerlof, G. 1970. The Market for Lemons: Quality Uncertainty and the Market Mechanism. *The Quarterly Journal of Economics*, 84, 488-500.

Brooks, F. P., and Sutherland, I. E. 1995. *Evolving the High Performance Computing and Communications Initiative to Support the Nation's Information Infrastructure.* Washington, DC: National Research Council.

Business Week. 1996. Web site for sale. (February 12), 8.

Berghel, H. 1996. The client's side of the World-Wide Web. *Communications of the ACM*, 39(1), 30-40.

Berners-Lee, T., Cailliau, R., Loutonen, A., Nielsen, H., and Secret, A. 1994. The World-Wide Web. *Communications of the ACM*, (37)8, 76-82.

Coase, R. H. 1937. "The Nature of the Firm, *Economica*, (November), 386-405.

Cohen, R. 1995. The economic impact of information technology. *Business Economics*, 30(4), 21-25.

Erkes, J. W., Kenny, K. B., Lewis, J. W., Sarachan, B. D., Sobolewski, M. W. and Sum, Jr., R. N. 1996. Implementing shared manufacturing services on the World-Wide Web. *Communications of the ACM*, 39(2), 34-45.

Garcia, D. L. 1995. Networking and the rise of electronic commerce: The challenge for public policy. *Business Economics*, 30(4), 7-14.

Kalil, T. 1995. Public Policy and the National Information Infrastructure. *Business Economics*, 30(4), 15-20.

Kambil, A. 1995. Electronic commerce: Implications of the internet for business practice and strategy. *Business Economics*, 30(4), 27-33.

Kendall, J. 1995. There's no place like home: The Web, the world, and you. *Journal of End-User Computing*, 7(3), 20-21.

Online Business Today. 1995. Newletter: 9511 1-20 (#15), (November 20).

Pearlman, A. 1995. Establishing a sophisticated presence on the Internet. *The American Lawyer*, 17(10), Supplement, 36-39.

Semich, J. W. 1995. The World Wide Web: Internet boomtown? *Datamation*, 41(1), 37-41.

Smith, J.A. 1937. *The Wealth of Nations*. New York: Random House, Modern Library Edition.

Strom, D. 1995. How to get Webbed. *Forbes*, 156(5), Supplement, 141-145.

Tirole, J. 1988. *The Theory of Industrial Organization*. Cambridge: The MIT Press.

Verity, J. W. 1996. What hath Yahoo wrought? *Business Week*, (February 12), 88-90.

Impact on Business II: Impact Assessment

A Statistical Assessment of the Impact of Information on Small Business Success

Liwen Qui Vaughan and Jean Tague-Sutcliffe
Graduate School of Library and Information Science
University of Western Ontario
London, Ontario

Abstract

A statistical methodology, LISREL, is applied to the problem of measuring the impact of information on small business development in Shanghai, China. Results show that information is the second most important factor in determining the success of small businesses, after the business environment. However, informal information channels are more important than formal ones.

Introduction

In the present economic climate of restructuring and accountability the questions 'What is its impact? What is its value?' are increasingly asked of services of all kinds. Information services have not escaped this scrutiny, but because of the indeterminacy of information, defining, let alone measuring, its impact is difficult. The problem is of particular concern to development agencies, government bodies which fund projects in developing countries, since they must justify their expenditures, ultimately, to the citizens of the funding country.

The International Development Research Centre (IDRC), an agency of the Canadian government, has embarked on a major investigation of ways to measure the impact of information on development. The framework for this imitative is given in the book <u>Measuring the Impact of Information on Development</u> (Menou, 1993) and some preliminary studies within this framework are reported in the proceedings of a 1995 Ottawa Conference (McConnell, 1995). The study we are reporting in this paper examines a methodology for assessing **quantitatively** the impact of information on development and so is meant to complement the earlier, more qualitative studies of this problem.

What we mean by impact and what we mean by development will always depend upon the particular environment studied. For this initial study, with the advice of IDRC, we decided to look at the impact of information in the small business environment, since this is a fast-growing sector in both developed and developing countries. Also, because of the current interest of the West in China, it was decided the use Shanghai as a test bed for our methodological approach.

This approach is called LISREL, an acronym which stands for Linear Structural RELations model. LISREL is a statistical methodology, usually implemented via the software of the same name, which analyzes causal relationships among variables by means of a path model which incorporates both observed and conceptual (or latent) variables.

To use LISREL we first had to define the model, which means identifying both variables which to some degree measure development or success in the small business environment (dependent variables) and variables which represent the factors, including information, which might contribute to this success (independent variables). In the model, dependent latent variables represent impact or results (such as small business success) and independent latent variables represent impacting factors (such as information). Each observed dependent and independent variable represents or, to some degree, measures a latent variable. The relationship between the latent variables and the observed variables of the model are displayed in a path diagram such as the one shown in Fig. 1. (The details of this figure will be explained later).

Data collected on all the observed variables are used to calculate correlation coefficients between all pairs of variables. Using this data, the LISREL software estimates the path coefficients, numbers which indicate the magnitude of the contribution of each independent latent variable to the dependent latent variable. Thus path coefficients have the potential of allowing us to assess quantitatively the impact of information on business success when the contribution of other factors to success is taken into account. LISREL also measures the validity of each observed variable to its corresponding latent variable, and these validity coefficients are represented by the numbers on the paths from observed to latent variables.

Before going to Shanghai to collect data and apply the LISREL methodology, we decided to carry out a pilot study on more familiar ground: London, Ontario. The initial step in this pilot was to speak with a number of local and international experts in the areas of small business and of information services evaluation. From this consultation we determined the input and impact variables to be used and developed an initial path model. The observed input variables in this initial model related to type of business, sources and kinds of information used by the business, and other factors which could be important in determining the success of the business such as location and financing. The observed dependent variables included length of time in business, growth in number of employees, profitability, and prospects for continued operation.

Data for the LISREL analysis was collected by means of a mailed questionnaire to 982 owners of small business in the London area. The response rate was 20% which, unfortunately, was insufficient for the procedures used in LISREL to estimate the path coefficients. Even a modification of the initial model failed to provide convergent estimates. Thus, the major value of the London pilot study was the indication of the changes that would have to be made in Shanghai in order to obtain results from a LISREL analysis. First, a larger sample than the one collected in London is necessary if the LISREL procedure is to work. Secondly, measures of business need to be designed so that business owners will feel confident and comfortable in providing the information.

Methodology of the Shanghai Study

The experience gained in the London pilot was very valuable in using the LISREL methodology. However, the whole survey instrument from questionnaire to sampling method had to be revamped because of the cultural, economic and social system differences between Canada and China. For this reason, we collaborated very closely with the Institute of Scientific and Technical Information of Shanghai (ISTIS). The Institute sent a researcher, Mr. Handong Wang, to Canada to gain firsthand experience with LISREL and help plan the Shanghai study. During the two months of summer 1995 when he was in London, we engaged in the extensive discussions about the Shanghai study. Other experts at the Institute were also consulted during this process and their suggestions incorporated into the final questionnaire. The actual survey was carried out in the fall of 1995 by the Institute. One of the Canadian research team member, Dr. Vaughan, spent two months in Shanghai to oversee the data collection process.

The original LISREL model for the Shanghai study consists of four latent variables: business environment, business expertise, use of information, and business success. The first three variables together contribute to (or influence) the last one, business success. These four latent variables were measured by a total of thirteen observed variables as follows. Business success was measured by the observed variables annual increase of fixed assets, liquid assets, sales amount, profit, and overall business prospects. Business environment was measured by availability of financing, location, technology development and marketing. Business expertise was measured by employees' expertise and composition of business leader team. The latent variable use of information, whose contribution is of most interest in this study, had two indicators (observed variables): use of informal information and use of formal information. Use of informal information was measured by the use of information from friends, relatives, customers, business conventions, trade shows etc. while use of formal information was measured by the use of a library, information institute, publicly available database, or similar service. Data on observed variables were obtained through a survey questionnaire.

Different types of business (service, manufacturing etc.) operate in different environments and may have different factors that will influence the success. In order to reduce the number of variables involved in the model, we chose a single type of business, namely manufacturing, for this study. There are different ways of defining a small business. The most common criteria used in China is the number of employees and the amount of fixed assets the business owns. Given the general situation with small manufacturing businesses in shanghai and the possibility of data collection, our Chinese colleague decided that 300 or fewer employees would be the best criterion for this study.

The electronic version of 1995 Business Directory complied by Shanghai Information Center was used to take random samples. The survey package included a cover letter and a self-addressed, stamped return envelope. The package was mailed to managers' offices rather than contact persons because only business heads can answer such questions as those about profit or fixed assets.

A total of 3,100 questionnaires were distributed. Follow up phone calls were made to over 70% of the subjects to encourage participation. The astounding pace of economic development in China and intense business competition has caused small business landscape to change rapidly. Most of questionnaires we sent out did not reach the targeted businesses for reasons such as address change or bankruptcy. Researchers in our collaborating institute estimated that only 30% of the questionnaires mailed actually reached their destination. The follow up phone call success rate confirmed this estimate. Assuming 30% of the mailed questionnaire were received, the adjusted return rate is over 40% for a total of 466 questionnaires returned.

The original LISREL model that we hypothesized for the Shanghai study did not fit the data collected. Data analysis by LISREL software and an examination of the questionnaire wording showed that two components of the model needed to be modified. First, the four observed variables (financing, location, technology development, and marketing) originally used as indicators of business environment were changed to measure two separate latent variables: business environment and business development. Financing and location measure the former while technology development and marketing measure the later. Second, the latent variable business expertise was removed from the model because one of the observed variables used to measure this concept, namely the composition of the business leader team, was biased in the data collection. Considering that the survey packages were mailed to managers' offices and most people filling out the questionnaires were business heads, it is not surprising that answers to this question had the highest average score and its variability was among the lowest.

Results of the Shanghai Study

These two modifications led to the final model as shown in Fig. 1. A chi-square goodness of fit test indicates that this model fits the data quite well (chi-square score with 30 degrees of freedom is 40.39, p=0.10). It should be noted that the chi-square value tends to be large in large samples because it is calculated as N-1 times the minimum value of the fit function, where N is the sample size (Jöreskog and Sörbom, 1993, p. 122). Considering the very large sample size in this study (over 400 data points), a p=0.10 fit is reasonably good. The LISREL estimate of the relationships between the four latent variables are indicated in the following equation:

$$success = 0.65 * business\_environment + 0.13 * develop + 0.2 * information\_use$$

The coefficient of determination for this equation is 0.8, meaning 80% of the variation in business success can be attributed to the variation in the business environment, in business development, and in use of information.

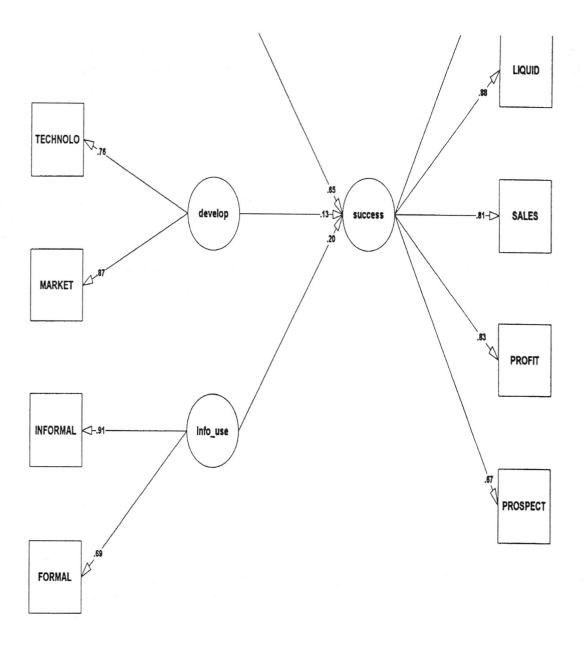

Figure 1 -- A final model that fits the data.

In the above equation, figures appearing in front of the * sign are the estimated path coefficients (the same figures are also displayed in the path diagram of Fig. 1). They indicate the relative magnitude of the effect of each factor on business success. Since all the coefficients are positive, it can be said that the contributions of all three factors to business success are positive.

As our main interest in this study is the contribution of information use, the statistical value of this coefficient was examined further. A T test value of 2.75 shows that the contribution of information is not only positive, but also statistically significant. Verbal comments received for the question "Please tell us your personal opinion on the impact of information on business management and development" echoed this statistical evidence. Most comments were very positive about the importance of information to business success, some even give examples of their own business success or failure to support their statements.

In Fig. 1, figures on arrows pointing from latent variables to observed variables can be interpreted as validity coefficients, that is they represent the validity of the observed variable as an indicator (measurement) of the latent variable. Comparing the two figures on the info_use latent variable in Fig. 1, we found that use of informal information is a better (more valid) indicator than use of formal information. This result does not surprise us because we reached the same conclusion in our London pilot study. Verbal comments obtained in both the London and Shanghai study help explain this phenomenon. Some subjects in the London study viewed the library as primarily a warehouse of information. Some respondents in the Shanghai study complained of difficulties they had at the information institute in finding information that is directly relevant and immediately useful to them. Some also attributed this lack of important information through formal sources to business secrecy due to competition.

The fact that informal information proved more valuable than formal information for small business sends a very important signal to libraries and information centres. Libraries and information centres can serve small business more effectively by promoting informal information sources, for example, by organizing activities which create opportunities for personal contacts and networking. Second, libraries should move away from the traditional stereotyped image of warehouse. Librarians should promote themselves as active providers of information and, in this way, build up personal relationships with the business community.

Summary

To summarize, this study shows that it is possible to quantitatively measure the impact of information on development (where development in this study refers specifically to business success). The LISREL model developed in this study shows that the use of information does indeed contribute positively to business success although its contribution is not as important as the business environment. It also found that in the small business sector, as in some other areas, use of informal information is more important than use of formal information.

Acknowledgements

The authors wish to thank our colleagues at the Institute for Scientific and Technical Information of Shanghai, especially Handong Wang, for their collaboration; Christian Sylvain, University of Western Ontario, the research assistant on this project; Pat Tripp, London Public Library, Charles Meadow, University of Toronto, Paul Kantor, Rutgers University, and Russell Knight, Western Business School, for help in developing the model; and the generous support of IDRC, which made the whole project possible.

References

Jöreskog, K. G. and Sörbom, D. (1993). LISREL 8: structural equation modelling with the SIMPLIS command language, Chicago, USA: Scientific Software International, Inc.

McConnell, Paul, ed. (1995). Making a difference; measuring the impact of information on development. Proceedings of a workshop in Ottawa, Canada, 10-12 July 1995. Ottawa: International Development Research Centre.

Menou, M.J., ed. (1993). Measuring the impact of information on development. Ottawa: International Development Research Centre.

Hispanic Managers Communicating Electronically in Anglo Businesses: Potential Interactions Between Culture and Technology

Carmen M. Bárcena and Gary P. Schneider
School of Business, University of San Diego
San Diego, California

Abstract

Increasingly, businesses are turning to groupware products that offer alternatives to in-person meetings among managers. Research on dehumanizing aspects of computerized communication technologies exists, but little or no research that examines the impact of cultural group differences on the effectiveness of communications technologies has been completed.

The participation of Hispanics in the managerial labor force in U.S.-based Anglo businesses is increasing. This paper argues that the experiences of Hispanic managers in Anglo businesses reflect a combination of three factors: specific characteristics of Hispanic culture, majority-minority relations, and elements of diversity within the Hispanic minority group. This paper examines the potential interactions between these three factors and the use of electronically-mediated communication technologies in Anglo businesses. The paper argues that, as Hispanic-Americans and other minorities increase their representation in the U.S. managerial work force, the interaction between culture and implementation characteristics of communication-facilitating technologies becomes a significant concern. The paper questions the implicit assumption that minorities must subsume their cultural values into those of the majority by acculturation.

The paper identifies literature on cross-cultural differences and suggests extensions to the case of Hispanic managers working in Anglo-owned and managed businesses. The paper identifies four dimensions—uncertainty avoidance, self and individualism, thinking and knowing, and doing and achieving—that combine the three factors: specific characteristics of Hispanic culture, majority-minority differences, and elements of diversity within the Hispanic minority group. The paper develops and presents propositions about the directions of differences between Hispanic and Anglo managers on each of these four dimensions.

Introduction

Increasingly, businesses are turning to groupware products that provide electronic communication and meeting capabilities (Wall Street Journal, 1995). These channels of communication offer alternatives to face-to-face meetings for managers' information gathering, strategy formulating, and decision making activities. Considerable research on the dehumanizing aspects of information and communication technologies does exist (e.g., Marx, 1990; Zuboff,

1988) as does research on the effectiveness of such technologies for specific tasks (e.g., McLeod and Liker, 1992; Zack, 1993). However, the impact of cultural group differences as mediators or causes of decreased effectiveness of communications technologies remains unexamined.

The 1990s are bringing major changes to the composition of the U.S. work force with African-American, Asian-American, and Hispanic-American participation in the labor pool increasing much faster than Anglo-American participation (Johnston and Parker, 1987; Saveri, 1991). The participation of Hispanics at all levels of management is increasing (Ferdman and Cortes, 1992). Many of the Hispanics that currently occupy managerial positions do so in businesses controlled by white, non-Hispanic Americans (Anglos).

The experiences of Hispanic managers in Anglo businesses reflect a combination of three factors: specific characteristics of Hispanic culture (Moore and Pachon, 1985), majority-minority relations (Ramirez, 1988), and elements of diversity within the Hispanic minority group (Cortina and Moncada, 1988). This paper examines the potential interactions between these three factors and the use of electronically-mediated communication technologies in Anglo businesses.

Electronic Communication and Meeting Technologies

Electronic communication technologies include electronic mail (email), file transfer software, and various kinds of groupware. Email sent via the Internet—once a tool for research scientists, librarians, and other academicians—has rapidly become ubiquitous in business, government, and not-for-profit organizations throughout the world.

In the United States alone there were 41 million email users by the end of 1994 sending some 18 billion messages per year (Burns, 1995). Increasingly, email software packages allow users to attach files to the text messages. These files may be spreadsheets, formatted text documents, databases, graphics, sound or video clips, or other types of formatted files.

Email software is one example of a category of software products called groupware. Groupware products allow people to communicate, work together, share information, and coordinate decision making. In addition to email, Haag and Keen (1996) identified six types of groupware:

- Group scheduling
- Electronic meeting support
- White board
- Video conferencing
- Work flow automation
- Electronic Data Interchange (EDI)

With the exception of video conferencing software, all of these products remove the visual cues that are an important part of human-to-human information transfer (Beamer, 1991; Limaye and Victor, 1991). Many of these technologies assume that users share a common world view.

Ibrahim (1991, p. 14) defines *world view* as a set of cultural variables that mediate and directly affect the "assumptions, modes of problem solving, decision making, and conflict resolution" that individuals bring to bear on workplace tasks. Other researchers (e.g., Bostrom, 1984; Heinen, 1977) have defined the term *frames* to capture a similar sense of world view. A frame is a filter through which an individual perceives the world and constructs an interpretation of its meaning (Goffman, 1974).

When designing the features of these work-enabling technologies, analysts and engineers bring their own frames and world views to bear. Differences between the designers' world views and the users' world views can lead to a number of problems (Leitheiser and Fouad, 1992). Similarly, we propose that differences among users' cultural backgrounds can create unintended problems. We believe that inconsistencies in users' world views or individual framings of communications received, communications composed, the organization of activities, and ordering of activities can all contribute to ineffective communication and work coordination.

In addition to the communication interference caused by differing world views, some research suggests that minority groups in the U.S. receive less training in software (Taylor and Munfield, 1991) and hardware (Boozer, et al., 1992) during the course of their primary and secondary education. Since computer hardware and software are either key or sole components of the emerging electronic communication technologies described above, all minority group members may begin with a deficit to overcome as they develop managerial skills in today's workplace.

A lack of familiarity with computer technology can induce computer anxiety, which researchers have found reduces performance levels on a number of computer-using tasks (Heinssen, et al., 1987; Igbaria and Chakrabarti, 1990; Premkumar, et al., 1993). The differential impact of computer anxiety on ethnic minorities is a significant problem in itself. It becomes an issue of even greater importance if the primary means of communication in information-age enterprise is electronically enhanced and computer based. Denying these minority groups access to computer knowledge and skills prevents them from participating fully in the management labor force.

Cultural Differences in the Workplace

During the 1990s and into the next century, the U.S. work force will expand more slowly than at any time since the 1930s—the rate of growth will be approximately half of that during the 1970s (Saveri, 1991). However, the labor force growth rates for minorities will be much higher—75% for Hispanic-Americans, who will also have a much lower median age, 26, than Anglos' median age of 39 (DOL, 1991; Johnston and Packer, 1987; Ponterotto and Casas, 1991). These drastic differences (see Table 1) in the composition in the work force at a time when the infusion of electronic communications technology is increasing suggest that an examination of culture-technology interactions is appropriate.

Table 1
Labor Force Projections for the Year 2000

Ethnic Group	Labor Force Growth Rate	Labor Force Median Age
African-American	32%	25
Anglo-American	17%	39
Asian-American	75%	28
Hispanic-American	75%	26

Adapted from DOL (1991), Johnston and Packer (1987), Ponterotto and Casas (1991), and Saveri (1991).

Managers who will use, supervise, plan, and implement the communication technologies of the present and the future must become sensitive to the ways a culturally diverse labor force will use these technologies. Since most of the managers who will plan and supervise the implementation of these technologies will not be members of the same ethnic groups as those who will use the technologies, managers' increased awareness of cultural difference impacts on communication technology use is extremely important.

Hofstede (1991, p. 5) defines culture in terms of a "collective programming of the mind." Harris and Moran (1991) identify culture as the acceptance of standardized ideas, habits, and attitudes that form a collective agreement on matters. This agreement manifests itself as tradition or custom within the cultural group. Beamer (1991), expanding on Kluckhohn and Strodtbeck's (1961) model, identified five dimensions of cultural orientation that might affect business communication processes: thinking and knowing, doing and achieving, self and individualism, organization of society, and universal conceptualizations.

Hofstede (1991) argued that cultural differences could be usefully classified in a hierarchical structure with each layer having significant, but not complete, dominance over layers that appeared further down in the hierarchy. The hierarchical structure of cultural layers followed the rough ordering that follows:

1. Nationality
2. Regional or ethnic affinity
3. Religious belief
4. Language or dialect
5. Gender
6. Generation or age
7. Social class
8. Organizational affinity

Although some researchers have disagreed with specific details of Hofstede's hierarchical structure of cultural layers (e.g., Hoecklin, 1995), most acknowledge that some layering occurs with individuals participating in multiple layers to varying degrees. Singer (1987) notes that communication efficiency is a product of how closely-matched the communicators are on dimensions of cultural group membership. Since the notion of power enters into many communications theories (e.g., Asante and Gudykunst, 1989; Gudykunst, 1991; Hoecklin, 1995; Ting-Toomey and Korzenny, 1991), the differing power of communications participants from different cultural groups becomes an important factor in the design of communications-enhancing and communications-coordinating technologies.

Complicating any examination of cultural communication issues are the findings that minority groups in the U.S. have large within-group variation (Knouse, et al., 1992) and have a tendency for cultural differences to be sublimated by acculturation (Marin and Marin, 1991). Acculturation is the process of minority group members changing their values to conform to those of the majority group (Marin and Marin, 1991) that can occur when members of different cultures come into contact with each other (Atkinson, et al., 1993).

Hispanic Managers

Hofstede (1984, 1991) identifies four dimensions of culture-related values: power distance, uncertainty avoidance, collectivism-individualism, and femininity-masculinity. He developed these dimensions while conduction an extensive study of IBM offices in some 50 countries. An examination of Hofstede's (1984) results for operations in Spanish-speaking countries reveals the following tendencies:

- Fairly high power distance scores, especially for Guatemala, Panama, Mexico, and Venezuela; however, the range of variation was significant with lower scores in Costa Rica, Argentina, and Spain.

- A clear clustering in the high end of the range on the uncertainty avoidance dimension.

- Fairly low scores on the individualism index, which indicates fairly strong collectivist tendencies.

- Mostly clustering in the middle of the femininity-masculinity scale, with a fairly large variation within the cluster.

Interestingly, the Spanish-speaking countries were all in the same power distance-uncertainty avoidance cluster when the two scales were plotted against each other. No clear clustering appeared on the individualism-gender plot. Notably, Hofstede's (1984) study included only one organization, and that organization was male-dominated—as were most large organizations at that time.

Of course, the study of culture in Spanish-speaking countries may provide quite different results from a study of Hispanic minority group members in the U.S. However, Hofstede's (1984, 1991) findings suggest two considerations that should help us design studies of culture-technology interactions in U.S. minority groups. First, if significant differences among cultures in Spanish-speaking countries exist, then we should expect to find cultural differences among Hispanic minority groups in the U.S. that trace their lineage to different countries of origin. Second, gender may be a factor that further mediates culture-technology interactions.

Diaz-Guerrero and Szalay (1991) provide an interesting communications lexicon that describes how residents of Columbia, Mexico, and the U.S. perceive themes such as family, society, and work. The goal of this lexicon is to identify differences in meaning that derive from perceptual and motivational dispositions that are likely to interfere in the process of communications across these three cultures.

Potential Culture-Technology Interactions

This section of the paper identifies research propositions about culture-technology interactions that might arise for Hispanic managers in U.S. Anglo businesses. These propositions are organized using Hofstede's (1991) four dimensions and Beamer's (1991) five dimensions. Because the Hofstede dimension of power distance overlaps considerably with Beamer's dimension of organization of society, we have combined these two constructs. For similar reasons, we have combined Beamer's self and individualism dimension with Hofstede's individualism. Therefore, we present a discussion of seven dimensions.

Power Distance and Organization of Society

Power distance is the extent to which managers assume that a hierarchical structure with embedded and formal authority structures is necessary. This dimension is difficult to develop into a proposition. Hofstede's (1984) results for Spanish-speaking countries included wide variation. Even within the U.S. Anglo majority, one might expect to observe regional variations in the intensity of this dimension that would, according to Hofstede's (1991) hierarchical model, dominate many other factors.

Uncertainty Avoidance

Uncertainty avoidance is the desire to avoid ambiguous situations or a preference for formal rules and interaction structures. We believe this dimension provides an excellent opportunity for developing a clear proposition. Not only did Hofstede (1984) find a clustering of Spanish-speaking countries on the high end of the range, but the U.S. and other Anglo countries (e.g., Canada, Great Britain, Australia, and New Zealand) clustered at a much lower end of the range. Consistent with these findings are the Mexican respondents in the Diaz-Guerrero and Szalay (1991, pp. 180-181) study that identified "hierarchy" as the strongest manifestation of "authority." Therefore, the proposition would be that Hispanic managers would desire a greater degree of structure and more formal rules than Anglo managers would provide in the communications technology.

Self and Individualism

The individualism dimension reflects the degree to which a person ranks concern for the individual more highly than concern for the group (collectivism). This dimension provides another excellent basis for a proposition. Hofstede (1984) found a clustering of Spanish-speaking countries near the low end of the scale, suggesting an Hispanic preference for collective loyalty to the group. The U.S. offices in Hofstede's study scored the highest of all on the individualism scale. This dichotomy could provide some compelling implications for communications technology design and implementation. Diaz-Guerrero and Szalay (1991, p. 61) also conclude that Hispanic-Americans are "gregarious people enjoying and cultivating a life of rich interpersonal relations."

Femininity-Masculinity

Hofstede (1984) found that Spanish-speaking country offices and U.S. offices both clustered near the middle of this scale. Therefore, we do not believe we can develop a clear proposition about differences, much less the direction of those differences, between Hispanic and Anglo managers on this dimension. As we noted earlier, gender differences are difficult to assess from the Hofstede (1984) data because of the male-dominated corporate environment that permeated his sample. We would expect gender itself to dominate this dimension as more females enter the managerial work force despite its low position in the Hofstede (1991) hierarchy. Diaz-Guerrero and Szalay (1991) did not examine gender specifically, but did compile a lexicon for "love and sex" that identified strong similarities between the Colombian and Mexican respondents that differed greatly from the U.S. respondents' lexicon.

Thinking and Knowing

This dimension describes how members of the culture obtain and accept the truth value of information. We would expect Hispanic managers to be somewhat less likely than Anglo managers to rely on linear, cause-and-effect thinking. We also would expect Hispanic managers to be more willing to accept that some elements of nature are essential mysteries (Carter, 1991). Therefore, we propose that clear differences between Anglo managers and Hispanic managers exist on this dimension.

Doing and Achieving

Some cultures value getting results over social relationships. Anglo managers may be one of the best examples of this type of culture in the world. Hispanic managers are more likely to value social relationships and ascribe successes to fate or good luck (Diaz-Guerrero and Szalay 1991). We propose that identifiable differences, with Anglo managers being much more directed to getting results, exist between all Hispanic cultural sub-groups and Anglos.

Universal Conceptualizations

Beamer (1991) identifies this dimension as a person's feelings about universal constants such as whether time is linear or cyclical, whether change is good or evil, and whether death is final or transitional. We believe that this dimension is too general and includes several important, but potentially conflicting, factors that might confound results—even within a cultural group. Therefore, we did not develop a proposition based on this dimension.

Summary and Conclusions

This paper argued that, as Hispanic-Americans and other minorities increase their representation in the U.S. managerial work force, the interaction between culture and implementation characteristics of communication-facilitating technologies becomes a significant concern. The paper questions the implicit assumption that minorities must subsume their cultural values into those of the majority by acculturation.

The paper identifies related literature on cross-cultural differences that have been found in studies that span countries and suggested, where possible, extensions to studies of Hispanic managers working in Anglo-owned and managed businesses. Of the seven dimensions of culture synthesized from the work of Hofstede (1984, 1991) and Beamer (1991), we identified four that were likely to produce culture-technology interactions that would affect the communications ability of Hispanic managers in Anglo businesses. We believe these four dimensions— uncertainty avoidance, self and individualism, thinking and knowing, and doing and achieving— combine the three factors that we identified earlier as affecting culture-technology interactions: specific characteristics of Hispanic culture, majority-minority differences, and elements of diversity within the Hispanic minority group.

Finally, we developed and presented propositions about the directions of differences between Hispanic and Anglo managers on each of these four dimensions. We hope that our identification of these differences provides an impetus for future research in this interesting area.

References

Asante, M. K. and W. B. Gudykunst, Eds. 1989. *Handbook of International and Intercultural Communication*. Newbury Park, CA: Sage.

Atkinson, D. R., G. Morten, and D. W. Sue. 1993. *Counseling American Minorities: A Cross-Cultural Perspective*. Fourth Edition. Dubuque, IA: Brown and Benchmark.

Beamer, L. 1991. Learning intercultural communication competence, *Journal of Business Communication*, 29, 285-303.

Bostrom, R. P. 1984. Development of computer-based information systems: A communication perspective, *Computer Personnel*, 9(4), 17-25.

Bostrom, R. P. 1989. Successful application of communication techniques to improve the systems development process, *Information and Management*, 16, 279-295.

Boozer, M. A., A. B. Krueger, and S. Wolkon. 1992. Race and school quality since Brown v. Board of Education. *Brookings Papers: Macroeconomics*, 269-338.

Burns, N. 1995. E-mail beyond the LAN, *PC Magazine*, (April 22), 102-108.

Carter, R. T. 1991. Cultural values: A review of empirical research and implications for counseling, *Journal of Counseling and Development*, 70, 164-173.

Cortina, R. J. and A. Moncada. 1988. *Hispanos en los Estados Unidos*. Madrid: Instituto de Cooperación Iberoamericana.

Department of Labor (DOL). 1991. *Occupational Outlook Quarterly*. Washington, DC: Department of Labor.

Diaz-Guerrero, R. and L. B. Szalay. 1991. *Understanding Mexicans and Americans: Cultural Perspectives in Conflict*. New York: Plenum.

Ferdman, B. M. and A. C. Cortes. 1992. Culture and identity among Hispanic managers in an Anglo business. In *Hispanics in the Workplace*, S. B. Kouse, P. Rosenfeld, and A. L. Culberston, eds. Newbury Park, CA: Sage, 246-277.

Goffman, E. 1974. *Frame Analysis: An Essay on the Organization of Experience*. New York: Harper & Row.

Gudykunst, W. B. 1991. *Bridging Differences: Effective Intergroup Communication*. Newbury Park, CA: Sage.

Haag, S. and P. Keen. 1996. *Information Technology: Tomorrow's Advantage Today*. New York: McGraw-Hill.

Harris, P. R. and R. T. Moran. 1991. *Managing Cultural Differences*. Third Edition. Houston: Gulf.

Heinssen, R. K., Jr., C. R. Glass, and L. A. Knight. 1987. Assessing computer anxiety: Development and validation of the computer anxiety rating scale. *Computers in Human Behavior*, 3, 49-59.

Hoecklin, L. 1995. *Managing Cultural Differences: Strategies for Competitive Advantage*. Reading, MA: Addison-Wesley.

Hofstede, G. 1991. *Cultures and Organizations: Software of the Mind*. New York: McGraw-Hill.

Ibrahim, F. A. 1991. Contribution of cultural worldview to generic counseling and development, *Journal of Counseling and Development*, 70(1), 13-19.

Igbaria, M. and A. Chakrabarti. 1990. Computer anxiety and attitudes towards microcomputer use. *Behaviour and Information Technology*, 9, 229-241.

Ivey, A. E., M. B. Ivey, and L. Simek-Morgan. 1993. *Counseling and Psychotherapy: A Multicultural Perspective*. Third Edition. Needham Heights, MA: Allyn and Bacon.

Johnston, W. B. and A. H. Packer. 1987. *Workforce 2000: Work and Workers for the 21st Century*. Indianapolis, IN: Hudson Institute.

Kluckhohn, F. R. and F. L. Strodtbeck. 1961. *Variations in Value Orientations*. Evanston, IL: Roe Paterson.

Knouse, S. B., P. Rosenfeld, and A. L. Culbertson, Eds. 1992. *Hispanics in the Workplace*. Newbury Park, CA: Sage.

Leitheiser, R. L. and N. A. Fouad. 1993. An exploration of the role of diverse cultures on the information requirements determination process. *Proceedings of the Fourteenth International Conference on Information Systems*, (December), 35-45.

Limaye, M. R. and D. A. Victor. 1991. Cross-cultural business research: State of the art and hypotheses for the 1990s, *Journal of Business Communication*, 28, 277-299.

Marin, G. and B. V. Marin. 1991. *Research with Hispanic Populations*. Newbury Park, CA: Sage.

Marx, G. T. 1990. The case of the omniscient organization, *Harvard Business Review*, March-April, 12-30.

McLeod, P. L. and J. K. Liker. 1992. Electronic meeting systems: evidence from a low structure environment, *Information Systems Research*, 3, 195-223.

Moore, J. and H. Pachon. 1985. *Hispanics in the United States*. Englewood Cliffs, NJ: Prentice-Hall.

Ponterotto, J. G. and J. M. Casas. 1991. *Handbook of Racial/Ethnic Minority Counseling Research*. Springfield, IL: C. C. Thomas.

Premkumar, G., K. Ramamurthy, and W. R. King. 1993. *Journal of Educational Computing Research*, 9(3), 373-398.

Ramirez, A. 1988. Racism toward Hispanics: The culturally monolithic society, In *Eliminating Racism: Profiles in Controversy*, P. A. Katz and D. A. Taylor, eds. New York: Plenum, 137-158.

Saveri, A. 1991. Realignment of workers and work in the 1990s. In *New Directions in Career Planning and the Workplace*, J. Kummerow, ed. Palo Alto, CA: Consulting Psychologists Press.

Singer, M. R. 1987. *Intercultural Communication A Perceptual Approach*. Englewood Cliffs, NJ: Prentice Hall.

Szapocznik, J., M. A. Scopetta, M. A. Arranndale, and W. Kurtines. 1978. Cuban value structure: Treatment implications, *Journal of Consulting and Clinical Psychology*, 46, 961-970.

Taylor, H. G. and L. Mounfield. 1991. An analysis of success factors in college computer science: High school methodology is a key element. *Journal of Research on Computing in Education*, 24(2), 240-245.

Ting-Toomey, S. and F. Korzenny, Eds. 1991. *Cross-Cultural Interpersonal Communication*. Newbury Park, CA: Sage.

Wall Street Journal. 1995. Groupware or webware? (November 7), A1.

Zack, M. H. 1993. Interactivity and communication mode choice in ongoing management groups, *Information Systems Research*, 4, 207-239

Zuboff, S. 1988. *In the Age of the Smart Machine: The Future of Work and Power*. New York: Basic.

Events-Based Financial Reporting:
The Potential of the Internet

Gary P. Schneider and Carol M. Bruton
School of Business Administration, University of San Diego
San Diego, California

Abstract

One of the most widely-accepted ways for publicly-held firms to communicate the results of their operations to stockholders, creditors, and other stakeholders outside the firm is to issue financial statements. Many critics have argued that the existence of multiple acceptable, yet not reconcilable, accounting procedures causes these financial statements to be inefficient and ineffective communication devices. These critics argue that investors and financial analysts must obtain information from sources other than a firm's financial statements. These critics further argue that the operation of an efficient capital market for most large firms effectively disseminates this additional information to investors, creditors, and others interested in the affairs of those firms. Unfortunately, recent research into the efficiency of capital markets suggests that these markets may not be efficient, especially for small firms and for firms with lightly-traded equity securities.

Accounting theorists have developed alternative approaches to recording economic events in relational databases that may provide a more efficient way to propagate information about all firms—even smaller firms—to investors, creditors, and other third-party stakeholders. These approaches, called *events accounting* or *database accounting*, identify semantic accounting phenomena of one sort or another as a first step. The approaches then make these semantic primitives available to accounting information users in various ways.

Although research into events and database accounting is still developing, a significant amount of work has occurred in managerial accounting applications. Managerial accounting is the set of accounting information that firms make available to managers and other decision makers inside the firm. These applications of events or database accounting are easier to develop because the reports need not comply with the detailed laws and accounting rules with which external financial reports must comply.

This paper discusses the prospects for extending the existing managerial accounting implementations of events accounting or database accounting to financial reporting applications. One major barrier to the extension of these accounting approaches to financial reporting has been the difficulty of delivering information stored in large databases to widely-dispersed users. The Internet appears to provide a means for overcoming this barrier. A second major barrier has been the need to restrict access to certain portions of the database while providing sophisticated querying capabilities. The currently emerging integration of advanced database manipulation tools with the World Wide Web (the Web) offers a potential means of overcoming this second barrier.

Introduction

Financial statements compiled in accordance with Generally Accepted Accounting Principles (GAAP) are an important source of information about publicly-traded business firms for investors, creditors, labor unions, and the general public (Chambers, 1966; Edwards and Bell, 1961; Paton and Littleton, 1940; Watts and Zimmerman, 1986). Unfortunately, GAAP do not require all firms to use identical assumptions, estimates, and accounting methods. The availability of alternative accounting treatments for the same transaction, all of which comply with GAAP, have inspired a long and continuing series of critics such as Canning (1929), Vatter (1947), Chambers (1964), and Briloff (1972). These critics argued that accounting numbers fail to provide financial statement users with consistent, meaningful, and useful information on which to base investment and credit decisions. Some of these critics, notably Briloff (1972), went so far as to argue that firms could—and did—intentionally mislead their investors.

Researchers have argued that investors obtain information from sources other than accounting reports (see Watts and Zimmerman, 1986, Chapter 2, for an excellent summary of these arguments). However, Beaver and Rappaport (1984) and Burton (1984) both noted that computing technology would soon cause financial statement users to increase their expectations about the level and quality of accounting information that firms should provide. Ten years later, the entrenched custom of issuing annual financial statements printed on paper to stockholders and other third parties has not changed significantly.

Alternatives to Annual GAAP-Based Financial Statements

Burton (1984) described annual financial statements as rigid disclosures. He noted that this rigidity was the logical result of the historically high cost of data accumulation and the time-consuming efforts required to aggregate financial data into financial statements. Financial statements became standardized for many of the same reasons that Henry Ford offered his Model T in any color the customer wanted—as long as that color was black. Automobile manufacturers like Ford operating early in this century found that they could standardize their manufacturing processes they could realize economies of scale. These economies of scale allowed them to produce large quantities of a homogeneous product at much lower costs than custom-manufacturing automobiles to customer orders would have permitted. These automobiles satisfied the transportation needs of many consumers well enough to be attractive, low-cost purchases. Similarly, accountants responded to the high costs of data accumulation and aggregation by producing a standardized product—financial statements in accordance with GAAP—that met the needs of a large number of financial information consumers.

While accountants were busy preparing their financial statements and developing new and more complex rules of GAAP, information technology was progressing at an impressive pace. Recently, the cost of gathering data and creating customized reports has dropped to such a low level that managers in firms have come to expect to have the information they want, when they want it, and in the form they would like to have it (Borthick, 1992). Users of accounting information inside firms now expect accountants to help them get this information rather than spend time and resources imposing rigid, periodic, historical cost-based statements (Elliot, 1992; McKinnon and Bruns, 1992).

Elliot (1996) identified five major defining attributes of existing GAAP-basis financial statements that, he argued, adequately capture only two of the three dimensions of a business enterprise. He stated that GAAP-based financial statements:

1. Are periodic statements issued annually or, at best, quarterly,
2. Show historical results long after these results are interesting to financial information consumers,
3. Rely on cost as the basis for measurement,
4. Include only financial information, and
5. Present information in a highly aggregated form.

Elliot argued that what financial information consumers really want is a resource that adequately presents all three dimensions—including time—of an enterprise and includes:

1. On-demand access to information,
2. Continuous information flow that can be intercepted and extracted at any time,
3. Values rather than historical costs as a basis for measurement,
4. A variety of information that includes, specifically, non-financial data, and
5. User-customizable formats with drill-down and drill-across capabilities.

Elliot (1996) predicts that the value chain linkages forged using electronic data interchange (EDI) over the past fifteen years (Borthick and Roth, 1993; Cathey, 1991; EDICA, 1990; Ferguson, et al., 1990; Powers, 1989) provide an excellent model that accountants could extend to financial statement users—the providers of enterprise capital.

Events-Based Accounting and Relational Databases

GAAP-based financial statements are based on double-entry bookkeeping—a technique that dates back some five centuries. Pacioli (1494) gave generations of accountants a valuable tool for identifying and recording essential business transaction elements. These procedures were well-suited to recording transactions in pen-and-paper information systems. Merchants needed to capture the essence of each transaction safely and efficiently. Recording transactions was still a time-consuming task, but Pacioli's bookkeeping procedures made it possible to accomplish the job. The double-entry nature of the technique provided an automatic internal control feature in manual accounting systems. Scholars continue to debate why Pacioli excluded negative numbers from his bookkeeping model (Peters and Emery, 1978; Scorgie, 1989; Thomsen, 1991). However, this exclusion has left modern accountants with a legacy of debits and credits that do not map well to computerized transaction recording systems.

Double-entry bookkeeping uses debits and credits to record changes in three categories of abstract entities called *accounts*: assets, liabilities, and equities. Accounting lore holds that summaries and aggregations of these three categories can provide information about firms' values and wealth changes (FASB, 1990; Ijiri, 1975; Sorter, 1969). Reducing every transaction to its effects on these abstract entities made record keeping feasible five centuries ago. For example, a double-entry bookkeeping system records a credit sales transaction as follows:

Date   Accounts receivable   *Amount*
            Sales   *Amount*
                               Explanation

This journal entry is an abstraction of the transaction that includes five items of information: a Transaction *Date*, two Account *Names*, a Transaction *Amount*, and an *Explanation* of the transaction. If the journal entry were posted to a subsidiary ledger, the customer name would also be recorded. The double-entry bookkeeping system records a maximum of six attributes of this transaction and records one of them, *Amount*, twice.

Sorter (1969) and Johnson (1970) argued that accounting should abdicate its role as aggregator of transaction data. They proposed that accounting systems store information about economic events and that accountants devote their energies to helping users obtain and aggregate information as needed. McCarthy (1979; 1982), Gal and McCarthy (1985), and others have used Chen's (1976) entity-relationship approach to model accounting events or similar concepts in relational databases (Parello, et al., 1985). Using an entity-relationship approach allows a much richer semantic representation of each accounting event. For example, the credit sales transaction described above could be recorded in a relational database that would store a virtually unlimited number of attributes for each sale.

Relational databases are increasingly being used in enterprise-wide information systems (Kendall and Kendall, 1995) while current accounting software packages continue to be no more than "computerized versions of journalizing and posting routines which use double-entry principles to define procedures and the chart of accounts to classify meaning of economic events" (Geerts and McCarthy, 1991, p. 160).

Computerized implementations of double-entry bookkeeping cannot use a relational database design—the artificial duality presents an obstacle to semantic modeling of the transaction processing activity. Although semantic models incorporate similar abstraction mechanisms such as aggregation and generalization (Reuber, 1988; Smith and Smith, 1977), they must contain the aggregation hierarchy within their own structures.

Transactions recorded in a double-entry accounting system have already been aggregated and abstracted. In manual systems, the dual nature of the accounting debit and credit model provides a built-in error correction mechanism. In automated systems, this same duality is inefficient and serves no control purpose. Many managers of automated financial reporting systems face problems that arise from the complexity of using computers to perform these manual tasks without re-thinking what tasks the systems should perform (McKie, 1995).

The Potential of the Internet

When Sorter (1969) and Johnson (1970) first envisioned events-based accounting, they hoped that it would give financial statement users direct access to large portions of firms' financial information. In an events-based accounting system, economic events are stored in a disaggregate form that allows users to specify the retrieval form. Sorter (1969) argued that this direct access would overcome concerns about aggregation and lack of comparability in firms' financial reports. Borthick (1992) echoed Sorter's arguments and noted that financial statement users have become less tolerant of the limitations of accounting reports. The Securities and Exchange Commission (SEC) recently introduced a program to make information about publicly traded firms available on the Web (SEC, 1996). These filings contain the firms' financial statements and other information; however, they do not provide the level of access and flexibility that events-based accounting would provide.

The level of access provided by events-based accounting databases combined with the world-wide connectivity of the Internet has the potential to revolutionize financial reporting. As the Internet becomes enabled with such features as the graphic user interface of the Web (Berners-Lee, et al., 1994) and increasingly sophisticated applications such as Java (Sun, 1996).

When Sorter (1969) first discussed events-based accounting, the computing technology did not exist to place large databases of accounting information on-line. Even if the computing technology had not been a constraint, database theory had not developed ways to store and retrieve data with sufficient efficiency to make events-based reporting feasible. Since that time, McCarthy (1979, 1982) and others (Gal and McCarthy, 1985; Geerts and McCarthy, 1991; Grabski and March, 1994; Hale, 1992; Schneider, et al., 1995; Weber, 1986) have applied evolving database theory to accounting systems and have described a number of functional events-based accounting applications.

Recently, books describing events-based accounting systems have also appeared (Denna, et al., 1993; Hollander, et al., 1996; Perry and Schneider, 1995). However, these applications have predominantly yielded internal or managerial accounting reports. Understanding the differences between financial and managerial accounting can help explain why events-based accounting databases were first developed for managerial accounting applications.

Differences Between Financial and Managerial Accounting

Accountants prepare *financial* accounting reports for information consumers outside the firm; they prepare *managerial* accounting reports for information consumers inside the firm. Events approaches to accounting database development have appeared first in managerial accounting applications (e.g., Grabski and March, 1994) because it is almost always in the best interest of a firm to make information available to decision makers inside the firm. Additional information generally improves a manager's ability to make decisions and should, therefore, generate additional profits for the firm (Hilton, 1985). Since a database containing all relevant attributes of each transaction provides a greater amount of information than any double-entry bookkeeping-based accounting system, all managers and their employing firms would prefer such a finer information system. A more fine information system is one that includes at least all of the information that exists in a less fine information system plus some amount of additional information (Blackwell, 1953; Hilton, 1985).

This choice is not so clear when a firm considers what to disclose to external third parties. As Demski (1973) noted, firms may have a significant incentive to limit the extent and nature of information disclosures to external consumers of financial information. The firm cannot move all interested third parties to a higher Pareto-optimum because the interested third parties may have conflicting utilities for additional information. For example, the firm's investors may become directly better off if they receive additional information about the firm. However, if that same information becomes available to the firm's competitors, government regulators, or labor unions, the investors may become indirectly worse off because private firm information becomes public and reduces the value of the firm.

Selective Access: A Solution?

As relational database management products become more sophisticated (Stamen, 1993), the idea of providing open access to large databases becomes realizable. Large databases, often called data warehouses (Cafasso, 1995; Celko, 1995; Fairhead, 1995; Strehlo, 1996) have become increasingly common in larger firms. Firms use these large databases as resources to maintain their competitive edge (Atre and Storer, 1995) by finding new relationships in existing data that they formerly kept in separate databases. This process is called data mining (Grupe and Owrang, 1995; Hedberg, 1995; Watterson, 1995).

More sophisticated tools for data mining and analysis are appearing regularly, including on-line analytical processing (OLAP) and multi-dimensional analysis products (Callaway, 1995; Mitchell, 1995; Ricciuti, 1994). These tools combine with graphical user interface enhancements such as the Web (Berners-Lee, et al., 1994) and Java (Sun, 1996) provide a basis for the development of Internet gateways that might allow external users to access large, firm-maintained, data warehouses of information about economic events.

Each firm will need to develop security guidelines to prevent third parties from using these analytic tools to access sensitive information or to combine information in separate records of economic events to assess or estimate sensitive information. By providing selective access to large databases of economic events, firms can provide financial information consumers with less aggregated, more timely, and more customized sets of information on demand. Until firms develop in-process audit and control software, external accesses should be closely monitored on an individual basis to ensure that no external party obtains sensitive information.

Summary and Conclusions

Publicly-held firms communicate the results of their operations to stockholders, creditors, and other stakeholders outside the firm by issuing financial statements. The existence of multiple acceptable, yet not reconcilable, accounting procedures causes these financial statements to be inefficient and ineffective communication devices. Therefore, investors and financial analysts must obtain information from sources other than a firm's financial statements.

Events approaches to accounting that use relational database technology are becoming prevalent in larger firms. These approaches identify semantic accounting phenomena of one sort or another and make these semantic primitives available to accounting information users in various ways. This paper examined how current advances in inter-entity networking—the Internet—and database storage and analysis software—data warehousing, OLAP, and data mining—could ultimately provide substitutes for periodic paper-based financial statements.

Finally, the paper noted some concerns about auditing and controlling third-party access to firms' databases to prevent extraction of sensitive information. The time for financial disclosures on the Internet that replace traditional financial statements is not here yet, but it is getting close.

References

Atre, S. and P. Storer. 1995. Data distribution and warehousing. *DBMS: Client/Server Computing*, 8, 54-63.

Beaver, W. H. and A. Rappaport. 1984. Financial reporting needs more than the computer. *Business Week*, (August 13), 16.

Berners-Lee, T., Cailliau, R., Loutonen, A., Nielsen, H., and Secret, A. 1994. The World-Wide Web. *Communications of the ACM*, (37), 76-82.

Blackwell, D. 1953. Equivalent comparisons of experiments. *Annals of Mathematical Statistics*, 6, 265-273.

Borthick, A. F. 1992. Helping users get the information they want, when they want it, in the form they want it: Integrating the choice and use of information, *Journal of Information Systems*, 6, v-ix.

Borthick, A. F. 1993. EDI for reengineering business processes. *Management Accounting*, 75, 32-37.

Briloff, A. J. 1972. *Unaccountable Accounting*. New York: Harper & Row.

Burton, J. C. 1984. What lies ahead for SEC's financial reporting? *Legal Times*, (October 8), A2, A9-A11.

Cafasso, R. 1995. Complexity rising on data access front. *Computerworld*, 29, 12.

Callaway, E. 1995. The flavors of OLAP. *PC Week*, 12, (July 17), 14-15.

Canning, J. B. 1929. *The Economics of Accountancy: A Critical Analysis of Accounting Theory.* New York: Ronald.

Cathey, J. M. 1991. Electronic data interchange: What a controller should know. *Management Accounting*, 73, 47-51.

Celko, J. 1995. Joe looks at data warehousing strategies, criticizes C. J. Date, and offers a new SQL puzzle. *DBMS: Client/Server Computing*, 8, 17-20.

Chambers, R. J. 1964. Measurement and objectivity in accounting. *The Accounting Review*, 39, 264-274.

Chambers, R. J. 1966. *Accounting, Evaluation, and Economic Behavior.* Englewood Cliffs, NJ: Prentice Hall.

Chen, P. P. 1976. The entity relationship model—toward a unified view of data, *ACM Transactions on Database Systems*, 1, 9-36.

Demski, J. S. 1973. The general impossibility of normative accounting standards. *The Accounting Review*, 48, 718-723.

Denna, E. L., J. O. Cherrington, D. P. Andros, and A. S. Hollander. 1993. *Event-Driven Business Solutions.* Homewood, IL: Business One Irwin.

EDI Council of Australia (EDICA). 1990. *EDI Control Guide.* Sydney: EDICA.

Edwards, E. O. and P. W. Bell. 1961. *The Theory and Measurement of Business Income.* Berkeley, CA: University of California Press.

Elliot, R. K. 1992. The third wave breaks on the shores of accounting. *Accounting Horizons*, 6, 61-85.

Elliot, R. K. 1996. The effect of information technology on the future of accounting and auditing. Keynote address at the Accounting Information Systems Research Symposium, Phoenix, AZ, February.

Fairhead, N. 1995. Data warehouses: Increasing the value of your decision makers. *Business Quarterly*, 60, 89-94.

Ferguson, D. M., N. C. Hill, and J. V. Hansen. 1990. Electronic data interchange: Foundations and survey evidence on current use. *Journal of Information Systems*, 4, 81-91.

Financial Accounting Standards Board (FASB). 1990. *Statements of Financial Accounting Concepts.* Norwalk, CT: FASB.

Gal, G. and W. E. McCarthy. 1985. Operation of a relational accounting system, *Advances in Accounting*, 3, 83-112.

Geerts, G. and W. E. McCarthy. 1991. Database accounting systems. In Williams, B. C. and B. J. Spraul (eds), *IT and Accounting: The Impact of Information Technology*. London: Chapman & Hall, 159-183.

Grabski, S. V. and R. J. Marsh. 1994. Integrating accounting and advanced manufacturing information systems: An ABC and REA-based approach, Forthcoming in *Journal of Information Systems*.

Grupe, F. H. and M. M. Owrang. 1995. Data base mining. *Information Systems Management*, 12, 26-31.

Hale, D. P. 1992. Modeling events accounting information systems, *Advances in Accounting Information Systems*, 1, 143-180.

Hedberg, S. R. 1995. The data gold rush. *Byte*, 20, (October 1), 83-88.

Hilton, R. W. 1985. *Probabilistic Choice Models and Information: Studies in Accounting Research #24*. Sarasota, FL: American Accounting Association.

Hollander, A. S., E. L. Denna, and J. O. Cherrington. 1996. *Accounting, Information Technology, and Business Solutions*. Chicago: Irwin.

Ijiri, Y. 1975. *Theory of Accounting Measurement*. Sarasota: American Accounting Association.

Johnson, O. 1970. Toward an "events" theory of accounting, *The Accounting Review*, 45, 641-653.

Kendall, K. E. and J. E. Kendall. 1995. *Systems Analysis and Design*. Englewood Cliffs, NJ: Prentice-Hall.

McCarthy, W. E. 1979. An entity-relationship view of accounting models, *The Accounting Review*, 54, 667-686.

McCarthy, W. E. 1982. The REA accounting model: A generalized framework for accounting systems in a shared data environment, *The Accounting Review*, 57, 554-578.

McKie, S. 1995. Financial accounting meets workflow. *DBMS: Client/Server Computing*, 8, 64-75.

McKinnon, S. M. and W. J. Bruns, Jr. 1992. *The Information Mosaic*. Boston: Harvard Business School Press.

Mitchell, L. 1995. *PC Week*, 12, (November 20), 74-77.

Pacioli, L. 1494. Summa Arithmetica Geometria Proportioni et Proportionalita. Venice: Paganinus de Paganinis.

Parrello, B., R. Overbeck, and E. Lusk. 1985. The design of entity-relationship models for general ledger systems, *Data & Knowledge Engineering*, 1, 155-180.

Paton, W. A. and A. C. Littleton. 1940. *An Introduction to Corporate Accounting Standards.* Chicago: American Accounting Association.

Peters, R. M. and D. R. Emery. 1978. The role of negative numbers in the development of double entry bookkeeping, *Journal of Accounting Research*, 16, 424-426.

Perry, J. T. and G. P. Schneider. 1995. *Building Accounting Systems: A Transaction Cycle Approach.* Cincinnati, OH: South-Western College Publishing.

Powers, W. J. 1989. *EDI Control and Audit Issues for Managers, Users, and Auditors.* Alexandria, VA: Electronic Data Interchange Association.

Reuber, A. R. 1988. Opportunities for accounting information systems research from a database perspective, *Journal of Information Systems*, 3, 87-103.

Ricciuti, M. 1994. Multidimensional analysis: Winning the competitive game. *Datamation*, 40, (February 15), 21-26.

Schneider, G. P., J. T. Perry, and C. B. Bruton, 1995. Modeling Accounting Information Systems: The Danger of Double-Entry Artifacts, *Proceedings of the Twenty-Fourth Annual Meeting of the Western Decision Sciences Institute*, April, 73-75.

Scorgie, M. E. 1989. The role of negative numbers in the development of double entry bookkeeping: A comment, *Journal of Accounting Research*, 27, 316-318.

Securities and Exchange Commission (SEC). 1996. *Electronic Data Gathering, Analysis and Retrieval System (EDGAR)*, (http://www.sec.gov/edgarhp.htm).

Smith, J. M. and D. C. P. Smith. 1977. Database abstractions: Aggregation and generalization, *ACM Transactions on Database Systems*, 2, 105-133.

Sorter, G. H. 1969. An "events" approach to basic accounting theory, *The Accounting Review*, 44, 12-19.

Stamen, J. P. 1993. Structuring databases for analysis. *IEEE Spectrum*, 30, 55-58.

Strehlo, K. 1996. Data warehousing: Avoid planned obsolescence. *Datamation*, 42(2), (January), 32-41.

Sun Microsystems, Inc. 1996. Java: Programming for the Internet. http://java.sun.com/.

Thomsen, C. T. 1991. The deep structure of an innovative accounting system, *Proceedings of the Twelfth International Conference on Information Systems*, December, 307-314.

Vatter, W. J. 1947. *The Fund Theory of Accounting*. Chicago: University of Chicago Press.

Watterson, K. 1995. A data miner's tools. *Byte*, 20, (October 1), 91-96.

Watts, R. L. and J. L. Zimmerman. 1986. *Positive Accounting Theory*. Englewood Cliffs, NJ: Prentice Hall.

Weber, R. 1986. Data models research in accounting: An examination of wholesale distribution software, *The Accounting Review*, 61, 498-518.

The Digital Revolution and the Cattle Ranching Community

Amanda Spink and Jane Hicks
School of Library and Information Sciences
University of North Texas
Denton, Texas

Abstract

A lack of research investigating the role of information and information needs currently hampers improvement in information services to rural industries. This paper provides preliminary findings from the first phase of a project investigating the role of information, including the use of networked information services by the cattle ranching community -- a major information user group in rural environments. Selected findings are reported from a national survey of 1600 cattle ranchers and members of the Red Angus of America. Results show the "electronic" or "digital" ranching community is in the early stages of development as "early adopters" begin to use networked information services. Implications are derived for the development of digital libraries for cattle ranchers.

Introduction

This paper reports preliminary results from the first phase of a study investigating the use of computer networks and information needs of cattle ranchers - a major group of information users in the rural environment of North Texas. Computer networks allow ranchers to access remote information sources and communicate through electronic mail and bulletin boards. The aim of the study reported in this paper is to provide data on the current use of computer networks by cattle ranchers -- the state of development of the "electronic" or "digital" ranch -- and investigate factors associated with network use by cattle ranchers.

Currently substantial national investment is funding the development of an information society and the National Information Infrastructure (NII) to facilitate technology transfer, increase research and development (R&D) and improve U.S. industrial competitiveness and productivity. The infrastructure requirements of agricultural industries are an important area requiring further research (Egan, 1992). The development of effective computer networks and information services, and policies governing their implementation and use, depends on a good knowledge of users' needs and requirements. This knowledge includes understanding the impact and outcome of networked information on industry productivity. Little empirical data exists regarding the role computer networks are beginning to play in ranching work, productivity and social life. Few researchers have previously examined the information-seeking patterns and information needs of ranching industry groups.

Related Studies

A small, but growing body of empirical studies has investigated the role of information in the resolution of human problems and the human process of information-seeking. Previous studies have investigated the information-seeking behavior of retired women (Chatman, 1992), battered women (Harris, 1988/1989), students and library users (Kuhlthau, 1991), health workers (Dee, 1990; Lundeen, Tenopir & Wermager, 1994) and university researchers (Ellis, Cox & Hall, 1993). Researchers have proposed models of human information-seeking processes and the role of information in human problem solving (Dervin & Nilan, 1986; Krikelas, 1983; Kuhlthau, 1991). Many studies have examined the role of public libraries in the provision of information services for rural communities (Dillman; 1991; Senkevitch & Wolfram, 1994; Wilkinson, 1991). Few studies have examined the information-seeking behavior and information needs of rural workers. The study reported in this paper seeks to redress this by undertaking an extensive research study investigating human information behavior in rural environments, beginning with a study of cattle ranchers.

A growing body of empirical research has also examined the characteristics, use and effects of computer network use (Bikson & Eveland, 1990; Sproull & Keisler, 1991) and the role of computer networks in rural communities (Egan, 1992; Hudson & Parker, 1990; La Rose & Mettler, 1989; U.S. Congress. OTA, 1991). In a recent study Bishop (1994) found that computer networks are used widely by aerospace engineers, and contribute to the efficiency and effectiveness of their work tasks. Delany and Chamala (1986) found little use of electronic media by Australian farmers and graziers. However, little is known about the use of computer networks by the United States ranching industry.

Cattle Ranchers

Cattle ranching is as a complex information and communication activity requiring ranchers to access diverse sources of information to support ranching tasks, including purchasing, sales, financial, veterinary, medical, commodities market, weather, cattle breeding, industry and community activities. The proliferation of personal computers, the growth of the Internet, and accompanying development of information and communication services, has given cattle ranchers potential access to many new services. We need to explore the types of computer technology and networks cattle ranchers access and for what reasons, e.g., ranching tasks or to reduce the barriers of rural isolation. Also, the types of information and communication services cattle ranchers need, including information-seeking patterns and network use by cattle ranchers following seasonal patterns with the changing tasks associated with cattle breeding, feeding and slaughter

The UNT - Center for Texas Studies is also conducting a five-year project "Ranching in Texas in the Twenty-First Century" to address common concerns of the ranching industry (Texas Studies Association Newsletter, 1995) including the preservation of the ranching way of life, developing a closer ranching coalition, government regulations, food safety, the environment and international trade relations. The project discussed in this paper provides a significant contribution to the Ranching in Texas initiative, as the issues of concern to the ranching industry involve the distribution of information (governmental, commercial or industry) and the need for increased communication within the ranching industry. The use of computer networks and services including information databases, E-mail, electronic bulletin boards and other appropriate services, could contribute to preserving the ranching way of life and the creation an integrated coalition of ranchers through the development of an electronic ranching community. The extent to which this electronic ranching community currently exists is explored in this study.

The results of the study also contribute directly to goals of the Red Angus Association's Strategic Mission 2000 to improve the provision of information and education to their members. The study provides pointers to new types of information services, networks or network features, and digital libraries for cattle ranchers. Understanding the relationships between ranchers' information-seeking behavior, network use, work and communication tasks will allow the impact of information services and electronic networks on the productivity of cattle ranchers to be assessed. The results also provide valuable data on the information requirements of cattle ranchers and suggest possible information-seeking patterns and network use by other types of ranchers and related agricultural groups, e.g., farmers.

The results are useful for librarians, including the Texas State Library and local public libraries, who are responsible for the provision of network-based and long distance information services to rural communities. Information science researchers will also be provided with valuable data to develop and enhance theoretical models of information seeking and use, network usage, and adoption of technological innovations.

Research Questions

The study reported in this paper was guided by the following research questions:

1)   What types of information do ranchers need to support their work tasks?

2)   What are the patterns of information-seeking exhibited by cattle ranchers?

3)   What types of computer technology and networks are currently used by cattle ranchers?

4)   What tasks and communication activities do cattle ranchers use computer networks to support?

5)   What are the impacts of network use on cattle ranchers' work tasks and communications?

6)   What is the current stage of development of the electronic ranching community?

7)   What are the characteristics of cattle ranchers who are "early adopters" of networked

information?

Research Design

Data Collection

A survey instrument (Appendix A) was designed and pretested during summer 1995, with the Executive Secretary of the Red Angus Association of America, Dr. Dick Gilbert and his staff, using examples of previous surveys of network usage (Bishop, 1994) and information needs (Dee, 1993; Lundeen, Tenopir & Wermager, 1994). The Red Angus Association of America is a national association of sixteen hundred Red Angus cattle breeders from 47 U.S. states and two Canadian provinces, headquartered in Denton, Texas. The association is dedicated to promoting and improving the breeding, feeding and marketing of Red Angus cattle (American Red Angus, 1995) and maintains a computerized registry of Red Angus breeding information.

The survey instrument with a cover letter from the Executive Director of the Red Angus was mailed to the 1600 members of the Red Angus Association of America with their monthly publication *American Red Angus*. A follow up notice was also sent in the next issue of the *American Red Angus*. This survey solicited information regarding members' information needs and network use, and the types of information services needed by members. The joint survey development generated data useful to both the researchers and Red Angus Association of America regarding their membership.

Additional data collection through site visits to cattle ranchers are currently being planned, to interview cattle ranchers regarding their use of computer networks, and information seeking patterns and needs. Interview volunteers were solicited during the survey. The interviews will also be used to establish sites for the collection of longitudinal data through an interview schedule over a twelve month period. A longitudinal study will provide data to assess the seasonal nature of network use, and information seeking and use by cattle ranchers.

Preliminary Results

A total of 209 (approximately10%) of Red Angus members responded to the survey. Initial data analysis indicates most respondents own and used a personal computer. Some 188 (90%) of respondents said they owned a computer, including 51 (24%) with a CD-ROM drive and 52 (24%) with a modem. Some 53 (25%) of respondents owned a satellite dish. Most respondents -- 175 (83%) said they did not use computer network services on their ranch. Of the 21 who did use computer network services, they had used computer networks for an average of 25 months and used them for an average of 5% of their average work week. A higher proportion -- 87 (41%) of respondents said members of their family used computer networks outside the home, mainly for school or work located away from the ranch.

The initial data analysis shows that respondents to the survey were ranchers using personal computers, including a small minority accessing computer networks.

Computer Network Services Used By Cattle Ranchers

Table 1 and table 2 provides the responses by Red Angus members regarding their use and the value of existing networked information services. The vast majority of respondents had not used networked information services - within a range of 1% to 11%. The largest group (about 11%) was using the Red Angus Sire Finder and Bulletin Board, the Internet or America Online. There was very little usage and value placed on agricultural networked information services.

Value of Information and Access Via Network

Table 3 shows the information valued by cattle ranchers and whether they accessed this information via computer networks. Respondents placed a high value on breeding information, auction values, general market information and veterinary information. Less interest was evident for other types of information.

Information Sources Used By Cattle Ranchers

Table 4 shows that word-of-mouth sources, such as customers, suppliers and other ranchers, and also industry magazines and ranching associations were major sources of information for cattle ranchers. Very few ranchers were accessing these sources of information electronically. Less used were libraries, political groups and bulletin boards. Overall, about a quarter of respondents showed an interest in using networks for electronic mail or information services.

Discussion

These preliminary results were based on a smaller group of respondents, but indicate some interesting findings. At this stage of development the "electronic" or "digital" ranch is only a gleam in the eye of the ranching industry. Most cattle ranchers do not own a personal computer or access networked information services. This may be due to many factors, including the advancing average age of ranchers, not familiar with computers, the predominance of telephone communication or the lack of suitable services for ranchers on the net.

However, there is a small group of technologically innovative ranchers or "early adopters" (Rogers, 1983) beginning to explore the vast and ever growing electronic information world for services suitable and applicable for a ranching business. Those ranchers venturing onto the net are seeking information particular to their particular business, such as breeding and ranching information. Most ranchers do not communicate with each other or the outside world via electronic mail from the ranch, although some family members are accessing the net from non-ranch locations, as they work and seek education off the ranch.

Conclusion

A major aim of this initial survey was to collect basic data to form the basis for a larger study. The survey also begins to identify those "early adopter" ranchers taking up the reins of technological innovation for further study. Due to the changing nature of the American economy and business the evolution of the "electronic" or "digital" ranching community seems inevitable. How this will occur and the nature of the evolving "electronic" ranching community will be fascinating to observe.

Acknowledgment

This study is being initially funded by a Research Initiation Grant from the University of North Texas. The authors would also to thank Dick Gilbert, Executive Director of the Red Angus Association of America and members of the Association for their contribution and assistance to this study. We also thank Judy Bateman and the UNT Computer Services for their invaluable assistance in the data analysis.

References

Bishop, A. P. (1994). The role of computer networks in aerospace engineering. *Library Trends, 42*(4), 694-729.

Center for Texas Studies. University of North Texas. (1995). *Texas Studies Association Newsletter.*

Chatman, E. (1992). *The information world of retired women.* Westport, CT: Greenwood Press.

Dee, C. R. (1990). *Information needs of the rural physician: A descriptive study.* Ph.D. dissertation. Florida State University.

Delany, N., & Chamala, S. (1986). Survey of Queensland farmers and graziers using interactive electronic media. *Proceedings of the First Australian Online Information Conference, Sydney, 20-22 January 1986* (pp. 248-263).

Dillman, D. (1991). Community needs and the rural public library. *Wilson Library Bulletin, 65*(9), 31-33.

Egan, B. L. (1992). Bringing advanced technology to rural America: The cost of technology adoption. *Telecommunications Policy, 16*(1), 27-45.

Ellis, D., Cox, D., & Hall, K. (1993). A comparison of the information-seeking patterns of researchers in the physical and social sciences. *Journal of Documentation, 49*(5), 356-360.

Eveland, J. D., & Bikson, T. K. (1987). Evolving electronic communication networks: An empirical assessment. *Office: Technology and People, 3,* 103-128.

Harris, R. M. (1988/1989). The information needs of battered women. *RQ, 28*(1), 62-70.

Hudson, H. E., & Parker, E. B. (1990). Information gaps in rural America: Telecommunications policies for rural development. *Telecommunications Policy, 14*(3), 193-205.

Krikelas, J. (1983). Information seeking behavior: Patterns and concepts. *Drexel Library Quarterly, 19*(2), 5-20.

Kuhlthau, C. C. (1991). Inside the search process: Information-seeking from the user's perspective. *Journal of the American Society for Information Science, 42*(5), 361-371.

Lundeen, G. W., Tenopir, C., & Wermager, P. (1991). Information needs of rural health workers in Hawaii. *Bulletin of the Medical Library Association, 82*(2), 197-205.

Red Angus Association of America. (1995). General information. *American Red Angus, 31*(4), 4.

Rogers, E. M. (1983). *The diffusion of innovation.* 3rd Edition. New York: Free Press.
Senkevitch, J., & Wolfram, D. (1994). Equalizing access to electronic networked resources: A model for rural libraries in the United States. *Library Trends, 42*(4), 661-675.

Sproull, L., & Kiesler, S. (1991). *Connections: New ways of working in the networked organization.* Cambridge, MA: The MIT Press.

Stinson, R. E., & Mueller, D. A. (1980). Survey of health professionals information habits and needs conducted by personal interviews. *Journal of the American Medical Association, 243*(2), 140.

U.S. Congress. Office of Technology Assessment. (1991). *Rural America at the crossroads: Networking for the future.* Washington, DC: USGPO.

Wilkinson, K. P. (1991). Information access in rural areas. *Rural Libraries, 11*(1), 53-67.

Table 1. Network Information Services Used. (No. Respondents = 209)

Type of Service	Have You Used This Service?					
	Yes		No		Missing Cases	
	Number	%	Number	%	Number	%
Red Angus Sire Finder	24	11%	167	80%	18	9%
Internet	23	11%	160	77%	26	12%
America Online	18	9%	159	76%	32	15%
Red Angus Bulletin Board	14	7%	175	84%	20	10%
CompuServe	13	6%	165	79%	31	15%
Prodigy	9	4%	167	80%	33	16%
Online Library Catalogs	8	4%	178	85%	23	11%
AG*SAT	8	4%	179	86%	22	11%
AGNET	5	2%	180	86%	24	11%
Other	4	2%	49	23%	156	75%
USDA Online	3	1%	181	87%	25	12%
AgriData Network	3	1%	183	88%	23	11%
AGRICOLA	3	1%	186	89%	20	10%
Commercial Networks	2	1%	136	65%	71	34%
AGRIBUSINESS	2	1%	185	89%	22	11%
The Source	1	<1%	170	81%	38	18%

Table 2. Value of Networked Services. (No. Respondents = 209)

Type of Service	Value of Networked Services				
	1 High	2	3	4 Low	Missing Cases
Red Angus Sire Finder		6			203
Internet		6	1	1	201
America Online		3	2	3	201
Red Angus Bull Board			1	2	206
CompuServe		1	1	2	205
Prodigy		3	2	2	202
Online Library Catalogs		3	1	2	203
AG*SAT			1	2	206
AGNET		7	6	4	192
Other		3	4	3	199
USDA Online		1	4	3	201
AgriData Network		1	1	2	205
AGRICOLA		8	6	3	192
Commercial Networks		4	1	2	202
AGRIBUSINESS		1	1	2	205
The Source				2	107

Table 3. Value of Information and Access Via Network. (No. Respondents = 209)

Type of Information	Value of Information				Access Via Network		
	1 High	2	3	4 Low	Yes	No	Would Like To
Breeding Information	155	28	4	3	3	185	101 (48%)
Auction Values	84	59	34	16	8	175	80(38%)
Gen. Market Info.	86	67	28	10	9	174	76(36%)
Veterinary Info.	84	67	32	10	2	181	83(40%)
Agric. Chemicals	19	45	70	55	1	178	53(25%)
Pest Management	31	54	55	47	2	178	56(27%)
Water Resources	23	44	53	63	1	173	43(21%)
Enviro. Regulations	23	53	63	47	3	175	52(25%)
Weather	67	57	33	27	17	158	65(31%)
Govt. Regulations	26	58	57	42	7	169	49(23%)
Community Info.	23	43	69	50	3	172	41(20%)
Education	75	63	27	19	12	166	61(29%)
Travel	11	33	61	73	8	163	42(20%)
Family Health	53	50	39	40	3	166	41(20%)

Table 4. Information Sources Used By Cattle Ranchers. (No. Respondents = 209)

Sources	Value of Information Sources					Use Network To Contact			
	1 High	2	3	4 Low	Miss. Cases	Yes	No	Miss. Cases	Want To
Customers	152	23	5	6	23	4	174	31	70
Suppliers	57	69	39	16	26	2	168	39	57
Other Ranchers	86	86	86	86	25	1	173	35	58
Ranching Assoc	40	74	49	16	28	1	170	38	53
Ext. Agents	45	62	46	27	30	4	166	39	50
County/State Health	10	43	68	54	29	1	163	45	36
Govt. Agencies	6	34	56	78	31	1	162	46	32
Libraries	11	39	54	68	34	5	161	43	38
Newspapers	33	61	54	30	36	3	164	42	31
Industry Mags.	79	70	21	14	37	2	169	38	49
Bulletin Boards	11	36	75	51	35	7	156	46	35
Political Groups	4	24	45	99	37	0	163	46	33

THE ELECTRONIC RANCH:
SURVEY OF COMPUTER NETWORK SERVICES USED BY CATTLE RANCHERS

For our purposes here, **computer networks** are defined as telecommunications links between computers. Examples of services include the commercial network providers such as America Online and CompuServe, the Internet, databases of information around the world, electronic bulletin boards and electronic mail services.

1. Do you use any of the following equipment? (Please check *all* that you use).
    ____ fax machine
    ____ modem
    ____ IBM compatible computer
    ____ CD-ROM drive
    ____ Macintosh computer
    ____ laptop/hand held computer
    ____ satellite dish
    ____ other _____

2. Do you ever use any kind of **computer network services** on your ranch?
    _____ **No**, I never use computer network services. Please go to question 3.
    _____ **Yes**, I personally use computer network services. If yes, please answer 2a, 2b, and 2c.

    2a. About what percent of your typical **work week** is spent using computer network services? _____ %
    2b. How long have you been using a computer network services?
    _____ years _____ months
    2c. Why did you start using computer network services?

3. Do you or other members of your family use computer networks outside the home?

    _____ **No**. Please go to question 4.
    _____ **Yes**. If yes, please check all that apply.

    At least one member of my family, staff, or I use computer networks at:

    3a. ____ school/college
    3b. ____ a work location away from the ranch
    3c. ____ library
    3d. ____ other _____

6. VALUE AND USE OF COMPUTER NETWORK SERVICES

Please indicate if you have used any of the following network services. If you have used a service, rate its value to you.

TYPE OF NETWORK SERVICE	HAVE YOU USED THIS SERVICE?			IF YES, PLEASE RATE THE VALUE OF THIS SERVICE			
	Yes	No	Don't know	High 1	2	3	Low 4
Red Angus Bulletin Board							
Red Angus Sire Finder							
AGNET (Agriculture Computer Network)							
AGRIBUSINESS U.S.A.							
AGRICOLA (National Agriculture Library)							
AgriData Network							
AG*SAT (Agricultural Satellite Corporation)							
Commercial networks:							
• America On Line							
• CompuServe							
• Prodigy							
• The Source							
Internet							
Online library Catalogs							
USDA Online							
Other (please list)							

5. INFORMATION SOURCES USED BY CATTLE RANCHERS

Please indicate the value of each business information source you use.

Business Information Sources	What is their value to you?				Do you use a computer network to contact these sources?		
	High 1	2	3	Low 4	Yes	No	If no, would you like to?
Customers							
Suppliers/Vendors							
Other Ranchers							
Ranching Associations							
Extension Agents							
County/State Health Dept							
Other Govt. Agencies							
Libraries							
Newspapers							
Industry Magazines							
Bulletin Boards							
Political alliance groups							
Other (please list)							

4.   TYPES OF INFORMATION NEEDED BY CATTLE RANCHERS

Please indicate the value of each type of information you need.

Type of Information	What is its value to you?				Do you use a computer network to find this type of information?		
	High 1	2	3	Low 4	Yes	No	If no, would you like to?
Breeding information							
Auction values							
General market information							
Veterinary information							
Agricultural chemicals							
Pest management							
Water resources							
Environment regulations							
Weather							
Government regulations							
Community information							
Education							
Travel							
Family health							
Other (please list)							

7. What do you think are the three biggest barriers to using network services?

8. What are the three most important factors that encouraged your use of network services, or that could encourage your use?

9. Overall, how would you **describe your reaction to computer network services?** (Please circle the number of the most suitable response).

    1 They could revolutionalize ranching.
    2 They are useful in many respects.
    3 I am neutral or indifferent to them.
    5 They are not useful in many respects.
    6 They are worthless and should not be implemented.

10. Will you please tell us the size of your herd?

       1-50   _____
      50-100   _____
     100- 300   _____
     over 300   _____

10. Are you interested in participating in follow-up research related to this survey, such as a telephone call or site visit regarding your network use and information needs? If so, please provide your name, address and contact information.

_____

_____

_____

MANY THANKS!

Impact on Education I:
Digital Libraries I

SOCIAL WORLDS OF KNOWLEDGE-WORK: HOW RESEARCHERS APPROPRIATE DIGITAL LIBRARIES FOR SCHOLARLY COMMUNICATION

Lisa Covi
Department of Information and Computer Science, University of California
Irvine, California

ABSTRACT

Although librarians have been assessing and integrating information technology (IT) into library systems and services for many years (Arms, 1990), digital library designers and system builders are still looking for new ways to understand and anticipate IT use. Knowledge-workers such as journalists, marketing researchers and in this study, academic researchers, depend upon access to digital libraries (DLs) for their livelihood. They not only need to work with electronic materials, but they often contribute to the corpora they search. However, despite promises and predictions of pervasive "effective" use of both Internet-oriented and library-oriented DLs, this study's researchers continue to depend on paper distribution channels, appropriating some DLs and not others which seem relevant for their work. As librarians and other IT providers are moving towards substitution of electronic services for paper collections, it is important to understand why knowledge-workers sometimes do not appear to effectively use DLs.

This paper explains why an exemplary set of knowledge-workers continue to depend upon paper collections and appropriate certain DLs and not others. This study investigates paper and electronic material use patterns of faculty and graduate student researchers from eight U.S. Research Universities in four diverse disciplines: molecular biology, literary theory, computer science and sociology. Within these disciplines are included researchers in multiple subspecialties who had diverse work habits and access to different resources. In order to explain major gaps and typical uses of DLs in organizations, this study contrasts two theoretical perspectives. Bounded database searching (BDS), a closed rational perspective is based on a caricature of information retrieval models (Lancaster and Fayen, 1973) and represents DL use as the interaction between an information-seeker and an archival database system. Although this is the predominant perspective in DL research, BDS does not explain how organizations influence DL use through work arrangements and work practices. Social worlds, as an open natural perspective (Becker, 1982) can supplement BDS by examining conventions relating to the focal activity of the work: scholarly communication. DL use from a social world perspective embodies social practices such as choosing acceptable resources, working with recognizable methods, and publishing in certifiable outlets. The social world perspective supplements the BDS perspective by explaining organizational patterns that influence how researchers appropriate, adapt and even fail to effectively use DLs. In addition, this paper argues that the social world perspective helps us better anticipate new patterns of knowledge work with changing technology and thus DL use in multiple diverse organizations.

INTRODUCTION

The Clinton-Gore administration has brought Information Technology (IT) and Digital Libraries (DLs) to the forefront of public discourse from proposals to network every school to deregulating telecommunications utilities creating competitive markets for content providers. Despite the initial speculation about commercial applications such as 500 channels of television programming and video on demand flowing over the National Information Infrastructure, federal research funds now focus attention on digital libraries (DLs) as the preferred content to flow over the Internet (NSF, 1994). Gore's early vision of the future use of DLs depicted a little girl from Tennessee accessing the Library of Congress from her home (Gore 1994). However, what do we really know about the ways people even currently use online information resources?

DL resources and services are not as novel as the popular press would lead us to believe. Librarians have been integrating IT into systems and services for many years (Arms, 1990) such as Online Public Access Catalogs (OPACs), Bibliographic databases and other indices and integrated library systems for circulation and back-office administration activities. The popularization of the Internet, electronic mail (email), gopher, and world wide web (WWW) adds a new set of evaluation issues to those of library-oriented DL services. The Internet-oriented DLs also include personal, group and organizational databases including such recreational and work-oriented concerns as travel information, fan club databases, genetic sequencing resources, telephone books, newsletters and even digitized texts.

In order to learn about how people use these resources, Rob Kling and I investigated the work practices of a group of people who have good access to paper and digital materials already and have strong incentives to make good use of them. This study examines DL use by academic researchers who are strongly motivated to produce material (usually articles and books) that become part of the growing archive of published knowledge. We visited eight U.S. research universities which have provided both library-oriented and Internet-oriented DLs for several years to their researchers. Our original research questions were

1. How accurately do faculty and students perceive the contents and formats of information that these services provide;

2. How much do faculty and students actually utilize these resources, and how do they fit their informational preferences;

3. Under what conditions do faculty and students prefer electronic information to be available in specific forms electronic for reformatting or restructure; paper for mobility or annotation;

4. To what extent do faculty and students use services where they have assistance from skilled help -- such as reference librarians or colleagues;

5. How do these patterns of preferences and usage vary with the different disciplinary traditions and working conditions

However, our questions began to change as we discovered a surprisingly similar pattern early in our site visit schedule. Although basic services such as provision of computers for word-processing and networks for electronic mail were fairly widespread, there were still major gaps in the DL use patterns in different disciplines. Why did the researchers adopt some DL resources and services and not others? Why did these researchers who had access to a high level of connectivity to DLs and were highly motivated to contribute their work to the cultural archive not take advantage of all relevant DLs for scholarly communication?

There has been recent empirical work that indicate social influences shape knowledge workers' adoption of information technology. Studies of email use and electronic conferencing have identified the role of organizational culture (Markus, 1994) and social cues (Sproull & Kiesler, 1992). The adoption of Lotus notes by consultants in a "big-10" accounting firm was shaped by incentive systems, organizational structure and resource flows (Orlikowski, 1992). The ways in which a particular community constructs and interprets the meanings of technological artifacts influenced the ways research scientists and engineers in a petrochemical company communicate electronically (Fulk, 1993). These studies share several characteristics. Several contrast efficiency or rational models with more social or natural models of behavior. These types of studies frequently emphasize the need to investigate narrow groups of workers in order to obtain precise results. This paper addresses both points. I build on these theoretical distinctions to understand how academic researchers use DLs to create new knowledge.

Drawing on sociological theory of organizations (Scott, 1992), I contrasted two broad analytical perspectives of organizational behavior: closed rational systems perspectives and open natural systems perspectives. These two perspectives best characterize the contrast between the rational model from Gore's vision of DL use and the results from our data which also suggested DL use is shaped by social influences.

ORGANIZATIONAL ANALYSIS: CLOSED RATIONAL AND OPEN NATURAL PERSPECTIVES

One theoretical perspective depicts DL use in a closed rational system of action. Rational systems perspectives describe organizational behavior as purposeful moving towards defined goals with formalized processes. They often take into account elements that constrain action such as costs, coordination efficiency, and performance measures. For example, rational analysts may focus exclusively on DL use from the point of view of how it facilities access to digital or paper materials by library users. When rational perspectives focus on influences contained by the focal system of action, the perspective is also considered to be a closed system. For example, to illustrate how DLs create more efficient access to materials, a closed rational perspective would focus on the users' information needs, the characteristics of the archival database, and benefits of search automation and features. An open rational analysis of service provision would include functional variables outside the focal system such as influences of the conditions under which the user accesses the database (a crowded library, a quiet campus workspace, home office), or influences of the organization of the database such as librarian preferences, availability of commercial databases, and interface assumptions.

I will call the closed rational model of DL use the bounded database search (BDS) perspective. It is a caricature of an information-seeking model (i.e. Lancaster & Fayen, 1973) which focuses on user interactions with databases which may or may not include social influences. The BDS perspective depicts DL users as information-seekers with clear goals and competent skill to interact with archival databases. It explains use patterns in terms of decreasing barriers to access (Okerson, 1991), increasing speed of research publication (Wiederhold, 1995) and making expensive scientific data more available and affordable (CSTB, 1993). The BDS perspective helps us understand DL use accounts particularly when researchers are working under deadlines or budget restrictions that (usually temporarily) prevent them from working outside the boundaries of their immediate work environment. The BDS perspective helps us understand DL use accounts when actors search for and obtain information from electronic systems which help them achieve predefined goals in a predictable manner without significant influences from factors outside their organizational context. It does not help us understand why researchers cannot access appropriate sources or describe rational strategies that are inconsistent with the purposes they espouse. The BDS perspective also doesn't explain why organizational systems may embrace or reject values or ambiguities.

The other analytical concept which I will employ comes from symbolic interactionist studies of social worlds (Becker, 1982) and draws upon an open natural organizational perceptive. Natural systems perspectives view organizations as competitive organisms who inherit organizational characteristics, develop and change their identities and respond to environmental factors with a strong motivation to survive. Organizational participants in natural systems perspectives develop informal arrangements with people and artifacts to shape goals which perpetuate their values and their existence. A social world is a social system of people who share an interest in some common activity and interact with one another. The conception of DL use in a social world embodies a natural systems perspective because it puts the identity of the user as researcher instead of database-user in the center of analysis (Ruhleder, 1991, Star and Ruhleder, 1994, Harnad 1990). Researchers belong to different social worlds, but the focal activity common to the three I analyze is scholarly communication via active publication in a research subspecialty. The social world perspective helps us understand DL use in terms of the conventions of different social worlds: what is acceptable source material, what types of projects and activities the researchers engage and social practices for the use of paper and digital materials.

Closed natural systems perspectives focus exclusively on human activity within the circumscribed organization. These explanations are not very useful to us unless we are only concerned with the internal mechanisms of perpetuating group values. Even so, the influences of values outside the group - the basis upon which the group survives, are difficult to analytically separate. Open natural systems perspectives provide a more holistic representation of organizational behavior which suits a wide variety of large complex organizations.

The social world perspective is an exemplar of open natural systems perspectives because researchers are simultaneously identifying themselves in terms of different social worlds. In this study, three key influential social worlds emerged from the informants' accounts: their workplace setting, their professional field (broad discipline) and their occupational niche (research subspecialty). Researchers balance these diverse and overlapping social identities making it difficult to examine one social world without taking into account other social worlds. I will use the social world perspective to begin to develop a richer understanding of DL use that will enable us to better analyze and predict use of technology. This analysis builds upon research contrasting closed rational with open natural perspectives to help understand other technological use practices (Boland & Pondy, 1983, Covi & Kling, in press, Kling & Jewett, 1995). I will refer to BDS and social world perspectives as exemplars of closed rational and open natural perspectives (summarized in Table 1).

Closed Rational Systems: Unified task systems in which upper managers guide subordinates toward clear goals through explicit strategies (Scott, 1992)	Open Natural Systems: Coalitions of shifting interest groups that develop goals by negotiation; the structure of the coalition, its activities and its outcomes are strongly influenced by tasks, technologies, and relationships with institutions, groups and people outside the focal organization. (Scott, 1992)
BDS Perspective: Models DL use as closed rational system. Information seekers have clear goals and competent skills to interact with archival databases. Focuses on influences within the system: users information needs, characteristics of the database, benefits of search features. (i.e. Lancaster & Fayen, 1973)	Social World Perspective: Models user in terms of social organization of work activity. Focuses on influences of social conventions on DL use: what is acceptable source material, what types of projects and activities are appropriate, social practices in use of paper and electronic materials. (i.e. Becker, 1982)

Table 1. Exemplars and Models from Sociological Theory of Organizations

METHODS AND DATA

This paper reports on a systematic empirical study conducted between February and August of 1995 by Lisa Covi and Rob Kling. We framed the study by focusing on the use and management of paper and DLs in eight major Carnegie I research universities[1]. We chose four public universities and four private universities in the northeast and west coast of the U.S. These universities vary in their library investments (per faculty member) from $3,200 to $37,500 and in their levels of library centralization from 2 to 76 branch libraries. At each university, we interviewed three faculty in each of four fields: lab science (molecular biology); artifact-based discipline (computer science); social science (sociology); and a humanities discipline (literary theory). In addition, when we could identify Ph.D. students in each field, we interviewed one or more for a total 124 faculty and student researchers. We supplemented informant accounts with 23 in-depth interviews with key DL resource providers such as the University Librarian, the Director of Academic Computing, an informant on the faculty senate library committee and other senior academic administrators such as a Provost. We sought data about ways that scholars use paper and digital research materials, patterns within the disciplines (e.g., roles of paper and electronic preprints), and data about university investments in library and computer support. During our visits to each campus, we also toured and utilized library and computing facilities to examine first-hand the resources and services that were the topic of discussions with our informants.

---

[1]The Carnegie I classification included 88 U.S. universities awarding 50 or more doctoral degrees and recieving at least $40 million in federal support each year.

The main form of data analysis has been to examine the ways that demand for digital and paper materials was reflected in three social worlds:

- the workplace setting of the informants: particularly temporal and proximate influences on DL use
- the professional fields of our informants: the practices and structure of the four disciplines broadly construed, and
- the occupational niche of the informant within their employing organization: the subspecialty or subspecialties that inform and shape their contributions.

These categories emerged from an inductive examination of the informants' accounts and site data we collected. The findings presented here are drawn from a theoretical sampling of informants' accounts (Strauss, 1987)

FINDINGS

In the introduction, I alluded to some patterns we found as we visited our first sites. The typical uses and major gaps in the researchers' use of both Internet-oriented and library-oriented DLs are summarized in Table 2.

	Internet-oriented DLs		Library-oriented DLs	
Discipline	*typical uses*	*major gaps*	*typical uses*	*major gaps*
Literary Theory	email net OPACs d-lists	e-journals e-texts	OPACs ARTFUL	MLA Bib b-databases CD-ROMs
Sociology	email	e-journals www d-lists net datasets	OPACs SOCIOFILE, ABI/INFORM datasets	CD-ROMs
Computer Science	email preprints tech reports HCI Bib. JAIR d-lists netnews (grads)	e-journals www search	rare	OPACs CD-ROMs
Molecular Biology	email GENBANK journals on CD-ROM	e-journals	MEDLINE BIOSYS	OPACs CD-ROMs

Table 2: Typical Uses and Major Gaps in Internet-oriented and Library-oriented DL use of Study Informants by Discipline

Electronic mail was widely used across all disciplines. On the other hand, electronic journals (e-journals) were widely ignored even when researchers were aware or curious about them. The only exception was the Journal of AI Research (JAIR) which I discuss in detail below. Online Public Access Catalogs (OPACs) were widely used chiefly in literary theory and sociology. In fact, literary theorists would use Internet tools such as gopher or telnet to connect to OPACs at other institutions across the network to order paper materials for interlibrary loan or browse other collections. Discussion lists (d-lists) were particularly prominent in computer science as a way of regularly communicating with colleagues and were conspicuously absent in sociology. In fact one of our informants in sociology asked if we could contact him if we found a discussion list on his area of interest. Sociologists and molecular biologists used bibliographic databases (b-databases) in their field more typically than literary theorists or computer scientists. Other conspicuous gaps are the lack of use of electronic texts (e-texts) by literary theorists and the lack of use of public datasets available on the Internet (net datasets) by sociologists. I will discuss the use of a widely-distributed set of public bulletin boards called "usenet news" (Netnews) by computer science graduate students below. Most informants did not make use of CD-ROMs (usually containing bibliographic databases or similar library indexes) that were available in their university library. However, molecular biologists were enthusiastic about the prospect of getting copies of their print journals on CD-ROM in their lab (in addition to the paper), several literary theorists made regular use of ARTFUL on CD-ROM and when CD-ROM collections were available over a local area network, researchers reported regularly using them.

To define effective DL use, I draw on the organizational perspectives described above. From the BDS perspective, effective DL use is efficient searching, matching predefined needs and well-organized DLs. The social world perspective of DL use would getting access to acceptable resources in appropriate ways that are easily integrated into social practice. Adopting only the BDS perspective that Gore and other DL designers use, Table 2 indicates major gaps in effective DL use in all disciplines. Why don't these researchers, as key stake-holders effectively utilize DLs? The social world perspective explains these major gaps. In each social world, I will introduce several exemplary accounts by the research informants and then explain the issue from the BDS perspective and the social world perspective. First I will discuss how the workplace setting shapes DL use by the boundaries of spatial (specifically physical proximity to resources) and temporal constraints on research activities. Then, I describe how the professional field: the broad discipline, shapes DL use via conventional conceptions and practices of how to use research materials. The third social world is the occupational niche: the research subspecialty (or subspecialties) that the informants most identify with and to which they contribute their work. The ways in which the researchers share materials with other specialists within or among their universities explain several major gaps in effective use.

The Workplace Social World: Proximate and Temporal Shaping of DL Use

Researchers work in a setting bound by location and time. Like other social worlds, the places where researchers work have resources, services, skills and people associated with them. Researchers workplaces include departmental offices, laboratories, libraries, home offices, kitchen tables, vacation homes and hotel rooms: any place where researchers think and meet, talk and write. The tasks they conduct in these places have temporal constraints such as deadlines, family demands, classroom responsibilities and a concern for the quality of time they require to think, write and read. In order to manage the multiple complex tasks they need to accomplish, researchers prefer flexible work settings with easy access to proximate resources. McGrath's work on temporal patterns in group work illustrate this need for flexibility (McGrath 1990, 1991).

The following account illustrates some key themes about proximate and temporal influences on DL use. This molecular biologist describes her experience with using color capabilities in publishing data in an article. She explains how, even though she has good access to color printing and displays for producing her work, the resource base available to the biologists who read her work in their workplace settings (i.e. expense and access to color photocopies) curtailed her initial efforts.

> This is the only one [article] that I have a lot of color and I'll never do it again because it costs so much money - it cost $8,000 to publish this paper.... We send these [color] articles out, they're in the journals, [but] people xerox them and give them to their students [to] read them. And nobody can make sense of them because you can't see poop because ... it has these color figures and you can't see anything.... he [her coauthor] should make these gray, these white and those black. Then you could xerox it. [Molecular Biologist]

The elements of color publication that affect her resource base were the journal's charge (paid by her grant) to include color copies in her illustration and the expense or lack of access to color photocopy facilities to reproduce the illustration. She also recognized that the resource base of the journal audience limits the power of her use of color illustration The lack of means, skill or access to transmit (communicate) her color illustration directly to the journal audience, and their access or expense of color photocopying limited the value of the color illustration.

This example has counterparts in the problems of reproducing black and white photography and charts and graphs. The molecular biologists we interviewed had, in general, good access to computing equipment and network access. Most molecular biologists heavily used MEDLINE or BIOSYS bibliographic databases to search for articles. However, when it came to transmitting data other than text, they did not, in general, have the resources to fully utilize the capabilities of Internet-oriented services. Thus the resources associated with work settings play an important role.

This same informant also gave us a good example of how temporal constraints figured into her appropriation of DLs into her research. Although her research was quite dependent on electronic resources, she selectively employs them within the constraints of her time, given that she isn't really a computerization aficionado.

> I would say I'm not totally [savvy about electronic resources]. It's mostly because my husband is really quite into it and I only take advantage of it once I decide I need something or somebody shows me... [Molecular Biologist]

Researchers rely on spouses (who may in this case also be colleagues), graduate students, technicians, support staff or colleagues to identify materials, learn skills or decide to appropriate IT into their research. They may compete with these people in their workplace, be it office or home for access to Internet or library-oriented DLs. In this case, the researcher organizes her time by capitalizing on her husband's enthusiasm for the resources and relying on him to spend the time exploring what's available before she considers incorporating resources into her work. Other informants relied upon graduate students to cull relevant materials from open discussion lists, and colleagues to explain how to use new DLs. Unless he or she saw an immediate benefit or was also a technophile, researchers would often choose to focus on traditional research practices rather than spend time learning new ones with uncertain benefit.

The two issues that this account illustrates concern the problems with communicating color data and identifying electronic materials within limited time constraints. The BDS perspective would suggest that greater access to color photocopy equipment or direct sharing of data without print mediation and improved search tools may alleviate this gap. In fact, authors with a BDS perspective argue that using DLs help researchers transcend time and place limitations (Okerson, 1991, Wiederhold, 1995). However, the social world perspective adds a new dimension to this understanding. Viewing this account in terms of the proximate and temporal limitations inherent in scholarly communication, the workplace shapes DL use. In the first case, the researcher's decision to move away from using color DL resources stems from her interdependence on readers who have social practices that blur the meaning of her color data. In the second, she depends on an intelligent human assistant who is aware of her preferences and needs to find tools that will be useful to her in a timely manner.

Besides the social world of the workplace, the social world of a professional field further elucidates the conventions of research work practices within an academic discipline to shape DL use.

The Professional Field Social World: Academic Discipline

The social world of the academic discipline mixes activities such as defining a domain for research interests, judging standards of evidence, and traditions of training. These activities help researchers identify themselves and distinguish themselves from other disciplines and with respect to societal interpretations of worklife. Although our informants identified themselves as molecular biologists, literary theorists, sociologists or computer scientists, they would make finer grade distinctions or interpret the terms differently depending on the context of their accounts. Some informants positioned themselves in more than one discipline. However primary academic appointments helped define a primary disciplinary identity. The disciplinary social world influenced DL use via shared norms (conventions) about appropriate ways to work and use of materials. Several disciplines had similar norms for certain activities such as computer science and molecular biology in the accounts below.

In the following example, a computer scientist explains how he has narrowed his search space to a small collection:

> My feeling is that within computer vision there are basically three conferences and two journals where most work that's interesting appears. And so ...[to direct students at material] I say, "Go read the last few proceedings of this conference, the last couple years of this journal." Often times I just know, I mean particularly being on the [journal] editorial board I see [the interesting papers]. So I try to keep up on things, attend these conferences.... [Computer Scientist]

Similarly, another computer scientist identifies materials based on the publication output of university departments, research groups and face to face conferences presentations:

> I follow stuff coming out of [western state university], ... I follow everything coming out of the HCI group in [midwest state university]... and the [inter-university ARPA-funded project] work. [The project] work has a mechanism for [following other

people's work], -- we have a workshop every nine months. Every single person talks and you know what they're doing. And then of course, you have to correspond [via email] with them to get the real details because the talks are only 10 minutes long. [Computer Scientist]

Besides having the resources and a disciplinary incentives to communicate and share documents electronically, the computer science informants relied on conference publishing which in most computer science departments contributed towards their tenure cases. Computer scientists however, did not privilege interaction via public discussion lists, relying instead on human agents to bring important work to their attention:

Netnews, I don't use at all. If anything interesting shows up there, I'm sure one of my students will tell me about it, since they waste much too much time on that. [Computer Scientist]

In molecular biology, researchers work in laboratory groups headed by a faculty member who manages their resources. Most molecular biologists in the study subscribed to a set of 5-10 print journals which they reviewed carefully usually in their lab groups. The following example illustrates the social process involved with identifying relevant source material for the lab's research.

What I do personally is to go through them as the journals come in. I will scan through their indexes to find articles that seem like they're relevant to what we are doing, and then I photocopy those abstracts .... And then I have those photocopies circulated amongst the people in the lab. And then they chose one or two papers out of those... on which we do a journal club... the whole laboratory, all seven or eight or whatever the number of us get together and we discuss that article and decide on the plus and minus points of it.... [Molecular Biologist]

More important than individuals getting access to specific relevant papers was the social process of digesting, interpreting and making strategic decisions based on the material. Scientific research results in molecular biology shape the direction of many expensive years of work and thus disciplinary practices guide the use of materials.

The issues in these accounts about disciplinary social worlds concerned conventions for identifying and evaluating both print and electronic source materials. In computer science, conference publishing and meetings held by project funders served as a source for keeping abreast of current research. In computer science and molecular biology, the faculty researchers, as principle investigators led their labs not only in formulating the work, but also delegating some search and evaluation tasks to the graduate students and research staff. In molecular biology, many labs conducted journal clubs where the lab would meet and review research publications from other labs.

A BDS perspective would suggest that DLs would supplement or supplant the conference meeting activities which may seem costly and exclude some interested researchers. The egalitarian nature of public access to important databases could reduce the difficulty of assembling a group of people at the same place and the same time to evaluate research work. However, the social world perspective highlights reasons the conference and meeting practices endure. As researchers become more influential in their discipline, materials (in both paper and electronic form) start flowing to them. For some informants, almost all relevant work flowed to them unsolicited making bibliographic database searching needless except as a reference tool. In the case of the molecular biologists, the social function of the journal club is not only to obtain material but to develop strategies and make decisions about how the laboratory project will proceed with relation to other work. This also serves as an important training function for junior researchers to learn how to function as a research group.

Even though this analysis identifies key norms and sanctions for DL use by discipline, even disciplines are not completely homogeneous. Researchers specialize in particular areas with their occupational discipline which focused their interaction outward from their workplace organization. I next turn to the social world of research subspecialties.

The Occupational Niche Social World: Research Subspecialty

The following quote illustrates a common reason researchers seek colleagues outside of their departments and universities with which to communicate their work.

> When it's research, let's face it, I have a couple of colleagues in the department whose research interests overlap with mine. I know what they do, but as you get away from your own domain, I don't really understand what other people do. [Computer Scientist]

Although researchers are grouped into departments within their universities, they often find themselves the local expert on a research subspecialty in their field without similarly specialized peers in their area. In addition, researchers evaluate each other in relation to their scholarly contribution within this subspecialty. I refer to this subspecialty as an occupational niche. Despite apparent commonalties in training, interest and teaching concerns within their departmental workplaces or broad disciplines, academic researchers must seek outside peers to communicate their work. These specialization patterns make economies of scale difficult to achieve in one department, discipline or university. Even when DLs help specialists connect and share resources with peers across organizational boundaries, learning may be slow and dependent upon activities in professional societies across organizations.

One of the more noticeable gaps in DL use is the lack of reading and publishing in electronic journals (Kling & Covi, 1995). The following account illustrates the contrast between the one exception to electronic journal use patterns in our study and the predominant lack of use. The Journal of Artificial Intelligence Research, known as JAIR, is published and distributed electronically free of charge. However, at the end of the year a scholarly publisher sells subscriptions of bound version to individuals and institutions. The papers published via JAIR are not immediately identifiable as electronic journal articles: the printed format (i.e. postscript formatting) looks like a photocopy from the bound volume. One informant explains his understanding of JAIR's value:

> The major journal of AI is the AI Journal [AIJ - paper] and it has a 2-year backlog and it takes a year to get papers reviewed... by the time they come out they're not relevant any longer. So [JAIR-electronic] was an attempt to do something [about this

problem]... It's not uncommon to try to get the reviews back in 6 weeks. You can get a paper published within two-three months of writing it....

The idea [behind using an electronic format that prints like a print journal] is ... if your deans are going to say, "Is this an electronic journal?" ... you can show him that it's a real journal, that the people using it can read it [in a print journal format]....

I guess I'm not quite sure [if it's "better" to get into AIJ-paper]. My feeling is that actually the [JAIR-electronic] is better. [AIJ] unfortunately has had the same editor for 20 years and he's been focusing it towards a certain class of research which is becoming less and less relevant to my own work.... [Computer Scientist]

In this account, the informant first depicts the value of JAIR from a BDS perspective: a faster way of publishing research before it gets out of date. However, as he goes on, the informant places JAIR in relation to the norms of his subspecialty, Artificial Intelligence (AI). JAIR met a need in the AI social world to have an additional publication outlet with a faster time to publish. In addition, he has marginalized the value of the older paper journal due to the content rather than the distribution mechanism.

However, the typical use of JAIR among AI researchers was an exception to electronic journal use patterns even in different subspecialties in computer science. The following account illustrates the predominant view of electronic publishing in this study, except that he actually published in one. Here a computer science researcher in a different research subspecialty describes his experience with an electronic journal.

I actually published in one [electronic journal]... To tell you the truth I haven't looked at it since then. In fact, I don't know whether it is still around or not.... Since I haven't come up for tenure, I think that [whether his article will count for tenure] will be fully answered only at that point. I only did it because I was curious about the whole electronic publishing area. This was... sort of a chapter from my dissertation which was my opinion about an issue.... I deliberately went to an outlet which I found was not controlled by the hierarchy so I could get my ideas published and get them out of my head and move on to something else. [Computer Scientist]

The sensitivity this informant has to tenure issues was further substantiated by the views of a senior professor in another institution who was involved with an new electronic journal in his subspecialty.

I can't answer [how e-journals figure into tenure and promotion decisions] very definitely because I do not know what quality these electronic journals will be. The conviction which we have for the [e-journal for which he is an associate editor] is that it will be fiercely written and so I would have no objections [to having e-journal articles count for tenure] if the evidence is strong that these are not just a sloppy way of getting papers published, you know - half-baked ideas.... [Computer Scientist]

As this informant describes electronic publishing, the issue is quality which is judged by the senior participants in a subspecialty (the invisible college who also legitimizes the research).

The issues that these accounts highlight is the lack of critical mass of subspecialists within the departmental workplace. One way of connecting with colleagues who care about and understand their work is publishing in scholarly journals. However, most informants do not read or publish in electronic journals. The BDS perspective suggests that electronic journals can bridge the critical mass gap by offering a more efficient means of publishing and disseminating their research. However, it does not explain why they wouldn't avail themselves of this new format for publishing. The social world perspective shows how conventions within a niche (such as format, acceptance, relevance and quality) influence the adoption of electronic journals. An important control mechanism that signifies the contribution of electronic journals is whether they are considered in the academic tenure review.

I have shown how the social world perspective explains several major gaps in DL use in this study. I next examine how social world analysis helps us retheorize DL use and informs the design and development of DLs by examining a publicly funded project in progress.

THEORETICAL IMPLICATIONS

This social world perspective of DL use can help us anticipate patterns of appropriation which in turn can help us improve the design of DL resources and services. I next apply this analysis of diverse overlapping social worlds to the University of California, Santa Barbara (UCSB) Digital Library project. The following example reinforces the contribution of the social worlds perspective to reconceptualize DL use. This demonstrates the way that the social world perspective supplements BDS perspectives by adding to the assessment of user requirements in order to inform the design and development of DLs that diverse groups of people such as college professors and school children can effectively use.

According to the UCSB proposal,
> The primary goal of the Alexandria Project is to design, implement, and deploy a digital library for spatially-indexed information....

> the main testbed system that we will design, develop, and test over the greater part of the project will provide a major test of our characterization of user requirements. This characterization will involve the various classes of users and their data needs; the classes of items of interest to the users; the sets of operations that users wish to apply to items; the nature of the interface(s) that are appropriate; and the levels of system performance that must be met. (Dozier et al, 1994)

The UCSB research team based their characterization of user requirements on 6 classes of queries which are associated with organizational roles:
> Research-Level Spatial-Data Query, Undergraduate Spatial-Data Query, K-12 Community Spatial-Data Query, Public Library Spatial-Data Queries, and Librarians' spatial data queries. (Dozier et al, 1994)

This view of DL use based on user requirements draws upon an BDS perspective. It bounds the human activity system to the interaction between users and the system in order to define the occasions of use in reference to the database they are creating. Because funders often judge DL effectiveness by how much it is used, viewing DL use only in this way may result in a major gap in effective use from the BDS perspective because the database is being created with an assumption that "if we build it [correctly], they will come" without careful consideration of the social worlds in which the DL is appropriated. Although DL use is predicated on the availability of a DL to use, even the existence of a well-designed DL does not alone ensure effective use. The BDS perspective of conceptualizing DL use by examining traditional user requirements of paper materials can benefit from an examination of the organizational influences of social worlds.

For example, the K-12 Community Spatial Data Query is based on observed use of the geographic collection: a teacher works with a reference librarian to develop a source list for his students. I choose this because of the contrast between the arrangements for use of DLs by school children via the teachers' lesson plan with the arrangements for university researchers in my study. This description describes the interaction with the collection from a BDS perspective:

> K-12 Community Spatial-Data Query: A high-school teacher is putting together a module for 8th-grade students to study the local ecosystem. The teacher asks first for any materials highlighting natural science subjects and discovers that many are of the local slough. He then refines the search for all information on the local slough to build a source list for the students. (Dozier et al, 1994)

The BDS perspective focuses on the teacher's use of the materials drawn from interactions within the library building. The teacher searches and then discovers materials on the local slough. The interaction is complete when the teacher has compiled a list of references for the students.

Examining the **work setting** of the high school teacher will reveal clues for how and where she teaches and in what time frame will influence the kinds of maps they prefer. A social world analysis of the work setting might include consideration of the role when and how often teachers prepare course material, and use of geographic information in the classroom. In addition whether the teacher would be accessing this DL from his home, classroom or public library will affect how he is likely to find it effective.

From the point of view of the **professional field**, the conventions surrounding teachers work in the school, classroom and community will give clues to how a teacher would be likely to utilize geographic information. The conventions of evaluating student work, standardized curricula, and controlling or entertaining activities to raise or maintain student interest will influence the kinds of materials teachers will find useful.

Within the high school teacher's **occupational niche**, or specialty subject of the high school teacher, teachers meetings and development interactions, pedagogical approaches within the specialty and the arrangements to share resources within and across school districts and regions in particular subject areas can also provide clues for how geographic information will be helpful.

Teachers, not unlike the researcher informants in my study have multiple roles. As DLs blur the organizational roles of users to create economies of scale, understanding DL use exclusively from the BDS perspective will become more difficult. There will be fewer teachers, school children and parents walking into public libraries for librarians to observe.

The very advantages of making a specialized resources as a geographical information system available to a wider group of people can make the process of analyzing what different professional groups find useful more difficult. Conceptualizing DL use from both the BDS perspective and in terms of diverse multiple social worlds has predictive power for understanding use of DLs and similar networked electronic resources.

CONCLUSION

This study initially identified major gaps in effective DL use by academic researchers. However, the informants appeared to be highly successful knowledge-workers, professional researchers at top U.S. universities -- how could they not be using these resources and services effectively? The social world perspective helps explain why they weren't actually failing to effective use DLs. It supplements the BDS perspective to view DL as supplementing scholarly communication in workplaces, professional fields and occupational niches. The social world perspective helps us understand better understand typical uses and major gaps in DL use. In addition this paper argues that the social world perspective can inform the design and development of DLs by retheorizing effective DL use. This study demonstrates that we can better predict use by understanding the ways organizations influence the occasions of DL use. Even among highly skilled knowledge-workers, the features of the three diverse social worlds enrich and constrain the ability of our informants to produce work that has value. The ways that DLs support research activities across these social worlds provide an important evaluative criteria for these professionals, librarians, publishers and all who have a stake in knowledge-work.

Acknowledgments

I would like to thank Rob Kling who collaborated with me throughout the project and with whom I conducted the field work. Brian Starr, Leysia Palen and Suzanne Schaefer provided helpful comments. I would also like to thank John King and Beki Grinter for providing formative feedback on this paper. This work was funded by the U.S. Department of Education's Office of Educational Research Initiatives (R197D40030).

References

Arms, C. R. (Ed.) (1990). Campus Strategies for Libraries and Electronic Information. Bedford, MA.: Digital Press.

Becker, H. S. (1982). Art Worlds. Berkeley: University of California Press.

Boland, R. J. & Pondy, L. R. Accounting in Organizations: A Union of Natural and Rational Perspectives. *Accounting, Organizations and Society, 8 2/3),* 223-234.

Computer Science Telecommunications Board (1993). National Collaboratories: Applying Information Technology for Scientific Research. Washington, DC: National Academy Press.

Covi, L. M. & Kling, R (in press). Organizational Dimensions of Effective Digital Library Use: Closed Rational and Open Natural Systems Models. *Journal of the American Society for Information Science.*

Dozier, J., Goodchild, M., Ibarra O., Mitra, S., Smith, T., Agrawal, D., El Abbadi, A., & Frew, J. (1994). Towards A Distributed Digital Library With Comprehensive Services For Images And Spatially-Referenced Information. National Science Foundation Proposal. Available as URL=http://alexandria.sdc.ucsb.edu/public-documents/proposal/0main.html

Fulk, J. (1993). Social construction of communication technology. *Academy of Management Journal 36(5)*, 921-950.

Gore, A. (1994). Remarks. Television Academy. Royce Hall, UCLA: January 11, 1994. Also available as URL=gopher://ntiaunix1.ntia.doc.gov:70/00/papers/speeches/gore_telecom_spch011194.txt

Harnad, S. (1990). Scholarly Skywriting and the Prepublication Continuum of Scientific Inquiry. *Psychological Science 1(6)*, 342-344.

Kling, R & Covi, L. M. (1995). Electronic Journals and Legitimate Media in the Systems of Scholarly Communication. *The Information Society 11(4),*: 261-271.

Kling, R. & Jewett, T. (1994). The Social Design of Worklife With Computers and Networks: A Natural Systems Perspective. In C. Marshall Yovits (ed.), *Advances in Computers 39* (pp. 240-293).. San Diego: Academic Press.

Lancaster, F. W., & Fayen, E. G. (1973). Information Retrieval On-Line. Los Angeles: Melville.

Markus, M. L. (1994). Finding a 'Happy Medium': The Explaining the Negative Effects of Electronic Communication on Social Life at Work. *ACM Transactions on Information Systems (12)2*, 119-149.

McGrath, J. E. (1990). Time Matters in Groups. In Galegher, J., Kraut, R. E., and Egido, C. (Eds.), *Intellectual Teamwork: Social and Technological Foundations of Cooperative Work* (pp. 23-61) Hillsdale, NJ: Lawrence Erlbaum Associates.

McGrath, J. E. (1991). Time, Interaction and Performance (TIP): A Theory of Groups. *Small Group Research 22(2)*, 147-174.

National Science Foundation (1994). NSF announces Awards for Digital Libraries Research. September 27, 1994. Washington, DC: National Science Foundation. Also available as URL=http://stis.nsf.gov/nsf/press/pr9452.html.

Okerson, A. (1991). The Electronic Journal: What Whence and When? *The Public Access Computer Systems Review, 2(1)*, 5-24.

Orlikowski, W. J. (1992). Learning from Notes: organizational issues in groupware implementation. In *CSCW '92, Proceedings of ACM 1992 Conference on Computer Supported Cooperative Work,*, (pp. 362-369). New York, NY: ACM Press.

Ruhleder, K. (1991). Information Technologies as Instruments of Social Transformation: The Computerization of Classical Scholarship. Ph.D. dissertation, University of California, Irvine.

Scott, W. R. (1992). Organizations: Rational Natural and Open Systems. Englewood Cliffs, NJ: Prentice-Hall.

Sproull, L. S. & Kiesler, S. B. (1992). Connections: New Ways of Working in the Networked Organization. Cambridge, MA: MIT Press.

Star, S. L & Ruhleder, K. (1994). Steps Towards an Ecology of Infrastructure: Complex Problems in Design and Access for Large-Scale Collaborative Systems. In *CSCW '94, Proceedings of ACM 1994 Conference on Computer Supported Cooperative Work,,* (pp. 253-264). New York, NY: ACM Press.

Strauss, A. L. (1987). Qualitative Analysis for Social Scientists. Cambridge: Cambridge University Press.

Wiederhold, G. (1995). Digital Libraries, Value and Productivity. *Communications of the ACM 38(4),* 85-96.

Digital Library Models and Prospects

Gregory B. Newby

Graduate School of Library and Information Science
University of Illinois at Urbana-Champaign

ABSTRACT

Digital libraries are the means by which people of the next millennium will access materials found in current libraries, yet the nature of digital libraries is only now being shaped. Different visions of the purposes for digital libraries include electronic access to materials previously found in print form, access to data stores, and access to scholarly (self-published) materials. In order to bring about significant progress towards the realization of full-scale digital libraries, print publishers must participate. Yet economic impediments to full participation of publishers exist, including fears of unauthorized duplication, distribution, or modification. Uncertainty about whether digital access to published materials may yield acceptable fees or royalties may be addressed through adoption of "pay as you go" or "buy once, use many" models, yet significant infrastructure development is needed to make these models feasible. The proliferation of scholarly reprint archives, moderated discussion groups, and electronic conferences and proceedings is helping to address some of the publisher concerns, as are developments in network access, browser standards, bibliographic standards, data security, and encryption.

THE DIGITAL LIBRARY

Conferences, journals, books, and projects have emerged in 1995 and 1996 on a topic which has been of only limited interest previously: digital libraries. The basic concept of the digital library may be traced back at least to such visionaries as Bush (1945), Licklider (1965) and Lancaster (1969). The sudden surge of interest in digital libraries is due primarily to the state of the Internet. The Internet has matured to the point of near-ubiquity in institutions of higher education, and sophisticated cross-platform browsing and display tools for the Internet are widely available (notably Mosaic and its offshoots). It's therefore to be expected that long-held visions of digital libraries can be implemented in earnest, with expectations of considerable progress by the millennium.

The basic concept of a digital library is subject to debate. All notions of digital libraries include electronic ("digital") storage of materials for retrieval or processing, but beyond this common base there are several major approaches to digital libraries. Some of the major approaches include data stores, electronic access to traditional library materials, and scholarly archives.

The data store is the least glamorous approach to digital libraries, yet is concerned with topics critical for the other approaches. For a data store, the goal is to make large collections of numeric, textual, images, or other data accessible in electronic form. Examples include an academic slide archive or a collection of nightly news programs from around the world. Important concerns for the creation of such a digital library include the storage of the data (what file formats to use, how to maximize for quick retrieval, how to make the data available across a local- or wide-area network); indexing and retrieving (what sorts of descriptions should be applied to the data, what retrieval methods should be used — for example, for browsing or for keyword searching); and standards (what standards for data organization should be used in order for people to be able to display or process the data?). None of these areas are trivial, and examples of the type described above are at the limits of what researchers and commercial developers are able to accomplish, especially on a large scale.

Electronic access to traditional library materials is the approach to digital libraries which may be the most obvious. The challenge is to make books, journals, vertical files, indexes, and other (print) materials found in libraries accessible to patrons in an electronic format, preferably from any location. While the storage of, for example, a book in a computer file is not necessarily challenging, since, after all, the book probably started out as a computer file, the surrounding issues are challenging. Making the contents of an electronic library searchable, insuring that access to materials is gained only by those to whom access is granted, delivering materials, agreeing on standards for display, search, and retrieval, and so forth are necessary issues to be addressed in order for this approach to digital libraries to come to pass. Note these issues are largely similar or identical to those for providing access to a data store — the main differences are that the data store is intended for post-processing, but traditional library materials are to be used more or less "as is," and traditional library materials are geared more towards the general public, versus a more specialized user group for the data store.

The final approach to digital libraries to be considered here is that of the scholarly archive. The primary idea is to bypass much or all of the existing publishing industry to make scholarly articles available. To this end, the main areas of development to date are scholarly pre-print archives and networked discussion groups (Harnad, 1996). But development must continue to achieved the goals of quick, ready, and equitable access to scholarly works. The main impediments to development include the technical problem of maintaining good quality control, editorial oversight, and other benefits that journal publishers provide, and the problem of insuring that scholarly publications which bypass publishers are seen as legitimate by the scholarly community and by tenure review committees. A further area of great concern is maintaining archival access to the scholarly publishing — insuring that a journal article will be available many years in the future is of concern of both the author and the researcher.

Common threads for these major approaches to digital libraries include primary areas of inquiry for information scientists. How can data collections be successfully searched by a variety of users with a variety of information needs? What indexing, abstracting, and organizational techniques should be applied to materials? What mechanisms should be utilized for timely retrieval and display of materials?

This paper will continue with an analysis of economic models which may be applied to digital libraries, with a focus primarily on the electronic access to traditional library materials and scholarly archives approaches. Then, prospects and challenges for developing economic models and other aspects of digital libraries will be examined.

ECONOMIC MODELS

Books cost money. The cost of producing a book includes fees, salaries and royalties paid to authors, editors, indexers, and others; cost of printing and binding; distribution costs; and others (Freeman, 1996). Because books cost money to produce (as do journals, indexes, newspapers, and most other items found in libraries), fees are charged to recoup the costs.

Individuals who purchase books receive a copy of the book to use at their discretion. Barring reproduction, almost any use is usually legitimate: giving the book away, sharing the book, storing the book indefinitely for later access, destroying the book, etc. For a library, similar rules apply: the library may make its own policies for how the book may be used, loaned, etc. For most materials found in libraries, responsibility for how the material is used is up to the individual library. Only in some instances (e.g., for CDROM databases or other materials which are updated frequently) does the publisher include stipulations for how a material may be used or disposed of.

For digital libraries, though, additional guidelines are needed to determine what sort of use is legitimate. According to Freeman (1996), the actual physical printing and production cost of a book is only 10-20% of the total cost of producing a book. Publishers want to make sure they are able to profit from their books in digital forms, as they do in print forms. But "buy once, then use as you wish," if applied to digital books or other materials, creates a threat to publishers due to the ease with which electronic materials may be copied, shared, and redistributed.

Consider the simple case of a book which has been transcribed to plain ASCII text, such as those produced since 1971 by Project Gutenberg (see ftp://uiarchive.cso.uiuc.edu/pub/etext/gutenberg). If one desires a copy of, perhaps, Henry Thoreau's <u>Walden</u>, she may retrieve it by anonymous FTP or other means. She may then print the text, reformat it, redistribute it, or destroy her copy. Gutenberg places almost no restrictions on what one may do with an etext they publish. But if they did, how would restrictions be enforced? There are no good methods to insure that the text is not printed, reproduced, retransmitted, modified and resold, etc.

As the forms of electronic books or other materials get more sophisticated, some of the things which people can do with plain ASCII texts become more difficult:

• SGML or other text markup schemes can make it more difficult for the layperson to modify a text.

• Larger bodies of work (such as a CDROM encyclopedia) are less likely to be transmitted or copied due to their size.

• Some browsers may limit printing, or create problems with reproduction. For example, an online hypermedia book may contain electronic movies, sounds, or other materials which are more difficult (again, for the layperson) to reproduce or retransmit.

• Legal copyright restrictions can also help to prevent unauthorized duplication or distribution, as they do with the photocopying of books and journal articles.

• Texts stored in non-copyable (or less-copyable) formats can include encrypted CDROM data or hardware ROM-based data. Or, text readers may be utilized which keep track of when a text is used.

Clearly, from the above, there is no guarantee that a publisher's work can be fully protected from uses the publisher would rather not permit. In the world of physical books, publishers cannot prevent pirate publishing operations from stealing their work wholesale, then reproducing and selling it on their own. However, such instances are relatively rare — as, for example, counterfeiting of US currency is relatively rare — due to the expense and expertise required.

In the world of the electronic book or other electronic material, unauthorized duplication and distribution is much easier. As the (estimated) billions of US dollars lost to software piracy annually attests, people are willing to duplicate and distribute electronic materials even when the law prohibits it.

The imperative for publishers to profit from their work in the electronic world is therefore at odds with the ease with which materials in electronic forms may be put to uses which, in the print world, are not legitimate. A major issue for digital libraries — and a crucial impediment for large-scale digital library implementation — has to do with how publishers can make their materials available in electronic form with confidence that the materials will not be put to uses they do not wish to permit.

Two major models for publishers to sell their products for digital libraries exist. A third model sidesteps the publishers. The two publisher models are "pay as you go," and "buy once, use many." The model which sidesteps the publishers is the author as publisher/distributor — as discussed for scholarly archive creation, above.

"Pay as you go" refers to the charging scheme currently employed for online databases, pay-per-view movies, and other things. In this model, publishers (or their agents, perhaps the digital libraries themselves) would make electronic materials available on-demand, but not transfer ownership of a copy to the user. In a world with ubiquitous access to the Internet or another network, the most likely scenario is that the central distribution point for a material would let a user view the material, but not actually provide a usable copy of the material.

One possible technical scheme for such distribution would be to have browsers/viewers that are capable of displaying materials sent using a one-time encryption key. This is not a perfect scheme, of course. The idea is to require the user to communicate with the distributor (and, presumably, pay some sort of fee) every time she wants to view a book, journal article, or other material. As with pay-per-view movies, the publisher would rely on a combination of the technical difficulty of making a personal copy and distributing it, the illegality of doing so, and the ease (and, one hopes, relatively low cost) of obtaining legitimate access to the material.

The necessary infrastructure for pay as you go schemes for digital libraries barely exists. Although the Internet may be used for access to publishers' (or others') materials, the Internet's emphasis is on free and open transmission of data. Access restrictions, encryption schemes, etc. for the World Wide Web, for example, are fairly limited and not yet reliable. Browsers for WWW data, as for email, Gopher, word processed files, etc. are not geared towards encryption, restrictions on such things as printing or editing, or restrictions on storage or redistribution.

Pay as you go is, however, probably the method most desired by publishers to sell their wares. It is fairly close in nature to existing models for how books and journal articles are sold, and is able to keep revenues fairly well synchronized to the amount of use for a particular material. Developers of digital libraries would need to invent the necessary infrastructure in order for pay as you go to work, should this prove to be a dominant model for digital library access.

The "buy once, use many" model is how libraries usually work. Libraries purchase a book and decide for themselves how to provide access. For most libraries, books and other materials are made available for loan to any authorized person. The digital library, in such a scenario, can know for certain the cost of a particular material. In the pay as you go model, the library cannot accurately predict the cost of a material, since it cannot know how many individual uses of the material may be made in the future. (One of the major issues that becomes apparent here is whether a digital library is something which is an independent organization, as traditional libraries are, or something run by the publishers or their agents.)

Under the buy once, use many model, a library would need to insure that restrictions of the publisher were enforced. For example, publishers might dictate that only one person may make use of a material at any one time (typical of software or CDROM licensing schemes currently in place). Or, libraries might be forced to insure that the sorts of encryption schemes and reproduction impediments described above are in place.

The "scholar as publisher" model is one which requires relatively few technical advances and is so occurring at a good pace already. Through pre-print servers, electronic conference proceedings, electronic mailing lists, and electronic journals in a variety of formats, scholars are now able to make their work widely available without the participation of publishers. In some cases, editorial boards and editorial processes are used. In others, there is little opportunity for editorial oversight, peer review, etc.

The main limitation of the scholar as publisher model for the creation of digital libraries is that the audience is relatively narrow: A digital library content would not be complete with only self-published scholarly works. Even if it were, scholarship does not take only the form of the journal article or conference paper — books, monographs, edited conference proceedings, and so forth are also important. Without good opportunities for compensation for the time spent at putting together such works, such materials would probably not be produced in any great quantity.

An additional important limitation of the scholar as publisher model is that indexing and abstracting services may be unaware of the published works, or unwilling to add such "gray" literature to their databases. Without being searchable, indexed, and abstracted, the value of scholarly works are lessened by their decreased accessibility.

This section has presented a summary of the issues surrounding the practical creation of materials to be stored and distributed by digital libraries. From the standpoint of publishers, who produce the vast majority of materials found in the collections of existing traditional libraries, important risks to revenues would be encountered by providing electronic copies of print materials for use in digital libraries, even on an experimental basis.

The problems are not insurmountable, but there does not yet appear to be an immediate financial imperative for publishers to solve them. Instead, the scholarly community is attempting to resolve the issues that face publishers and other stakeholders in digital library development. Some of these prospects and developments are discussed in the next section.

PROSPECTS AND DEVELOPMENTS

The analysis in the previous sections has focused on the role of the publishers — who create the majority of materials which are found in current libraries, and so could be expected to contribute greatly to digital library development. There are other areas of work, though, which this section will briefly address. These areas include data browsers, network development, network security, electronic publication of scholarly materials, and developments in resource sharing for libraries.

Data browsers for network access have been ubiquitous on the Internet since about 1990. Gopher, WAIS clients, and the World Wide Web all became available at about that time. The advantage of these types of data browsers over older methods (cf. telnet and FTP) are that they remove the need for an information seeker to know the network location of the item he is looking at. The first graphical browser for the World Wide Web, Mosaic, became available in 1993 and added greatly to the capability of network users to "publish" (usually informally) work with visual appeal, greater depth, and better organization. In the near term, network data browsers (the progeny of Mosaic, Netscape, and others) will incorporate the ability to display data from a variety of formats, most notably SGML. SGML is the standard employed by most publishers in the creation of their work. Thus, the union of SGML capability with networked browsers will yield browsers which are capable of directly accessing the data in a digital library in their most likely format.

Network development. Thanks to the ease of use for the Internet which tools such as Mosaic have helped to bring, to the favorable press coverage the Internet has received, and to the increased role of the microcomputer for home and office use, Internet access is now commonplace throughout US society. In higher education, Internet connectivity and basic access for faculty, students, and staff is nearly universal. This widespread access to the Internet from the home, office, schools, etc. means that access to digital libraries, when they exist, obtainable.

Network security. Along with the interest that many individuals have taken in the Internet over the past few years has been a surge of interest in the private sector. The largest area of growth on the Internet in 1994 and 1995 has been the commercial domain (according to the Internet Society: http://www.isoc.org/). The outcome of this growth which most closely effects digital library implementation is the need of commercial applications on the Internet for security for data delivery. Security is especially needed for customers to make credit-card purchases on the Web, but also for return delivery of data and for ensuring customer confidentiality.

As discussed above, the ability of materials found in digital libraries to be encrypted and transmitted securely may be important to publishers. The ability of digital libraries (or publishers) to identify and bill users of materials appropriately is also likely to be extremely important. These needs of digital libraries will be directly met by commercial interests in security for Internet transactions.

The future of *scholarly self-publishing* for digital libraries is not entirely clear, as it may be that such publishing is superseded by the digital libraries of the future (hopefully to the satisfaction of all parties and purposes involved). Current efforts for edited electronic journals, refereed preprint collections, and moderated electronic discussion are all relevant practice for large-scale digital library development.

Resource sharing. A final area of development relevant to digital libraries is continued progress with bibliographic standards (MARC, as applied to electronic materials) and bibliographic interchange formats (Z39.50, used to query databases remotely, including over the Internet). These developments have been underway for a long time with relatively few real-world applications, partially due to a relative lack of real materials being used in real libraries that require such services. Both academic libraries and library automation vendors, among others, are making gradual progress towards remote queries and bibliographic standards for electronic materials.

Other areas of development for digital libraries are underway as well. Issues for effective storage and delivery hardware are not trivial, as are increases in network speed and reliability. Interface design is another area of research with key implications for digital libraries. Many user studies are underway which can help to identify the information needs, situations, individual factors, and other components that must be combined appropriately to create environments for effective information retrieval.

CONCLUSION

The exact role of the digital library for the 21st century is far from certain. In order to develop digital libraries sufficiently so that their role in public, organizational, and academic life might begin to emerge, many steps must be taken. Research is underway, most notably at universities (ACM 1995), which will address some of the fundamental issues for digital libraries.

The role of the traditional publisher for the digital libraries of the future is of particular interest, due to their centrality to libraries of the present. But in order for publishers to start making a transition to participation in digital library formats, solutions to the problems of illicit copying, distribution, access, and modification of publishers' materials are needed. Publishers might prefer a "pay as you go" model, in which only temporary access is given to electronic materials, with some sorts of usage meters or restrictions. Libraries are more familiar with a "buy once, use many" model, in which ownership of a copy of a material is made to a library, then the library loans or otherwise provides access to that material as it sees fit.

Developments in scholarly self-publishing may help to guide the transition to digital access to materials from commercial publishers by creating standards, identifying demand, and providing materials for a test market. The creation of public-access data stores — for example, for US Census data, Supreme Court decisions, and geographic data — also can help lead to standards and provide a test market.

There is no doubt that the digital library, not the print library, will be the basic access point for information of all types within only a few years — for scholars, for business uses, and for the general public. The nature of the digital libraries of the future is currently being shaped by researchers, scholars, government funding agencies, publishers, and commercial interests. This work has attempted to characterize some of the important areas of concern for the development of digital libraries, and to discuss current work and some anticipated outcomes.

REFERENCES

Association for Computing Machinery (ACM). 1995. Communications of the ACM special issue on digital libraries. June.

Bush, V. 1945. "As we may think." Atlantic Monthly 176: 101-108.

Freeman, Lisa. 1996. "The university press in the electronic future." in Peek, Robin P. & Newby, Gregory B. (Eds.). Scholarly Publishing: The Electronic Frontier. Cambridge, MA: The MIT Press.

Harnad, Stevan. 1996. "Implementing Peer Review on the Net: Scientific Quality Control in Electronic Journals" in Peek, Robin P. & Newby, Gregory B. (Eds.). Scholarly Publishing: The Electronic Frontier. Cambridge, MA: The MIT Press.

Lancaster, F.W. 1969. Conceptual Alternatives to the Scientific Journal. Bethesda: ERIC.

Licklider, J.C.R. 1965. Libraries of the Future. Cambridge, MA: The MIT Press..

Impact on Education II: Challenges to Traditional Libraries

Electronic Indexes and the End User

Enid L. Zafran and Michael G. Bernier
The Bureau of National Affairs, Inc.
Washington, D.C.

ABSTRACT

The purpose of any index is to enable users to gain access to the information they need. Indexes must, therefore, be built with end users in mind. Yet published research has little to offer on the cognitive approaches of index users. In the realm of electronic delivery of information, the construction of and need for indexes may change from traditional models.

The purpose of this paper is to highlight issues involved in indexing for the electronic environment and to identify how researchers are using indexes on CD-ROM products. Hypotheses based on how sophistication of users, complexity of material, ease of use of CD software, etc., impact users' perceptions of and responses to electronic indexes will be explored in a limited case study.

INTRODUCTION

Since 1990, The Bureau of National Affairs, Inc. (BNA)[1] has expended an increasing amount of time and effort to produce tax, human relations, payroll, and environmental information on CD-ROM. The original plan to transfer print products into the new medium[2] did not include indexes, but due to market reaction the indexes were added as a later enhancement. The indexes are now part of the design of all new CD products. Currently over 20 indexes are maintained monthly on our CD products.

BNA has chosen Folio VIEWS (TM) as the software engine for its CDs. Folio VIEWS is licensed to BNA by the Folio Corporation. Data on the CD is organized into large segments of material called infobases. These infobases are connected through hypertext links and can be searched individually or several infobases may be searched at once, depending on the capacity of the end user's

---

[1] BNA is the largest private publisher located in Washington, D.C. Offering more than 200 news and information services that cover both federal and state governments as well as international developments, BNA products are available in paper, on-line (through Westlaw, Lexis, Lotus Notes Newstand), and CD-ROM formats.

[2] While the first CD products were mirror images of their print counterparts, BNA has since enhanced them with information not published in their print counterparts. Additionally, new products have been developed that are available only in CD format.

machine to have several infobases open simultaneously. BNA CDs are offered on the DOS and MS-Windows (TM) platforms.

Several approaches are available to users to find information within infobases: full-text searches using a single term or phrase or a Boolean search; tables of contents; templates on Windows versions which assist in structuring types of searches;[3] and the indexes. The indexes on CD look much like print indexes. Alphabetically organized, headings and subheadings divide the material by topic. We expect users to access the indexes by either browsing or implementing full-text searches of the indexes. Those with print counterparts may use page numbers as the links to the material while unique numeric identifiers or simply link tokens may appear in index entries for CD-ROM only material. By activating the link, the user calls up the material.[4]

The decisions we have made about the indexes on the CDs have been based on anecdotal, random feedback.[5] For most of BNA's market the medium is new, and they have not established any definite preferences and methods of research. The decision was made to add the indexes after it was clear that users had made an analogy to the corresponding printed products and that they missed the index which facilitated their research in that format. It was also theorized that the indexes might be needed only temporarily while users became more familiar with CDs and the power of full-text searching.[6] Other theories have been advanced that indexes are

---

[3] For example, a BNA environmental CD allows users to limit their searches to a specific state, history of statute, or certain EPA regions only. This assists the users in getting the hits most relevant to their research question and limits the amount of false drops that would occur if searching the CD at large.

[4] Depending on the type of link (i.e., page number or unique identifier), the user may be exactly at the location of the relevant material or as much as two screens away from the actual location. For example, a BNA looseleaf product page may require several screens to display the entire page's contents.

[5] As Milstead pointed out much of what we know about indexes is based on "folklore and intuition." Milstead, J. "Needs for research in indexing," *J. of the Amer. Soc. for Info. Sci.,* *45(8)*:577-82 (1994).

[6] The inadequacy of full-text searching has been extensively documented in recent literature. *See* Blair, D.C., & Maron, M.E., "An evaluation of retrieval effectiveness for a full-text search document retrieval system," *Communications of the ACM, 28(3)*:289-99 (1985); Gillaspie, D., "Why online legal retrieval misses conceptually relevant documents," *Proceedings of the 55th Annual Meeting of the Amer. Soc. for Info. Sci., 29*:256-59 (1992); Gillaspie, D., "The role of linguistic phenomena in retrieval performance," *Proceedings of the 58th Annual Meeting of the Amer.*

only really useful if
  1/ the users have an advanced educational background,
  2/ the subject matter is conceptually complex,
  3/ the design of the product is overwhelming to the average user,
  4/ the user previously relied on the index in print, or
  5/ the software platform inhibits searches across infobases making the index the primary method for cross-infobase searching.

The goal of our research is to determine which CD products benefit from the use of indexes, and what alterations from the traditional print index may be needed to best suit the electronic medium. We are also interested in determining how users vary in attitude toward CD indexes in terms of educational background, prior experience with CDs or electronic products, complexity of subject matter on the CD, and amount of information presented on the CD.

DISCUSSION

Indexes on BNA CD-ROM products supplement full-text searching. The shortcomings of full-text searching lie in its inability to add synonyms, distinguish homographic terms, express concepts, and handle acronyms. It also cannot overcome omissions in the text, for example, where the subject is understood but not expressed. Since passing references are picked up with the significant ones,[7] the end users must spend too much time paring down their "hit list." Folio VIEWS CDs are literal in their full-text search.[8] A

Soc. for Info. Sci., *32*:90-96 (1995); and Corbett, M., "Indexing and Searching in Statutory Text," *Keywords*, *3(1)*:7-10 (1995). Corbett makes clear that "no matter how sophisticated the parser," an automated search cannot derive from the text that which "is not there in the words of the text itself." *Id* at 10.

  [7] Relevancy ranking has been touted as the answer to this problem but even that has inherent flaws requiring searchers to spend additional time structuring "perfect" search strings. For example, a search for "deposit insurance" in a banking product may turn up instances of the "Federal Deposit Insurance Corporation" where it is off-point and yet ignore "FDIC" where it is relevant. The number of times these terms appear in an article may produce deceptive results. Indexers separate the casual references from the significant and pinpoint the true subject under discussion. Many of the problems Bella Hass Weinberg recognized in postcoordination searching still exist in and distort search results when ranked by frequency of terms' appearances. Weinberg, B.H., "Why postcoordination fails the searcher," *The Indexer*, *19(3)*:155-59 (1995).

  [8] While Folio VIEWS offers a thesaurus capability, it has yet to be developed in a manner that will assist in most searches. For example, the thesaurus does not handle phrases, only individual

search for "automobile" will not locate "car" or "motor vehicle." State statutory materials frequently use different terms to refer to the same issue. Driving a car under the influence of alcohol may be referred to as driving while intoxicated (DWI) in one state's statute and as driving under the influence (DUI) in another. A search of the index on CD will, however, locate the synonymous term as a cross-reference to the postable heading where all information is located.

The legal area is full of acronyms such as RICO for Racketeer Influenced and Corrupt Organizations Act and SLOB rules for separate-line-of-business rules. The text discussion may only use the spelled out version of the term so that a search for RICO or SLOB will have no hits when in fact the CD does contain discussion of these topics. Or, for RICO too many false drops may occur by failing to exclude "Puerto" in the search and picking up references to "Puerto Rico." To be assured of locating all information on SLOB rules, the user must not only include the acronym and the full term, but must also worry about the use or non-use of hyphens in designing the search. Any missing character or variation in spelling can throw the search off. The index will have a cross-reference from the heading SLOB RULES to the heading SEPARATE LINES OF BUSINESS RULES, where all information will be organized, regardless of the CDs use of the acronym or inconsistent use of hyphens.

Conceptual terms and phrases also affect search results. An index provides access by concept and not just by the specific phrase or language used in the CD's full text, allowing users to locate information without knowing all the terms of art used on the CD. For example, tax specialists looking for information on estate planning on one BNA CD can look in the index for a heading ESTATE PLANNING without needing to know or search for specific types of estate planning tools, such as the marital deduction, the unified credit against estate tax, or family limited partnerships. Similarly, users can locate information using the terms and phrases they know. For example, a major welfare reform proposal in 1995 was entitled the Personal Responsibility Act. A major tort reform provision in 1995 was known as the Common Sense Legal Reforms Act. Users interested in reading BNA analysis of this legislation could access the index headings for WELFARE REFORM and TORT REFORM without needing to know the specific act names. Blair and Maron's study of legal documents[9] shows that conceptual issues often result in poor results in full text searching. Anaphora, a later-

---

words. A compound phrase like "motor vehicles" will be split by the thesaurus into "motor" and "vehicles," and a thesaurus-based search will yield too many irrelevant hits. Until this capacity is enhanced, it is better left unused.

[9] Blair, D.C., & Maron, M.E. (1985)

abbreviated reference, also favors the use of indexes in a full-text search environment.[10]

The specificity of the material may affect the need for indexes in information retrieval. A travel book on CD may not require an index. Information on Phoenix or San Diego may be located readily enough via full-text searching. Similarly, a search for all references to a named individual will also prove successful in the full-text search environment.

Casual references also impact search results.[11] The indexer has eliminated minor and casual references in building the index. Full-text searching on BNA CDs cannot distinguish a casual from a relevant reference. For example, a researcher interested in Social Security rules and regulations would not want to locate information that proposed welfare reform legislation is a large policy shift akin to the enactment of Social Security. Significant discussion areas are often best located on CDs using the index. A search for discussion on defined benefit plans, which is a major type of pension plan, on a BNA employee benefits CD retrieves 657 occurrences of the term while the index unequivocally points to the place of primary discussion. Polysemy, same words with different meanings, can also impact search results.[12] Unlike the problems inherent in full-text searching, the cognitive processes of indexers and end-users have received little attention from researchers. Cognitive studies of indexers have shown that indexers commonly assign different terms to the same material.[13] Background, education, and experience of the indexer all affect the terms and keywords chosen in their indexes. While more research is clearly needed in this area, it is outside the scope of the present study.

The lack of cognitive studies of end-users is well stated by Milstead.[14] Studies completed to date have often yielded results

---

[10] The legal area is full of such references, such as "said party," "respondent," "petitioner," etc., where the party involved is mentioned without specifying the name, such as Smith Manufacturing, or John Doe. *See also* Gillaspie, D. (1992 and 1995).

[11] *Id.*

[12] Hersch, W.R., & Hickman, D., "Information Retrieval in Medicine: The SAPPHIRE Experience," *J. of the Amer. Soc. for Info. Sci.*, *46(10)*:743-47 (1995).

[13] David, C., Giroux, L., Bertrand-Gastaldy, S., Lanteigne, D., & Bertrand, A., "Indexing as problem solving: a cognitive approach to consistency," *Proceedings of the 58th Annual Meeting of the Amer. Soc. for Info. Sci.*, 32:49-55 (1995).

[14] Milstead, J. (1994)

that might surprise the experienced indexer. Users frequently do not understand the index and may not use the index as the indexer intended.[15] Scanning the index was found to be a common tactic to locate information.

Having identified the index as a valuable tool for CD-ROM researchers, we wish to identify how they will utilize the index so that we may better serve their needs. As one study previously noted, it is difficult to assess usefulness of indexes on CDs when so little is still known about the traditional print indexes.[16] While it is the aim of the present study to learn more about indexes in the new medium, it is expected that the results will also yield information applicable to the use of print indexes.

RESEARCH METHOD

A group of users numbering ten to twelve will be identified by a BNA product manager. Users will be geographically dispersed, with varying educational backgrounds. They will represent the major market segments that use the CD product. Some will have the same product in both print and CD formats. Participants will be interviewed and asked questions on their research methods and preferences. The results of this study will be reported at the session at San Diego in May.

RESEARCH ISSUES

Five years have passed since we started including the indexes on CD. Have users altered how they work with an index? Or, do they rely on the same practices that they employed with print indexes, and in particular, on scanning of the index? A well-known study of library school students has shown that they did not intuitively understand cross-references.[17] Does the display of cross-references as a linkable zone reduce confusion on part of the users?

---

[15] Liddy, E.D. & Jorgensen, C.L., "Reality check! book index characteristics that facilitate information access," *Proceedings of the 25th Annual Meeting of the Amer. Soc. of Indexers* (1993). Liddy and Jorgensen studied the cognitive processes of information science students as they attempted to retrieve information from a text. Different indexes and index styles were studied. User assumptions about a good index or successful retrieval were often different from that of the indexer. Form and layout were found to be important factors in how the index was used. Also see a study done of accountants' use of an index to a large financial services document. Forrester, M., "Indexing in hypertext environments: the role of user models," *The Indexer*, 19(4): 249-56 (1995).

[16] Forrester, M. (1995)

[17] Liddy & Jorgensen (1993)

Good indexing practices in print required multiple posting of entries. For example, the use of x-ray equipment in dental offices would be indexed under both a heading for DENTISTRY and a heading for X-RAYS. In print, this was a very helpful practice since the letter D may be many pages (or even volumes) away from the letter X. But, a full text search of the index would yield duplicative hits. How necessary are multiple postings? These are a few examples of the types of questions we will explore with our users.[18]

CONCLUSION

Study and further discussion is needed on how index professionals can best meet the needs of end users as the digital revolution continues. While this study of CD user's cognitive processes is limited, it will serve to begin as a focus for further study of how indexes will function in an electronic world.

_____

[18] See also Introduction for list of other issues to be explored.

EXTENDING THE KANTOR-SARACEVIC *DERIVED TAXONOMY OF VALUE IN USING LIBRARY SERVICES*: THREE DEFINITIONS FROM THE MICROSOFT LIBRARY USE-STATISTICS DATABASE

Michael Stallings
Microsoft Library

ABSTRACT

The Microsoft Library use-statistics data model defines three concepts that can reasonably be seen as additions or extensions to Kantor and Saracevic's *Derived Taxonomy of Value in Using Library Services*. The concepts and their definitions were derived from an analysis of library services by the Microsoft Library Systems Group. They are useful for organizing and classifying library services, library users, and the interaction between services and users in a way that both accurately reflects the real world and that makes sense to the Library organization. This paper discusses the three user-centered concepts and their relationship to and effect on the Kantor-Saracevic taxonomy. The combination of the two taxonomies is found to have a focusing effect on the Kantor-Saracevic taxonomy and interview process, and to add depth to the Microsoft data model.

1. INTRODUCTION

The Microsoft Library use-statistics database was developed by the Library Systems Group in response to a request by Library managers to develop a database that counts use of Library services by Microsoft employees. An additional constraint was added that the data model be useful in the Library's ongoing efforts to develop a cost-benefit analysis of its services. The data model was implemented in a relational database (MS SQL Server 6.0) and is successfully tracking library use statistics today. As of March 1 1996, it held over 6 million rows of data. Each month it produces dozens of reports on the use of Library Services by the Library's customers.

2. METHODOLOGY

The Systems Group approached the task using a modified form of the Systems Development Life Cycle, specifically the database design phase (Jordan & Machesky; McFadden & Hoffer). The database design process is data-driven, in that it seeks to conceptually model a real-world situation in such a way that data streaming in from the situation can be stored and retrieved using standard database tools.

First, Library managers' requirements for the database were defined. Then primary entities were identified and relationships between them derived from library staff and analysts' own experience and knowledge of Library services. Attributes were then assigned to these entities based on available information about the real-world use of Library services by its customers. The data model was normalized to 3rd normal form (Date) and displayed in an Entity-Relationship Diagram (McFadden & Hoffer). This process was repeated until the group was satisfied it had ported the real-life situation of customers using Library services into a model that could be implemented in a relational database.

Use of the relational model and its constraints of normalization were a key factor in the shape of the final product. For instance, the relational model requires that the attributes of an entity be organized around a single defining attribute that distinguishes it from other instances of that entity. In relational vocabulary, this defining attribute is called the "primary key" (Date). The primary key for the entity "Library Service," for example, is the name of the service, so every Library Service is listed once and only once with a unique name. This requirement leads to the necessity, and benefit, of creating an authority list of Library Services. These kinds of constraints help organize and clarify empirical information about library customers and library services into a model that can store and retrieve data logically.

3. THE MICROSOFT DATA MODEL

Three entities emerged to form the core of the data model: User, Library Service and Information Transfer. These entities are discussed in detail in the sections that follow.

3.1 USER

User is defined as a customer of the Library, which in turn is anybody allowed by the rules of the institution to use it. At the Microsoft Library, every Microsoft employee is a customer. The primary key is formed on the attribute of the user's email alias. Access to the company's employee database provides the ability to characterize the customer with other attributes, some of which are listed in Table 1.

Table 1. Sample of Microsoft employee attributes.

Email Alias
First Name
Last Name
Title
Building
Room
Hire Date
Department
Division
Employee Type
Manager

These additional attributes are useful in grouping service usage along a customer axis. For instance, it is possible to aggregate use of Library services by user departments. This might prove useful in a future project for valuing Library Services if, for example, the Library wanted to target different groups with different types of surveys.

3.2 LIBRARY SERVICE

Library Service is defined as the tool that delivers information to the user, as seen from the user's point of view. In other words, the service is the customer's perception of the mechanism that dispenses the information. From the user's perspective, the mechanism is usually denoted by an icon on a computer screen, a library person or a physical location; consequently, the process for identifying a service usually means finding the interface the customer approaches with their information need. For example, customers use an icon captioned with the word "NewsEdge" on their computer screen to start the newswire service; thus that icon represents the customer-perceived boundary between the service "NewsEdge" and the customer. In another example, the customer might request help from someone at the reference desk; the combination of the physical reference desk and the librarian staffing it represents the boundary of the service "Library Assist."

Although the user's perception of the service is the criteria for isolating it as a service, the service's name is not limited to the user's name for it. For example, the user might have "requested an article," but the service will be called "Document Delivery" based on an expert interpretation of their statement. Users often refer to the Library Catalog as "MLO" (Microsoft Library Online) when the acronym MLO actually refers to the Visual Basic shell that holds the icon that starts the Library Catalog. These variations are sifted to create an authority list of Library Services.

This process results in a set of user-centered definitions of Library Services. Although the customer's view of library services has not been empirically determined by interviewing the customer, the database design process has elicited that view from the library staff's own experience as users, and their experience with users.

The authority list in the Microsoft use-statistics database has grown to approximately 135 services, a sample of which is shown in Table 2.

Table 2. Sample of Microsoft library services.

Archive Item
Company Profile
Dialog Alert
Document Delivery
Internet Training
Library Assist
Library Briefing
Library Tour
Museum Visit
Research Project
Researcher Consultation

The only required attribute, or characteristic, of a Library Service is that it have a unique name to provide the primary key. However, it is possible to add an unlimited number of characteristics to the entity to facilitate grouping and reporting. For instance, one characteristic requested by Library managers is that it be amenable to grouping by the medium of the Library Service, so a medium-type field was added. Some possible values are listed in Table 3.

Table 3. Sample of possible medium-types of a library service.

AudioCassette
Email
Floppy Disk
In-Person
Object
Paper
Phone
Server
VideoCassette

With the addition of this attribute, Library Services can now be grouped by medium-type and their use explored from that angle.

3.3 INFORMATION TRANSFER

An <u>Information Transfer</u> (IT) is a single output of a Library Service in response to an expressed user information need. The user's information need is signaled when the user interacts with a Library Service. The request may be transitory ("What's the capitol of New Hampshire?") or permanent (a Dialog Alert), it may be implicit (subscribing to an in-house, email-based news service and subsequently receiving mail) or explicit ("What's the capitol of New Hampshire?"). We look no deeper into it than that the user approached and activated a Library Service and received information as an output. An additional constraint on an Information Transfer is that it cannot be "meta-information," or information about getting information. For instance, a result set in a library catalog search is meta-information, but a book checked out as a result of retrieving that information is an Information Transfer.

This is a user-centered definition in that the identification of an IT is based on an expert interpretation of what the customer sees as an output. The IT is defined as what the user sees as a single item, even if it is, from the Library's point of view, a compound item. A user may ask for a competitor profile and receive a document with many parts, each of which is the result of a search by a different researcher. This is the work of possibly 40 hours, and is counted as a single IT by our user-oriented definition. On the other hand, a user may open a document retrieved from a third-party online database; this is the work of 5 seconds and is also an IT.

It is obvious that, with this definition, IT's are not aggregable in a meaningful sense in the same way that you cannot count the number of bills in a random collection of currency and come up with a sense of value. Some bills are worth $1, some 5$ and some $20, etc. If you had 100 bills, you could have a value in the range between $100 and $10,000. This limiting definition of the IT is necessary if the model is to avoid an overwhelming complexity that might prevent it from accomplishing its original task of counting instances of the use of library services. It should be noted, however, that the IT concept does not obliterate the notion of value, it defers it. Other processes and entities, building on the IT and related concepts, should be able to determine cost and value.

3.4 THE DATA MODEL

The User entity and the Library Service entity have a many-to-many relationship: a Library Service can be used by 0:N Users, and a User can use 0:N Library Services. An "associative object" or "correlation table" is required at the intersection of a many-to-many relationship. In this case, the correlation table is the Information Transfer table. Following relational rules, the key to this table starts with the key from each parent table. A date-time field representing the time the transfer was started completes the defining primary key that makes each row in the table unique. A simplified version of the final model is shown in Figure 1.

Figure 1. Simplified data model of the Microsoft use-statistics database.

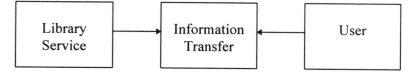

4.0 COMBINING THE TAXONOMIES

4.1 THE MICROSOFT USE-STATISTICS DATA MODEL AS A TAXONOMY

It is also possible to view the Microsoft model as a classification scheme using Bailey's definition of classification: "the ordering of entities into groups or classes on the basis of their similarity," seeking to "minimize within-group variance, while maximizing between-group variance." Minimizing within-group and maximizing between-group variance corresponds closely to the idea of 3rd Normal Form (3NF) in the relational model, where all attributes of an entity must describe the entity's defining primary key, the whole primary key, and only the primary key (Date).

Whether or not this model is more like a typology or a taxonomy is open to question. As defined earlier, the database design process tries to conceptually model real-life data, a statement close to Bailey's definition of a taxonomy as a "classification of empirical entities." It is sufficient for our purposes here to say that the Microsoft model is an empirically-based classification scheme similar to a taxonomy in the way that Kantor and Saracevic's taxonomy might be said to be an empirically-based classification scheme similar to a typology at its uppermost classes (discussed in the next section).

The three Microsoft entities form the top-level classes of a taxonomy in the same way that they form the primary entities in the database world's Entity-Relationship Diagram. Table 4 illustrates the top-level classes of the resulting taxonomy. Although it is also possible to position the attributes of each entity as leaves in a taxonomy, it is of more use here to focus on the main entities.

Table 4. Microsoft data model top-level classes.

1.	User
2.	Library Service
3.	Information Transfer

4.2 THE KANTOR-SARACEVIC "DERIVED TAXONOMY OF VALUE IN USING LIBRARY SERVICES"

Kantor and Saracevic developed their taxonomy as part of a larger study. Taking a user-centered approach, the study is based on a foundation of value "as perceived and defined by users," and focuses on "the specific task or project that brings the user to the library." The study does not try to determine the value of library services to the sponsoring institution, but instead seeks to determine the value of those services to individuals associated with the institution, assuming informally that value experienced by the individual equates to value experienced by the institution. (Kantor et al)

This user-centered approach is manifested in the user-interview process that provides the data-gathering framework for the study. Users were interviewed in libraries (and phone follow-ups) about their recent interaction with a library service. Table 5 shows a sample of questions used in the interviews.

Table 5. Sample of questions from Kantor-Saracevic interview process.

xxx = library service
What did you get out of using **xxx** on that occasion?
On a scale of 1 to 7 ... how helpful was what you got to your actual project or work?
... how confident are you that you can rely on the information you got from using **xxx** on that occasion?

(Kantor et al)

These interviews were then transformed by a coding and analysis process into data that was organized into the empirical taxonomy. The derived taxonomy was then extracted from the empirical taxonomy. Over 500 interviews were taken in 5 major research libraries. The resulting taxonomy has 3 broad classes, several major subclasses, and a large number of sub-subclasses. Table 5 shows the classes and major subclasses.

Table 6. Major classes/subclasses of Kantor-Saracevic taxonomy (Kantor & Saracevic).

1.		REASONS for using a library service
	a)	For a TASK
	b)	For PERSONAL reasons
	c)	To get an OBJECT or perform an ACTIVITY
2.		INTERACTION with a library service
	a)	RESOURCES, SERVICES
	b)	USE of resources, services
	c)	OPERATIONS AND ENVIRONMENT
3.		RESULTS of using a library service
	a)	COGNITIVE results
	b)	AFFECTIVE results
	c)	ACCOMPLISHMENTS in relation to tasks
	d)	Meeting EXPECTATIONS
	e)	TIME aspects
	f)	MONEY estimates

The study proposes that the user interaction with the library takes place in three phases: Acquisition, Cognition and Application. As well, although we are concerned mostly with the taxonomy here, the study also produced or displayed several other tools for valuing library services. Among them is a methodology for developing cost estimates using functional cost analysis (Kantor et al).

4.3 COMBINING THE MICROSOFT TAXONOMY AND THE KANTOR-SARACEVIC TAXONOMY

There appears to be no explicit guidance for combining independently-developed taxonomies or typologies in Bailey or elsewhere. However, both taxonomies were developed with a user-centered approach to valuing library services, and both used defensible, empirical methodologies. Thus we should find that they complement, strengthen, or otherwise connect with each other. Table 6 offers a likely configuration. The Microsoft classes form the top level classes, with the Kantor-Saracevic top-level classes becoming major subclasses of the Microsoft class "Information Transfer."

Table 7. Combined taxonomy showing origins of classes.

	Combined Taxonomy		Origins
1.	USER		Microsoft definition
2.	LIBRARY SERVICE		Microsoft definition
3.	INFORMATION TRANSFER		Microsoft definition
	a)	REASONS for using a library service	Kantor-Saracevic top-level class
	b)	INTERACTION with a library service	Kantor-Saracevic top-level class
	c)	RESULTS of using a library service	Kantor-Saracevic top-level class

Since the primary goal of both the Microsoft and the Kantor-Saracevic models is to evaluate library services, it might appear that the Kantor-Saracevic classes REASONS, INTERACTION and RESULTS belong under the Microsoft class LIBRARY SERVICE rather than INFORMATION TRANSFER. However, the definition of an Information Transfer ("a single output of a Library Service in response to an expressed user information need") makes the IT the more precise location because REASONS, INTERACTION and RESULTS more accurately refer to transactions between users and services than to the services themselves. This arrangement permits the evaluation of services at the most atomic level of a single transaction between the user and the library service. The evaluation of the service can be undertaken by aggregating the results of IT evaluations. Then the resulting Library Service evaluations can be aggregated into an evaluation of the whole library in its role as information provider.

That is the underlying assumption of this move: that the thing that's under study here is the library's role as an information provider. In that light, the most appropriate measure of the library's value is a measure of the value of the information provided, not a measure of the efficacy of the services that provide the information. One effect that cascades from this assumption is that a transaction-based approach will not measure the instances of users who come away completely empty-handed, nor will it fully capture the frustration of the user who comes away with less information than they wanted. Neither will it capture the value of the library as a copy center, a place to study, or a provider of meeting rooms. It may be important to capture all of these kinds of data, but it is not pertinent to a study of the net value of the information provided by the library.

This rearrangement and the resulting re-focus arguably causes some displacement in the subclasses of the Kantor-Saracevic taxonomy. For instance, subclass A.3 ("REASONS for using a library service—To get an object or perform an activity") in the

Kantor-Saracevic taxonomy can be supplanted with the more robust authority list of Library Services. Subclass B.3 ("Operations and Environment") more fittingly belongs in a different model, one that attempts to value the library shell as a sort of meta-service. Other adjustments may be appropriate as well, but that discussion is more useful at a time when the model is brought on-site at a specific library or type of library.

It is important to note that changing or extending the taxonomy does not necessarily require changing the interview process or any other part of the study. Taxonomic development in its narrowest sense takes the opposite approach, trying to discern order in masses of empirical data. However, insofar as classification is a means for understanding the world, and then organizing and communicating this understanding, then the development of taxonomies and data models can and should be an iterative process where the end results of one phase cycle back into and improve the other phases. The following section is an example of this process in action.

4.4 WHAT THE MS DATA MODEL BRINGS TO THE KANTOR-SARACEVIC TAXONOMY

As previously discussed, Kantor and Saracevic collected open-ended responses from users about the tasks and projects that brought them to the library, and the impact of recently-used library services on those tasks or projects. Their interview process was, to some degree, transaction-based in that they approached the user immediately after his or her interaction with the service. However, the Microsoft model is much more strictly focused on transactions (i.e., Information Transfers). The Kantor-Saracevic method is brought more closely into alignment with this approach by locating the three Kantor-Saracevic classes under Microsoft's Information Transfer class. This adjustment helps correct three closely-related problems that arise from excessive broadness in Kantor and Saracevic's interview process.

First, as Kantor and Saracevic state in more than one place, it is sometimes difficult during the interview to maintain a user's focus (Kantor et al). For instance, users often have difficulty isolating their underlying reason for coming to the Library. In their minds, "getting a book" stands in for "writing a paper" because they are getting the book in order to write the paper. This problem should be lessened to some extent if the questioning is explicitly about, for example, a recent transaction involving checking out and using the book "Graphic Arts Handbook." A transaction-based interview process provides this kind of focus by letting the user answer questions about specific pieces of information rather than about their general contact with the service. Table 7 shows a comparison of how the interview process might be changed with the transaction focus. The Kantor-Saracevic questions are taken from Appendix A of their Final Report. It should be clear how the focus on a single transaction eliminates a level of uncertainty in the questions that should be repaid by less uncertainty in the answers and the analysis of the answers.

Table 8. Some Kantor-Saracevic interview questions compared to transaction-focused interview questions.

KANTOR-SARACEVIC question	Transaction-focused question
What did you get out of using the Art and Archaeology Library on that occasion?	You checked out "Graphic Art Design Handbook"; what did you get out of that book?
On a scale of 1 to 7 ... how helpful was what you got to your actual project or work?	On a scale of 1-7 ... how helpful was "Graphic Art Design Handbook" to your actual project or work?
... how confident are you that you can rely on the information you got from using the Art and Archaeology Library on that occasion?	... how confident are you that you can rely on the information you got from using "Graphic Art Design Handbook?"

Not all of Kantor and Saracevic's interview questions would be improved to this degree. For instance, it is difficult to get more precise about the use of the reference desk than by conducting, as they do, an exit interview about the user's most recent contact with the reference person. However, most of their evaluated services would benefit. Questions about a collection or branch library could be narrowed to questions about items checked out of the collection or consulted at the branch library. Questions about documents retrieved from a document delivery service could be aimed at extracting a notion of the value yielded by a single, specific document. This is bound to have a clarifying effect on the interview process as it focuses the user on a specific, tangible piece of information.

Second, a transaction-based approach helps detach the evaluation of the service from the evaluation of the platform that forms the shell for the service. For instance, asking questions about a user's experience with the Music and Media Center in an exit interview invites extraneous variables into the user's response. These variables might include whether the person staffing the desk was friendly or unfriendly, whether the material was difficult to locate in the catalog or find on the shelf, and whether certain items were checked out or not. These aspects of the experience play a part in the user's perception of the Music and Media Center, but not in the value the user receives. A transaction-based approach tries to capture the net value of the information dispensed by a service, not whether the service itself was good or bad. The Music and Media Center is just a platform for the transaction; it is the transaction and its subsequent use that provides value. As previously stated, a successful information transfer does not include the answer "No, we don't have that item," because this is meta-information, or information about information. Neither does it include those who could not find a service to operate; and we do not care if the user found the service unfriendly or obtuse. It defers study of those situations to another model, along with other questions about the library as a whole. This deferral allows us to discover the value of library services rather than the character of those services. Stating this deferral in terms of the Kantor-Saracevic study, we can say that the revised model defers evaluation of the Acquisitions phase.

Third, Kantor and Saracevic speak of a prominent limiting factor in their interview process (Kantor et al). Their focus on the user's most recent interaction with a service, called the "local context" factor, interferes with the ability of the interviewee to compare the present interaction with other interactions. Although the Microsoft transaction-based interview might seem to exacerbate this condition, in fact just the opposite is true. For instance, in their example of an interviewee who is happy with the library that day because he or she was able to copy an article, the problematic result of asking them how well the library served them at that moment is that they may respond that the library served them very well (because the copier worked). This has nothing to do with the impact of the article on their work or life. By focusing on Information Transfers (not the library service shell, and not the meta-information they may have gathered in the process of retrieving their information), the interviewer might not have approached the user at all, or might have approached the user and found that he or she had not even looked at the information yet and so could not respond. In that case, the interview would, correctly, not take place. The incidence of the limiting factor is diminished by reducing the number of occasions in which it might appear.

4.5 WHAT THE KANTOR-SARACEVIC TAXONOMY BRINGS TO THE MICROSOFT DATA MODEL
The strength of the Microsoft data model is in its deferral of the complexity required to determine value, a deferral taken in order to count transactions well. This obviously makes for a one-sided model. The Kantor-Saracevic taxonomy remedies this deferral by adding that dimension. By porting the combined taxonomy back to the data model and then into the relational database, it should be possible to correlate values with individual transactions. This is a subject for another paper.

5.0 APPLICATION OF THE EXTENDED TAXONOMY
One likely application of the extended taxonomy comes with the ability to group library services. For instance, once an authority list of services has been established, they can be characterized and classified in any way that makes sense to the organization. They could be broken out by whether or not they are compound documents; by originating library department; by media type or bibliographic format. Once broken out this way, they can be evaluated for cost and value in ways that are appropriate for that grouping.

Another application depends on the ability to group users. In a corporate environment, where access to personnel records at some level is assumed, there are many ways to characterize an employee. If the employee's office location is part of the data available, it is possible to classify use of library services based on proximity to the library or one of its branches. If the employee's title or job level is available, library use can be broken out that way.

On the costing side, services that generate compound documents could have more elaborate costing routines attached to them than services with simpler output.

The transaction-based approach strongly suggests the use of electronic data-gathering in order to begin the process at that pinpoint level. Survey forms that pop open immediately following the opening of a document in an online database, for instance, would be ideal. The ability to do follow-ups based on circulation records or other data gathered electronically about user transactions would also be a plus. This brings up a couple of issues. First, the user may react negatively to a perceived violation of his or her privacy; and second, it is difficult to prompt users for more detailed responses as Kantor and Saracevic have done using live interviewers.

6.0 CONCLUSION
The Microsoft Library data model is a counting tool. Its almost simplistic definitions provide a narrow focus that defines and organizes library services and counts instances of user interaction with them. The Kantor-Saracevic taxonomy is a valuation tool, embracing the complexity of determining value using the rich chaos of user response. The Microsoft model brings into play a user-centered but library-aware focus in its authority list of Library Services and Users; Kantor and Saracevic appropriately classify their data in a fully user-based framework. The combination of these two tools adds a needed dimension to the Microsoft model, and sharpens the approach of the interviewing and interpretation instruments built around the Kantor-Saracevic taxonomy.

The combination has a practical side as well, for it provides a way to store data gathered in the library valuation process. Areas for further work here include the incorporation and normalization of entities involved with costing, as well as further work on normalizing the Kantor and Saracevic subclasses and sub-subclasses.

NOTES
Bailey, K. D. (1994). *Typologies and taxonomies. An introduction to classification techniques.* Thousand Oaks CA: Sage Publications.

Date, C.J. (1986). *Relational database.* Reading MA: Addison-Wesley Publishing.

Jordan, E. And Machesky, J. (1990). *Systems development.* Boston: PWS-Kent Publishing.

Kantor, P.B., Saracevic, T., & D'Esposito-Wachtmann, J. (1995). *Studying the cost and value of library services: Final Report.* New Brunswick, NJ: School of Communication, Information and Library Studies, Rutgers University. Available in electronic form from: ftp://scils.rutgers.edu/pub/APLab/cost.value.study

Kantor, P. and Saracevic, T. (1995). Studying the Value of Library and Information Services: A Taxonomy of Users' Assessments. *Proceedings of the 58th Annual Meeting of the American Society for Information Science 32,* 35-44.

McFadden, F. And Hoffer, J. (1991). *Database management.* New York: Benjamin/Cummings Publishing.

The Mann Library Gateway -- A Cataloger's Tale

Gregory A. McClellan
Albert R. Mann Library, Cornell University
Ithaca, New York

This paper explores the changing role of the cataloger in a modern research library. The architecture of the Mann Library Gateway is discussed along with the cataloging division's role in the development of the Gateway, one of numerous digital library initiatives now underway at Cornell's Mann Library.

The Gateway is a World Wide Web interface to hundreds of remotely accessible resources. Intellectual access to these resources is provided by several methods, including lists by title and subject and a searchable keyword index. The cataloging department oversees the design, development, and maintenance of these features.

The implementation and mainstreaming of the Gateway has necessitated that the role of the professional cataloger be reexamined and redefined. Mann's experience with the Gateway has made clear a few of the new roles and responsibilities that the cataloging profession must embrace in order to continue to provide adequate intellectual access to library resources. Some of these functions are: database design and management, computer programming, system administration, and systems analysis.

Providing access to networked information resources is one of the most interesting and exciting areas of development within the digital library. The cataloging profession must remain flexible and dynamic in order to face the new challenges of the digital revolution. Catalogers should not miss out on this great opportunity to expand the responsibilities and definition of their jobs.

Impact on Education III:
Digital Libraries II

A Hybridized Hypertext and Boolean Retrieval Model for Bibliographic Databases

Dietmar Wolfram
School of Library and Information Science, University of Wisconsin
Milwaukee, Wisconsin

ABSTRACT

The author proposes an information retrieval model for bibliographic data that combines aspects of traditional Boolean-based querying and browsable hypertext access. The search advantages of each method are combined in a descriptive model resulting in a very flexible search environment for bibliographic records. By using a Boolean approach to first narrow search options combined with hypertext browsability of the retrieval set and surrounding documents, a rich search environment is created. Users are able to further focus retrieved search sets for browsing by following hypertext linkages of common occurrences of terms such as authors and descriptors among records. The author demonstrates the feasibility of the retrieval method by example in the context of an existing hypertext retrieval system.

INTRODUCTION

The increasing availability of information in digital form, whether as document surrogates such as bibliographic records, or as full-text databases, has made the design of effective information retrieval systems more important than ever. One the products of the Digital Revolution has been commercial hypertext/hypermedia information systems. With the popularity of networked resources such as the world-wide web and multimedia encyclopedias on CD-ROM, hypertext/hypermedia access has entered mainstream popularity.

Within a purely hypertext-based retrieval system, there is no formal retrieval set to be viewed. Searchers navigate the system by traveling from node to node via linkages that take the form of 'buttons' or 'hotwords' on the screen. These linkages represent relationships that exist between nodes (i.e. a semantic link or common occurrence of a search term). Searchers begin their investigation by entering one point of the hypertext database, usually via an index, and then traverse a network of links to locate relevant items until the information need is met. The linkages, in essence, create structure within largely unstructured information environments.

The use of hypertext for highly structured textual information such as bibliographic records has not been widely implemented. Traditionally, bibliographic retrieval systems have relied on query-based methods (e.g. Boolean, probabilistic) to access relevant database contents which have not been well-suited for system browsing. In standard Boolean-based search systems relying on inverted file organization, searching depends on the retrieval of a set of documents or document surrogates that match entered query terms. The retrieval process is relatively straightforward, from which a list of potentially relevant documents is compiled. Once part of a retrieval set, the documents are viewed linearly according to some sequence (chronology, weighted relevance, accession numbers). The advantage of this search approach is that documents which share a set of search terms can be isolated to allow sequential inspection, thereby eliminating examination of large numbers of documents. But this model for retrieval has several well-known weaknesses. Potentially relevant documents that are not part of the retrieval set are missed because searchers are limited to viewing documents contained within the retrieval sets. Retrieval sets may also become too large if queries are too general or incorporate search terms that appear in numerous documents. Query modification involving the use of more specific or additional terms is then necessary, which may further exclude relevant items. Searchers are unable to browse retrieval sets in a non-linear fashion and documents are not grouped in other meaningful ways to show inter-document relationships.

Hypertext-based systems, although providing superior browsing capabilities, may not be useful as a sole method for bibliographic retrieval. Using common occurrences of fields such as authors, descriptors, title and abstract keywords, and citations if available, links may be established between bibliographic records for easy traversal of the database. But in bibliographic retrieval systems where keywords and descriptors form the basis for retrieval as linkages between documents, the number of items to be viewed may become too large due to the Zipfian nature of the distribution of terms. The method, therefore, becomes impractical for large databases. Also, since documents may contain large numbers of keywords or descriptors, the number of inter-record linkages may also become overwhelming. Finally, the hypertext strategy is useful for expanding one's searching options, but does not by itself allow one to easily focus a search strategy.

If bibliographic systems could be designed that take advantage of the querying strengths of Boolean systems for better search focus, and the browsability strengths of hypertext systems, a more effective retrieval system could be developed. A hybrid model for retrieval which combines the best features of both methods is described here.

PREVIOUS STUDIES

The design of more effective information retrieval systems is an ongoing endeavor in information science research. Most commercial systems still rely on variations of Boolean-based retrieval. However, more innovative approaches using natural language, probabilistic, and clustering techniques are becoming available. Hypertext access to information, although existing at least conceptually for fifty years, has only received much attention in the research literature since the late eighties.

Comprehensive models for information retrieval combining existing techniques and proposing new methods for a range of textual retrieval environments have taken many approaches, encompassing functional aspects of systems design and user-centered, conceptual approaches. Crouch and Nance (1984) developed a description of a generalized IR system by decomposing the system into functional modules and abstract processes which could be applied to traditional models such as a Boolean-based system. Croft and Thompson (1987) developed a model entitled Intelligent Intermediary for Information Retrieval (I^3R) that combined several existing information retrieval strategies, providing a range of facilities for the IR process, from query formulation to the evaluation of results through the use of intelligent intermediaries. A browsing expert was be used to graphically represent a network of linkages between documents, in effect providing a form of hypertext linkage for system navigation. Tague, Salminen and McClellan (1991) developed a Grammar/Hypergraph model for an IR system that permitted searchers to navigate database contents through static and transient hypergraphs.

The importance of browsing and retrieval system navigation has been espoused more recently in online searching and has been incorporated in retrieval models. Bates (1989) developed a 'berrypicking' model of information retrieval in which the retrieval process is likened to the process of searching for isolated berries scattered in a forest. To facilitate this approach, browsing, citation searching, and area scanning are among several techniques suggested for inclusion in online retrieval systems. Jacobson (1991) relied on the communication theory of 'sense-making' to describe the search processes of novice searchers in a multi-file, full-text database environment.

Incorporation of search features suggested by these models is possible in hypertext-based retrieval systems, and have been implemented into a number of studies that combine traditional and novel approaches with hypertext-based retrieval. Croft and Turtle (1993) integrated hypertext linkages of citations and nearest neighbor bibliographic records in a probabilistic retrieval system using Bayesian inference nets. The authors concluded the inference net approach was at least as effective as previously used spreading activation techniques. Belkin, Marchetti & Cool (1993) developed an intelligent prototype interface called BRAQUE that supported a variety of searcher behaviors referred to as 'information seeking strategies' and demonstrated by example how the BRAQUE interface could be used. Nelson (1991) developed an interface for an OPAC that used implicit hypertext linkages of key words after searchers have initially narrowed records to be browsed via Boolean queries. Watters and Shepherd (1990) introduced a transient hypergraph-based model that supports both browsing and querying of databases. The generalized model was shown through demonstration to be applicable to several traditional information retrieval models and types of data, including bibliographic retrieval systems. Through the use of transient hypergraphs (i.e. linkages which only exist for the duration of the search session) processing overhead is reduced. However, the model does not support browsing of the system without first formulating a query.

The existing research demonstrates that the integration of hypertext browsing capabilities with more established query-based retrieval approaches is feasible. But many avenues remain to be explored, and further user studies of system performance need to be carried out. In this paper the author presents a hybrid model that combines the querying strengths of Boolean retrieval with the browsing advantages of hypertext as a precursor to a user-based retrieval system study.

MODEL DEVELOPMENT

The proposed model is presented in the context of an existing prototype hypertext bibliographic retrieval system, called HyperLynx, that was developed using Asymetrix ToolBook, a Windows-based hypermedia authoring system. HyperLynx was designed to study hypertext system design and usage for highly structured information (Dimitroff & Wolfram, 1993,1995). The system consists of a subset of the NTIS database, containing close to 3,000 records on library and information science covering 1989-1991. Fields contained in each record include author, title, notes, descriptor, and abstract fields.

Access to database records is initiated through an introductory menu which takes the searcher to separate indexes for authors, titles, and descriptors. The linking of records with common terms provides an important connection between possibly related records, especially for descriptors, since they summarize the subject content of a record. To enter the database of bibliographic records the searcher clicks on the desired search term in the indexes. For authors and descriptors, if more than one record exists for a search term, the searcher is taken to the first record in a circular list of linkages for that term. The searcher may then navigate to the next or previous record in the list containing the term by clicking on a 'next' or 'previous' button. If a searcher wishes to alter the search path, the searcher merely clicks on a different descriptor or author hotword appearing on the page. Records, in effect, act as the intersection point of many possible search paths, thereby allowing searchers to shift their focus without having to return to an index to modify their query. Searchers may also return to the different indexes for new terms to search at any time.

The main advantage of this approach is that searchers are able to browse many avenues, altering their search path as other possibly relevant search terms are revealed in the records. A rich browsing environment is created. Because browsing of records sharing a search term is performed sequentially on single terms at one time, a drawback of this search method is the possibility of lengthy search chains. As the database grows this can become a significant problem (Savoy, 1992). The Zipfian nature of the frequency of occurrence of terms in databases creates difficulties, particularly with the small percentage of search terms that occur with great frequency. The browsing capability in this case becomes a hindrance, with no mechanism for reducing the number of records to be searched, as in a query-based system where subsets of the database are first isolated. The searcher must either be very patient, or select another search term.

A retrieval environment that first enables the searcher to isolate a subset of the database to which browsing techniques can be applied is needed. For more effective searching several system features are desirable:

- A method of isolating a subset of records within the database

- A method of grouping records with common terms within the subset

- Flexible browsing within the subset

- A method of exploring beyond the subset without having to reformulate the query

The existing hypertext web of linkages within the HyperLynx system may serve as a mechanism for searching the entire database, but modifications are needed to incorporate the desired system features.

The traditional Boolean model provides an easily implemented approach to isolating subsets of the database. No term weights within the existing database need be assigned as in probabilistic retrieval systems. Also the combination of Boolean terms need not be as specific as traditional systems since a more browsable interface is provided, allowing the searchers to view different groups of records within the subset. Once a reasonable subset of the original database has been selected, the browsing capabilities inherent in hypertext systems may be applied.

By integrating the hypertext model into the retrieved subset, browsability becomes more practical. Browsing will be initiated by selecting search terms from a list of all search terms existing within the subset. The list of search terms and the frequencies of occurrence will also follow a Zipfian distribution. But the frequencies of occurrence which determine search path lengths will be smaller than the complete database, but will still provide a rich set of linkages for exploration. These terms could be presented to searchers in alphabetical order or in descending order of frequency of occurrence.

Common terms within the subset, such as authors and descriptors, may be used to create transient hypergraphs, as described by Watters and Shepherd (1990) within the subset to support browsing. Transient hypergraphs exist only for the duration of a search session and are built as the searcher selects navigation options such as 'next' when browsing through records containing the common term. The common term occurrences represent semantic linkages between records and allow grouping and viewing of all records containing the term in sequence. The use of transient hypergraphs is also computationally more efficient since the entire set of linkages of the subset of records need not be developed--only those search paths selected.

The approach also accommodates flexible browsing by allowing searchers to focus on all records containing the selected term. Conversely, the user may opt to select a new term to view a different path of records, thus allowing different permutations of the subset of records to be browsed.

Finally, the searcher need not be limited to records within the subset of records retrieved. By relying on the existing web of hypertext linkages of the entire system, a searcher may opt to investigate records containing a promising search term revealed by the retrieved records, but which were not part of the initial subset. If a search term is selected that proves to be especially relevant to the query, and more records exist within the database containing the relevant term, the existing hypertext linkages for the complete database may be used to allow the searcher to continue exploration beyond the initial retrieval set without having to formulate a new query.

Thus the system empowers the searcher by presenting available options for exploration. Unlike systems incorporating natural language processing or artificial intelligence techniques, it does not try to second guess the searcher's intentions. The system simply presents other options for the searcher to explore. The hypertext linkages help to refine the initial query if it is not initially very specific.

A representation of the relationships among records appears in Figure 1. An example of how the hybrid system would operate using a descriptor-based search in the HyperLynx database follows.

EXAMPLE

A searcher is interested in finding bibliographic records about 'public library services.'

1)   Search terms used to establish an initial retrieval set are identified:

Descriptor	Frequency of Occurrence
Library-Services	**250**
Public-Libraries	**182**

Note that the browsing of linkage chains for either term in a purely hypertext-based system would be tedious.

2) The two search terms are used to formulate a Boolean query resulting in a browsable subset of the database consisting of 116 hits.

The initial set of records has now been reduced to a more manageable level. However, 116 items may still be too large. One alternative would be to add extra search terms to the query to reduce the number of records in the browsable set. This may reduce recall at the expense of precision. The searcher, not willing to eliminate any possibilities at this point, uses this set.

3) A list of terms existing within the browsable set is provided to the searcher (see Figure 2).

In the browsable set, the Zipfian relationship of term sizes and frequencies is also present, but maximal values of frequencies are much smaller than in the overall database (the maximal value in this case being 39). The searcher is able to browse the set contents using other descriptors present within the records. The list of terms is also beneficial in allowing the searcher to discover other potentially useful search terms with paths for exploration. In this case, there are 37 other descriptors that occur in at least 10 records of the set. The searcher opts to select the descriptor 'Program-Development' with 14 postings. Subsequent visitation of records using transient hypertext linkages reveals records of particular interest to the searcher.

4) The searcher continues the investigation outside of the retrieval set.

The searcher, encouraged by the number of relevant items produced by this search path decides to continue by investigating other records containing this descriptor outside of the browsable set by relying on the existing non-transient hypertext structure. Browsing outside the set reveals that another 6 records in the database contain this descriptor. Subsequent visitation of these records results in several additional relevant items without having to reformulate the query.

Thus the searcher is able to take advantage of the focusing abilities of Boolean retrieval as well as the broadening abilities of the hypertext linkages.

CONCLUSIONS

The author has presented a model for bibliographic retrieval that combines aspects of Boolean retrieval for querying and hypertext retrieval for browsing. By providing the searcher with transient hypertext linkage options on a retrieved set, a more flexible search environment is presented which may allow searchers to explore records both within the initially retrieved set and surrounding records.

The next phase of this project will involve the implementation of the model using the HyperLynx system and performing a user study to determine system search effectiveness and searcher attitudes to the model.

Acknowledgments:

The author would like to thank the National Technical Information Service for allowing the use of data from the NTIS database.

REFERENCES

Bates, M. J. (1989). The design of browsing and berrypicking techniques for the online search interface. Online Review, 13, 407-424.

Belkin, N. J., Marchetti, P. G. & Cool, C. (1993). BRAQUE: Design of an interface to support user interaction in information retrieval. Information Processing and Management, 29, 325-344.

Croft, W. B. & Turtle, H. R. (1993). Retrieval strategies for hypertext. Information Processing and Management, 29, 313-324.

Croft, W. B. & Thompson, R. H. (1987). I^{3}R: A new approach to the design of document retrieval systems. Journal of the American Society for Information Science, 38, 389-404.

Crouch, C. J. & Nance, R. E. (1984). An approach to the functional description of an information retrieval system based on a generalized model. Information Technology: Research and Development. 3(3), 168-179.

Dimitroff, A. & Wolfram, D. (1993). Design issues in a hypertext-based information system for bibliographic retrieval, ASIS '93: Proceedings of the 56th ASIS Annual Meeting, 30, 191-198.

Dimitroff, A. & Wolfram, D. (1995). Searcher response in a hypertext-based bibliographic information retrieval system. Journal of the American Society for Information Science, 46, 22-29.

Jacobson, T. L. (1991). Sense-making in a database environment. Information Processing & Management, 27, 647-657.

Nelson, M. J. (1991). The design of a hypertext interface for information retrieval. Canadian Journal of Information Science, 16(2), 1-12.

Savoy, J. (1992). Bayesian inference networks and spreading activation in hypertext systems. Information Processing and Management, 28, 389-406.

Tague, J., Salminen, A. & McClellan, C. (1991). Complete formal model for information retrieval systems. In SIGIR '91: Proceedings of the Fourteenth Annual International ACM/SIGIR Conference on Research and Development in Information Retrieval (A. Bookstein, Y Chiaramella, G. Salton, and V. V. Raghavan, Eds.), Baltimore: ACM Press. pp. 14-20.

Watters, C. & Shepherd, M. A. (1990). A transient hypergraph-based model for data access. ACM Transactions of the on Information Systems. 8(2), 77-102.

FIGURE 1- Sample Search

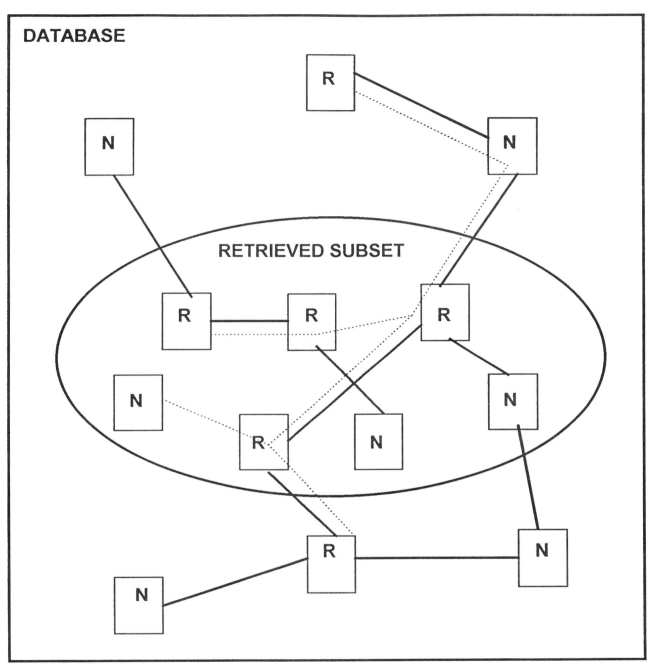

R = Relevant Record
N = Non-relevant Record
_____ Existing System linkages
.... Search Path (including transient linkages
within the retrieval set)

FIGURE 2 - Intra-Set Search Index

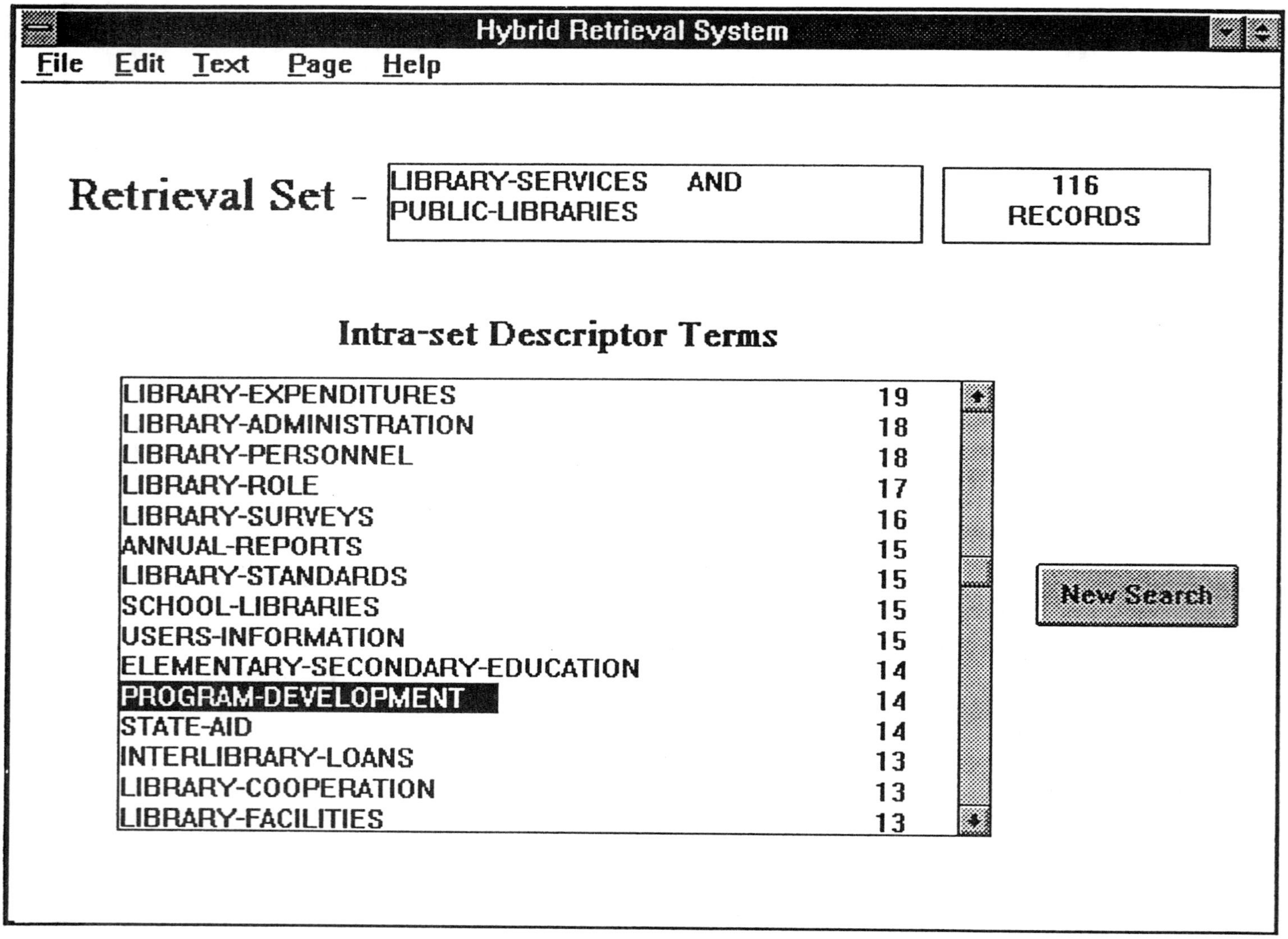

Hybrid Retrieval System

File   Edit   Text   Page   Help

Retrieval Set - | LIBRARY-SERVICES   AND
PUBLIC-LIBRARIES |

| 116
RECORDS |

Intra-set Descriptor Terms

LIBRARY-EXPENDITURES	19
LIBRARY-ADMINISTRATION	18
LIBRARY-PERSONNEL	18
LIBRARY-ROLE	17
LIBRARY-SURVEYS	16
ANNUAL-REPORTS	15
LIBRARY-STANDARDS	15
SCHOOL-LIBRARIES	15
USERS-INFORMATION	15
ELEMENTARY-SECONDARY-EDUCATION	14
PROGRAM-DEVELOPMENT	14
STATE-AID	14
INTERLIBRARY-LOANS	13
LIBRARY-COOPERATION	13
LIBRARY-FACILITIES	13

New Search

Fuzzy Matching as a Retrieval-Enabling Technique for Digital Libraries

T. R. Girill
Lawrence Livermore National Laboratory
Livermore, California

Clement H. Luk
Department of Computer Science, California State University
Chico, California

Abstract

This paper advocates an often-neglected search-support technique, approximate or "fuzzy" matching of user search terms. When properly deployed, fuzzy matching can significantly enhance the benefits of other, more common approaches to end-user answer retrieval from online reference collections. We compare crude with more sophisticated approximation techniques to explain how astute fuzzy-match software can convert many different near-miss situations (such as those involving faulty prefixes or suffixes, character misplacement, nonstandard word stems, or unanticipated redescription of concepts) into more adequate results. We also suggest practical ways to overcome fuzzy matching's own major drawbacks (namely, problems with search speed, search imprecision, and misinterpretation of search results). The resulting analysis clarifies how to deploy fuzzy matching for maximum effectiveness. We conclude that appropriate fuzzy matching enables more frequent, more flexible search success than do ordinary retrieval-improvement techniques used without it.

Introduction

Online documentation spreads along a spectrum from very focused help passages deeply integrated into a particular application (Duffy, Palmer, and Mehlenbacher, 1992) to large, general, digital libraries of reference material potentially relevant to answering many questions in many contexts (Girill and Tull, 1988). At the latter end of the spectrum, effective search tools are vital if users--both casual end users and busy help-desk consultants--are to reliably yet easily locate the answer passages they need (Girill, Griffin, and Jones, 1991). We have a working prototype search interface for online documentation that incorporates fuzzy matching (syntactic approximation) of search terms. Its behavior convinces us that this feature enhances the searching of large reference databases, even though this application has not been a primary focus of the literature on fuzzy matching techniques in the past.

Recent publications on syntactic approximation or fuzzy matching most often emphasize office-automation situations and the automatic indexing of business papers, legal briefs, or other office memos (e.g., Kent, Sacks-Davis, and Ramamohanarao, 1990; Faloutsos and Christodoulakis, 1987). This is the context of document preparation (or database construction) rather than the context of answer search. And the implied goal of fuzzy matching tools here is creating text collections without attentive human intervention; i.e., replacing human with artificial intelligence to minimize processing time or reduce collection-development costs. Our work suggests, on the other hand, that fuzzy matching can be applied jointly with semantic techniques (such as extensive aliasing) to improve performance during the search process itself, not just during presearch text preparation. We believe this search-time approach is best viewed as amplifying the native intelligence of the human searcher (by promoting more flexible pattern recognition) rather than replacing the human role (Wegner, 1983).

Anthropologist Bonnie Nardi, after a study of how reference librarians add value to the information gathering that occurs among professionals at work, proposed that "electronic search agents may be usefully modeled on reference librarians" (Nardi, 1994; Nardi, 1993). The sections below show how astute inclusion of fuzzy matching in a search interface to an online reference collection pursues this anthropological hint more thoroughly than do interfaces without it. Enriching a literal search by including a tolerance for imprecise input, through the use of appropriate approximations, is one way every seasoned reference librarian intuitively adds value to the search process.

Fuzzy-match software captures that professional intuition in algorithms that let even unwitting end users add (some of) the same value to every search they run. Of course, trivial approximation yields trivial improvement (discussed below), and approximation alone is insufficient for search success. But we believe a closer look at the problems it solves supports our conclusion that fuzzy matching at search time is a key enabling technique that maximizes the value to end users of the reference collection searched and of the usual semantic techniques jointly applied to search that collection.

The next section examines four typical failures of literal-only search systems and shows how fuzzy matching can overcome each one. We then look at the potential problems fuzzy search systems encounter and discuss the practical solutions to them that our prototype has suggested. The resulting analysis reveals the practical value of fuzzy-match searching as a user services tool.

Characteristic Cases

Faulty Prefixes or Suffixes

Omitting or misstating prefixes, suffixes, or plurals is the most simple case of a syntactic flaw that prevents the otherwise successful match of a user's search term and a database descriptor. The many common and meaningful variations on the stem COMPIL, for example, such as

```
[pre]compil|e
             |er
             |ers
             |ing
             |ation
```

show why this pitfall is so prevalent.

Here, the easiest approximate-match response is also well known: stemming or filters ("wildcards"). This most basic fuzzy matching technique appears in two forms.

(A) User Activated: allow the user when constructing the search to overtly specify with special filter characters how to truncate the front, tail, or other parts of the search term to increase the number of hits (mostly by eliminating prefixes or suffixes where unintended variations are greatest). The UNIX metacharacters are one simple example (e.g., Sobell, 1995, pp. 108, 435).

(B) System Activated: use automatic stemming rules or a built-in dictionary to detect the stem of search terms and database descriptors before comparing them for matches. This form works whether or not users remember to invoke it, but they consequently have less control over the search. The WAIS stemming algorithms are one simple example (Liu, et al., 1994, pp. 111, 115, 116).

Although stemming and filtering address well the specific problem of mismatches caused just by faulty prefixes or suffixes, they are inherently limited as fuzzy matching techniques. Each can generate only proper substrings of the original search term. Syntactic flaws lurking within such substrings can still prevent otherwise desired matches unless they are overcome by additional, more subtle approximation techniques.

Character Misplacement

Missing, extra, transposed, or erroneous characters, especially inside the stem of a search term, pose a more challenging approximation problem. Examples faced by our prototype system include

```
v e k t e r i s a t i o n
F o u r i e r  t r n a s f o r n
f u o r e i r  t r a n s f o r m
f o r i e a   t r a n s f r m
l e g e n d e r  p o l i n o m i a l
```

As these examples show, multiple character misplacements often occur in the same search term. Simple mistyping, spelling errors, faulty memory of unfamiliar technical terms, and input from nonnative speakers all contribute to these syntactic problems, sometimes simultaneously. These problems are frequent: 80% of user syntactical errors involve character misplacement (Ho, 1995). But filters and autostemming seldom suffice to overcome such misplacements because the flaws are usually not localized in the word parts discarded or ignored by those two techniques alone.

Getting practical benefit from fuzzy matching thus demands more elaborate, more comprehensive approximation techniques than the two most common ones. First, we need to compare not literal terms but rather abstract representations ("signatures") of search terms and database descriptors. These representations should be specific enough to preserve important semantic similarities yet coarse enough ("fuzzy signatures") to ignore (most) character misplacement flaws sprinkled through the compared terms. For example, the fuzzy signatures (bit strings) for 'vectorization' and for 'Fourier transform' should allow them to be properly distinguished, but the signatures for 'vectorization' and for 'vekterisation' should allow their dominant syntactic similarities to yield an approximate match that would otherwise be missed.

Second, good systems must also allow users to adjust at search time the coarseness with which these abstractions (signatures) are themselves compared. User control of the signature fuzziness is impractical (database signatures are generated in advance). But user control of the fuzziness with which signatures are compared is both possible and desirable. Different fuzzy-comparison levels (different percentages of overlapping 1 (one) bits) will be appropriate in different verbal contexts. When there are few near terms, for example, letting *'vekterisation'* match *'factorization'* as well as *'vectorization'* may be acceptable. When the term space is more crowded with interesting near neighbors to *'vectorization'* this matching may be much too coarse, yielding too many irrelevant hits.

There is more than one way to construct plausible syntactic approximations (fuzzy signatures) of search terms and database descriptors. We have tried several approaches in different prototype systems, sometimes noting unexpected side effects (such as varying sensitivity to term length, or to length differences between compared terms). This is not the place to defend one specific, signature-generating approximation algorithm over others, but rather to stress the value they all add to mere stemming and filters as worthwhile retrieval-enhancing techniques.

Nonstandard Word Stems

Highly relevant descriptors (and hence related answer passages) sometimes occur in families most members of which would be missed by a searcher who only retrieved exact matches. For example, in the Boeing Computer System extended mathematics (subroutine) library are many subroutine families with names such as

```
hssqft
hdsqft
hcsqft
hzsqft
```

which solve sparse linear equations using (respectively) single precision, double precision, complex, and double complex arithmetic. Theoretically, filtering could find all of these terms if a user happened to request h*sqft, but all other filter variations would fail because of how the family names are constructed. Likewise, no natural language stems are present from which to trim prefixes or suffixes automatically. So here again practical retrieval enhancement (finding all four hits by name) results from, but only from, deploying a sophisticated fuzzy matching technique of the kind described in the previous section (along with the usual semantic search mechanisms).

Unanticipated Redescription

Even with extensive aliasing, some serendipity hits present themselves only after aggressive fuzzy matching. For example, using our prototype system a search for "foreign countries" yielded a hit on "sensitive countries" (the descriptor for the relevant list of countries) even at the default level of approximation coarseness. These beneficial syntactic surprises are another, admittedly less predictable, way in which fuzzy matching enhances standard searches.

Potential Problems

Search Acceleration

The primary problem with fuzzy-match search systems is that their very strength--an increased number of matches--causes side-effect weaknesses. Without compensatory measures, for example, they do not scale well; they can run very slowly on large text databases.

Although a hash function is used to generate the signatures that enable fuzzy matching, the comparison of a search-term signature with database-descriptor signatures cannot be accelerated by using a hash table. For exact-match searches, one can use a hash function to compute a (bucket) address for storing each database term, then locate the matching bucket quickly at search time by applying the same hash function to the user's search term. The speed of this approach is independent of the number of terms searched, and varies only with the hash function, bucket size, and overflow handling.

Fuzzy matching, however, requires finding all the terms that "almost" match the search term (over a specified range of approximation). Such syntactically varied terms may not all fall into the same hash bucket, or even into adjacent buckets. So comparison with every (database-descriptor) signature must occur, a process whose time increases along with the number of signatures. Unless this comparison is accelerated, the resulting search may grow too slow for practical use, a problem encountered in our earlier prototypes (Girill, Griffin, and Jones, 1991).

Signature trees provide one possible solution. "A signature tree is formed by grouping signatures and then superimposing (ORing) them to form a new 'super'signature at the next higher level in the tree" (Kotamari and Tharp, 1990, p. 80). Matching a search-term signature to a high level in such a tree is a necessary condition for matching it to any lower levels, so irrelevant branches can be quickly pruned from further searching. This scheme for limiting additional signature comparisons to only those branches that have high-level matches depends for its practical value, however, on a low degree of signature saturation (filling with 1s). The hash function, signature length, and signature grouping all affect how quickly a tree level saturates, and a level whose (super)signatures are (almost) all 1s provides (little or) no help in pruning the tree.

A related response to slow fuzzy-match searches that avoids this saturation problem is partitioning of the database signatures (without a hierarchy). One can group the text signatures, for example, by the number of bits turned on (1s bits), and then compute the number of bits turned on in the search-term signature. Exact matches fall only in the group with the same number of bits turned on (n) as the search term; increasingly coarse approximate matches lie in the groups with n±1 turned on, n±2 turned on, etc. The amount of search acceleration this provides depends on how uniformly the signatures spread among the bits-on groups. Our prototype experimented with variations on this approach to accelerate fuzzy searches (Ho, 1995).

Finally, on machines with more than one CPU, multitasking can help compensate for search slowness. Our database of descriptors drew from several independent sources. So we searched the signature sets for each source in parallel, as separate tasks running simultaneously. The search software then merged the parallel results for sorted presentation to the user (see the interface comments below).

Search Precision

Precision is the percentage of search hits that are relevant to the search term. Irrelevant hits were retrieved in error. A recent trend in user service admits the inevitability of such errors and stresses error recovery instead of error avoidance, with a focus on guides, prompts, and help messages that "aim to avoid the consequences of errors, rather than the errors themselves" (Oatey, 1994, p. 7) This is certainly appropriate for fuzzy-match systems, because the very fuzziness that overcomes syntactical flaws in the input introduces some syntactically close but irrelevant hits into the output set. The more coarse the approximations used to build signatures of the database terms in advance, and the more coarse the comparison of search-term and database signatures at search time, the lower is the precision of the fuzzy searches that result.

One way to compensate for this imprecision is to let users adjust the fuzziness or coarseness of the signature comparisons each time they supply a search term. User-specifiable match fuzziness gives a sense of control that psychologically balances the extra, unwanted terms retrieved by searching with approximations. It also lets users adapt their search precision to the perceived density of the search space. The (dense) math-library case (cited above) probably calls for modest match fuzziness, for instance, while for other terms in a sparser space (e.g., "disk space preallocation") much higher match-fuzziness levels with much lower precision are more appropriate.

Result Interpretation

As Hildreth notes, for the user interface of any information-retrieval system to be adequate, it must "facilitate the semantically demanding cognitive tasks of user comprehension [of hits] and decision making [among them]" (Hildreth, 1995, p. 7). Interpreting the results of a fuzzy search can be confusing, especially for those unfamiliar with how the approximation(s) to their search term were built. Hence, offering fuzzy matching in the context of an astute user interface that combines it with known, strong interpretation-support features is vital for user acceptance.

Our prototype interface, for instance, signals the waiting user that their search is multitasking, then ranks the merged hits in relevance order from exact matches on aliased terms through exact matches on nonaliased terms and into increasingly distant approximations. The degree of approximation and the source document name appear with each listed hit. And the length of the whole hit list is controllable by the user (from just the best few to many hundreds if found and wanted). These task-related cues and adjustability show again how fuzzy matching, deployed jointly with other techniques, yields beneficial results not possible by using those techniques alone.

Conclusions

Fuzzy matching of user search terms is a very helpful retrieval-enabling technique. It allows other techniques to perform better because if implemented astutely, using an approximate-signature approach, it overcomes the most common syntactical problems that otherwise thwart retrieval. And, if deployed jointly with search-space partitioning, user-adjustable approximation levels, and a supportive interface, fuzzy matching's potential problems can themselves be avoided.

Acknowledgments

This work was performed in part under the auspices of the U.S. Department of Energy by Lawrence Livermore National Laboratory under contract W-7405-Eng-48. We also acknowledge the thoughtful collaboration of Lai Fong Ho on parts of this project.

References

Duffy, T. M., Palmer, J. E., and Mehlenbacher, B. (1992). *Online help: design and evaluation*. Norwood, NJ: Ablex Publishing. 260 pp.

Faloutsos, C. and Christodoulakis, S. (1987). Description and performance analysis of signature file methods for office filing. *ACM transactions on office information systems,*, 5 (3): 237-257.

Girill, T. R. and Tull, C. G. (1988). Comparative access rates for online documentation and human consulting. In *Proceedings of the ASIS 51st Annual Meeting* (pp. 48-53). Medford, NJ: Learned Information, Inc.

Girill, T. R., Griffin, T., and Jones, R. B. (1991). Extended subject access to hypertext online documentation. *Journal of the american society for information science*, 42 (6); 414-426.

Hildreth, C. (1995). The GUI OPAC: approach with caution. *Public-access computer systems review*, 6 (5): 6-18.

Ho, Lai-Fong. (1995). *A fuzzy string matching technique for text retrieval.* M.S. thesis, California State University, Chico. 68 pp.

Kent, A., Sacks-Davis, R., and Ramamohanarao, K. (1990). A signature file scheme based on multiple organizations for indexing very large text databases. *Journal of the american society for information science*, 41 (7); 508-534.

Kotamarti, U. and Tharp. A. L. (1990). Accelerating text searching through signature trees. *Journal of the american society for information science*, 41 (2): 79-86.

Liu, C. Peek, J., Jones, R., Buus, B., and Nye, A. (1994). *Managing internet information services.* Sebastopol, CA: O'Reilly and Associates. 630 pp.

Nardi, B. (1993). *A small matter of programming: perspectives on end user computing.* Cambridge, MA: MIT Press. 162 pp.

Nardi, B. (1994). Toward a diverse information ecology. Tenth Annual Apple Library Users Group Meeting (June 28, 1994). Miami, FL.

Oatey, M. (1994). Trial and error versus instructions. *Communicator*, 4 (February), 7-8.

Sobell, M. G. (1995). *Hands-on unix: a practical guide.* Redwood City, CA: Benjamin/Cummings Publishing. 832 pp.

Wegner, P. (1983). Paradigms of information engineering. In F. Machlup and U. Mansfield (Eds.), *The study of information: interdisciplinary messages* (pp. 163-176). New York: John Wiley.

Selective Feedback for Optimal Search

Valery I. Frants
Computer and Information Sciences Department, Fordham University
Bronx, New York

Nick I. Kamenoff
Department of Software Engineering, Monmouth University
West Long Branch, New Jersey

The problem of optimal search has been always considered to be important in the design of information retrieval systems. However, there are two major difficulties in implementing optimal search: first, the lack of an effective method which automatically can choose the system's best state, and second, even if we could determine the system's best state, there is no mechanism which allows the change from a given system's state to the best state. In this paper solutions to both of these problems are proposed. The most promising approach to achieve "optimal search" is to provide the system with a set of different algorithms for constructing query formulations. A proof is presented so that the system's best state can be defined by the expression

$$\sqrt{\frac{r^2}{N \cdot C}} = \sqrt{R \cdot P}$$

where, r = number of relevant documents in the output, N = number of documents in the output, C = number of relevant documents for the request under consideration in the collection of documents, R = the recall, and P = the precision level.

To implement the optimal search a method is proposed which combines the static search (new query which does not intersect with any previous query formulation) with the dynamic search (improved previous query formulation) . Algorithms for an optimal search with selective feedback for both static and dynamic collections of documents are presented.

Introduction

The problem of optimal search was always considered to be important in designing information retrieval (IR) systems. However, there are two major difficulties in implementing optimal search. The first, is the lack of a simple and effective method able to automatically choose the system's best state for a specific search request of an individual user. The second, even if we could determine the system's state, a mechanism does not exist which would allow the change from a given system's state to the best state. In this paper we propose solutions to both of these problems.

The notion of "optimal search" means the best possible search in a specific system for a specific request. Such a system must realize more than one way to perform a search. Several papers by Frants, Shapiro, and Voiskunskii (1991, 1992) discussed different approaches to designing IR systems capable of performing an optimal search. In these papers it was shown that the most promising approach is to provide the system with a set of different algorithms for constructing query formulations which allow the formation of different outputs. In the next section we describe a method for determining the system's best state.

Criterion for Selecting the System's Best State

To choose the best, among available query formulations, we will consider the outputs from different query formulations obtained by different algorithms. The best query formulation under consideration is the one which gives the greatest value of the quantity r^2/N as a result of a search in the same collection of documents. Here, r is the number of relevant documents in the output and N is the number of documents in the output.

We will briefly discuss the justification for using this criterion (see Voiskunskii, 1984 and 1987 for more details). We denote by symbol C the number of relevant documents for the request under consideration in the collection of documents. Since all query formulations under consideration were constructed for the same request, the best query formulations with respect to the quantity r^2/N are also the best with respect to the quantity,

$$\sqrt{\frac{r^2}{N \cdot C}} = \sqrt{R \cdot P}$$

where R is the recall and P is the precision level. This is easy to prove, keeping in mind that the value of C is the same for all query formulations. We will prove it, or more precisely, we will prove this assertion: in the case of any two query formulations (i and j) for the same request, the signs of the differences

$$\left(\frac{r_i^2}{N_i} - \frac{r_j^2}{N_j}\right) \quad \text{and} \quad \left(\sqrt{R_i \cdot P_i} - \sqrt{R_j \cdot P_j}\right)$$

coincide. It is obvious that the desired conclusion follows immediately from this result. Thus:

$$\sqrt{R_i \cdot P_i} - \sqrt{R_j \cdot P_j} = \frac{\left(\sqrt{R_i \cdot P_i} - \sqrt{R_j P_j}\right)\left(\sqrt{R_i P_i} + \sqrt{R_j P_j}\right)}{\left(\sqrt{R_i P_i} + \sqrt{R_j P_j}\right)} =$$

$$\frac{R_i P_i - R_j P_j}{\sqrt{R_i P_i} + \sqrt{R_j P_j}} = \frac{\dfrac{r_i^2}{N_i C} - \dfrac{r_j^2}{N_j C}}{\sqrt{R_i P_i} + \sqrt{R_j P_j}} =$$

$$\frac{1}{C\left(\sqrt{R_i P_i} + \sqrt{R_j P_j}\right)} \times \left(\frac{r_i^2}{N_i} - \frac{r_j^2}{N_j}\right)$$

Since the quantity $\dfrac{1}{C\left(\sqrt{R_i P_i} + \sqrt{R_j P_j}\right)}$ is nonnegative, then the signs of the differences

$$\left(\frac{r_i^2}{N_i} - \frac{r_j^2}{N_j}\right) \quad \text{and} \quad \sqrt{R_i P_i} - \sqrt{R_j P_j} \quad \text{in fact coincide.}$$

We consider two vectors K and V, where $K=(K_1, K_2, \cdots K_n)$ is the vector evaluating the relevance of documents in the collection by the user, and vector $V=(V_1, V_2, \cdots V_n)$ evaluates the relevance of documents in the same collection by the system (as the result of a Boolean search), i.e.

K_i = 1 if the i-th document of the collection is considered relevant by the user
= 0 otherwise.

V_i = 1 if the i-th document of the collection is included in the output
= 0 otherwise.

We will show that $\sqrt{R \cdot P}$ equals the cosine of the angle between vectors K and V, and thus provide some justification for using the quantity $\sqrt{R \cdot P}$ and consequently r^2/N for comparison of query formulations and for the choice of the best among them. Thus:

$$\cos \Psi = \frac{(K, V)}{\sqrt{(K, K)}\sqrt{(V, V)}} = \frac{\sum\limits_{i=1}^{n} K_i V_i}{\sqrt{\sum\limits_{i=1}^{n}(K_i)^2}\sqrt{\sum\limits_{i=1}^{n}(V_i)^2}} =$$

$$\frac{r}{\sqrt{C}\sqrt{N}} = \sqrt{\frac{r^2}{C \cdot N}} = \sqrt{R \cdot P}$$

In fact, there are C ones (among the coordinates of vector K) and the rest are zeroes, since for C documents and only for them we have $K_i =1$; among the coordinates of vector V we have N ones, and the rest are zeroes, since for N documents and only for them we have $V_i=1$; and, finally, vectors K and V have r coordinates where they both have values of 1, since for r documents and only for them we have $V_i =1$ and $K_i =1$ simultaneously. Consequently,

$$\sum_{i=1}^{n} K_i \cdot V_i = r, \quad \sum_{i=1}^{n}(K_i)^2 = C \text{ and } \sum_{i=1}^{n}(V_i)^2 = N$$

concludes the proof.

We note that in developing a criterion for comparison of query formulations, it is desirable to apply retrieval characteristics (for example, $R+P$) whose use for evaluating the quality of the search is pragmatically justified. Retrieval characteristics have been actively investigated, and are being investigated in information science (see for example, Bollmann,1987; Cleverdon, 1970; Copper,1973; Kraft & Bookstien, 1978; Lancaster, 1979; Raghavan, et al.,1989; van Rijsbergen, 1979; Salton & McGill,1983; Sparck Jones,1978). However, all known retrieval characteristics, except the one given above, require a very time-consuming user's evaluation of the documents in the collection (to determine the number of relevant documents). In our proposed criterion for comparing query formulation we used the retrieval characteristic $\sqrt{R \cdot P}$, which is much more time-efficient.

One should also note that since in the developed criterion the evaluation of the output is necessary (with the goal of determining r), this criterion assumes the presence of iterations in the search and consequently the presence of user's feedback. Thus, the IR system realizing the optimal search, in addition to the known processes realized in the mechanism of feedback, must have a mechanism to evaluate each alternative of the search with the goal of choosing the best alternative, i.e. the feedback must be selective.

Selective Feedback

The importance of feedback and its algorithmization in IR systems has been extensively discussed in literature. A detailed discussion of this problem (and references) including the nature and characteristics of feedback in an IR system can be found in Frants & Shapiro (1991b). Here they also show that the character of feedback depends on the character of the collection of documents, i.e. a static collection (for example, in the course of one session of On-Line search) and a dynamic collection (for example, in the system realizing SDI).

In realizing feedback for a static collection of documents, the task of control consists of an attempt to find relevant documents which were not found during the previous search in the same collection. Every subsequent search assumes the lowest possible noise. The feedback algorithm in this situation will construct a new query formulation which will be used in an attempt to find new (presumably relevant) documents.

In realizing feedback for a dynamic collection of documents, the task of control is different from that of the static collection. In the static collection we try to obtain a new query formulation (at every new iteration) which does not intersect with any of the previous query formulations, because otherwise in a new iteration we will obtain the

documents which were given previously to the user. In a dynamic collection we only try to correct (improve) the previous query formulations. In other words, we try to remove all subrequests[1] which led to the unsuccessful search, and add new (original) subrequests which will presumably give us relevant documents. Hence, in the case of a dynamic collection our task is not to find relevant documents which were not found during a previous search, but to have a more successful search of a new collection of documents, i.e., we want to construct a new query formulation (by correcting the previous one) so that if we performed two searches in the same collection using the previous query formulation and the new one, the latter search would give us better results.

The proposed feedback algorithms, which consider the choice of an optimal alternative for the search, are oriented to the static and dynamic collection of documents. The developed selection criterion r^2/N permits evaluation not only of the query formulations, but also of each of the subrequests of each query formulation; this is especially important for a dynamic collection of documents.

Thus, in developing feedback algorithms we will assume that in an IR system realizing an optimal search the Boolean search criterion is used, and this system includes some set of algorithms for constructing query formulations in Boolean form. This set could, for example, consist of the algorithms proposed by Voiskunskii and Frants (1974), Dillon et al. (1983), Salton et al. (1985), Frants and Shapiro (1991a), etc. In each of these algorithms it is possible to use a marked set of documents as a search request (see Frants & Shapiro, 1991a), and each of the algorithms constructs a query formulation in Boolean form. For these reasons all further discussions are applicable to all algorithms for constructing query formulations which we assume are a part of an IR system.

Before the initial search for a given search request, the query formulations are constructed by each of the available algorithms. The initial search is then conducted by each of the constructed query formulations and all outputs are combined. In other words, a combined output will be formed as a set union of all the outputs obtained by each query formulation.

---

[1] The notion of a subrequest was defined in Frants & Shapiro (1991a). For example, in the following query formulations, given in the Boolean disjunctive normal form,

$A \vee B \vee (C \wedge D) \vee (C \wedge K \wedge L \wedge M)$, where

A, B, C, D, K, L, M, are descriptors in some IRL, there are four subrequests: A, B, C∧D, and C∧K∧L∧M. More formally, a subrequest is a conjunction of descriptors (or one descriptor) which appears before ∨, or after ∨, or between two ∨. Then the document from the collection will be included in the output if the document profile contains all the descriptors from some subrequest in a given query formulation.

Algorithm for Static Collection of Documents

As was indicated above, the initial search is performed for each of the query formulations, and all the outputs are combined into one output (duplicates are removed) that is given to the user. The user evaluates this output , i.e. indicates which documents are relevant to her/his information need, and gives the result back to the system. This algorithm begins by checking if there are any relevant documents in the output. If no relevant documents are found then the algorithm stops since the user did not provide additional information about her/his information need[2]. In general, it does not mean that there is no more interaction between the user and the system. For example, the user can reformulate his request, or change the search parameters, such as the acceptable number of documents in the output.

In case relevant documents exist in the combined output, the feedback algorithm computes the value r^2/N for each individual output (corresponding to a specific query formulation), containing at least one pertinent document. The output with the largest value r^2/N indicates that the algorithm or algorithms which constructed the corresponding query formulation is the most appropriate (gives the best results) for the given search request and a specific user. This algorithm will be used in subsequent iterations of the feedback algorithm. (It is also possible that two or more outputs may have the same largest value of r^2/N. We consider this case later).

Denote by A the algorithm or algorithms which constructed query formulations (PQ) with the best output (largest r^2/N). The feedback algorithm constructed a new marked set by combining the pertinent documents found by the user in the previous output. Then, on the basis of this new marked set the algorithm A constructs a new query formulation, denoted by AQ (auxiliary query formulation). This query formulation is then compared to PQ, and the algorithm constructs a query formulation, denoted by NQ, by removing from AQ all subrequests that appear in PQ and also subrequests that contain any subrequests appearing in PQ. For example, if a,b are descriptors from the systems dictionary, and a∧b is a subrequest of PQ or if either a or b is a subrequest of PQ. The reason for this removal is quite clear, because all of the documents that may be found by these removed subrequests have been seen by the user.

It is possible for NQ to be empty (if all subrequests of AQ were removed). In this case, the algorithm stops since no new documents can be found. If NQ is not empty then another search is performed and new documents not appearing in previous outputs (if such exist) are given to the user. This is the end of one feedback iteration.

In cases where several outputs have the same largest value r^2/N i.e., there is more than one "best" algorithm, all of these algorithms are used to construct their AQ's and then the logical operator OR (∨) is used to join them into one query formulation (AQ). Notice that this AQ is also in a disjunctive normal form. Then NQ is constructed by removing from this AQ all the subrequests which either coincide with subrequests I the PQ's constructed by the best algorithms or containing those subrequests as proper subsets (see example above). The NQ is used to perform the search and the new documents (not appearing in previous output) are given to the user.

The process described above can continue through several iterations when the user's evaluation of the output is given to the system. At each iteration, a new AQ and NQ are constructed. The decision to remove some subrequests to construct NQ from AQ takes into consideration the query formulations constructed at all previous iterations and the removal of subrequests from AQ is performed as described above. All the documents seen by the user at previous iterations are not included in the output. The feedback algorithms stops in the following cases:

(a) no evaluation of the output is provided by the user;
(b) no relevant documents are found (by the user) in the output;
(c) no new subrequests are constructed (NQ is empty);
(d) no new documents are found by the system.

The main steps in the feedback algorithm for the multiversion IR system with a static collection of documents are:

1. Selection of relevant documents from the previous output (using user's evaluation).
2. If the previous search was based on a combined query formulation, constructed by more than one algorithm, then these algorithms are compared using the criterion (or more precisely r^2/N) and the best algorithm is selected.
3. The best algorithm (algorithms if there is more than one) is used to construct an auxiliary query formulation (AQ) (combined from several query formulations in the case of more than one algorithm).
4. A new query formulation (NQ) is constructed by

---

[2] By additional information about the user's information need we mean information which is contained in relevant documents, i.e. information which may be useful in finding new relevant documents

removing from AQ all subrequests which appear in PQ and subrequests which include subrequests of PQ.

5. If NQ is not empty the search is performed and the preliminary output is obtained.

6. A new output is formed by removing all the documents appearing in the previous outputs from the preliminary output. Then the new output (if not empty) is presented to the user.

Algorithm for Dynamic Collection of Documents

The user's evaluation of the output will be used by the feedback algorithm as additional information about the POIN[3]. The algorithm can proceed only when the user's evaluation is given to the system. In the first stage the algorithm tests if there are any relevant documents in the output. If there are none, the algorithm stops since no additional information about user's POIN is available. In the case of the existence of relevant documents, the algorithm determines by which query formulation(s) they are found, and then further analysis is applied to those query formulations by which at least one relevant document is found. The best, from the point of view of the criterion $\sqrt{R \cdot P}$, query formulation or combination of query formulation indicates also the best algorithm that was used in its construction. We recall that for determining the best query formulation or its combination from the point of view of criterion $\sqrt{R \cdot P}$, one must calculate the value of r^2 / N of the corresponding output of each query formulation and select the one or combined with the largest value of r^2 / N.

After determination of the best algorithm (or best algorithms, if the same best values of $\sqrt{R \cdot P}$ are attained in more than one version of query formulations), best subrequests are selected in all query formulations which are not among the best. This is done for the following reasons. First, there may be subrequests which do not appear in the best query formulations and which give good results for the search. Such subrequests can prove to be effective for subsequent searches. Second, as was indicated above in the discussion of the character of feedback in a dynamic collection of documents, the best algorithm(s) will be used later for obtaining a new corrected query formulation. This means that there is no need to select the best subrequests in other than the best query formulation, the same criterion $\sqrt{R \cdot P}$ is used, and the best subrequests are considered to be those for which

the value $\sqrt{R \cdot P}$ is not *lower than* the value of $\sqrt{R \cdot P}$ for the best query formulation.

Then the relevant documents obtained from the user are added to those on the basis of which the best algorithms constructed the best query formulation. In those cases when there is more than one best query formulation, relevant documents are added to the original request in the case of the algorithms which constructed the best query formulation. After this, the best algorithm(s) constructs a new, *preliminary* query formulation, where occurrence frequencies of descriptors in document profiles of the new collection are used. Those original subrequests that were selected before, are added to the obtained query formulation(s), and thus the final query formulation is constructed. Then a new search is performed using this new final query formulation and the new output (obtained in the collection of documents) is given to the user. This is the end of first feedback iteration.

Beginning with the second output, the system realizes optimal service, since the best possible alternative was used for the search. The basic steps of the feedback algorithm for an optimal search in an IR system with a dynamic collection of documents are:

1. Selection of relevant documents from previous output (at first stage from the output that was formed using the combined query formulation), based on evaluation of this output by the user.

2. In the case when a combined query formulation constructed by more than one algorithm was used in the previous search, an evaluation of available algorithms proceeds with the help of the criterion $\sqrt{R \cdot P}$. The highest value of this criterion determines the choice of the best algorithm(s).

3. With the help of the same criterion $\sqrt{R \cdot P}$, best original subrequests are determined among other than the best query formulations and those subrequests whose criterion value is not smaller than the highest value are selected for the use in the search on the new collection of documents.

4. Relevant documents found during the previous search are added to those on the basis of which the previous query formulation was constructed, i.e. a more precise search request is obtained.

5. On the basis of the new marked set (more precise request) a new preliminary query formulation is constructed by the best algorithm(s).

6. The final query formulation is constructed by adding the best original subrequests (see step 3) to the preliminary query formulation.

7. A search is performed using the final query formulation, and a new output is given to the user.

---

[3] POIN- problem oriented information need. The documentary IR systems are created to satisfy POIN (Frants & Brush, 1988).

In conclusion, we have shown how to implement an optimal search in IR systems. It is important to point out that an optimal search is performed for each request of each individual user. This leads to the increased quality of information service for the user community.

References

Bollman, P. (1978). A comparison of evaluation measures for document retrieval systems. Journal of Information, Vol 2, No.1.

Cleverdon, C.W. (1970). Evaluation of tests of information retrieval systems. Journal of Documentation,Vol 26, 55-67.

Cooper, W.S. (1973). On selecting a measure of retrieval efectiveness. JASIS, Vol. 24, 87-100.

Dillon, M. Ulmschneider, J., & Desper, J. (1983). A prevalence formula for automatic relevance feedback in Boolean systems. Information Processing and Management, Vol.19,27-36.

Frants, V.I.,& Brush, C.B. (1988). The need for information and some aspects of information retrieval systems construction. JASIS, Vol. 39, No. 2, 86-91.

Frants, V.I., & Shapiro, J. (1991a). Algorithm for automatic construction of query formulations in Boolean form. JASIS, Vol. 42, No.1, 16-26.

Frants, V.I., & Shapiro, J. (1991b). Control and feedback in a documentary information retrieval system. JASIS, Vol. 42, No. 9, 623-634.

Frants, V.I., Shapiro, J., Voiskunskii, V.G. (1992). Multiversion information retrieval systems and feedback with mechanism of selection. JASIS.

Kraft, D & Bookstien, A. (1978). Evaluation of Information retrieval systems: a decision theoretic approach. JASIS, Vol. 29, 31-40.

Lancaster, F.W. (1979). Information retrieval systems:characteristics, testing, evaluation. New York, John Wiley & Sons.

Raghavan, V.V., Bollman, P., & Jung, G.S. (1989). Retrieval system evaluation using recall and precision: problems and answers. (Extended abstract). Proceedings of the Twelfth Annual International ACM SIGIR Conference on Research and Development in Information Retrieval, Cambridge, Massachusetts, 59-68.

Salton, G., & McGill, M.J. (1983). Introduction to modern information retrieval. New York, McGraw Hill.

Salton, G., Fox, E.A., & Voorhees, E. (1985). Advanced feedback methods in information retrieval. JASIS, Vol. 36, 200-210.

Spark Jones, K. (1978). Performance averaging for recall and precision. Journal of Informatics, Vol. 2, 95-105

Van Rijsbergen, C.J. (1979). Information retrieval. 2-nd edition. London, Butterworths.

Voiskunskii, V.G., & Frants, V.I. (1974). Algorithmization of the translation of a request from a natural language to a descriptor language in a documentary information retrieval system. Nauchno-Teknicheskaya Informatsiya (NTI), Ser. 2, No. 11, 17-22.

Voiskunskii, V.G. (1984). The distance in n-dimensional vector space and search characteristics. Nauchno-Teknicheskaya Informatsiya (NTA), Ser. 2, Vol. 18, No. 1, 18-20.

Voiskunskii, V.G. (1987). Applicability of search characteristics. Nauchno-Teknicheskaya Informatsiya (NTI), Ser. 2, Vol. 21, No. 12, 18-24.

Approaches to Facilitating Query Formulation and Interpretation in Database Searching

Peter Jacso
University of Hawaii

Manuscript not received at time of publication.

Impact on Education IV:
Digital Libraries III

Integration of Model-Based Interfaces and Intelligent Systems to Digital Libraries

S. Narayanan, Nagesh Reddy, & Scott Walchli
College of Engineering & Computer Science, Wright State University
Dayton, Ohio

ABSTRACT

We need a principled methodology to ground design and development of interfaces to digital libraries in a comprehensive understanding of the information seeker and the nature of documents. We present a methodology to designing effective interfaces to library information. Our methodology integrates three phases: (1) field studies and models of information seekers in libraries, (2) development of library information systems, and (3) design, implementation, and evaluation of interfaces derived from models. In this article, we outline the phases of our methodology in the context of our research at an University library. We present an operator function model of the information seeker and describe our field study at the library. We discuss the implications of the model results on the information retrieval system. We also present a prototype system we developed on the internet infrastructure using a world wide web server, common gateway interface scripts, and hypertext markup language interfaces. Our system features direct manipulation interface access to multiple databases, full-text access and document delivery, and is a gateway to information.

INTRODUCTION

New advances in computing technologies continue to be made, but users and designers of systems providing on-line access to bibliographical databases and catalogues acknowledge that system users face major limitations in information retrieval (Rasmussen et al., 1994). The problems arise due to several reasons including the content of the information retrieval systems, the vocabulary used in bibliographic records, and mismatches in user-system interaction. Flexible and easy to use techniques to organize and retrieve information through computer systems are needed (Denning and Smith, 1994).

Recent advances in digital libraries particularly in commercial web services enable library information systems to go beyond a simple text-based interface and facilitate direct access to information in multiple forms including text, graphics, and other media. However, most interfaces to library information still appear to reflect the classification schemes of database suppliers and are not based on user's view of the domain of interest. Incompatibilities exist between the language used by the information seekers and the database providers, which makes seamless access of information very difficult. We need a principled methodology to ground design and development of interfaces to digital libraries in a comprehensive understanding of the information seeker and the nature of documents.

We present a methodology to designing effective interfaces to library information. Our methodology integrates three phases: (1) field studies and models of information seekers in libraries, (2) development of library information systems, and (3) design, implementation, and evaluation of interfaces derived from models.

We demonstrate the methodology in the context of a prototype system we developed on the internet infrastructure using a world wide web server, common gateway interface scripts, and hypertext markup language interfaces. The system features direct manipulation interface access to multiple databases, full-text access and document delivery and is a gateway to information.

First, we present an overview of our approach. We then describe the field studies and analysis of the domain. We then present a model of the information seeker and describe the prototype system that integrates model-based interfaces and intelligent searches in the context of information retrieval. Finally, we discuss our approach in the context of related research in the literature.

OVERVIEW OF THE METHODOLOGY

Our methodology integrates three phases: (1) field studies and models of information seekers in libraries, (2) development of library information systems and (3) design, implementation, and evaluation of interfaces derived from models. Figure 1 illustrates the three phases.

Field study involves interviewing librarians, information seekers, and analyzing elements of the library domain to better understand the nature of the enterprise and the complexity of the interactions in it. The model of the information seeker is developed based on observations and protocol analysis during the information retrieval task. The following sections detail the phases of the methodology.

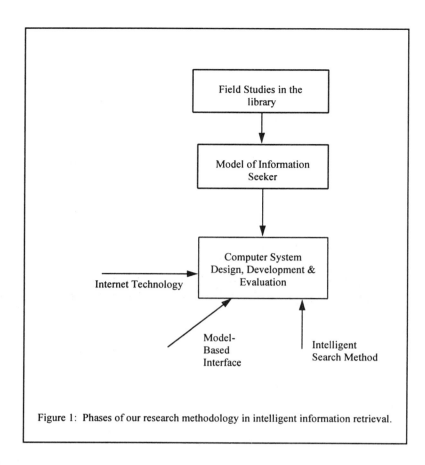

Figure 1: Phases of our research methodology in intelligent information retrieval.

FIELD STUDIES AND ANALYSIS

The interviews with the librarians revealed several features of the library domain (Narayanan et al., 1995). First, the complexity of the domain is due to the large number and variety of documents, types of users, and the rapid growth of the volume of information. Second, information is distributed among several databases (e.g., technical information in applied science and technology, science citation index). Each database has its unique set of fields. For example, some databases have an abstract whereas some do not. Third, most library search systems have Boolean search capabilities, but typically do not contain other search capabilities (e.g., relevance ranking, or statistical association-based search). Finally, there is an increasing awareness among the librarians of the capabilities of the internet and many available resources on the world wide web.

A MODEL OF THE INFORMATION SEEKER

Figure 2 illustrates a model of a typical information seeker. The modeling framework is called an operator function model (OFM) developed by Mitchell (1987). OFM has been applied to describe and prescribe operator activities in supervisory control. The model depicted in Figure 2 is the first application of the OFM in an information retrieval task.

The OFM is a network in which nodes represent operator activities. Activities are structured hierarchically, representing operator goals or functions at the highest level and individual actions at the lowest level. Actions can be physical or cognitive. The OFM provides a means to structure and organize

156

observed behavior, permitting a modeler to hierarchically abstract low level actions into meaningful higher groupings.

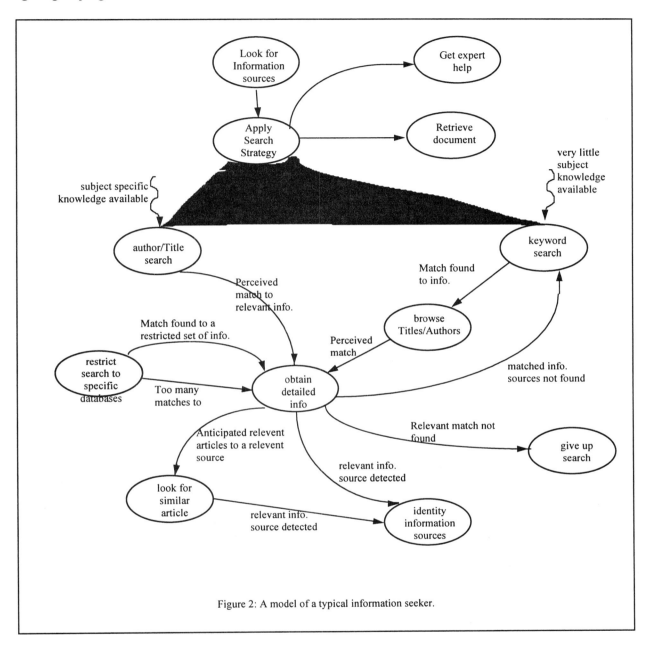

Figure 2: A model of a typical information seeker.

In the model, nodes represent activities of the information seeker and the labeled arcs represent enabling conditions in the next step of the information retrieval process. The top-level model shows the sequence of possible primary functions including (a) look for information source(s), (b) apply search strategy, (c) retrieve document(s), and (d) get expert help. An information seeker typically obtains help from librarians if the search system did not yield a relevant information source.

The lower-level of the model illustrates the details of search strategies during the information retrieval process and associated enabling conditions and actions. When the information seeker has subject-specific knowledge available, the author/title search strategy is applied. In contrast, if the information seeker does not have specific knowledge available, (s)he enters the keyword search mode. The keyword search strategy involves browsing the matched list of sources. Both strategies involve obtaining details of the information record and may involve restricting search to specific databases if too many matches are found during the search process. If successful, the net result of the search process is the identification of a set of information sources. If not, the seeker reaches out for expert help.

The model has several implications in the development of the information retrieval system. First, the system should not force the information seeker to specify information about databases. Users who do not have specific information on the authors or about the subject will be severely limited by such an enforcement. Second, information must be presented progressively. Users do not look for detailed information unless they find a perceived match to their search. Third, the system must have the capability of enabling users retrieve "similar" information sources once a relevant match is found. Documents can be similar in terms of having the same author, same salient key words, or appearing in the same Proceedings (for conference articles). Finally, it will be useful to provide full-text access and enable cheap and efficient document delivery.

Our prototype system provides many of the above capabilities. Users have the capability of beginning the search using the keyword match or the author/title strategy. The information seeker can restrict the search to a specific database (or format) at any time. Information is presented hierarchically, where detailed information about a record is provided at a later stage (upon user request). The system has hypertext links to other documents by the same author, having the same keywords, or appearing in the same Proceedings. Our system also provides access to full-text information (whenever available). The information seeker can directly obtain the digital information through a hypertext link. Details of the prototype system are provided below.

PROTOTYPE SYSTEM

The prototype system is built on top of the internet. It consists of the following components: clients, a server and a search engine, databases (information sources), and database interface scripts. A client is the computer used by the information seeker. It can be any equipment with internet access (PC, Mac, or UNIX workstation).

The server is implemented on a UNIX system. Its url is http://isis.cs.wright.edu:1947/cgi-bin/weblib/search/wsulib. Upon receiving a request from any client, it triggers the search engine (Common Gateway Script, CGI, written in Perl). Results obtained from the search engine are embedded in HTML and sent to the client. Functionality of the entire system is depicted in Figure 3. The following paragraph briefly describes the backend (search engine, databases, and database interface scripts) of the system.

Our system is built using WebLib (Dorfman & Anthony, 1995). Databases are organized into catalogs (any database can appear in any number of catalogs). Catalogs are created based on the subject(s). For each catalog there is a file describing about its contents (format of the constituent databases, location of the databases, executable to be used to search the database), *databases.conf*. Database can be in any format (refer, MARC, PRO-CITE, or any RDBMS database). For each database format we need an executable, called DBI (Database Interface) script, to search the database(s). If a database resides on a remote machine, its url is used in specifying its address in the *databases.conf* file. Current version of search engine searches only the databases in the selected catalog. When ever the search engine is triggered it first reads the configuration file. It then activates the corresponding DBIs. It also passes the information, obtained from the server, requested by the user to each DBI. DBIs can be activated concurrently to perform searches.

The main advantage of this architecture is the extensibility of formats. In order to add a new format we just need to add/write a new DBI. Databases are also added in modular fashion. It also reduces lot of data redundancy when a particular database needs to be placed in more than one catalog. We just have to create new entries in the corresponding *database.conf* files.

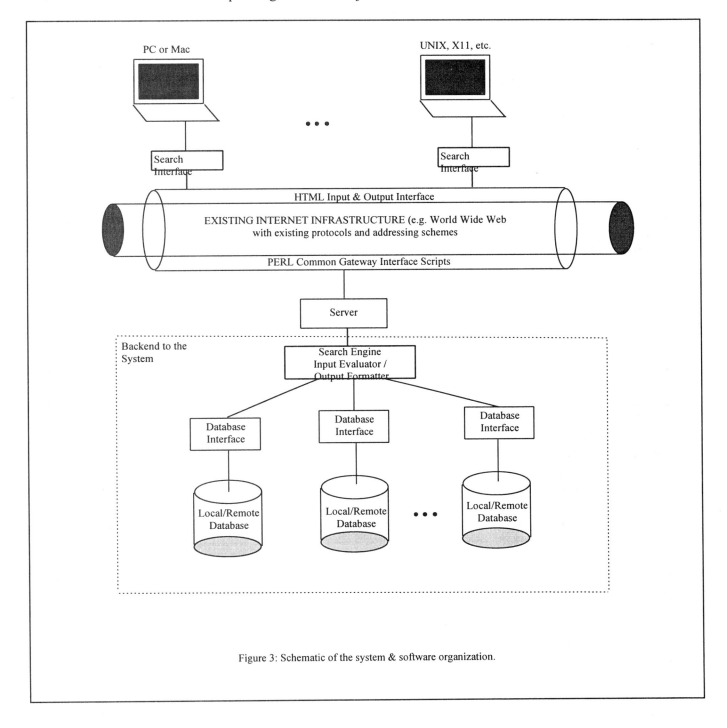

Figure 3: Schematic of the system & software organization.

Figures 4 and 5 show some of the features of the input and output interfaces. A sample query is shown in Figure 4. A user requests for the books/articles having the word **programming** with **Stroustrup** as the author. Users can fill in any of the text boxes with additional details. The first text box, labeled *Search words in title/subject/abstract*, can be used if the user does not have specific knowledge about the information source.

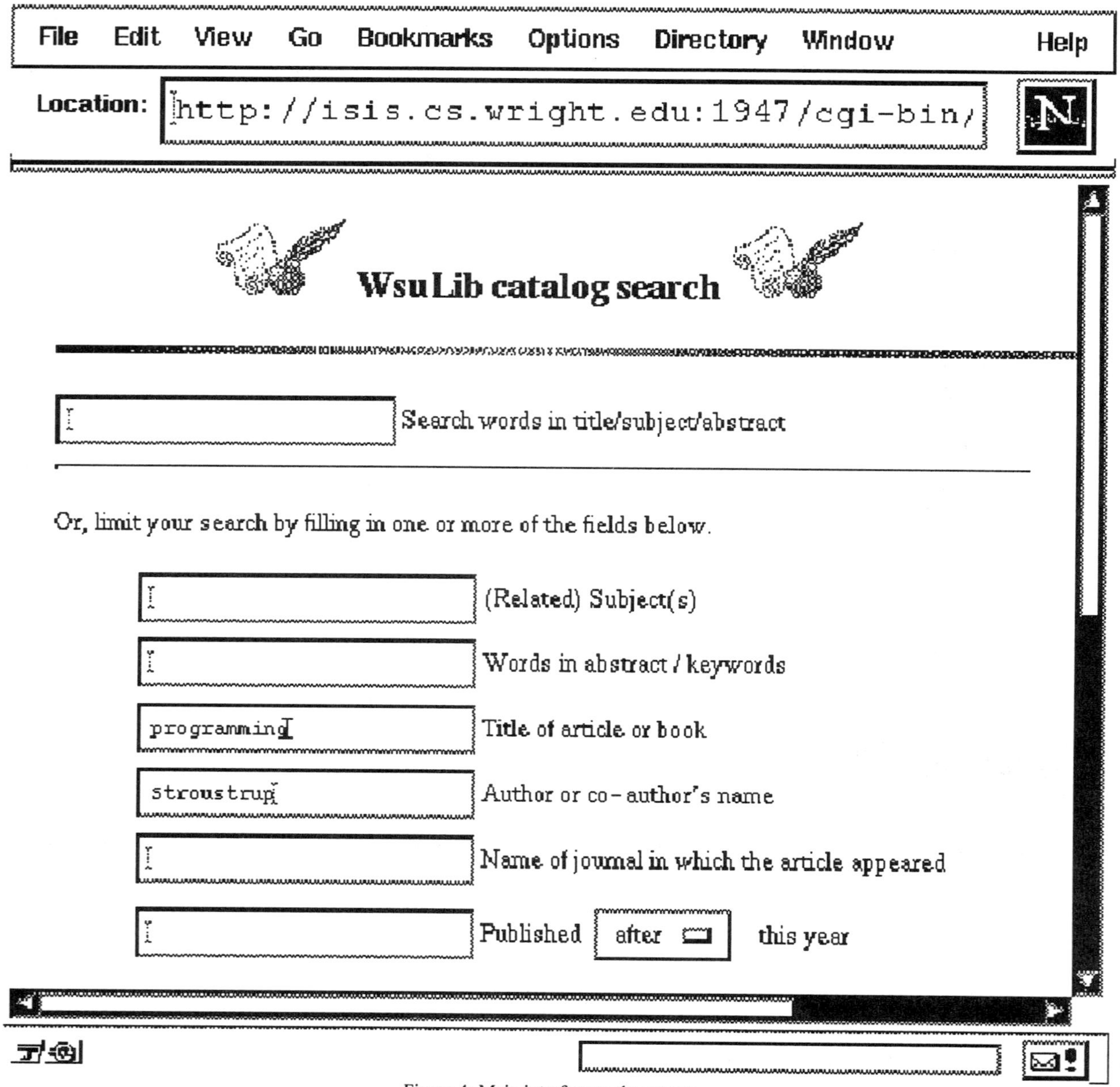

Figure 4: Main interface to the system.

Intermediate results of the search are shown in Figure 5. Each hit is shown by a card symbol with title and author details underneath it. Users can get more details about the book/article by just clicking on the required card symbol (which is a hyperlink to the detailed description of the corresponding match).

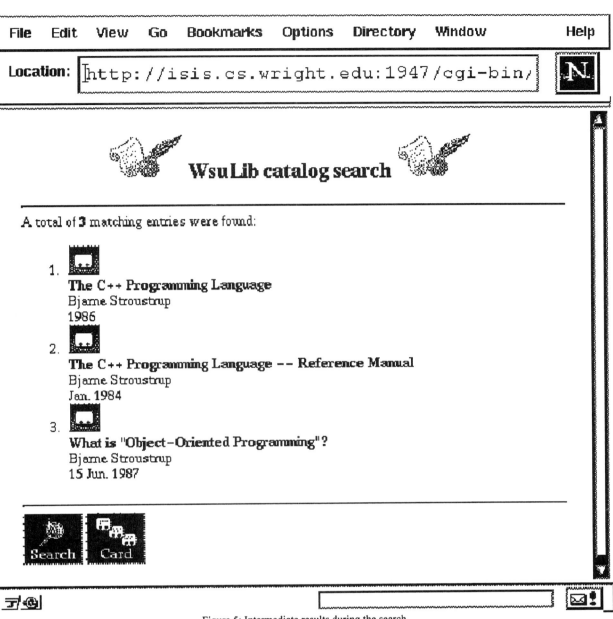

Figure 5: Intermediate results during the search.

DISCUSSION

Our research is interesting in many ways. First, our work is grounded in the understanding of the current library domain and users. This is in contrast to many current research efforts on digital libraries that often make incorrect assumptions about the nature of documents, the technology and the workplace (Levy and Marshall, 1995). Second, our research goes beyond the traditional text-based interface and provides direct access to information in multiple forms including text, graphics, and other media (Narayanan, et al., 1995). Third, the interface to our system is not driven from the database perspective, but is oriented towards the information seeking process thus potentially making seamless access to information easier (Rasmussen et al., 1994). Fourth, from a modeling perspective, the information seeker OFM is the first application of the framework in a non-control task.

The system currently has two major limitations. First, the total set of databases used in the prototype system is relatively small (in the order of hundreds of records). Second, the search methods perform a direct match and do not have "intelligence" to detect typographical errors or infer intent on topical areas. In the future, we plan to study issues of scalability and incorporate visualization capabilities in the system. We will also formally evaluate the effectiveness of the system in the information retrieval process. We also plan to incorporate additional intelligent search methods including semantics search methods on a specific set of topics into the system.

ACKNOWLEDGMENTS

This research was supported in part by the Wright State University Research Council.

REFERENCES

1. Denning, R., and Smith, P. J. (1994). *Interface design concepts in the development of ELSA, an intelligent electronic library search assistant.* Information Technologies and Libraries, Vol. 13, No. 2, June, pp. 133-147.

2. Dorfman, E., and Anthony, T. (1995). *Welcome to WebLib 2.0!, reference manual,* available on http://selsvr.stx.com/~weblib/.

3. Levy, D. M., and Marshall, C. C. (1995). *Going digital: A look at assumptions underlying digital libraries.* Communications of the ACM, April, pp. 77 - 84.

4. Mitchell, C. M. (1987). *GT-MSOCC: A research domain for modeling human-computer interaction and aiding decision making in supervisory control systems,* IEEE Transactions on Systems, Man, and Cybernetics, SMC-17(4), 553-572.

5. Narayanan, S., Walchli, S. E., Reddy, N., A. L. Wood, & Reynolds, B. K. (1995). *Developing intelligent information retrieval systems - Issues in database organization, distributed processing, and interface design.* Proceedings of the 1995 IEEE International Conference on Systems, Man, and Cybernetics, Vancouver, British Columbia, October.

6. Rasmussen, J., Pejtersen, A. M., and Goodstein, L. P. (1994). *Cognitive Systems Engineering.* John Wiley and Sons, Inc. New York.

In the trenches of the digital revolution: Intellectual freedom and the "public" digital library

Howard Rosenbaum
School of Library and Information Science. Indiana University
Bloomington, Indiana

Abstract

The development of the Internet and the increasing popularity of the World Wide Web have opened up a new realm of information access, storage, and delivery for librarians and information professionals. Libraries and schools are striving to respond to the pervasive and persistent growth of global networking and manage the demand for access to this dynamic new medium. Currently, 35 percent of American public libraries have some form of internet access and more than 650 K-12 schools are connected to the internet (Sackman, 1995). Working in the trenches of the digital revolution, librarians and information professionals are beginning to offer internet services to patrons; their work marks the beginning of the grassroots implementation of the "public" digital library. Such efforts do not come without their attendant risks, and it is extremely important that those who are becoming network service and resource providers and content producers clearly understand what is involved in their participation in the digital revolution from an issues- and policy-oriented perspective.

This paper will outline one subset of the range of critical issues that are part and parcel of the world of networked information and discuss their impacts on librarians and information professionals. It will discuss questions of access, privacy, copyright, and the protection of intellectual property and suggest that librarians and information professionals discuss and develop reasonable acceptable use policies early in the implementation process that will allow them to effectively person the front lines of the digital revolution.

Introduction

Capturing the attention of researchers, policy-makers, funding agencies, and practitioners alike, the concept of the "digital" or "virtual" library is a new organizational form that is expected to be linked in some way to physical libraries. Although at best an elusive concept, the digital library has acquired the cachet of a powerful meme, driving research and thinking throughout this decade. In fact, the definition of a digital library is by no means clear; despite the awarding of millions of dollars to develop components of digital libraries and several conferences devoted to the topic, there does not seem to be a consensus on the meaning of the term (Digital Libraries '95, 1995; Digital Libraries Conference, 1995; Digital Libraries '94, 1994). Micksa and Doty (1994) wonder whether the term is even appropriate, considering that the use of the term has been asserted "not by librarians (who might have been expected to choose it) but rather by computer and information scientists." According to Nürnberg, Furuta, Leggett, Marshall, and Shipman (1995):

The emerging field of digital libraries brings together participants from many existing areas of research. Currently, the field lacks a clear agenda independent of these other areas. It is tempting for researchers to think that the field of digital libraries is a natural outgrowth of an already known field... [It] will be limited if viewed only as a subfield of prior research interests.

Despite this confusion, throughout this decade, librarians and information professionals have moved to the front lines of the digital revolution as a consequence of their interests and in response to increasing customer demand, providing Internet services to a wide range of patrons in a wide variety of settings. This is in keeping with the role that the Federal government has described for libraries in the National Information Infrastructure; according to the NRENAISSANCE Committee (1994; 135):

Libraries complement both research and education. They figured first into the NREN and now into the vision of an integrated, broadly useful NII. The High Performance Computing Act of 1991 (PL 102-194) envisioned libraries as both access points for users to utilize the network as well as providers of information resources via the Internet. The [Clinton] administration's characterization of the NII carries forward this expectation, expanding it to include a training function.

Predictably, most of the well-publicized work that has been done on digital libraries has occurred in academic settings and has focused on the technical issues involved in digitizing, storing, organizing, and providing access to the content of these libraries (for example, see Bishop, 1995; Fox, 1993, 1994; and the NSF/ARPA/ digital library projects, Informedia, 1996; University of Illinois at Urbana-Champaign, 1996; University of California at Berkeley, 1996; University of California at Santa Barbara, 1996; University of Michigan, 1996; Stanford University, 1996). However, this only represents one of two major streams of work on digital libraries, the high end, well-funded, testbed projects taking place in research and educational institutions.

The second stream of work is taking place in the trenches of the digital revolution, where librarians and information professionals in public libraries and K-12 schools are in the midst of attempts to provide to their patrons what will certainly become important components of digital libraries (Libraries for the Future, 1996; Saint Joseph County Public Library, 1996; Sackman, 1995; Abrahams, Clement, and Parris, 1995). Their work is typically underfunded and done "on-the-fly," yet they "have the potential to generate some of the most innovative educational uses of the evolving national electronic networked environment for meeting the needs of the widest range of individuals" (McClure, Ryan, and Moen, 1993; 7).

Public and school librarians are working typically without a blueprint, under time and economic constraints and, with a few exceptions, little assistance from the research community (these exceptions include the work of McClure and his study teams, notably McClure, Bertot, and Beachboard, 1995; McClure, Babcock, Nelson, Polly, and Kankus, 1994). Their efforts do not come without their attendant risks, and it is extremely important that public and school librarians who are becoming network service and resource providers clearly understand what is involved in their participation in the digital revolution from an issues- and policy-oriented perspective. For these reasons, this paper will concentrate on the second stream of digital library work, the emergence of front-line digital libraries in public and school libraries, and will focus on an underappreciated but critically important subset of issues dealing with intellectual freedom: free speech, access, privacy, and intellectual property.

Intellectual freedom and the public digital library

There is a range of issues and concerns that must be considered by those who building and managing digital libraries which will vary with the setting within which the development effort takes place. Academic, special, and public/school libraries operate under varying institutional, social, and economic constraints and it is reasonable to expect that researchers and practitioners exploring the possibilities of digital libraries will have access to different resources and will face different problems in their work. One key difference is that the academic digital library projects are taking place under the aegis of the university and the major funding agencies; these projects may allow the public access to their services and resources, but they are not really "public." On the other hand, many of the efforts of public and school librarians take place without the same kind of institutional safety net and are intended for immediate public use. They are creating a new organizational form - the "public" digital library.

Therefore, the setting of interest in this paper is public libraries and their K-12 counterparts, because of their unique position; currently, about 35 percent of public libraries have some form of internet access and more than 650 K-12 schools are connected to the internet (Sackman, 1995). As the media continues to define the internet as the broadcast television of the 1990s, the general public discovers the vast world of resources and services on the internet, and politicians attempt to impose a regulatory framework on the American portion of the internet, public and school librarians find themselves on the front lines of provision of access to the net. There have been cogent arguments that this is appropriate because public and school libraries are the natural points of access to the internet (Isenstein, 1992; 2; Henderson, 1993; 1). As librarians and information professionals begin to offer Internet services to patrons, they are in the trenches of the digital revolution and their work marks the beginning of the grassroots implementation of the digital library.

The complexity of the technical challenges that must be faced and overcome in these settings is neither trivial nor easily managed. However, there is an equally challenging set of issues focused loosely around the concept of intellectual freedom which also must be faced and managed. These are issues that have been recognized as being central to the professional compass of librarianship, as critically important in the electronic networked information environment, and, in the context of public and school libraries, little discussed and analyzed[1]. Responding to an internal document staking out the American Library's position on the role of libraries in the NII, the ALA's Intellectual Freedom Committee (1996; 25) comments that:

An atmosphere of urgency about issuing a statement on the national information infrastructure pervaded the 1994 conference. Bills on the subject were pending before Congress. Nevertheless, the Intellectual Freedom Committee felt that ALA's basic intellectual freedom policies were being swept aside, at least to some degree, in the rush by many library organizations to become 'players' in the discussions taking place in Washington on the structure of the national information superhighway.

In an effort to return intellectual freedom concerns to the debate over the implementation of the digital library, this paper raises four of these issues that quickly arise in any public library and many school libraries that offer patrons and student access to the internet. The purpose of this paper is to bring these issues to the foreground in an attempt to initiate a dialog between researches and practitioners; there will not be an attempt to resolve them here for many quickly shade off into intricate legal discussions. Rather, by explicitly bringing them into view, practitioners and interested researchers can begin to wrestle with them. This is a necessary first step towards one reasonable resolution of these issues, which is a

well-thought out and defensible acceptable use policy that protects the institutions while not infringing on the rights of users.

According to the American Library Association (1995):

Issues arising from the still-developing technology of computer-mediated information generation, distribution, and retrieval need to be approached and regularly reviewed from a context of constitutional principles and established policy, so that fundamental and traditional tenets of librarianship are not swept away.

In each of the following sections, a brief scenario will be presented to focus the discussion of the issues; these scenarios are descriptive and are intended to provoke thoughtful reflection. This will be followed by questions intended to sharpen the issue and excerpts from the American Library Association's (1996) recently adopted resolution about patron access to electronic information, services, and networks, which stakes out the broad guidelines for the profession. This is an important document to consider because it provides a basis on which acceptable use policies can be built.

Free Speech

- A patron brings a disk in to the library, uploads a document that contains hateful material denigrating particular ethnic groups and advocating racial separation, and sends it as email to the White House, hundreds of listservs and USENET groups, and some selected individuals. Each time the message arrives at its destination, it carries header information identifying it as having come from the library.

Can the library deny the patron's right to broadcast the document? What are the limits of a patron's constitutionally protected speech when using the public library's internet connection to engage in communication with others (privately and in computer conferences)? According to Cavasos and Morin (1995; 67), "the right to speak one's mind without fear of government retribution is perhaps the most cherished of all the rights guaranteed by the U.S. Constitution." What should be the position of the library on the issue of the protection of the patron's right to freedom of expression, which "encompasses the freedom of speech and the corollary right to receive information" (ALA, 1996)? More specifically, the question concerns the extent to which the rights of the patron using the library's internet access to participate in public and private electronic communications must be balanced against the responsibilities of the library as the provider of the resources and services. Are there or should there be any restrictions on a patron's ability to use an email account or other internet resources provided by the library to send or receive any type of electronic message to another person, organization, or computer conference? This situation is exacerbated by the fact that many libraries are experimenting with WWW access, using browsers such as Netscape™, Mosaic™, or Internet Explorer™, all of which allow the user to send email without closing the browser and with varying degrees of anonymity.[2]

The ALA (1996), in its document "Access to Electronic Information, Services, and Networks," recently clarified its position on the issue of free speech by asserting that "Users should not be restricted or denied access for expressing or receiving constitutionally protected speech." This would seem to indicate that, in the above scenario, the patron should be allowed to carry on. This raises the dilemma of "finding the right balance of editorial control and tolerance" in an official policy statement of user rights, responsibilities, and acceptable use (Cavazos and Morin, 1995; 70). If a given computer conference and other site where the patron engages in the potentially hateful communication can be defined as "limited public forum," then the case for restricting speech is weakened, because "the owner of that particular forum no longer has the right to control and censor speech activities there" (Cavazos and Morin, 1995; 70). This matter is further complicated by the realization that the issue of the ownership of the internet is far from clear.

The protection of patron's rights to freely express themselves using the internet facilities in their public library is also supported by the National Research Council (1994), albeit for different reasons:

Providers that assert the right to control the content of public traffic may be subject to a more stringent liability (e.g., for defamation) for that traffic than those that do not assert such a right ... Information services supported by public funds, operated by government, or otherwise deemed public cannot discriminate among users on the basis of their electronic communications for First Amendment reasons ... Service providers of all types are well advised to establish the rules under which they provide their services, preferably in advance and perhaps in consultation with their users.

Public and school librarians would do well to heed this advice and have a set of clearly established rules and procedures covering the range of internet resources and services they intend to offer in advance of establishing their internet connection.

Privacy

- After the library has been running its forms- and email-based electronic reference service through its WWW site, the systems librarian asks what to do with the archives of the email messages and the information in the files that are created when users visit and use the WWW pages. She informs you that the files contain personal information about the patrons.

If a library operates an internet reference desk, as is being done at the Internet Public Library (1996), all incoming reference questions and outgoing responses can be easily captured and stored in a searchable database. This enable the amassing of detailed statistics that will provide the librarians with a clearer understanding of the efficiency of their reference work, the diversity of questions that arrive as email, and the usefulness of their reference collection. This information, however, also raises privacy concerns, because the header information that is attached to each email question is also captured. Unlike the face-to-face reference interview, where the question can be logged and time-on-task recorded, electronic, networked reference work allows the capturing of personal information about the sender of the question the confidentiality of which the library must be careful to preserve.

A similar concern is raised by MOO-based reference work[3], where users must log on, again providing the host (in this case the library) with personal information. In addition, a line-by-line verbatim transcript can easily be saved and stored, each of line of which can be matched to the userID of the person who keyed it in. This obviously is a boon to the researcher interested in careful textual analysis of the reference interview interaction, but again, the librarian must be concerned with the preservation of the patron's privacy. A related privacy concern arises in the instance where the library hosts computer conferences, through their WWW site, using listserv software, or through the creation of a USENET group. The library is then in possession of the database of subscribers, containing their names and email addresses and, if archived, a complete transcript of all of the messages posted to the conference.

One prevailing opinion is that this information should receive the same protection as is afforded to circulation information. The ALA (1996) seems to agree, arguing that, in the electronic, networked, information environment:

Users have both the right of confidentiality and the right of privacy. The library should uphold these rights by policy, procedure, and practice. Users should be advised, however, that because security is technically difficult to achieve, electronic transactions and files could become public.

One good example of language in a policy statement intended to deal with the ease with which personal information can be collected about individuals using the "public" digital library's resources and services is found in the "Server Access Log Policy" of the Internet Public Library (1996):

No Library records shall be made available to the public, press, or governmental agency, except by such process, order, or subpoena authorized by national, state or local law. The Director of the Library shall resist such process, order, or subpoena until there is a proper show of good cause. Any costs incurred by the Library in any search of records shall be charged to the agency demanding such a search.

The importance of such language cannot be underemphasized, because of the need to protect the confidentiality of the patron's personal information.

<u>Access</u>

- One patron has gotten into the habit of using the WWW search tools to run searches for sites with sexual themes. He takes delight in downloading and displaying images and multimedia that he finds on web sites and in USENET groups on the high resolution monitor. he asks at the reference desk for help in printing them out on the library's printer. A milder form of this scenario might be the patron requesting that the library provide access to certain USENET computer conferences in the .alt hierarchy that espouse racial warfare and separation of the races.

Can the library deny this patron access to the internet connection? Would the situation be different if the patron was searching for politically sensitive information, such as pro- or anti-abortion sites? Are there reasonable grounds for refusing a patron access to the library's internet services and resources?

The ALA (1996) does not believe that there are a priori grounds for denying patrons access to networked information resources and services, arguing that "electronic information, services, and networks provided directly or indirectly by the library should be equally, readily and equitably accessible to all library users". Further, librarians should not be placed in the position of having to make decisions about the quality of the resources and services that patrons may access and, on the touchy issue of allowing minors access to the full range of the internet, ALA (1996) states forcefully that access restrictions are the provenance of parents:

Providing connections to global information, services, and networks is not the same as selecting and purchasing material for a library collection. Determining the accuracy or authenticity of electronic information may present special problems. Some information accessed electronically may not meet a library's selection or collection development policy. It is, therefore, left to each user to determine what is appropriate. Parents and legal guardians who are concerned about their children's use of electronic resources should provide guidance to their own children.

Libraries and librarians should not deny or limit access to information available via electronic resources because of its allegedly controversial content or because of the librarian's personal beliefs or fear of confrontation. Information retrieved or utilized electronically should be considered constitutionally protected unless determined otherwise by a court with appropriate jurisdiction.

Perhaps questions of access can be handled by education; librarians may wish to consider developing programming to educate their patrons about the complexities, rights, and responsibilities of internet use, following the observation of the United States National Information Infrastructure Advisory Council (1995) that "schools, libraries, and community centers have an interest in encouraging their constituents to use information in lawful and ethical ways."

Intellectual property

- The library is publishing its own web pages. The person in charge is proud of her work and points out that the markup was simplified because she was able to access other pages and easily cut and paste their markup into the library's pages, including a "guestbook," and could quickly and efficiently download most images directly to the library's pages.

The trend seems to be for public and school libraries to establish their internet presences on the WWW, especially since the primary markup language (Hypertext Markup Language or HTML) has proven to be fairly easy to learn and use. In the scenario described above, are the various elements that constitute a WWW page fair game simply because most browsers allow users to access the markup code for any page on the web? Is there any problem in copying and using images and "scripts" from other people's sites? It is clear that current networking hardware and software make the copying and transfer of digital information simple and relatively painless, especially when using WWW browsers. It is much less clear what type of copying and use of what can be found on the WWW is legitimate and what constitutes a violation of copyright.

Current copyright legislation protects the "original expression" of a fact or idea or of "compilations of facts" or ideas as soon as the work is fixed in a tangible medium (Cavazos and Morin, 1995; 49; 50). It also establishes the conditions under which use of the copyrighted material is legitimate; when, then can the downloading and use of the images, arrangement of HTML tags, and CGI or Java scripts of another web page be considered fair use?

The ease with which one WWW page designer can link to another using HTML tags is at least partially responsible for the phenomenal growth of the WWW. It is also important to note that linking is mostly a one-way phenomenon; because I link to your site, you are under no obligation to link to my site. At present, there is no protocol beyond HTML which determines the procedures by which two sites can be linked and nothing more binding that common courtesy determining the appropriateness of the resulting links. In a sense, the owner of a web page cannot prevent another from making use of the page through linking and cannot prevent the subsequent display of her or his intellectual property. The designer or owner of a public digital library site has little more then his or her powers of persuasion in the event that his or her page has been linked to a site that, by the standards and policies of the library, is deemed unacceptable.

Conclusions

It is clear that there is a strong emphasis on the extension of digital libraries into public and school libraries in some as-of-yet undetermined form. According to the NTIA Office of Telecommunications and Information Applications (1995):

Connecting every classroom, library, hospital, and clinic in the United States to the National Information Infrastructure (NII) is a priority for the Clinton Administration. It is critical for these public institutions to become and remain active participants in the NII, since they can use telecommunications and information technologies to benefit all Americans.

Putting aside for a moment the technical and economic issues involved in creating and maintaining a digital library in a public or school library setting, this paper has argued that there are layers of complexity involved in applying the principles of intellectual freedom to public digital library service. There is a set of issues that must be separated and carefully studied by librarians and information professionals so that they can clarify the policies that are necessary to ensure, to the fullest extent, that they and their patrons "can escape the whims of the censor and enjoy the full benefit of freedom of expression under the First Amendment" (Krug, 1996; x).

These issues include the preservation of free speech when communicating on the global internet, the right of the patron to privacy, particularly in the realm of personal information in electronic form, the provision of access to electronic, networked resources and services in the public or school library, and the protection of digital intellectual property. Examples of acceptable use policies created by public and school libraries that attempt to come to grips with these issues have been gathered by Champelli and a sympathetic critique this type of policy is offered by Kinneman (1996). These are not trivial matters to resolve, and this paper represents a call to librarians and information professionals to begin a critical public discussion towards two complementary ends: the clarification of the range of positions that be taken in the profession on these issues and the development of practical and workable policies that can provide assistance and support to those in the trenches of the digital revolution.

Notes:

1. The recent passage of the Communications Decency Act raises additional questions for librarians concerned with intellectual freedom issues. A full discussion of the implications of this legislation are beyond the scope of this paper.

2. It is possible, if the site maintainer has sufficient technical expertise, to disable some of the features of WWW browsers, effectively preventing user from being able to invoke the mailing and newsgroup posting functions, but this is a neither trivial nor obvious procedure.

3. The MOO at the Internet Public Library <http://www.ipl.org/moo/> is explained as follows:

    A MOO is a Multi-User Object Oriented environment, an interactive system accessible through telnet by many users at the same time. Moos are based on the MUD - (Multi-User Dungeon) concept, but include more possibilities for interaction and real time communication learning experiences.

    Why telnet to the MOO?

    The Internet Public Library is a place where a library community can form, where people can get together and interact in real time. In this environment the community can help shape their surroundings and make it a place that fits their needs. One of the benefits of the moo is that interaction with other visitors and objects (desks, chairs, cat etc.) creates a mood conducive to virtual community. We have formed the framework where librarians and information seekers can gather together, talk, and provide reference services.

Bibliography:

Abrahams, J., Clement, J., Parris, M. (1995). A list of schools in the United States with high-bandwidth connectivity to the Internet.

  Available at: <http://k12.cnidr.org/janice_k12/states/current_march.html>

American Library Association. Office of Intellectual Freedom. (1996). Access to Electronic Information, Services, and Networks: an Interpretation of the LIBRARY BILL OF RIGHTS [Adopted 1/24/96]

  Available at: <gopher://ala1.ala.org:70/00/alagophx/alagophxfreedom/electacc.fin>

Bishop, A.P. (1995). Working towards an understanding of digital library use: A report on the user research efforts of the NSF/ARPA/NASA DLI projects. D-Lib Magazine, October.

  Available at: <http://www.dlib.org/dlib/october95/10bishop.html>

Cavazos, E.A. and Morin, G. (1995). Cyberspace and the Law: Your Rights and Duties in the On-line World. Cambridge, MA" The MIT Press.

Champelli, L. (1996). The Internet Advocate: A Web-based Resource Guide for Librarians and Educators Interested in Providing Youth Access to the Net

  Available at: <http://silver.ucs.indiana.edu/~lchampel/netadv.htm>

Digital Libraries '95. (1995). Proceedings of the Second International Conference on the Theory and Practice of Digital Libraries. Austin, Texas, USA. June 11-13, 1995.

  Available at: <http://bush.cs.tamu.edu/dl95/README.html>

Digital Libraries Conference. (1995). Singapore Information Technology Institute. March 27-28, 1995.

  Available at: <http://www.iti.gov.sg/personal/kwanghan/dl/dl.html>

Digital Libraries '94. (1994). Proceedings of the First Annual Conference on the Theory and Practice of Digital Libraries. College Station, Texas, USA. June 19-21, 1994.

  Available at: <http://bush.cs.tamu.edu/dl94/README.html>

Fox, E. (1993). Digital Library Source Book, 1993, ed.

    Available at: <http://fox.cs.vt.edu/DLSB.html>

_____. (1994). Digital Libraries - NSF/ARPA/NASA Research.

    Available at: <http://ei.cs.vt.edu/~cs5604/DL/DL3.html>

Henderson, C. (1993). The role of public libraries in providing public access to the internet. Presented at Public Access to the Internet. John F. Kennedy School of Government, Harvard University. May 26-7, 1993.

Informedia. (1996). The Informedia (tm) Digital Video Library project. Carnagie Mellon University.

    Available at: <http://fuzine.mt.cs.cmu.edu/im/>

Internet Public Library.

    available at: <http://ipl.sils.umich.edu/>

Isenstein, L.J. (1992). Public libraries and electronic networks: The time to act is now. Electronic Networking. 2(2). 2-5.

Kinneman, D. (1996). Critiquing Acceptable Use Policies.

    Available at: <http://gnn.com/gnn/meta/edu/features/archive/aup.html#whose>

Krug, J.F. (1996). Preface. In Office for Intellectual Freedom. Intellectual Freedom Manual, 5th ed. Chicago. IL: American Library Association. ix-x.

Libraries for the Future. (1996). Local Places, Global Connections: Models of Public Library Connectivity.

    Available at: <http://www.inch.com/%7Elff/technology/local.html>

Liddy, E.D., Eisenberg, M.B., McClure, C.R., Mills, K., Mernit, S., and Luckett, J.D. (1994). Research Agenda for the Intelligent Digital Library.

    Available at: <http://www.csdl.tamu.edu/DL94/paper/liddy.html>

McClure, C.R., Babcock, W.C., Nelson, K.A., Polly, J.A., and Kankus, S.R. (1994). The Project GAIN Report: Connecting Rural Public Libraries to the Internet. Liverpool, NY: Nysernet.

McClure, C.R., Bertot, J.C., and Beachboard, J.C. (1995). Internet Costs and Cost Models for Public Libraries. Washington D.C.: U.S. National Commission on Libraries and Information Science.

    Available at: <http://istweb.syr.edu/Project/Faculty/McClure.NCLIS.Report.html>

_____, McCabe, H. and Scoville, S. (1995). Policy Initiatives and Strategies for Enhancing the Role of Public Libraries in the National Information Infrastructure (NII).

    Available at: <http://istweb.syr.edu/Project/Faculty/McClurePaper1.html>

McClure, C.R., Moen, W.E., and Ryan, J. (1994). Libraries and the Internet/NREN: Perspectives, Issues, and Challenges. Westport, CT: Mecklermedia.

_____., Ryan, J., and Moen, W.E. (1993). The role of public libraries in the use of internet/NREN information services. Library and Information Science Research. 7-34.

Miksa, F.L. And Doty, P. (1994). Intellectual Realities and the Digital Library.

    Available at: <http://www.csdl.tamu.edu/DL94/paper/miksa.html>

National Research Council. (1994). Rights and Responsibilities of Participants in Networked Communities. Washington, D.C.: National Academy Press.

    Available at: <http://www.nas.edu:70/nap/online/rights>

National Research Council. Commission on Physical Sciences, Mathematics, and Applications. Computer Science and Telecommunications Board. NRENAISSANCE Committee. (1994). Realizing the Information Future: The Internet and Beyond. Washington, D.C.: National Academy Press.

Nürnberg, P.J., Furuta, R., Leggett, J.J., Marshall, C.C., and Shipman, F.M. (1995). Digital Libraries: Issues and Architectures.

    Available at: <http://www.csdl.tamu.edu/DL95/papers/nuernberg/nuernberg.html>

Sackman, G. (1995). HotList of K-12 Internet School Sites - USA - Nov 1, 1995.

    Available at: <http://www.sendit.nodak.edu/k12/>

Saint Joseph County Public Library. (1996). SJCPL's List of Public Libraries with Internet Services.

Available at: <http://sjcpl.lib.in.us/homepage/PublicLibraries/PublicLibrary Servers.html>

Stanford University. (1996). Stanford University Digital Libraries Project .

Available at: <http://diglib.stanford.edu/diglib/>

United States Department of Commerce. National Telecommunications and Information Administration. Office of Telecommunications and Information Applications. (1995). Connecting The Nation: Classrooms, Libraries, and Health Care Organizations in the Information Age.

Available at: >http://www.ntia.doc.gov/connect.html>

United States National Information Infrastructure Advisory Council. (1995). KickStart Initiatives: Connecting America's Communities to the Information Superhighway.

Available at: <http://www.benton.org/KickStart/kick.privacyresources.html>

University of California at Berkeley. (1996). UC Berkeley Digital Library project.

Available at: <http://elib.cs.berkeley.edu/>

University of California at Santa Barbara. (1996). Alexandria Digital Library Project.

Available at: <http://alexandria.sdc.ucsb.edu/>

University of Illinois at Urbana-Champaign. (1996). Digital Library Initiative: Federating Repositories of Scientific Literature.

Available at: <http://www.grainger.uiuc.edu/dli/>

University of Michigan, Ann Arbor, Michigan. (1996). The University of Michigan Digital Library Project

Available at: http://www.sils.umich.edu/UMDL/HomePage.html

Measures for the Academic Networked Environment: Strategies, Guidelines, and Options

Cynthia L. Lopata and Charles R. McClure
School of Information Studies, Syracuse University
Syracuse, New York

ABSTRACT

As budgets for academic networking resources and services grow, so do demands from academic administrators for evidence of the effects of networking on campus. Also, as academic computing departments face increasing user demands for networked resources and services, they may find it difficult to plan and allocate resources without information on the use and performance of their campus networks.

The purpose of this study was to investigate the state of networking at academic institutions and to develop measures to assess network performance. Data were collected via focus groups, site visits, and interviews, all of which involved academic computing administrators and staff, library administrators and staff, and campus network users.

The results of this study include a manual of techniques and instructions for their use in evaluating networks as well as a set of issues which must be resolved by evaluators prior to and during the assessment of network performance.

INTRODUCTION & BACKGROUND

One aspect of the Digital Revolution is the development, implementation, and rapid growth of computer networks at academic institutions. Budgets to expand campus networks to include dorms and offices and to provide access to the Internet for all members of these institutions have increased greatly in the past few years. However, there has been little evaluation of networking on campuses and academic administrators are now beginning to ask questions concerning the value, importance, and impacts of networking (Fleit, 1994; Heterick, 1994).

Evaluation and performance measures are important, in any organization, for several reasons. First, they help managers obtain information which can be used to answer questions about whether their units are doing what they are supposed to be doing and how well they're doing that. Such information may be required, or at least useful, in justifying resource requests. Second, evaluation and performance measures provide information which managers can use in making decisions about the allocation of resources and planning.

In addition to these internal uses of this information, there are other external uses for it. In an increasingly competitive environment, academic institutions are becoming more aware of how they compare to other institutions which may be competing for the same students, faculty, and resources. Network resources and services constitute one point of comparison.

This paper presents an overview of a study, funded by the U.S. Department of Education, and conducted by a study team at Syracuse University's School of Information Studies, to investigate the state of networking at academic institutions and to develop measures to assess network performance. Results of this 18-month study include:

- descriptions of academic network configurations and networked resources and services offered at selected institutions;

- a model developed from those descriptions;

- a typology of driving forces behind network development;

- a typology of barriers to network assessment;

- an analysis of network assessment efforts at selected academic institutions;

- and a set of suggested performance measures and assessment techniques for use in the evaluation of academic networks.

The performance measures and assessment techniques developed during this nvestigation are the subject of this paper.

METHODOLOGY

Assessment of networking in the academic environment is an area in which little research, applied or theoretical, has been done (McClure, 1991). For that reason, an exploratory, inductive approach, using a variety of qualitative methods, was taken. Among the methods used were: focus groups, site visits, and interviews with individuals and small groups. Participants included people involved in the design, implementation, support, and use of networked resources and services. Among these were academic library administrators and staff, academic computing administrators and staff, faculty, and students.

Data collection activities included, specifically: two focus groups and a small group interview to get input to development of the measures, assess the current state of network evaluation, and identify problems associated with network evaluation; two site visits to test the measures; two focus groups to get feedback on the measures during and after their development; and an ongoing electronic discussion to explore issues related to network evaluation and the measures. These data collection activities were supplemented by informal interviews with knowledgeable individuals and feedback from a formal advisory group of experts in the field. Thus multiple sources were used and multiple perspectives were represented. Data analysis included content analysis of audio tapes and notes from the focus groups, interviews, and site visits.

The focus of this investigation was research universities meeting the following criteria:

- Listed as Carnegie Research I or II institutions and ARL members

- Demonstrated an interest and ability to participate in the study

- Actively involved in the development and implementation of academic networking

(Note: the number of institutions meeting the first of the criteria listed above is 87 (The nation: Doctorate-granting institutions, 1994).) Individuals from institutions which met these criteria were invited to participate in focus groups and interviews. The institutions which were selected for site visits met all of the above criteria and one additional criterion: the institutions had to be located within a reasonable proximity to Syracuse, NY, where the study team was based.

Traditional evaluation criteria as defined below, were used as a beginning model for network assessment in this investigation:

- Extensiveness: how much of a product or service has been provided, how widely it was made available, how many people used it, and how much use they made of it.

- Efficiency: how much time and money, or other resources, were required to provide a given amount of a product or service.

- Effectiveness: how well the networked information service met the objectives of the provider or the user.

- Impact: how a service made a difference in some other activity or situation.

Aspects of academic performance which were considered were those traditional areas of activity and concern at universities: teaching, learning, research, and student support.

RESULTS

As stated above, the results reported here do not include all aspects of the study. Rather they are confined to those results which are directly relevant to the development of performance measures and assessment techniques for use in the evaluation of academic networks. However, data on the current state of network assessment will first be briefly reviewed in order to set the context for the introduction of these measures and techniques.

The need for performance measures was stated clearly by academic computing administrators who described budgeting processes and conditions in their respective institutions. According to one focus group participant,

> "Nobody is throwing capital dollars at networking [at our institution]...they are expecting to see some sort of supporting improvement, or some sort of recovery scheme to come back to recover the capital costs."

Another participant added, "... we're certainly not immune from all the cost cutting measures going on throughout the rest of the institution...we've got to make arguments and internal kinds of decisions on trading some things off..."

However, indications from people who were interviewed and who participated in focus groups were that assessment of networking on most campuses is at a very early stage if and when it is being done at all. It appears that currently used networking evaluation measures are primarily at the extensiveness level, with the use of some efficiency measures. Effectiveness and impacts of networks are largely unmeasured and cannot be measured without a foundation of extensiveness and efficiency measures.

Approaches to measurement which focus on ROI (Return on Investment) have, so far, revealed few financial benefits associated with investment in networking. One computing administrator commented, "The one thing I know is that we haven't lowered costs. And some people look to [networking] to lower costs. And I think that is probably a holy grail that I don't know how to get to."

Other measures currently in use are of an anecdotal nature. For example, one faculty member commented, "I have a small class and there's another fellow in Nebraska with a small class, and we are collaborating using the Internet. There are all kinds of things like that that you can point to that you can say that those are things that could not have happened any other way. So those are tangible outcomes but you can't measure them."

Another participant reported on a study done to determine if students believed that their use of electronic information services affected their work or their grades. "Again, you know, it's still soft in the sense that they are asking users their view, not that there's an external quantitative measure. But there is an effort at that kind of measurement."

Still, there appears to be a need for data on use of specific resources. One library staff member commented, "If I had data on the [use of] journals in my collection and I had data on the [use of] databases that we had mounted on the network and I could compare the use and the cost per use that would be something that I could use very, very easily. Now, when I talk to faculty they say this is great, we've got to have it. But when

I say it's going to cost $20,000 and we're going to have to cut nine journals to do it, they say oh...but if I could show much more specifically that we were getting much more bang for the buck it would be worth it."

Participants also reported on their efforts to develop measures of networking's impact on research. One person described a study in which he compared the number and value of research grants received by faculty who were active users of the network to those received by faculty who were not active network users.

"There was an amazing correlation....between those that had the network connection and substantially higher amounts of research dollars that came in....I did it within humanities, I did it within hard sciences and did it within engineering, did it within medicine...it was there, it was indisputably there. [But] there are probably a lot of intervening variables."

The focus group and interview data were used to construct a preliminary set of measures which were then reviewed by individuals who are knowledgeable about academic networking and which were also presented to panels of individuals at site visits to two academic institutions. The measures were further developed and revised as a result of feedback from the site visits and they were then compiled in a manual for use and further development by academic institutions. The manual includes:

- a set of quantitative measures of academic performance
- a review of qualitative techniques and instructions for their use in assessing academic networks
- and a survey instrument for use in collecting data from network users

In addition to the measures, a number of issues were identified which must be addressed by any institution before an evaluation effort can begin and the measures can be used. Possible approaches to dealing with these issues are discussed in the manual.

Quantitative Measures

The quantitative measures developed in this study cover the following broad areas: network users and their usage of, and satisfaction with, the network; traffic on the network; costs to develop, maintain, and support the network; and network services, including applications and support. For each of the performance measures, the manual provides an operationalized definition, issues that may have to be resolved prior to obtaining data to produce the measure, data collection procedures, and suggestions for developing related measures. The measures presented in the manual are intended for use as a menu from which evaluators will select those measures which are most useful in the context of their organizations. A more detailed list of the individual measures is presented in Appendix A.

Qualitative Techniques

Techniques for the collection and analysis of qualitative data are especially appropriate for use in investigating research problems which are not well defined, in research settings which are not well understood. Because evaluation of academic networking is in its infancy, problems associated with it are not yet well defined. Also, campus networking is developing rapidly as new technologies and new uses for those technologies emerge. Thus campus networks constitute rather unstable environments which are not well understood. For these reasons, a portion of the manual developed in this project was devoted to the identification and explanation of techniques for collecting and analyzing qualitative data.

Included in the techniques covered are: benchmarking, focus groups, critical incidents, activity logs, interviews, group process surveys, site visits, scenario development, and observations. Also, criteria for selecting the appropriate techniques for evaluation in a specific situation are discussed. Evaluators must consider the amount of time, money, training, involvement and commitment required for each technique. In addition to the techniques, a group of networking topics and issues which would be appropriate to investigate using these techniques is presented. These include: teaching, learning, research, administration, library use, professional development, collaboration, the campus social and cultural environment, and network help resources.

User Survey

An evaluation of campus networking would not be complete without feedback from users of the network technologies, services, and resources. For this reason an instrument for use in surveying network users was developed as part of this project. This survey instrument covers: user demographics and computing experience; patterns of access and use; perceptions of network availability and reliability; applications use and perceptions of their usefulness; and support for network users. The instrument is comprehensive, with 53 questions, but it is not intended for use as is. Rather network administrators who are interested in using the survey will have to determine which parts of the questionnaire are appropriate to their institutions and they will likely want to use only selected questions from the survey. Issues and methods related to the administration of surveys also are discussed in this section of the manual.

CONCLUSIONS

One result of this investigation was the realization that for the purposes of assessing academic networking, a one-size-fits-all approach would not be appropriate. The institutions studied were different from each other in a variety of ways: their networking configurations were different; the range of network services and resources they offered varied; and their support structures were different.

Although the manual describes standardized procedures for data collection and computing performance measures, the resulting measures are unlikely to be comparable across different academic institutions. The networking infrastructure and the manner in which data on networking may be collected in different institutions vary considerably. Furthermore, different institutions may use different definitions for key terms. Evaluation results must be judged in the context of each individual institution.

To some degree, these performance measures might be best seen as estimates of the extensiveness, efficiency, effectiveness, or impact of a service or activity rather than a precise measure of that particular service or activity. Even if these measures are best seen as estimates, such estimates are a significant improvement over the very limited set of performance measures that are currently available and being used.

Clearly, measurement of the impacts of networking, and of the adequacy of individual institutions' network capabilities, is problematic. Financial measures seem inappropriate, yet newer, more appropriate measures have not yet been developed. While this investigation has not produced a set of refined performance measures ready for use in any given institution, the instruments and procedures developed in this study and presented here provide a starting point for individual institutions to develop evaluation plans for networking on their campuses.

Information on obtaining a copy of the completed manual can be obtained by sending a request via email to the following address: kreschen@istweb.syr.edu.

REFERENCES

Fleit, L. (1994). Self-assessment for campus information technology services. Boulder, CO: CAUSE

Heterick, R. (1994). A stone soup. Educom Review, 29(6), 64.

McClure, C. (1991). Planning and evaluation for the networked environment. EDUCOM Review, 26(3-4), 34-37.

The nation: Doctorate-granting institutions. (1994). The Chronicle of Higher Education Almanac Issue, XLI(1), 42.

APPENDIX A

QUANTITATIVE MEASURES OF NETWORK PERFORMANCE

Count of Network Users

Count of Active Network Users

Annual Information Technology Expenditures

Router Traffic as a Measure of Overall Campus Network Activity

Modem Traffic into the Campus Network
Dial-up user rate
Saturation rate

Internet Traffic
Incoming Internet volume
Outgoing Internet volume
Saturation

Frequency of Email Use
Percentage of frequent email users
Percentage of infrequent email users

Use of Clusters or Public Sites to Access the Network
Ratio of network users to available public terminals
Occupancy rate of public sites

Network Applications
Count of "hits" on applications
Use of applications by specific user groups

Internet Access to Shared Servers
Count of accesses via commercial provider
Count of accesses via dial-up connection

Online Library Catalog Measures
Number of remote logins to the online library catalog
Number of non-remote logins to the online library catalog
Number of searches made from remote and nonremote terminals
Cost of online library catalog per remote login
Cost of online library catalog per non-remote login

Campuswide Information Systems (CWIS)
Total number of visitors to the CWIS
Total number and/or percentage of faculty/students/staff/others visiting the CWIS
Frequency of Visits from each visitor or group (i.e., faculty, students, staff, others)
Sites visited within the CWIS for each visitor
Location of visitors after they leave the CWIS

Distance Learning
Number of distance learning classes offered in a given semester
Distance learning classes as a percentage of all offered classes
Number of faculty offering distance learning classes in a given semester via the network
Percentage of faculty teaching via distance learning in a given semester via the network
Number of students enrolled in distance learning classes in a given semester
Percentage of all students enrolled in distance learning classes in a given semester
Distance learning student grade point average compared to non-distance learning student grade point average
Unique costs associated with distance learning classes

Help Desk
Volume of requests
Types of requests
Response time
Accuracy of response
Courtesy of staff

Network Repair and Services
Response time
Accuracy of response
Courtesy of staff

Availability of Networked Resources
Percentage of classrooms with at least one computer
Percentage of classrooms with LCD or other type of projector display for computing/networked services or resources
Percentage of classrooms that have access to the campus network
Average number of computers per networked classroom
Average number of network connections per networked classroom
Percentage of networked classrooms with LCD displays
Percentage of faculty offices connected to the campus network
Percentage of administrative offices connected to the campus network
Percentage of student dorm rooms connected to the campus network

Network Support Staff
Ratio of support staff to users
Ratio of support staff to active users

Network Training
Number of users participating in training
Number of users seeking training
Annual training hours received
Number of training activities offered
Ratio of application-specific training to available applications

Training expenditures as a percentage of total information technology expenditures

Network Documentation Available to Users
Count of print-based documentation available
Count of electronic-based documentation available
Usefulness of documentation
Annual cost of documentation

Impact on Education V: Teachers and Learners

Information Seeking Behavior of Science and Engineering Faculty: The Impact of New Information Technologies

Julie M. Hurd
Science Library, University of Illinois at Chicago
Chicago, Illinois

Ann C. Weller and Karen L Curtis
Library of the Health Sciences, University of Illinois at Chicago
Chicago, Illinois

Abstract

This paper describes preliminary findings from an ongoing study of a group of university faculty who are engaged in use and production of scientific and technical information. It examines the extent to which the Digital Revolution has altered their information seeking behavior and other scholarly activities. Innovations in information delivery that were investigated include locally-mounted databases, client/server databases, and Internet resources, as well as opportunities offered for training in use of the Internet. The focus in this paper will be on the analysis of data derived from a survey conducted during autumn 1995 of basic sciences and engineering faculty at the University of Illinois at Chicago. Comparisons will be made to a baseline study that was carried out during autumn 1991 of faculty in the same departments who were surveyed regarding their use of library resources, particularly those paper and electronic indexes and abstracts that provide access to journal literature.

Introduction

Electronic information resources and information technologies are now provided by every major research library and, at most universities, represent a rapidly-growing expenditure in library budgets. Libraries are faced with more possibilities for purchase than budgets will support, and decisions on which resources to acquire are complex and difficult. Often the promise of enhanced access through networking and powerful searching capabilities drives decisions more than cost alone. Furthermore, electronic resources represent "big ticket" purchases that demand much more from library staff than purchase of a comparable paper resource; there are typically on-going systems costs for people, hardware, and software and public services and staff and user training issues as well. Monitoring use of these costly resources provides essential data to fund managers who desire assurances that scarce resources are being allocated wisely. The user survey described in this paper represents an effort to document use of information technology and electronic resources by science and engineering faculty at The University of Illinois at Chicago. The survey population also included health sciences faculty in the Colleges of Medicine, Pharmacy and Nursing; analysis of that data will be reported in another paper to be presented at the spring 1996 meeting of the Medical Library Association.

The University of Illinois at Chicago (UIC) is one of 88 Carnegie Research I institutions in the United States. The University offers doctorates in 54 specializations and master's degrees in 93 disciplines. UIC enrolls over 25,000 students and employs 11,000 full-time faculty and staff and is the largest institution of higher learning in the Chicago area. UIC is a member of the Association of Research Libraries and the Committee on Institutional Cooperation (CIC), a consortium of large midwestern research institutions that includes the members of the Big Ten athletic conference and the University of Chicago. The Library is an active participant in various CIC initiatives that promote resource sharing and sponsor technological approaches to shared collections and electronic resources.

The UIC Library has developed its computer-based systems to accommodate several characteristics of its primary user community:

- Users may be remote from library resources they need. The campus has two major sites in Chicago and three regional sites associated with the College of Medicine in Urbana, Peoria, and Rockford. The University Library is decentralized with materials located in eight separate buildings in Chicagoand at the regional sites.

- Users may be engaged in interdisciplinary research and need materials in more than one campus library. Purchases of duplicate materials, particularly costly scientific journals, have declined in recent years.

- The computing environment is rich and diverse; it includes a mainframe-based Academic Data Network (ADN) as well other local area networks serving dedicated user groups. A wide variety of equipment is used to connect to campus networks and the Internet, and many users also connect from home locations.

- There is no large residential community near the Chicago campus so faculty, staff, and students live through out the greater-Chicago region and may commute to campus from significant distances.

Both the decentralized nature of library resources and the geographic distribution of users has long argued for a networked approach to providing library resources, and that philosophy has driven development of UIC's library systems and services. The library's online catalog has been available over the campus computing network for many years as has a set of bibliographic databases that can be used to search the journal literature. In addition, library documentation on the network and a system based on electronic mail informs users and supports communication with the library. Recent developments have included more specialized tools based on client/server systems such as Grateful Med which allows searching of over twenty two National Library of Medicine databases and the Beilstein database of chemical information. Encyclopedia Britannica Online is available in campus libraries and on the network to affiliated users. The Library has also installed a number of workstations, both networked and stand-alone, that provide access to data, information, and citations in government documents, pharmacy, public health and more. Still other electronic resources are under consideration for addition to this array.

In autumn of 1991 we conducted a survey of science, engineering, and health sciences faculty that provided baseline data on use of paper and electronic resources. [Hurd, Weller and Curtis, 1992; Curtis, Weller and Hurd, 1993] That earlier survey provided a snapshot of scientists as they were beginning to incorporate computer-based resources into their work habits. At that time there was a sizable group, as many as 50% in some departments surveyed, who had not yet obtained computer accounts; we saw considerable variation among disciplines studied and noted the lack of an appropriate technological infrastructure in some campus buildings. That survey suggested directions for both the library and the Computer Center in providing and promoting resources and training. The survey that will be described here was distributed to faculty in the same departments as the earlier survey. Questions were included that probed faculty use of computer-based information services that the library offers as well as use of other network resources and training opportunities.

Related Research

In 1991 most published user studies had been conducted prior to widespread use of networked resources; only a very small number of studies examined faculty use of locally-mounted databases and other information technologies. Some of these user studied are referenced in the above two publications that describe findings from our earlier survey. The intervening years have seen several investigations that have contributed to our understanding of use of networked resources and have provided background to inform this study. Judith Adams and Sharon Bonk (1995) studied faculty at four campuses of the State University of New York (SUNY) to determine availability of equipment and network connections and to measure factors affecting use of electronic resources. The authors identified variant use patterns by discipline as well as perceived obstacles to use of electronic information technologies. They list mandates for libraries in the areas of promoting understanding of available resources, user training, allocation of funding, and service delivery options. Another study by Eileen Abels, Peter Liebscher, and Daniel Denman (1996) explored factors that influenced adoption and use of electronic networks and network services by science and engineering faculty in six smaller universities and colleges in the southeastern United States. They found physical access to appropriate workstations to be the biggest significant determinant of adoption of network use. They are continuing to study the user population and are preparing additional reports on their research.

Survey Demographics and Response

The population we surveyed consisted of faculty in the UIC Colleges of Engineering, Medicine, Nursing and Pharmacy, and the science departments in the College of Liberal Arts and Sciences. The total survey population consisted of 1121 faculty. Faculty in the humanities and social sciences, as well as those in professional programs such as social work, business and education were excluded from this study as we hypothesized that their information use patterns would differ significantly and require a different survey instrument. This paper reports only the findings from the analysis of returns from faculty in the basic sciences and engineering.

As in the earlier baseline survey, we elected to survey our entire population rather than employ a sample. A total of 202 questionnaires were mailed to all faculty in the departments of biological sciences, chemistry, geological sciences, mathematics, statistics and computer sciences, and physics. 107 questionnaires were mailed to all faculty in the College of Engineering. 101 surveys were returned from science faculty, 49 from engineering faculty for a response rate of 50% from the sciences and 46% from engineering. The typical survey respondent was male (92%) and tenured (71.3% with the rank of professor or associate professor) with an average of 15 years on the UIC faculty. This profile of respondents matches the entire population in these characteristics so we are confident that our response group reflects demographically the full population.

Methodology and Survey Instrument

The survey instrument was patterned after that used in the 1991 baseline survey. It included questions that explored use of major indexing and abstracting services in both paper and electronic formats. Frequency of use of resources was queried. During the time elapsed since the 1991 survey the library had added numerous electronic resources so new questions were written to document use of these. In addition, the World Wide Web and other Internet tools had become widely available and faculty were queried about these as well. Other questions probed faculty access to computer networks from both campus and home and asked about participation in training opportunities offered by the library. An open-ended question invited comments on library-related issues. The survey instrument is not reproduced here but is available from the authors upon request.

The questionnaire was designed with assistance from the university's Office of Survey Research, a consulting service available to faculty. It was also reviewed by the university's Institutional Review Board which monitors all proposals for research by faculty involving human subjects. The survey was pre-tested on a small number of faculty to identify any ambiguity in questions asked. A cover letter explaining the purpose of the survey accompanied the questionnaire which was distributed early in the Fall Semester of 1995 after classes were underway. A reminder postcard was sent, and non-respondents received two additional survey mailings.

Data from returned questionnaires were entered in Microsoft Excel for Macintosh and analyzed in that application. Coding on questionnaires permitted sorting by departments and colleges as well as tracking of individual returns. The Excel database used for analysis did not identify respondents by name as anonymity was assured to all in the original cover letter that accompanied the survey. Only aggregate data will be reported in any presentations and publications of survey findings.

A major goal of the survey was to measure use of indexing and abstracting services by faculty who frequently had multiple format options available to them, including paper. To date, the library has not canceled any paper secondary publications even though a number are duplicated by electronic services. It also continues to offer mediated searching of databases by librarians and supports end-user searching of commercial databases by providing passwords and account management for faculty. Selected major secondary services are available on the campus computing network through the Illinois Bibliographic Information Service (IBIS) a set of locally-mounted databases searchable through a customized interface based on BRS Search. IBIS databases include all sections of Current Contents, the ERIC database, PsycLit (Psychological Abstracts in electronic format), and a subset of H.W. Wilson databases. In addition, access is available through OCLC's FirstSearch to many of the same databases, for example, ERIC and PsycLit, and several others, such as Biological Abstracts and the OCLC database WorldCat. UIC-affiliated users may also search twenty two National Library of Medicine databases using Grateful Med software at library workstations or by loading the software, available at no charge to users, on office or home computers. Encyclopedia Britannica Online is offered on library workstations across the campus. Just as the survey was distributed two new databases were made available to the campus. The Beilstein database of organic chemical information, funded through a CIC initiative and searchable through a client/server system, was loaded on library workstations and offered as well, similar to Grateful Med, for office and home use. The MathSci database, the electronic version of Mathematical Reviews and other mathematical databases, was made available through the online catalog interface supported again by CIC collaborative efforts. Databases providing information in the health sciences and on government documents could be found on stand-alone workstations in campus libraries.

To summarize: campus library users have available a diverse array of constantly-changing electronic resources covering many disciplines and searchable on various interfaces from multiple locations. The library provides workshops, course-integrated instruction, and point-of-use training to all who wish it, but it is reasonable to assume that many users may be unaware of all that is offered or lack the skills needed to search suitable systems most effectively.

The survey also questioned faculty about their use of library resources and services, including the online catalog, other library catalogs searchable online, document delivery and interlibrary loan. As in the baseline survey, faculty were asked about how they used the library to obtain journal articles and whether they used other research libraries. In the time since the earlier survey Internet resources had proliferated so use of these was explored in another survey question. Faculty were also questioned about their participation in library-sponsored training on automated systems.

Findings

Science and engineering faculty reported use of many of the major indexing and abstracting services provided by the library in both paper and electronic formats. The most frequently used services by all the faculty appear to be the multi-disciplinary publications of the Institute for Scientific Information (ISI). 39% of the scientists and 22% of the engineers responding reported use of the library's paper Science Citation Index. A smaller percentage reported searching the electronic version of the Citation Index as a mediated online search or through an end-user account. (The UIC Library has not purchased the CD ROM version of the Citation Index, but some individuals reported use of the CD ROM in other area libraries.) ISI's Current Contents publications were also used across all departments surveyed. The locally-loaded electronic Current Contents files were used within the last year by 30% of the responding science faculty and 28% of the engineers. Paper versions of Current Contents were reported used about a third as much by both groups and are under consideration for cancellation by the library. UIC Science Library paper copies of Current Contents were formerly tattered and worn after a period on the shelf; they now sit in nearly pristine condition in order received by the Library. The only other multi-disciplinary source for which significant use was reported as the full-text Encyclopedia Britannica Online used by 13% of the chemists and engineers.

Subject specific bibliographic databases and their paper equivalents show patterns of use that correlate to specific disciplines. Faculty in the department of Biological Sciences are the heaviest users of Biological Abstracts; 30% report use of the paper version and 9% use electronic versions whether through OCLC's FirstSearch service or through mediated or end-user searching. Somewhat surprising is the fact that a larger percentage of the biologists (43%) use some form of Index Medicus, most as Grateful Med. The convenience of access to Grateful Med in the library or individual office may be a factor in its use; the user-friendly graphical interface may be another feature that makes this more popular with biologists than the service directed toward their own discipline. It is also possible that some biologists' research focuses on medical applications.

Chemists and chemical engineers are the heaviest users of Chemical Abstracts; 61% of the chemists use the paper version as do 20% of the chemical engineers. 33% of the chemists and 40% of the chemical engineers report either mediated or end-user searching of the Chemical Abstracts database. Nearly all the end-user searching done by UIC science faculty is through Chemical Abstracts' STN service and its favorably-priced Academic Plan. The Beilstein database of organic chemical information had just become available on a library workstation and to end-users as this survey was underway. Although only a small amount of promotion to faculty had been done at the time of the survey, 17% of the chemists and 9% of the chemical engineers reported searching Beilstein. We believe that this usage will grow quickly given the number of "early adopters" measured in this survey.

Scientists and engineers in all campus departments report use of the library's online catalog; in several departments 100% of the faculty used the online catalog with the least use reported by mechanical engineers (64%). The library's catalog interface also provides access to the catalogs of other CIC institutions and 77% of the scientists and 53% of the engineers reported using this feature. Faculty were asked which other libraries they used, and many reported use of specific CIC collections naming the University of Chicago and Northwestern, the closest CIC libraries, most frequently. We hypothesize that the ability to search these catalogs from campus or home facilitates planning of trips to these libraries. As a group, scientists and engineers appear to have assimilated use of online catalogs into their research behavior.

At the same time these faculty continue to make use of the library's paper journal collections and their own personal collections. 78% of the scientists and 54% of the engineers read journals in the library; larger percentages photocopy from the library for later reading at other locations. For materials not held locally by UIC or other area libraries, use of interlibrary loan is favored over document delivery from CARL Uncover to which the library provides network access. Electronic journals were reported used most frequently by physicists who obtain pre-prints from the Los Alamos e-prints archives and by mathematicians who use Internet-based electronic journals from the American Mathematical Society. Engineers reported no use of electronic journals.

Science and engineering faculty reported use of Internet resources with electronic mail being the most frequently-used network service. 87% of the scientists and 79% of the engineers use e-mail. The World Wide Web is another popular network application used by 79% of the scientists and 72% of the engineers. Sizable numbers also FTP, gopher and telnet; a preliminary analysis suggests discipline-dependent variations in use of these features and this will be the subject of further exploration. Use of listserves and discussion groups was reported less often by respondents as was use of the library's Web page which was under development at the time of the survey. As yet only a small percentage of faculty have personal home pages, 15% of the scientists and 20% of the engineers. We hypothesize this will change rapidly as many respondents expressed interest in receiving training in use of html and creation of Web pages. These respondents did not report much participation in training offered by the library. The most popular library training program appeared to be the class in the Internet, "Take the e-train", that was delivered to subscribers over the campus computer network as a series of e-mail "lessons".

The 1991 baseline survey documented the existence of a sizable group of faculty who lacked convenient connections to campus networks or who had no active computer account. Both these factors appear to have changed significantly in the intervening four years. In this survey only six respondents of the 150 total reported having no computer account. 79% of the respondents have computers in their offices or labs and many report available equipment in multiple locations. 49% are now connecting from home as well which represents almost a four-fold increase over the earlier survey.

Conclusions

This survey has provided details of use of automated information services and networked resources by a group of university faculty. Even though these individuals are well-established in their careers, tenured with over fifteen years average service, they appear to have adapted to an increasingly automated environment and have adopted new tools provided by the library and the Computer Center. We can speculate that the campus culture which encourages use of electronic communication has contributed to this as has a campus-wide initiative to upgrade the computing infrastructure. UIC faculty appear compare in their use of technology to those SUNY faculty studied by Adams and Bonk [1995]. The majority of UIC faculty report ready availability of equipment and network connections, and they are making use of network resources. Abels, Liebscher and Denman found that "Accessibility appears to be a key factor influencing the adoption of the electronic network." [1996, p. 154] This observation supports our data.

Our findings provide documentation of use of CIC-supported resources and suggest that this collaborative program has already enriched information access for faculty. The major effort to provide access to all CIC online catalogs is an important part of the CIC's Virtual Electronic Library (VEL) Project. The VEL Project employs Z39.50 protocol to build a technical infrastructure that allows users at any CIC institution to search other members' online catalogs through their own local catalog interface. Also under development is a complementary system that will permit patron-initiated requests from other CIC libraries in support of resource-sharing among consortium members. It appears that UIC faculty are making use of CIC resources even as systems are under development; we can expect that they may prove receptive to additional enhancements in the VEL effort to become a model for a national distributed research collection.

Analysis of data from this survey is continuing. We plan additional exploration of discipline-related differences in use of resources and technology and will be making further comparisons to data collected in the baseline survey and reported by other investigators. Our findings will also provide information to support decision-making on resource allocation and to suggest additional needs for tools and training.

References

Abels, Eileen G., Liebscher, Peter, and Denman, Daniel W., (February 1996) "Factors that Influence the Use of Electronic Networks by Science and Engineering Faculty at Small Institutions. Part I. Queries" Journal of the American Society for Information Science, 47, no. 2, 146 - 158.

Adams, Judith A. and Bonk, Sharon C. (March 1995) "Electronic Information Technologies and Resources: Use by University Faculty and Faculty Preferences for Related Library Services" College and Research Libraries, 56, no. 2, 119 - 131.

Curtis, Karen L., Weller, Ann C. and Hurd, Julie M. (October 1993) "Information Seeking Behavior: A Survey of Health Sciences Faculty Use of Indexes and Databases" Bulletin of the Medical Library Association, 81, no. 4. 383 - 392.

Hurd, Julie M., Weller, Ann C. and Curtis, Karen L. (1992) "Information Seeking Behavior of Faculty: Use of Indexes and Abstracts by Scientists and Engineers" Proceedings of the 55th Annual Meeting of the American Society for Information Science. Pittsburgh, PA, October 1991, pp. 136 - 143.

Some Thoughts About the Relationship Between Information and Understanding

Michael O. Luke
Atomic Energy of Canada Limited
Whiteshell Laboratories
Pinawa, Manitoba

That there is a relationship between information and understanding seems intuitively obvious. If we try to express this relationship mathematically, however, it soon becomes clear that the relationship is complex and mysterious. Knowing more about the connection, however, is important, not the least because we need more understanding as our world becomes faster paced and increasingly complex. The influence of increasing the amount of information, increasing the effectiveness of information mining tools and ways of organizing information to aid the cognitive process are briefly discussed.

Introduction: Why the Relationship Matters

Those of you who are expecting to learn something definitive about the relationship between information and understanding, or to find out the results of some project investigating it, will I hope be disappointed with this talk. My subject is indeed the relationship between information and understanding, but this is not something I can tackle in any standard way. I am afraid that you are going to have to do some of the work. What you will see from me is a great deal of ignorance - great dark stretches in the map of understanding the relationship - lit up faintly, here and there with some gleams of insight (I hope you will agree that there are some gleams).
So then what is the relationship between information and understanding? And why even

pose such a question? Is there really any value in considering the relationship in any detail? What am I doing even putting the two terms on the table and drawing an arrow from one to the other with a question mark after it? After all, I know only a little about information and understand not much about understanding. What can possibly justify my temerity in raising such an issue at this conference and taking up a half hour of your time dealing with it?

In my own defense, let me suggest that this is one of the most important questions that an organization like ours, contemplating at this conference, as we are, the digital future, possibly can deal with. We practice information science and call ourselves information scientists. As scientists we seek to understand - the thirst to comprehend, to know how things work is, after all, the passion that drives science, for it certainly can only be the thirst to know and not money or fame! We seek to know and we have been puzzling at it for a long time. In this century in particular we seem to have made enormous progress in understanding as our stockpiles of information have grown at a dizzying rate. As information scientists we are interested in information. How does it work?

Surely, then the question of the relationship between these two things, information and understanding, should be no stranger to us, no alien skulking unobtrusively in our midst, but a constant companion. So maybe I am the only person in this room who doesn't understand the relationship fully. I guess if so that would eminently explain why I am up here squirming. I'll tell you a little story before I embark upon the major theme. When I came actually to write this paper, having been e-mailed that the deadline was March 1, it was -40 degrees Celcius at the time, and the sun was coming through the window of my office flat, straight across the farm land, the black soil that grows the world's best durum wheat invisible beneath a heavy mantle of glaring, gleaming white. It was a cryogenic Manitoba winter morning, bright and brittle, and we consoled ourselves by saying, "but it's a dry cold" and thinking of the mosquitoes, black fly, and deer fly we didn't have right now. So putting together the presentation proposal seemed a good idea at the time!

And in fact I still believe it is. So what is the justification for raising the question in this forum? I think it is that we are not really interested in information just for its own sake, revelling merely in piling it up and moving it around. We recognize information as a means to an end. It is what it can do for us, what it has done for us, what we might do to make it do even more that drives us. And what it can do is to promote understanding and to help us acquire knowledge and give us the basis for action, for decisions, for planning and doing. Information is useful - it helps us understand and when we understand we can do useful things, like invent things, develop better strategies for business success, and we even feel better. I am richer not poorer in the face of the rising sun for understanding something about how it may have formed, for how it creates the heat and light that enable life, for knowing how long the light has been travelling before streaming through my window and I an enriched for knowing its relative insignificance in the overall scheme of things in the universe.

It isn't useful in any economic sense this particular knowledge but it helps clear up some of the mystery around me if not the brooding stuff in the background. Information above all is useful, helping education and commerce, powering art and science, driving technology and innovation before it, commerce and industry. Knowing more about the relationship should help us to exploit it more effectively.

And that's not all! My final argument is right now, at this of all times, when we seem to stand poised at the edge of a node of almost cataclysmic change, with not much help of controlling it, maybe thinking ourselves lucky if we can just survive as the storm of change breaks around us, we shall need understanding if we are to have any hope at all of avoiding the perils and steering as best we can for safer ground. Understanding then is a prescription above all for managing, if that's the word, or perhaps more realistically coping with the future, the next millennium and beyond.

I should say that some people have higher aspirations and little patience with lowly old understanding. They have loftier things in mind as the titles of their books attest: "The Wisdom of Teams", "Working Wisdom" and the "The Wisdom of Science", the latter considerably older than the others and not a bad book. Well, I have no quarrel with wisdom? If occasionaly one can stumble across it, recognize it for what it is, and use it, so much the better! I just think that realistically there is more pay dirt in the more prosaic relationship we will explore in this session.

Considering an Equation

Now one of the things that scientists do when contemplating relationships is to seek a law, typically a mathematical expression that links the phenomena in some way, a notational short hand for the force hiding in the action. $E=mc^2$ and that sort of thing. Rarely has something so potent been expressed so economically.

Here's another pithy and profound one, thanks to Edwin Hubble: $v=Hd$

Is there a law linking information and understanding, lurking in the cognosphere, teasing us with tantalizing glimpses? (Fig.1).

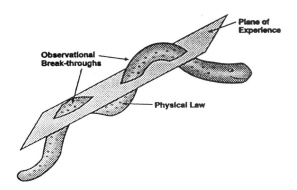

FIG.1. Tantalizing Glimpses of a Coy Law

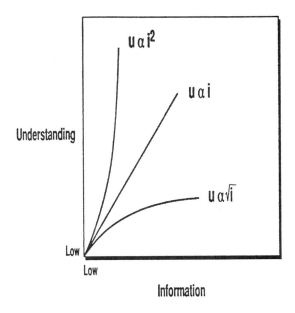

FIG. 2. Some Possible Mathematical Expressions

Perhaps. But why look for one? In answer, let me quote (I should caution you that I'll be doing quite a bit of name dropping in this presentation). David Chalmers (1995) said, "The ultimate goal of a theory of consciousness is a simple and elegant set of fundamental laws, analogous to the fundamental laws of physics.....What might the fundamental laws be? No one knows, but I don't mind speculating. I suggest that the primary psycho-physical laws may centrally involve the concept of information........Perhaps information, or at least some information, has two basic aspects: a physical one and an experiential one............It might even be that a theory of physics and a theory of consciousness could eventually be consolidated into a single grander theory of information." As far as I'm concerned that's all the justification I need to link anything mathematically!

But if we were to attempt to link information and understanding in such a mathematical harness, what might the equation look like? Some possibilities are shown in Fig. 2.

Does anyone think that any of these expressions might be true?

Does anyone already know the answer?

Of course we could draw an almost infinite number of possibilities. Maybe instead of any of these smooth lines a critical amount of information has to accumulate and then there is a sudden burst of understanding and then it goes flat for a while as information builds up again and then it jumps some more, like a condenser discharging episodically as charges accumulate relentlessly. In other words it might look like this. Or maybe even something like this!

Now if we think about the implications of some of these possibilities and then suppose that our very life depended on choosing the right expression, supposing that there is one, we would I am sure have no choice but to choose randomly, simply to gamble. I think this shows that looking at things like this is useful if for no other reason for showing us pretty clearly, as may have seemed obvious from the first, that the linkage between information and understanding is not one we understand very well.

Thus our instinct is that none of these equations can be right. Even so let's just write i over here on the left and put u up here on the right (Fig.3).

i   u

FIG. 3. Linking i and u.

Constructing a Galaxy Cruiser

What we're trying to do here is to bridge the gap between information and understanding. In fact what we want to do is to find a way of increasing the stock of u. What do we have to do to i to get more u? How do we cross that vast, dark gulf? It is as if information were the Milky Way and understanding, Andromeda, 1.1 million light years away, about 7 million trillion miles, whatever that is. Some measure of it is to consider the candle power - hundreds of billions of stars shining out brightly, hundreds of billions of fusion reactors blasting away at full throttle but so feeble with distance that the whole thing barely registers as a dim smudge on the darkest nights to the keenest eyes.

So how do we construct our galaxy cruiser? The first thing I'm going to do is to draw the information space as a kind of cylinder here. This is the information mine, the orebody and I think it is clear that making it bigger is one of the things we have to do to build our cruiser. Bigger rigs, more data, more complex experimental circuitry allow us to build better mathematical models for example that more closely approximate reality so that we can probe deeper into actual behaviour under all kinds of different conditions. The Hubble space telescope allows us to see deeper and clearer and so our understanding of such phenomena as star formation is improved. In terms of medical science, it is I think quite obvious that to manage serious and complex diseases like various forms of cancer and AIDS, one needs very deep and sometimes very broad understanding and that this can come only from a great deal of information. Similarly in the area of nuclear research, which is the mission of the laboratory where I work, a very sophisticated understanding of materials behaviour, or radionuclide transport over geological time periods, of complex thermodynamics is needed to develop and maintain the CANDU reactor program. Piling up

more information certainly is one of the methods we use to help us develop better understanding, to solve the puzzles we have set ourselves. But we of all people well know that there is more to it than simply adding to the information glut. Even the biggest computer system, with the most information stored in it, doesn't have a single clue after all. Just having it in short isn't nearly enough, although its a good start.

Information Objects

Here's where I introduce my collection of information objects. They are not really the sort of thing that computer people mean when they talk about information objects. Anyhow, let's pull them out of the bag and put them on the table. (Those who want to see what they are have to come to the presentation, or if that's in the past when you read this you can e-mail me).

How does information get into these objects in the first place and how is the information read? What do these things have in common? Anybody? Yes, the information is organized. It's not just piled up randomly, it's got structure, ordered concrete, steel, biological etc. expression. So if we go back to our equation we have to add another step that involves all the ways of organizing and retrieving information. We need to mine the information, to classify it and index it, to generate metadata about it, to organize it and reorganize it, and these are the mining tools for our orebody. We'll show this as another cylinder above the other one, reaching towards understanding. In this respect it is interesting to note the work of Swanson (1993, 1990) and Gordon and Linsay (1996) who have replicated and extended it, on undiscovered literature connections, which proves that just mining the existing information using existing tools can produce new understanding.

We have now reached the stage when we can draw something that roughly represents at least the first stages of how we can configure information so that it ultimately yields understanding. This is attempted in Fig. 4.

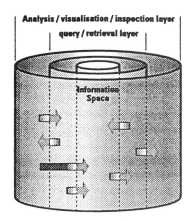

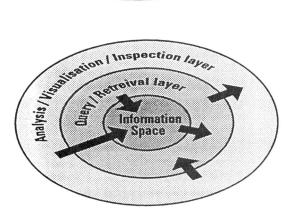

FIG. 4. Processing Information Towards Understanding

In this area it is clear that the challenge is on us to find better tools if the predictions of Bruce Shatz (1995) of "a billion machines with high-speed physical connections to the Net (containing) a trillion (one million each) logical objects" is to be of any value to us. Even if we had such tools, however, there would still be a gap. What can we do to fashion something to bridge it?

The Cognitive Black Box

Clifford Stoll (1995) said "There's a relationship between data, information, knowledge, understanding, and wisdom. Our networks are awash in data. A little of it's information. A smidgen of this shows up as knowledge. Combined with ideas, some of that is actually useful. Mix in experience, context, compassion, discipline, humour, tolerance, and humility, and

perhaps knowledge becomes wisdom. Minds think with ideas, not information."

Ideas! Minds! Thinking! The process clearly connects at some stage with the cognitive process. Now I really don't anything about cognitive stuff so I'll go back to our picture and just draw a black box here. Somehow understanding is one of the products and magically it seems that understanding also feeds back in some way into the information itself suggesting new arrangements, new organizations, so that it reaches out and influences information, opening new layers of it up, exposing new veins of thought, new wisps of connection, new insights, maybe just by providing the context for it.

The Need for Understanding-Technology

Is that the end of the story? Orebody, mining tools and cognition? I am curious as I stand here what it might be like thinking about such things a hundred years from now: 2096 instead of 1996. The budget is balanced, the debt has been retired, we've all got health care, and our pensions schemes are fully funded and substantial. We are gathering here to celebrate the maturity of the digital era, looking forward to the 22nd century. Perhaps some foolish fellow will be giving a virtual talk about the relationship between understanding and wisdom. If we were to index the current store of information and of understanding each at 1, how would we expect the stock to have changed by then? I think it is safe to say that we could express i as follows: i (2096) >>>> i (1996).

But what about u? Stuart Kauffman (1995) said, "We live on a self-organized sandpile that sheds avalanches down the critical slopes with each footstep. We have hardly a clue what will unfold." We need u badly and I think u needs some help. We can fiddle around in the first two parts of our expression, can work on the amount of i and the tools for organizing and retrieving it. But what about this last bit, the black box of the cognitive process. Kauffman (1995) said, "Evolution can have sampled only the tiniest reaches of "protein space"". I think similarly we can have barely tasted the full range of ideas that are open to us. This gives a germ of an idea. In a sense we need a kind of understanding-technology instead of information-technology here, ways of organizing the information we collect in precise combinations, 2-pieces long, 3-pieces long and so on, arranging and re-arranging them in precise spatial and contextual and conceptual orientations and stereoforms (cognoforms?), pinning them temporarily into fixed positions, pinning them transitionally into idea strings and complex templates and testing them against the filters and contextual templates of the mind. I can't draw a picture for you of what this looks like but I can kind of see it in my mind, see the faint impression of it at least, a ghostly image flickering there, dream or reality.

We feel in many ways the coming ignition of science - like a protostar that has been gravitationally contracting and is about to initiate fusion. Perhaps we are at the dawn of understanding, can feel its first faint vibrations, sense its gathering life. To study it is wise, it seems to me, for we shall surely need its help!

References

Chalmers, David J (1995). The Puzzle of Conscious Experience. *Scientific American*, *273*(6), 80-86.

Swanson, D. R. (1993). Intervening in the life-cycles of scientific knowledge. *Library Trends*, *41*(4), 606-631.

Swanson, D. R. (1990). Medial literature as a potential source of new knowledge. *Bulletin of the Medical Library Association. 78*(1)M 29-37.

Gordon, M.D, and Kindsay, R.K. (1996). Towards Discovery Support Systems: A Replication, Re-Examination, and Extension of Swanson's Work on Literature-Based Discovery of a Connection between Reynaud's and Fish Oil. *Journal of the American Society for Information Science, 47*(2), 116-128.

Stoll, Clifford (1995). Silicon Snake Oil. Second Thoughts on the Information Highway. Doubleday, New York.

Schatz, Bruce R. (1995). Information Analysis in the Net: The Interspace of the Twenty-First Century.
http://csl.ncsa.uiuc.edu/ISWWW/america21.html

Kauffman, Stuart A. (1995). At Home in the Universe: The Search for Laws of Self-Organization and Complexity. Oxford University Press, New York.

The Impact of Distance-Independent Education

Howard Besser and Maria Bonn
University of Michigan School of Information and Library Studies
Ann Arbor, Michigan

Distance-independent learning has the potential for a fundamental and beneficial transformation of higher education. By combining the best aspects of our present university and college system with the opportunities offered by recent developments in communications and information technology, distance-independent learning could lead to high quality, highly individualized instruction and the creation of intellectual communities that transcend the limitations of time and space.

This potential infuses the rhetoric of the proponents of distance-independent learning. But much of the rhetoric around distance education is misleading and fails to articulate the potential negative effects of widespread adoption of these new instructional delivery vehicles.

In this article the authors examine the motivations behind proponents of distance education, as well as the potential impact of distance learning upon instructors and students. They also raise questions as to curricular subjects and pedagogical styles that may not be appropriate for this type of instructional delivery.

The authors emphasize that the educational community must consider not just the benefits but the costs of relying on distance independent educational delivery. They must not see distance education as a universal innovation applicable to all types of instructional situations, but must carefully analyze the appropriateness of distance-independent learning to various types of instructional situations.

The full text of this article will appear in a special Perspectives issue of JASIS later this year.

Impact on Social Structures I: Information Policies

Alexandria Declaration of Principles and the GII

Ching-chih Chen
Simmons College
Boston, Massachusetts

Alexandria Declaration of Principles is derived from the NIT '94 Conference (7th International Conference on New Information Technology). A general consensus of agreement for development of the GII was created for many to use. It is intended to serve as a checklist to indentify issues that should not be overlooked and to state them without political implications.

This document has been utilized by many governmental and non-governmental agencies in both developed and developing countries as a baseline document, and deserves to be shared more with the ASIS members.

Big Brother is Watching You: The Panopticon in the Information Age

Julie M. Albright
University of Southern California
Los Angeles, CA

The notion of surveillance has always been both intriguing and frightening to people, perhaps because in Western societies privacy has been thought of as such a basic human right and need. The recent development of computer and other surveillance technologies, and their use as an ever-widening oculus for monitoring private citizens both within and outside of the workplace has been cause for alarm and increased vigilance among those protective of this notion of privacy. This paper will attempt to outline the parallels between Foucault's Panopticon and high tech surveillance systems by showing they too embody panoptic features: The automization of power, visibility of the subjects, and separation and categorization of individuals. Case studies of the effects of such surveillance on employees are included, as well as a discussion of the potential for control of private citizens outside the workplace. Specific suggestions are made for what policy makers can do to insure that surveillance technologies can and will not be used to create what Foucault has termed a "carceral society".

Assessing Impact from the Outset: Establishing a Strategic Research Program for a New Community-Based Information System

Linda Schamber
School of Library and Information Sciences
University of North Texas

Abstract

The most common approach to the development of community-based electronic information systems has been, "build it and they will come." Considering that many existing systems are still little more than prototypes, offering limited services, their popularity has been remarkable. However, with the sudden growth in public-access Internet provision and related information services, along with the availability of sophisticated search engines, it is likely that potential users' demands for quality of content and interactivity will have increased accordingly. Yet most community system developers have failed to study the needs and expectations of users early in the design process, when decisions are made on content, formats, and interface design. Researchers who have surveyed users of some of the first operational systems have concluded that system design might have benefited from studies conducted before the system was actually implemented. The results of such early studies can be used to identify appropriate information and resources for a specific community and to attract and retain new users. This paper describes a strategic research program intended to assess the impact of a particular community system from initial conceptualization through implementation and continuing development over the long term. Local responses to the program, along with the first phase of data collection, are described.

Introduction

Despite all that has been written and said about providing universal electronic access to information, only about three dozen community-based information systems are fully operational nationwide and fifty worldwide. Yet the concept is so popular, probably due in part to the recent widespread provision of Internet access, that at least 120 communities are currently planning their own systems (Schuler, 1995). Generally, communities have approached network development on the basis of "build it and they will come." Many developers are open about the problems they have encountered and strategic changes they have made. Although early and ongoing evaluation of such large-scale projects is of vital importance, very few developers have conducted market surveys prior to implementation or planned for ongoing usage studies after implementation.

This paper presents suggestions for a strategic research program intended to lay a foundation for long-term evaluation of a community system from design through implementation and continuing development. An appropriate place to begin such a program is with a community system in its earliest planning phase. The target for the research program described in this paper is DentonNet, a project recently approved by the City of Denton, TX, as part of a 15-year municipal improvement campaign. DentonNet will provide public access to a wide range of local information through libraries, kiosks, and home computers. These information sources will include government, education, public services, business, and entertainment. DentonNet is currently under active discussion and exploration by a citizen task force. This paper describes initial responses to the research program by the task force and the first phase of data collection.

Previous Research

Public-access electronic systems include community-based systems, networked public libraries, and various Internet-accessible digital libraries. Most operational community systems are only two or three years old and provide limited services, although many are rapidly gaining in sophistication.

The literature on public-access systems shows many to have been developed ad hoc, with no well-defined program for evaluation. Generally, previous evaluation studies have tended to neglect user needs analysis prior to design of the system, lack foresight in collecting baseline data for longitudinal evaluation, exclude system nonusers (potential users) as respondents, or employ methodologies that are not yet thoroughly adapted to this relatively new information setting.

Reports on evaluations of three of the most successful projects illustrate experiences that can be applied in developing a research program for a new community system. The most ambitious of community systems to date is the Blacksburg Electronic Village. A pilot study conducted just after the 1993 beta test of the system yielded findings on users' motivations for joining, present and future uses, problems, and positive/negative impacts. It also led to recommendations for improvements in data collection techniques, better coordination between researchers and project staff, and increased interdisciplinary research efforts (Patterson, Bishop, & Kavanaugh, 1993; Bishop, 1994).

A user study of a project providing Internet connectivity in rural public libraries in upstate New York was able to identify critical success factors, make recommendations for achieving social equity among various community members, and address politically sensitive budget issues. In the end, the authors stated, "the qualitative data were actually more valid and useful than the quantitative" (McClure, Babcock, Nelson, Polly, & Kankus, 1994, p. 150). Finally, a preliminary report on user needs evaluation for a digital library at UC Berkeley emphasized the importance of creating an evaluation research base early in the life cycle of the project. The author suggested combining and adapting a number of methodologies from user-centered system design research, usability testing, and library evaluation for a holistic evaluation strategy (Van House, 1995).

In addition to these formal research efforts, a plethora of less formal information and advice is widely available directly from World Wide Web sites, in mass media coverage, and through various organizations. One key source is the National Public Telecomputing Network (NPTN) founded by Tom Grundner, instigator of the 10-year-old Cleveland Free-Net (Schuler, 1995).

Research Strategy

When researchers are able to participate in ground-floor conceptualization and planning of a new system such as Denton's, they have an ideal opportunity to build and improve on the experiences of others through a strategic research program. In order to make a maximum contribution, they must consider both basic and applied research concerns and a group of broad research issues. On the basic side are academic interests in system use patterns, users' information-seeking behaviors, impacts of content and usage, methodologies, and research ethics. Applied or practical research concerns include funding, hardware and software selection, user support, interface design and system maintenance. Community concerns with social and ethical impacts and research policy questions are examples of broad issues that are important when conducting either type of research.

Basic Research Concerns

The largely unexplored territory of community systems is rich with ore for theoretical discovery. Because the provision of inexpensive or free electronic access to information is in its infancy, little is known about the uses, effectiveness, or impacts of electronic systems from the individual user's or the community's perspective. Nor is much known about human information-seeking behaviors (for example, the role of browsing) in this relatively uncontrolled environment. Further, researchers have only a rudimentary understanding and awareness of the psychological, social, and economic implications of this new form of mass communication and information exchange. Research in these areas suggests the study not only of system users and potential users, but also of a new group of electronic information providers--providers such as local business owners who are not necessarily knowledgeable in standards and practices of electronic delivery.

Clearly the choice of appropriate evaluation methodologies is still in question: in just the three projects cited above, the researchers employed at least 15 data collection techniques with varying success. For example, previous researchers have suggested that certain types of qualitative data, collected in addition to quantitative usage data, would have been able to contribute to a deeper understanding of the real psychological and social effects of a community system on individuals and the community as a whole. The potential impacts of community systems in sociological terms differ markedly from the individual impacts traditionally studied in information science (e.g., human-computer interactions, cognitive effects) and call for techniques, such as the focus groups used in all three projects, that have not been mainstream to the field. At both individual and community levels, the field currently lacks a full understanding of users' criteria for effectiveness or of techniques for measuring satisfaction, particularly for open-ended systems such as community systems. It seems evident that a strategic research plan should consider the best ways to adopt, adapt, and develop methodologies for studying electronic system use.

Finally, the academic research community is quite aware of potential logistical and ethical problems involved in the conduct of research. However, there appears to have been no concerted attempt in previous projects to develop a research policy that fully addresses the cooperative mission of a community system. Considering that Denton is home to two universities (some 36,000 students make up more than half its population), DentonNet is likely to be seen as a laboratory for basic and applied research by academics as well as for consumer studies by businesses. Without a research policy, at best, there is the potential for duplication of research efforts that may annoy and drive away some users, especially at the outset when the user pool is small. At worst, there is the potential for unscientific, invalid, and unethical conduct of studies. A research policy can be supported by procedures to coordinate research efforts, provide guidelines for novice researchers, and establish a common database for sharing research results.

Applied Research Concerns

On the applied research side are the practical concerns of system developers with funding, user and system support, hardware and software selection, information provider identification, interface design, and economic impact. Decisions to be made with regard to funding and technology are complicated, involving choices between private and public sources. With the recent passage of the new telecommunications law, telecommunication companies are eager to jump into local markets, and may initially offer information, design, and maintenance services at little or no cost. Large commercial firms may cut deals on hardware and software. Several private foundations offer grants for studying and expanding the role of information and interactive communications technology in society. Public funding sources at all levels offer grants for research and development, for example, through schools and libraries. The city itself, local businesses, public libraries, and universities are all potential sources of equipment, and system and user support. A large academic community such as Denton's can supply students and researchers to help develop and evaluate the system and provide some user support. The question is not whether a new community system can be funded, but how much support can be obtained, of what kind, from whom, and for how long. A research program can help this effort through the ability of the researchers to obtain grants and to collect information and data on comparable projects.

Another practical concern is system content and interface design. System developers have tended to provide whatever information is available, from whatever source, in order to establish prototype systems. This allows them to get immediate user feedback on quality of content and ease of use to help in improving system content and design. As the system improves, however, they often do not follow through with a series of surveys to assess users' satisfaction within a fuller range of criteria and interests. For example, users may be queried about their satisfaction with the information available, but not about the specificity of information they prefer or their uses of other media and information sources. Where surveys are employed, they may not reach all potential users of the system, some of whom may have special needs. A scientific approach to sampling and survey design can contribute, ultimately, to a better quality and more widely used system.

Broad Research Issues

Beyond individual users and uses are the community's concerns with social, political, and economic impacts. Information providers and potential providers within the city and the business community can provide valuable data about their expectations and knowledge with regard to content, presentation, and desired user responses. Surveys of information providers have rarely been conducted in the community system environment. Yet a comprehensive and systematic research plan may yield unexpected bonuses in innovative ideas for system design as well as provide a baseline for ongoing evaluation of community impacts. For example, instead of merely posting minutes from local public meetings, officials can seek citizen input online before or after the meetings or even conduct meetings online. Enhancing interactive features of the system may benefit the community by involving more citizens, including the disabled and homebound, in the political process and local economy.

In order to develop a comprehensive research program, researchers must address several broad concerns. One is what should be studied. Beyond the needs, goals, frustrations, and expectations of the individual user are those of potential users and information providers--all of whom contribute to the community as a whole. Another concern is when studies should be conducted. Research conducted at the earliest phase of the project may prevent mistakes and result in a truly beneficial user-oriented system that will continue to evolve over the long term. Finally issues such as equity of access, censorship, and privacy must be considered.

Community Orientation

Obviously, a research program must accommodate the unique features of the specific local community. Denton is a medium-size city of 66,000. Although to some extent it can be considered a bedroom community of Dallas and Fort Worth (about 30 miles away), Denton is unique in having a population that is almost evenly divided between university students and personnel and individuals involved in small businesses and agriculture. Of special interest to the task force is providing access to electronic information and communications for the non-university population, some of whom are uninformed about, uninterested in, or unable to afford hardware, software, or commercial access fees. One goal of the project is to provide public access from the public library and community computer literacy training center.

The concept of DentonNet was officially born in July 1995, when the city approved a 15-year municipal improvement plan that includes an electronic information system. DentonNet is intended to link local government offices, the University of North Texas, Texas Woman's University, and public schools and libraries. It will provide public access through libraries, kiosks, and home computers to a wide range of local information and probably to the Internet. High-speed transmission of data, voice, and video is possible via a citywide fiber optics network that has been implemented since 1990. The universities have offered support in the form of hardware, software, and technical support. Under the direction of the citizen task force appointed in September 1995, DentonNet is slated for design through 1996 and for implementation and testing through 1997.

Strategic Research Program

Although the research program was developed for DentonNet, it is hoped that it will also be of use to other communities developing comparable systems. The strategic research program is divided into three parts: before system implementation, during early implementation (within the first 12 to 24 months), and over the life of the system. It allows data collection for both basic and applied research interests.

Pre-implementation

1. Data collected before implementation of the system are intended to help guide initial design and form a baseline for continuing evaluation as the system evolves.

2. Collect local community data: Obtain existing data about Denton's population, telecommunication capabilities, businesses and industries.

3. Conduct community system national survey: Visit existing sites. Survey site owners.

4. Conduct focus groups with potential users: Ask small groups of individuals to evaluate an existing system and suggest features appropriate for the proposed system.

5. Survey potential users: Collect data, by mail and telephone, on demographics, media usage, computer skills and usage, and expectations for the system.

6. Survey potential information providers: Collect data, by mail and telephone, on professional goals and activities, media and computer usage, and expectations for the system.

Early Implementation

Data collected during early implementation are intended to elicit responses from users in order to improve system design and content and to gain new users. Some user data may be collected in computer training classes. Data from both users and information providers can be applied in publicity campaigns.

1. Survey actual users: Collect data, online, on demographics, media usage, computer skills and usage, and satisfaction with the system. Select some users to interview, observe directly, or participate in focus groups.

2. Survey actual information providers: Collect data, online, on demographics, media usage, computer skills and usage, and satisfaction with the system. Select some providers to interview or participate in focus groups.

3. Develop a long-term evaluation strategy. Draft it to parallel system development and have it approved by the city. Incorporate results of user and provider surveys and recommendations from comparable surveys elsewhere. Suggest methods for eliciting perceptions of the system and for evaluating impacts on individuals and the community at key intervals.

4. Develop a cooperative research policy. Develop policy and procedures for approval by the city. The policy will state a commitment to cooperation in interdisciplinary research so as avoid duplicating efforts and overtaxing user respondents (especially at the beginning when the user population is small).

Long-term Evaluation

Ongoing evaluation will help monitor success and constantly improve the system.

1. Implement long-term evaluation strategy. Conduct user surveys online, by mail, and interview. Update community demographic data periodically. Target nonuser populations for further study.

2. Implement cooperative research policy and procedures. Establish and maintain a public research database of research statistics and reports. Coordinate individual studies by business and academic researchers.

Initial Data Collection

Again, although much of the technical infrastructure for DentonNet is in place, the system has not yet been designed or implemented. Thus data collection is in the pre-implementation phase. As the five studies are conducted during spring and summer 1996, a great deal of data for system development will become available.

The first step, collection of local community data, has essentially been done. Most of the data are readily available through city offices and the chamber of commerce. The second step, a community system national survey, is underway. Results should be available for presentation at the ASIS meeting in May. The survey consists of three parts:

(a) Direct observation of community system sites: Collect data on managers, hardware and software, user support, fees, types of information and links, interactive features, and so forth. Compare to information and data about community systems elsewhere, available on sites such as those listed in Schuler (1995).

(b) Email survey of site managers: Collect responses on design and development, research, user and system support and maintenance, and funding. See appendix for questionnaire.

(c) Email or telephone survey of selected site managers: Conduct in-depth follow up to email survey.

Questions for the third step, focus groups with potential users, have been drafted and slated for pretests before the ASIS meeting in May. The fourth and fifth steps, surveys of potential users and information providers, will be undertaken during the summer. Local data will be studied for purposes of determining sample populations, and the surveys will be developed based in part on those used for projects such as the Blacksburg Electronic Village.

Portions of the pre-implementation research studies were developed in direct response to questions and suggestions from members of the DentonNet task force. The task force consists of about a dozen interested residents and representatives from city council, the universities, schools, libraries, and the local telephone company. Their immediate concern, for purposes of developing the prototype system, is in learning from the experiences of other community system developers, some of whom they have invited to make presentations. The researchers have responded by sharing literature on comparable community system. Some task force members also expressed confusion about the purpose and methods of user studies. The researchers made a presentation on the range of possible methods and types of data and offered to involve task force members as participants in the first user focus group pretest. Finally, the general interest in economic factors for the municipal improvement campaign contributed to the idea of surveying potential information providers.

Conclusion

Electronic community systems represent a relatively new information setting that can serve as a naturalistic laboratory for research. The purpose of the strategic research program is to lay a sound scientific foundation for long-term evaluation of a particular system, from initial design through implementation and continuing development. The program can benefit information scientists and practitioners in terms of potential research findings about individual and social effects; methodological development; and establishment of a common research database. It is hoped that, ultimately, the research effort will be able to contribute to the success of the target project, DentonNet, as a model facilitator of community interaction and cooperation.

At least two observations can be made on the success of this effort to date. One concerns the importance of working closely with community representatives in development of the research program. The response of task force members has been overwhelmingly positive. Not only have their comments been integral to the development of the program, but they have also been able to contribute to and share in the process of seeking and obtaining research grants. The other observation concerns the importance of assessing impact from the outset of system planning and development. This also takes into account the fact that a successful research program, like a successful system project, must continue to be dynamic and flexible in order to adapt to the user community's changing information needs over time.

Acknowledgments

This research project is supported in part by a grant from the University of North Texas. The author gratefully acknowledges the assistance of Judy Bateman doctoral candidate and Doug Bateman, Coordinator, UNT Campus Wide Information Systems.

References

Bishop, A. P. (1994). A pilot user study of the Blacksburg Electronic Village. Navigating the Networks: Proceedings of the ASIS Mid-Year Meeting, 18-38.

McClure, C. R., Babcock, W. C., Nelson, K.A., Polly, J., & Kankus, S. R. (1994). Connecting rural public libraries to the Internet: Project GAIN -- Global Access Information Network. Navigating the Networks: Proceedings of the ASIS Mid-Year Meeting, 142-160.

Patterson, S. J., Bishop, A., & Kavanaugh, A. (1993, Summer). Preliminary evaluation of the Blacksburg Electronic Village. Executive Summary. Available URL: Http://www.bev.net/project/research/summer93.html.

Schuler, D. (1995, December). Public space in cyberspace. Internet World, 89-95.

Van House, N. (1995). User needs assessment and evaluation for the UC Berkeley Electronic Environmental Library Project: A preliminary report. Digital Library '95 Proceedings, 71-76.

Appendix: Survey of Managers, Community Based Information Systems

Please accept our compliments on _____! We've looked it over and like what we see, especially the _____.

We're in Denton, TX, which is a medium-size university town just north of Dallas. Denton is planning to start its own system soon, and we're on the task force for the project. We're also university researchers who have volunteered to collect some information from various system developers as part of our contribution to the task force. Would you be willing to share some of your expertise with us? We have nine basic questions:

1. What advice can you offer to a city considering setting up a community system? (Could some problems be avoided by other system developers?)

2. From what types of domains do users access your system? (Schools or colleges? Commercial Internet providers? Other?)

3. What features of your system are most popular with users?

4. Would you say your system is successful? Please explain.

5. What individuals or groups were most active in getting your system started?

6. Have you conducted any market studies? If so, when? (Before or after implementation?)

7. How is your system funded? (City funds? Private funds? Donations? User fees?)

8. Who maintains your system? (Do one or more people maintain the system, update information, moderate content, etc. on a part-time or full-time basis?)

9. Who provides user and system support and maintenance and how is this funded? (Volunteer labor? Paid labor? Fees to a commercial service provider?)

That's it! As we said, we're collecting information on a number of community systems. Would you be willing to help us further? If so,

- May we contact you again, by email or telephone?

- Would you object to our sharing your responses (anonymously, if you prefer) with others in a research report?

- Would you be interested in receiving a report yourself?

Thank you for responding! Our task force has a lot of complicated decisions to make and we appreciate the help getting started.

Sincerely,

Linda Schamber, Ph.D.
Judy Bateman, Ph.D. candidate
University of North Texas
P.O. Box 13796, Denton, TX 76203
Members, DentonNet Task Force
schamber@lis.unt.edu or
bateman@lis.unt.edu
Voice 817-565-2445; Fax 817-565-3101

Impact on Social Structures II: Access and Control

The WebSCOUT Resource Discovery and Presentation System for the World-Wide Web

William Rosener
University of Tennessee
Knoxville, Tennessee

Locating valuable information quickly on the World-Wide Web (WWW) can be a very challenging and time-consuming task. The difficulties arise because the WWW is built upon a distributed hypertext environment where information is decentralized, dynamic, and diverse. As the information continues to grow at ever-increasing rates, it is becoming more and more difficult to locate relevant information. What is needed is a system which can easily and consistently retrieve specific information based on user-defined search criteria. Our approach which we are calling WebSCOUT will drastically eliminate the weaknesses of current approaches. This system will make finding valuable information less challenging by performing a more complete search and by taking an innovative approach to the presentation of the retrieved results.

Over the past few years numerous approaches on the WWW have been taken to simplify the problem of locating information, often called the resource discovery problem. Based on user-defined keywords, these approaches have been designed to quickly return a list of hopefully relevant Universal Resource Locators (URLs). The user is then forced to sequentially retrieve individual URLs and analyze them to determine their usefulness. Depending on a user's connection and the time of day, this approach can be a very time-consuming and frustrating task. Many impatient users will often fail to retrieve some of the more useful documents because they will terminate the retrieval process prematurely after having waited only a few seconds for a host to be contacted or a slow response. While these approaches appear to quickly return results, obtaining an array of information requires the user to exert a great deal of time and energy.

WebSCOUT will help to solve the resource discovery problem by 1) performing a more complete search, 2) creating a more interactive dialogue between the end user and the WWW, and 3) providing an innovative approach to the output presentation of the results. Rather than just consulting one database of indexed information, WebSCOUT can automatically query multiple databases simultaneously. Similarly, rather than just returning a list of URLS which maybe of possible interest, the user can dynamically interact with our system to help narrow the search process. Once this has been performed, the system will not only retrieve the desired information but will allow the user to specify how to format or extract excerpts from the documents. When viewed, the user will quickly be able to determine the relevance of a document. The hands-on time required by the user to retrieve information will become significantly less since there will be one long wait time - as compared to many short waits for the browser to return information. The user will no longer continuously see the message "connecting to host" or watch the file size slowly increase as the document is being transferred. Instead, after waiting a specified amount of time, the user will be presented with a complete and formatted collection of information. Using our approach, the user will be able to pursue other activities while the search process is going on in the background.

Let us compare our system with current approaches by using an analogy of finding a book in a library. In both our system and other approaches, the user first enters a list of user-defined keywords to base the search on. Once this has been performed, the differences become evident. In the other approaches, the results returned by the system tell the user where in the library a book can be found and, if lucky, a brief description of that book. When using these approaches, regardless of the search terms used, the same description is always returned. Our approach, on the other hand, not only finds the books but also retrieves them and places them on the user's desk. If that is not enough, it will even highlight and extract information from those books so that the user is not required to skim through each book to determine its relevance. One of the big advantages of this approach is that this system can be setup on a machine which has a fast connection to the Internet. Under this approach, the multiple retrieval process can be performed using a fast connection, and only the final formatted results will be delivered over a slow connection.

Supported Features

To simplify and alleviate the problems of locating valuable information on the Internet, WebSCOUT will support the following features:

1). Capable of pulling multiple links into a single document
Current WWW search systems prompt the user for search terms. Based on the entered terms, the user is presented with a list of URLs. The user must then retrieve each document separately and examine it to determine its usefulness. Again, depending on the connection type and the time of day, this can be a very time-consuming task. To overcome this shortcoming, WebSCOUT will be able to automatically gather the information from multiple URLs and place them into a single document. The user will not be forced to continously interact with the system. As the information is being retrieved, the user can even have the information filtered. For example, the keywords can be bold-faced so that they stand out when browsing through the results. Similarly, the user will be able to specify the number of lines of leading text returned before the matching string, as well as the number of lines of trailing text returned after the matching string.

At this point, someone may be questioning if users commonly terminate retrievals after a short wait, why would they tolerate one longer wait. The answer to this question involves an understanding of the difference between response time and turnaround time. Response time is the elapsed time from submitting a request to receiving the first response. While ideally response time should be 1 second or less, on the web users have been trained to endure response times as slow as 10 to 15 seconds. On the other hand, turnaround time is the elapsed time it takes for the entire job to complete. Typically there is no maximum time limit associated with turnaround time, since it varies directly with the task being performed. Our experience indicates that users will tolerate a longer search turnaround time if they feel the results returned are more complete and the relevance of the results can easily be determined.

2). Search multiple databases
Search engines such as WebCrawler often fail to warn users of the limited resources which their databases have indexed. Beginning users may be unaware of the many indexed databases that exist on the WWW. Even users who are aware of these numerous resources may not want the hassle associated with going from one search engine to the next.

To help users find the information they are looking for, WebSCOUT will allow the user-defined search terms to be submitted simultaneously to multiple search engines. Depending on response time and the number of documents that a given database has indexed, the default databases that WebSCOUT accesses will be able to dynamically change.

3). Begin searching from a specified location

The information behind most familiar indexed databases is gathered from robots which automatically navigate the Web and bring back information. Because the Internet is not completely connected, these robots may often fail to find valuable information. For these reasons, better search results might be obtained by starting at a location which is known to contain similar information rather than relying on indexed databases.

Another problem with relying on indexed databases is that most robots like the Webcrawler have adopted exploring algorithms which emphasize server coverage. These algorithms give higher priority to URLs on a different server and consequently may fail to retrieve additional information from a server which has already been represented. Hence, even databases containing thousands and thousands of documents, may have failed to index information which the user feels is important. To overcome this weakness, WebSCOUT will allow the user to perform either a depth-first or breath-first search starting from a specified location.

4). Perform domain restrictive searching

Many search results can be improved by limiting the domain of the URLs to be searched. For example, if someone was interested in finding local information about procedures and policy concerning the University of Tennessee, many non-relevant results might be returned when domain restrictions are not applied. However, by limiting the domain to URLs ending with "utk.edu" more relevant results might be returned. Without this feature, the user would have to determine which keywords (e.g. Tennessee, University, Knoxville, etc.) best limit the scope of the search without being so restrictive that some desired documents get filtered out.

Our system will also be capable of several types of document-specific searches. For example, only documents with a file size between 5k-10k should be examined. Similarly, more weight might be assigned to those documents which have fewer or more links on a page.

A more challenging feature to design would be an option which allows the user to specify the *types* of documents to be searched. As more individual and corporate homepages are being created, some of the best technical information is being hidden between high glossy advertisements and individual homepages. The ability to search documents that only contain a certain type of information could prove very helpful. With current standards, there is no simple solution to this question; however, any attempt to solve this problem should be investigated. The capability to limit searching by type or category is shared by many people as illustrated by the following quote.

"Most Web sites belong to individuals for whom the novelty of sharing favorite peeves with the entire planet proves just too appealing to resist. Wading through that soup in search of valuable information can wear down the most patient researcher. [4]"

A final issue which this proposal will address is how to more easily find information for a *second* time. This task is trivial if the user has bookmarked a site. However, often times, a user will mistakingly assume that they will not need to revisit the information they are currently viewing. Re-finding information can prove even more frustrating to the user, because they now know that the information exists and will relentlessly try to find it again. To help solve this problem, we will investigate how thumbnail images and color can be used to help provide "landmarks" when trying to relocate the same document twice. Altogether, the features outlined in this proposal should greatly help alleviate the challenging and time-consuming task of locating information on the Web.

Prototype of WebSCOUT

The WebSCOUT interface will be as simple and user-friendly as possible. The interface will be designed for today's users who quickly want to get started on a productive searching task without having to read pages of documentation and instructions before starting. Our research indicates most Web users are best motivated by self-initiated exploration and many of the people using search engines today are unfamiliar with boolean logic and quickly become intimidated by difficult options and features. All of these considerations will be taken into account when designing the WebSCOUT interface. Shown in Figure 1 is a prototype of the top level interface to our system.

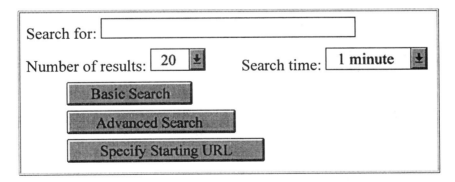

Figure 1

One of the most innovative features with this system is the approach taken towards presenting the retrieved results. Not only is the system capable of finding and retrieving information, but it will also be capable of formatting and extracting excerpts from the documents. Before examining the output presentation that our system will use, let us examine how other systems display results. The output shown in Figure 2 is returned when the keywords "medical ethics" are submitted to the Webcrawler search engine.

```
100 Medicine
090 Faculty of Medicine, Queensland Medical Education Centre
078 http://www.uihc.uiowa.edu/pubinfo/upcom.htm
069 About the JBE
066 MacLe an Center for Clinical Medical Ethics
064 Index
```

Figure 2

As shown by these results, Webcrawler displays the title of an article and a hyperlink to the document along with a relevant score normalized between 0 - 100. Other search engines provide similar feedback but may also display a brief abstract of the document. For example, the results shown in Figure 3 are returned when the keywords "medical ethics" are submitted to the InfoSeek search engine. Regardless of the search terms entered, the same description of the document is always returned. Often times, this description is simply the first few sentences of the document.

```
Clinical Ethics Fellowship Program
-- http://ccme-mac4.bsd.uchicago.edu/CCMEFellowship.html (Score: 56, Size: 3K)
The MacLean Center for Clinical Medical Ethics at the University of Chicago invites
applications for highly competitive positions in a unique year-long training program
that begins annually in July. The goal of this program is to prepare ...

Science Ethics Resources on the Net
-- http://www.chem.vt.edu/ethics/vinny/ethxonline.html (Score: 55, Size: 13K)
Compiled by Vince Hamner. Online Resources. The American Association for the
Advancement of Science (AAAS) is sponsoring Science magazine's first interactive
www project. Readers may comment on the June 23, 1995 Special News Report
```

Figure 3

As shown by these two examples, current search engines force the user to sequentially retrieve individual URLs and analyze them to determine their usefulness. Depending on a user's connection and the time of day, this approach can be a very time-consuming and frustrating task. To overcome this task, WebSCOUT will be able to automatically gather the information from multiple URLs at once and place them into a single document. The user will not be forced to continously interact with the system.

When the "Basic Search" option is selected from the top level interface shown in Figure 1, results similar to those shown in Figure 4 will be displayed. As shown in this figure, the user can select multiple documents that they wish to review. WebSCOUT will then retrieve all selected documents at once and format them so that the user can quickly detemine the usefulness of these documents.

```
☒ 100 The Sociology of Bioethics
☐ 090 Current Fellows of the MacLean Center for Clinical Medical Ethics
☐ 078 American College of Forensic Examiners
☒ 069 Evaluation of Bioethics
☐ 066 Bioethics and Medical Humanities Texts
```

Figure 4

User-defined options will allow a user to determine how the output is presented. For example, the user will be able to specify whether keywords should be in bold-face, blink, or regular text. Similarly, the user will be able to specify the number of lines of leading text returned before the matching string and the number of lines of trailing text returned after the matching string. Figure 5 shows an example of the output presentation from this system.

```
The Sociology of Bioethics
http://ccme-mac4.bsd.uchicago.edu/DPS/DPS15/Reviews.html
Why have bioethical questions become so important in the last two decades? What gave
rise to professional bioethics? How has this emergent profession organized itself and its
relation to existing medical occupations and institutions? By failing to explore these
questions, the authors tacitly accept medical definitions of "ethical" problems. After all,
the focus of ethnography is life in the wards. And yet, if we are to make sense of
bioethics, we must know how the tough, and the ordinary, medical decisions of the
1960's became the "ethical" questions of the 1990's.

Evaluation of Bioethics
http://wings.buffalo.edu/faculty/research/bioethics/eval.html
Everyone acknowledges that bioethics is an important component of patient care and it
should be taught to medical students, and post-graduate trainees. However, very little is
known about how best to evaluate them. Ethics is now regarded as an essential
component of medical education (Scott et al, 1991). By 1989, 43 of the 127 U.S.
medical schools had separate required courses on ethics while 100 covered medical
ethics within required courses (Miles et al, 1990).
```

Figure 5

As shown in Figure 5, by boldfacing the user-defined keywords and presenting text that contains these keywords it is easy to determine the relevance of a document. An interface similar to the one shown in Figure 6 will allow users to begin searching from a specified location. This feature will be especially helpful when trying to locate information from a websites that has not indexed their Web documents.

```
┌─────────────────────────────────────┐
│  Specify Starting URL                │
│  URL: ┌─────────────────────────┐    │
│       │ http://                 │    │
│       └─────────────────────────┘    │
│    ⊙ Depth first    ○ Breath first   │
└─────────────────────────────────────┘
```

Figure 6

Finally an interface similar to the one shown in Figure 7 will allow the user to perform domain restrictive searching and to specify which indexed databases should be searched. In this example, three databases will be searched but only documents residing on machines at the University of Tennessee (i.e., *.utk.edu*) will be returned.

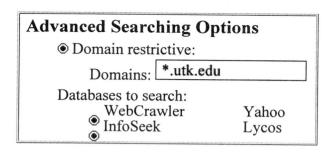

Figure 7

Conclusion

The WebSCOUT system will drastically help solve the resource discovery problem on the World-Wide Web. This system can accomplish this by performing a more complete search and providing a more innovative presentation of the information. The system will be capable of automatically retrieving documents on the Web in a presentation format in which the relevance can be quickly determined. The hands-on time required by the user to retrieve information will be significantly reduced. WebSCOUT will make locating valuable information on the Web a much less challenging and time-consuming task.

References

1. Anders Ardo, Franck Falcoz, Traugott Koch, Morten Nielsen, and Mogens Sandfoer, Improving Resource Discovery and Retrieval on the Internet, 1994. (http://www.ub2.lu.se/W4/summary.html)

2. Brian Pinkerton, Finding What People Want: Experiences with theWebCrawler, University of Washington, 1994. (http://info.webcrawler.com/signidr/Slide1.html)

3. David Glazer, Lessons Learned Implementing a Navigation Server for the Web, Verity, Inc., 1994.

4. David Habercom, Phyllis Moore, and Mary Hook, Did You Know, University of Tennessee, Knoxville, TN, 1994.

5. Michael F. Schwartz, C. Mic Bowman, Peter B. Danzig, Darren R. Hardy, and Udi Manber, The Harvest Information Discovery and Access System, 1994. *(http://www.ncsa.uiuc.edu/SDG/IT94/Proceedings/Searching/schwartz.harvest/schw*

6. Paul De Bra and R. D. J. Post, Searching for Arbitrary Information in the World Wide Web: the Fish-Search for Mosaic, 1994. *(http://www.win.tue.nl/win/cs/is/debra/wwwf94/article.html)*

7. Roy T. Fielding, Maintaining Distributed Hypertext Infostructures: Welcome to MOMspider's Web, First Internation World-Wide Web Conference, 1994. *(http://ezinfo.ethz.ch/general_info/www94/2nd_day_momspider.html)*

8. Theresa Kasper, *Untangling the Web - The role of text retrieval in a hypertext environment*, Information Dimensions, Inc., 1994.

Information Retrieval in Cyberspace

Dania Bilal Meghabghab
Instructional Technology Program, Valdosta State University
Valdosta, Georgia

George V. Meghabghab
Department of Mathematics and Computer Science, Valdosta State University
Valdosta, Georgia

Abstract

This paper reports research that examined the effectiveness of five World Wide Web search engines: Yahoo, WebCrawler, InfoSeek Guides, Excite, and Lycos. The study involved five queries which were searched in each of the engines in original and refined formats; totaling to fifty (50) searches. The queries varied in terms of broadness, specificity, and level of difficulty in finding Internet resources. We devised new measures to judge relevance and precision of the retrieved URLs. The results of the study revealed that Yahoo had the highest precision ratio for both original and refined queries. InfoSeek maintained a second place with respect to refined queries, and Lycos with respect to original queries. Query refinement resulted in a higher precision ratio. The addition of promising pages increased precision in all queries and across all engines.

Introduction and Background

The Internet has become one of the major revolutionary forces that is reshaping the way users, academicians, scientists, and businesses generate, seek, evaluate, and utilize information. In July 1995, the Internet had twenty to thirty million users (MIDS, 1995).

The World Wide Web, one of the most popular Internet servers, was introduced to the public in 1991 (December, 1991). Since then, the number of resources, Web traffic, and the number of users have increased at an astounding rate. As of January, 1996 there were over eighteen (18) million Uniform Resource Locators (URLs) available on the Web (Lycos, 1996), in addition to home pages, newsgroups, File Transfer Protocol sites, and other resources. The Web's "information explosion" is unique in the history of information science in terms of information storage, codification, distribution, management, access, effectiveness, and efficiency.

While access to Web resources has been facilitated by the introduction of search engines, the lack of an on-line thesaurus of controlled vocabulary results in relying on keyword as the single method of searching. In addition, the absence of a human intermediary (i.e., information professional) to assist users in refining their queries and identifying their true information need prior to accessing the engines leads to querying the engines poorly. Users find themselves drowning in superfluous, redundant, and erroneous information which is associated with low precision. As Randall (1995) states: "Finding what you want on the Internet can be even more frustrating and time consuming than finding a bagel in Biloxi."

This study examines the effectiveness of five World Wide Web search engines: Yahoo, WebCrawler, InfoSeek Guides, Excite, and Lycos and suggests methods for improving access to Web resources. For description of the engines, the reader is referred to (Lester; Bertland; Scoville; Randall; Notess, 1995; Tennant, 1996).

Studies that examined the effectiveness of search engines are sparse. Leighton (1995) assessed the performance of InfoSeek, Lycos, Webcrawler, and World Wide Web Worm (WWWWorm) on eight queries. He developed the following four measures for judging relevance and precision:

1. "Bad" or duplicate URLs to total Hit ratio within the top ten URLs returned.
2. Total number of good Hits not counting duplicates.
3. Ratio of good Hits to the total number of retrieved URLs not counting duplicates; also called total precision.
4. Ratio for good Hits to the total number of retrieved URLs in the top ten returned URLs not counting duplicates; also called top ten precision.

Leighton found that the first three measures were irrelevant statistically and that only measure four had statistical significance for analyzing the results. His study revealed that WWWWorm had a high number of "bad" or duplicate URLs followed by WebCrawler, InfoSeek, and Lycos. Lycos maintained the highest relevant hits without duplicates; InfoSeek was rated second, Webcrawler third, and WWWWorm fourth. The study also showed that InfoSeek held the highest precision ratio without duplicates; Lycos came in second, WWWWorm third, and Webcrawler fourth. An ANOVA analysis of the top ten precision ratio of the results without duplicates uncovered that Lycos endured the highest ratio followed by InfoSeek, WWWWorm, and Webcrawler. Both Lycos and InfoSeek were found to be the best index services. A two-way analysis of variance (ANOVA) indicated that the significant difference in the results lied in the search engines not in the queries. Leighton's study was criticized by his major professor for not being statistically thorough.

Winship (1995) examined indexing techniques and search features of WWWWorms, WebCrawler, Lycos, Harvest, Galaxy, and Yahoo. He tested the engines on database content, the search interface, search features, output of results and performance, using three queries. Although the results of the queries were reported, the relevance and precision ratios are not indicated.

Berns (1995) evaluated the performance of WWWWorm, InfoSeek, Webcrawler, JumpStation, and Lycos for classroom use. Using three queries, the researcher found that InfoSeek was the most valuable source since it retrieved one-hundred percent (100%) relevant hits without duplicates. The results of this study cannot be generalized because of the limited number of searches performed.

Randall (1995) studied fourteen engines, including those providing meta-searches (i.e., All-in-One Search-Page). The engines' performance was judged on their descriptions, usability, and effectiveness. The study revealed that the most thorough engines were InfoSeek, WebCrawler, and WWWWorm followed by Lycos and OpenText. The number of queries used in this study was not stated; the exact search statements employed were not mentioned; and the research methodology was unclear.

These studies overlooked query refinement as a criteria for judging the engines' performance. Query refinement is essential for increasing precision in large databases, such as the World Wide Web.

Method

This experimental, preliminary study comprises Yahoo, WebCrawler, InfoSeek Guides, Excite, and Lycos which are available for access via the World Wide Web and its Netscape browser. The study was designed in November 1995 and the experiment started in January 1996.

Five queries were searched in both original and refined formats in each engine; totaling to fifty (50) searches. The queries varied in terms of broadness, specificity, and level of complexity in finding resources (Table 1).

TABLE 1. Queries.

Query	Type	Information Sought
1. Science experiments	broad, complex	science projects for children and or teachers to use at home or in the classroom
2. CIA World Factbook	specific, average	the publication itself, 1995 edition.
3. Search engine	average, average	seeking studies and other publications about the effectiveness or performance evaluation of WWW search engines
4. Dania Meghabghab	specific, easy	Dania B. Meghabghab's home page
5. Lesson plans	broad, complex	lesson plans for teaching English literature, composition, grammar, etc.

Search Procedures

Each of the five queries completed was searched in each of the engines using keywords. Each query statement was refined in a second search using selected features provided by the engines (e.g., Boolean operators, etc.). Query refinement was conducted to provide more specificity to search statements and, hence, increase precision. The URLs retrieved as a result of both original and refined searches were examined, analyzed, and evaluated. Although we explored the engines' search features, we did not employ them in full because we aimed to uncover the kind of experiences end-users might encounter during searching. To obtain a user perspective on searching the engines, we asked ten graduate students enrolled in "Information Sources and Services" class, and who possessed some experience in searching the engines, to select keywords and assist with formulating the query statements. All searches were conducted by the researchers.

The formulation of the query statements varied based on the search features employed in each engine. We used the "good search" and "matching all terms" features in Lycos, for example, in the original searches. In the refined searches, we included new terms, applied the "good search", and selected the AND feature. Considering the size of Lycos database, we considered a "good search" as equivalent to a standard search in other engines. We applied both the concept and the keyword searching in Excite, and employed the plus sign (+) in InfoSeek Guides to indicate the operator AND.

Judging Relevance

Relevance was judged on the following criteria: Presence of keywords in the headings and/or abstracts, as provided; confidence level, as applicable; and relevance of URLs' contents to the information need. Each URL retrieved was tested for availability and browsed thoroughly.

Measuring Relevance

We adapted measure four that was developed by Leighton (1995), but we made minor changes. We added relevant promising pages to the total precision ratio and used the top twenty-five URLs returned, instead of the top ten for examination. Therefore, our total number of relevant hits (RE) is determined by the number of relevant hits (RH), plus (+) the number of promising pages (PP). Promising pages are those containing relevant resources which were found through URLs links. The number of total relevant hits is illustrated as:

$$RE = RH + PP$$

Measuring Recall

Recall is defined as the number of relevant documents retrieved divided by the number of relevant documents (Harter, 1996). Since it is impossible to determine the total number of relevant documents on the Web, we relied on precision to measure the search engines' performance.

Measuring Retrieved URLs

The total number of URLs retrieved (RT) is assessed as the top twenty-five URLs returned (T), as applicable, minus (-) the number of duplicate URLs (DUP), minus (-) the number of non-clickable sites (NS), minus (-) the number of mirror sites, plus (+) promising pages (PP). This is shown as:

$$RT = T - DUP - NS - MS + PP$$

Measuring Precision

Precision is defined as the number of relevant documents retrieved divided by the number of retrieved documents (Harter, 1996). This formula suits measuring precision in on-line databases. In applying it to Web documents, however, we had to omit duplicate URLs, mirror sites, and non-clickable URLs. Therefore, our precision is defined as the total number of relevant hits (RE) divided by the total number of URLs retrieved (RT), as seen below:

$$P = \frac{RE}{RT}$$

Findings

The results of the searches indicated that the precision ratio of the URLs retrieved without and with promising pages varied. The ratio of Query 1 was higher in the refined searches than in the original searches (Table 2).

TABLE 2. Query 1. Science Experiments.

Engine	Original and Refined Queries	Useful/Relevant Hits + Weight	Duplicate URLs	Non-clickable Sites	Mirror Sites	Precision without PP	Promising Pages	Precision with PP
WebCrawler (25 out of 1,946)	Science experiments	1 (0.54)	9	3	3	1/10 (0.10)	2	3/12 (0.25)
Webcrawler (25 out of 175)	Science experiments and kids	5 (0.76; 0.24; 0.13; 0.09; 0.09)	6	0	0	5/19 (0.26)	4	9/23 (0.39)
Yahoo (25 out of 42)	Science experiments	2 (N/A)	0	0	0	2/25 (0.08)	0	2/25 (0.08)
Yahoo (2 out of 2)	Science experiments and kids	1 (N/A)	2	0	0	1/2 (1.0)	0	1/2 (1.0)
InfoSeek (25 out of 100)	Science experiments	1 (0.50)	0	0	0	1/25 (0.04)	0	1/25 (0.04)
InfoSeek (25 out of 100)	Science experiments +kids	12 (0.51-0.50)	0	1	0	12/24 (0.50)	0	12/24 (0.50)
Excite (concept search); 25 out of N/A)*	Science experiments	0	0	0	0	0/25 (0)	0	0/25 (0)
Excite (concept search); 25 out of N/A)	Science experiments and kids	7 (0.86-0.83)	0	0	0	7/19 (0.28)	6	13/31 (0.42)
LYCOS (good search; match two terms); 25 out of 59)	Science experiments	5 (1.0: adj 0.9; 0.89 : adj 0.7; 0.59;0.52-0.51)	7	0	0	5/18 (0.28)	0	5/18 (0.28)
LYCOS (good search; match all terms with AND); 4 out of 4)	Science experiments kids	2 (1.0; 0.98)	0	0	0	2/4 (0.50)	0	2/4 (0.50)

*Excite does not provide the total number of URLs returned. It submits ten URLs at a time.
+PP=Promising pages.

In this original query, which we characterized as broad and complex, Lycos provided the highest precision ratio (28%) without and with promising pages followed by WebCrawler (10%),

Yahoo (8%), and InfoSeek Guides (4%); Excite retrieved zero returns. In the refined query, both Lycos and InfoSeek Guides had the same precision ratio, (50%), followed by Excite (28%), and WebCrawler (26%). The refined query with promising pages indicated a higher ratio than without them in both WebCrawler (39%) and Excite (42%). The ratio in the other engines remained the same.

The total precision ratio of the original Query 1 without promising pages was (5%) compared to (13%) with promising pages. A significantly higher precision ratio was obtained in the refined query without promising pages (50%), and a slightly higher (56%) with promising pages. The refined queries resulted in a higher precision ratio without and with promising pages than the original queries.

TABLE 3. Query 2. CIA World Factbook.

Engine	Original and Refined Query	Useful/Relevant Hits + Weight	Duplicate URLs	Non-clickable Sites	Mirror Sites	Precision without PP	Promising Pages	Precision with PP
WebCrawler (25 out of 460)	CIA World Factbook	1 (0.45)	2	2	16	1/5 (0.20)	17	18/23 (0.82)
Webcrawler (25 out of 175)	CIA World Factbook 1995	1 (0.45)	2	2	3	1/18 (0.06)	0	1/18 (0.06)
Yahoo (13 out of 13)	CIA World Factbook	7	6	0	0	7/7 (1.0)	0	7/7 (1.0)
Yahoo (2 out of 2)	CIA World Factbook 1995	1	1	0	0	1/1 (1.0)	0	1/1 (1.0)
InfoSeek (25 out of 100)	CIA World Factbook	6 (0.57-0.55)	0	0	0	6/25 (0.24)	0	6/25 (0.24)
Info Seek (25 out of 100)	CIA World Factbook 1995	3(0.53-0.52)	0	0	0	3/25 (0.12)	0	3/25 (0.12)
Excite (concept search; 25 out of N/A)	CIA World Factbook	4 (90-89%)	0	0	17	4/8 (0.50)	0	4/8 (0.50)
Excite (concept search; 25 out of N/A)	CIA World Factbook 1995	2 (95-94%)	0	0	8	2/17 (0.12)	0	2/17 (0.12)
LYCOS (good search; match two terms; 25 out of 15,126)	CIA World Factbook	1 (0.86)	8	0	0	1/17 (0.06)	13	14/30 (0.47)
LYCOS (good search; match all terms with AND; 25 out of 15,126)	1995 CIA World Factbook	1 (0.86)	8	0	0	1/17 (0.06)	13	14/30 (0.47)

The specific title search in Query 2, (i.e., CIA World Factbook) showed that Yahoo resulted in the highest precision ratio for the original query without promising pages (100%) followed by Excite (50%), InfoSeek Guides (24%), WebCrawler (20%), and Lycos (6%). Promising pages increased the precision ratio in the original query from (20%) to (82%) in WebCrawler, and from (47%) to (96%) in Lycos; the ratio remained the same in the other engines (Table 3).

Surprisingly, when we added the date of publication to refine the original Query 2, the precision ratio decreased from (50%) to (12%) in InfoSeek Guides, and from (20%) to (6%) in WebCrawler. Lycos maintained its low ratio, whereas Yahoo sustained its high ratio. Search refinement with promising pages showed an increase from (6%) to (47%) in Lycos. The ratio remained unchanged in Yahoo (100%), InfoSeek Guides (12%), Excite (12%), and in WebCrawler (6%).

The total precision ratio of the original Query 2 without promising pages was (40%) compared to (60%) with promising pages. The total precision ratio of the refined Query 2 without and with promising pages, however, was (27%) compared to (35%) in the original query.

The results of Query 2 revealed that Yahoo was the most effective is engine for searching topics with a publication date. Yahoo limited the search results of this Query to the year 1995, whereas other engines added the date as a new search term. The latter caused the return of more but less precise URLs. One may infer that a specific title search may not result in a high precision.

In Query 3, (Table 4), we sought studies or other publications about the effectiveness or performance evaluation of the World Wide Web search engines. The precision ratio of this Query in both the original and refined formats without and with promising pages was very low. The precision ratio of the original query without promising pages submitted by Excite was (10%), WebCrawler (5%), InfoSeek Guides (4%), and Lycos (4%); Yahoo returned zero URLs. Promising pages did not increase the precision ratio in the original query. Query refinement without and with promising pages generated zero URLs in Yahoo, WebCrawler, and Lycos. The ratio remained unchanged in InfoSeek Guides in the refined Query without promising pages, but increased from (4%) to (17%) with promising pages. The ratio in Excite without promising pages increased from (0%) to (10%) and from (0%) to (25%) with promising pages. Both WebCrawler and Lycos returned zero URLs for the refined query without and with promising pages for which relevant URLs were retrieved in the original query.

The total precision ratio of the original Query 3 without promising pages was (0.026) and (0.044) with promising pages. The total precision ratio for the refined query without promising pages remained low (0.028), but increased slightly with promising pages (0.084).

To perform a search for which we knew URLs existed, we employed a specific query; we assumed that all engines would return a high precision. We searched the home page of the first researcher (i.e., Dania Meghabghab), (Query 4, Table 5). Both Yahoo and Lycos retrieved (100%) precise URLs in the original query without and with promising pages. Excite returned (6%), InfoSeek Guides (4%), and WebCrawler (0%). In the refined searches, which included the first letter of the researcher's first and last name in upper cases, Yahoo maintained the same precision ratio, (100%), while InfoSeek Guides ratio increased from (4%) to (100%) in the refined query. The ratio in Excite remained at (6%), whereas it decreased in Lycos from (100%) to (8%). It is noteworthy that in both the original and the refined searches (i.e., dania meghabghab; Dania Meghabghab), the two terms were adjacent one hundred percent (100%) in Lycos but resulted in different precision ratios. The total precision ratio of both the original and the refined query without and with promising pages remained at 42%.

TABLE 4. Query 3. Search Engine.

Engine	Original and Refined Query	Useful/Relevant Hits + Weight	Duplicate URLs	Non-clickable Sites	Mirror Sites	Precision without PP	Promising Pages	Precision with PP
WebCrawler (25 out of 7721)	search engine	1 (0.15)	3	2	0	1/20 (0.05)	1	2/21 (0.10)
Webcrawler (25 out of 235)	search engine evaluation	0	0	0	0	0 (0)	0	0 (0)
Yahoo (25 out of 606)	search engine	0	1	0	0	0 (0)	0	0 (0)
Yahoo (5 out of 5)	search engine evaluation	0	0	0	0	0 (0)	0	0 (0)
InfoSeek (25 out of 100)	search engine	1 (0.51)	0	0	0	1/25 (0.04)	1	2/26 (0.08)
Info Seek (25 out of 100)	search engine + evaluation	1 (0.50)	0	0	0	1/25 (0.04)	4	5/29 0.17)
Excite (keyword search; 25 out of N/A)	search engine	0	2	0	0	0 (0)	0	0 (0)
Excite (keyword search; 25 out of N/A)	search engine evaluation	2 (88-87%)	0	1	4	2/20 (0.10)	4	6/24 (0.25)
LYCOS (good search; match two terms; 25 out of 492)	search engine	1 (.91; adj 1.0)	1	0	0	1/24 (0.04)	0	1/24 (0.04)
LYCOS (good search; match all terms with AND; 0 out of 0)	search engine evaluation	0	0	0	0	0 (0)	0	0 (0)

Table 6 exhibits the results of Query 5 dealing with lesson plans. We characterized this query as broad and complex and we sought to find resources about lesson plans dealing with teaching English literature or composition or grammar. The results of this search revealed that Yahoo had the highest precision ratio (35%) without promising pages followed by Lycos (29%), InfoSeek Guides and Excite (28%), equally; and WebCrawler (17%). The addition of promising pages to the original query resulted in a higher precision ratio in all engines; it increased to (62%) in Yahoo, (75%) in Lycos and InfoSeek Guides, equally; (68%) in Excite, and (51%) in WebCrawler.

The refined searches without promising pages showed an increase in precision from (28%) to (32%) in InfoSeek Guides and from (17%) to (24%) in WebCrawler. The precision ratio of Excite, Yahoo, and Lycos decreased, however, from (28%) to (16%); (35%) to (9%); and (29%) to (0%), respectively.

In all engines, the refined query with promising pages resulted in a higher precision ratio than without them, except in Lycos. The ratio increased from (32%) to (79%) in InfoSeek Guides, from (9%) to (65%) in Yahoo, from (24%) to (60%) in WebCrawler, and from (16%) to (40%) in

Excite. In comparing the precision ratio of the refined query to that of the original query, including promising pages, we found that it rose from in (75%) to (79%) in InfoSeek Guides, from (62%) to (65%) in Yahoo, and from (51%) to (60%) in WebCrawler. Surprisingly, the precision ratio dropped from (75%) in the original query to (0%) in the refined query in Lycos and from (68%) to (40%) in Excite.

TABLE 5. Query 4. Dania Meghabghab

Engine	Original and Refined Query	Useful/Relevant Hits + Weight	Duplicate URLs	Non-clickable Sites	Mirror Sites	Precision without PP	Promising Pages	Precision with PP
WebCrawler (zero out of zero)	dania meghabghab	0	0	0	0	0 (0)	0	0 (0)
Webcrawler (zero out of zero	Dania Meghabghab	0	0	0	0	0 (0)	0	0 (0)
Yahoo (2 out of 2)	dania meghabghab	1	0	0	1	1/1 (1.0)	0	1/1 (1.0)
Yahoo (2 out of 2)	Dania Meghabghab	1	0	0	0	1/1 (1.0)	0	1/1 (1.0)
InfoSeek (25 out of 91)	dania meghabghab	1 (0.77)	1	0	1	1/23 (0.04)	0	1/23 (0.04)
Info Seek (1 out of 1)	Dania Meghabghab	1 (0.86)	0	0	0	1/1 (1.0)	0	1/1 (1.0)
Excite (keyword search; 16 out of 16)	dania meghabghab	1 (72%)	0	0	0	1/16 (0.06)	0	1/16 (0.06)
Excite (keyword search; 16 out of 16)	Dania Meghabghab; Dania and Meghabghab	1 (72%)	0	0	0	1/16 (0.06)	0	1/16 (0.06)
LYCOS (good search; match two terms; 1 out of 1)	dania meghabghab	1 (1.0; adj. 1.0)	0	0	0	1/1 (1.0)	1	2/2 (1.0)
LYCOS (good search; match all terms with AND; 25 out of 25)	Dania Meghabghab	1 (1.0; adj. 1.0)	1	0	0	1/24 (0.04)	1	2/25 (0.08)

The total precision ratio of the original Query 5 without promising pages was (27%) compared to (22%) in the refined query. The ratio of the original query with promising pages was (66%) compared to (48%) in the refined query. The original query resulted in a higher precision ratio than the refined query.

In summary, this study uncovered that Yahoo had the highest precision ratio for all original and refined queries without and with promising pages. In the original queries, Lycos scored second, WebCrawler third, and Excite and InfoSeek fourth. In the refined queries, however, InfoSeek Guides was rated second, Excite third, WebCrawler fourth, and Lycos fifth.

TABLE 6. Query 5. Lesson Plans.

Engine	Original and Refined Query	Useful/Relevant Hits weight	Duplicate URLs	Non-clickable Sites	Mirror Sites	Precision without PP	Promising Pages	Precision with PP
WebCrawler (25 out of 625)	lesson plans	4 (0.13-0.09)	2	0	0	4/23 (0.17)	16	20/39 (0.51)
Webcrawler (25 out of 73)	lesson plans and teaching and english	6 (1.0-0.03)	0	0	0	6/25 (0.24)	23	29/48 (0.60)
Yahoo (25 out of 29)	lesson plans	8	2	0	0	8/23 (0.35)	16	24/39 (0.62)
Yahoo (25 out of 645)	lesson plans and teaching and english	2	3	0	0	2/22 (0.09)	35	37/59 (0.65)
InfoSeek (25 out of 100)	lesson plans	7 (0.55-0.52)	0	0	0	7/25 (0.28)	46	53/71 (0.75)
InfoSeek (25 out of 100)	lesson plans +teaching +english	8 (0.52-0.50)	0	0	0	8/25 (0.32)	56	64/81 (0.79)
Excite (keyword search; 25 out of N/A)	lesson plans	7 (86-82%)	0	0	0	7/25 (0.28)	32	39/57 (0.68)
Excite (keyword search; 25 out of N/A)	lesson plans and teaching and english	4 (95-92%)	0	0	0	4/25 (0.16)	10	14/35 (0.40)
LYCOS (good search; match two terms; 25 out of 130)	lesson plans	7 (0.96-0.77)	1	0	0	7/24 (0.29)	45	52/69 (0.75)
LYCOS (good search; match all terms with AND;0 out of 0)	lesson plans and teaching and english	0	0	0	0	0 (0)	0	0 (0)

The total precision ratio of the original query without promising pages was (27%) compared to (22%) in the refined query. The ratio of the original query with promising pages was (66%)

compared to (48%) in the refined query. The original query resulted in a higher precision ratio than the refined query.

In summary, this study uncovered that Yahoo had the highest precision ratio for all original and refined queries without and with promising pages. In the original queries, Lycos came in second, WebCrawler third, and Excite and InfoSeek fourth. In the refined queries, however, InfoSeek Guides was rated second, Excite third, WebCrawler fourth, and Lycos fifth.

Discussion

This preliminary study shed light on the complexity of searching a high volume of data through the World Wide Web selected engines. It revealed that promising pages increased the precision ratio in all engines, and indicated that Yahoo and InfoSeek Guides provided the best results for the refined queries. Query refinement did increase the precision ratio, but not as much as we hoped it would. This can be attributed to the ineffectiveness of boolean implementation by Lycos, WebCrawler, and Excite.

Precision remains the most critical problem in the engines' performance. Despite that a higher precision ratio was obtained by refining the queries and adding promising pages, Yahoo was the only engine that attained a precision ratio for all queries above fifty percent (50%). Lycos had a precision ratio of fifty-one percent (51%) but with respect to the original queries only, including promising pages. The lowest precision ratio among all engines was (4%). These ratios are displayed in Figures 1 and 2.

The confidence level (i.e., probability of relevance) applied to the URLs retrieved by selected engines was not as indicative of relevance as we thought. We found URLs with confidence level of (50%) or lower, for example, to be more relevant to the information need than URLs with higher levels. In addition, the presence or absence of relevant keywords or terms in URLs headings did not always designate relevance. In Query 2 (i.e., CIA World Factbook), for example, we located relevant links under the heading Recommended Links. We also found irrelevant hits under URLs headings that contained the appropriate keywords or terms. Similarly, the adjacency score employed by Lycos did not result in precision, in many cases.

The application of the boolean operator AND in Lycos and Excite increased rather than decreased the number of URLs retrieved and resulted in a lower instead of a higher precision ratio. This is attributed to the ineffectiveness of the implementation of the boolean operator AND by these engines.

Methods for Improving Access

Because this study is preliminary, we suggest basic methods for improving the access to these engines. These methods involve the efforts of both the engine service providers and the end-users. We believe that the engines' service providers need to include on-line thesaurus to assist users in selecting appropriate terms. To alleviate the "information overload" problem, we suggest that redundant URLs be made an option for users to add to or delete from their search results.

Improving the implementation of boolean operators, providing some type of query negotiation, and including optional on-line tutorials are additional areas for consideration. We recommend that end-users read the instructions or search options provided by the engines, identify their information need prior to searching the engines, use the features provided by the engines, and examine the URLs retrieved thoroughly.

Concluding Remarks

This study revealed that Yahoo was the most effective engine. Earlier studies which excluded Yahoo showed that Lycos and InfoSeek were the best indexing services (Leighton, 1995), and that InfoSeek was the most thorough engine (Randall, 1995).

Precision was found to be the most critical problem of the search engines. Only Yahoo provided the highest precision ratio for the original and refined queries without and with promising pages; the lowest ratio it attained was (49%) and the highest ratio was (73%). Lycos's ratio was (51%) for original queries with promising pages only. The ratio in the other engines remained below (40%).

The addition of promising pages did increase the precision ratios in all queries and across all search engines. On the average, the refined queries resulted in a slightly higher precision than the original queries. Confidence levels assigned to retrieved URLs by selected engines and the presence or absence of relevant keywords in the URLs headings were not indicative of relevance, in most cases. This suggests that users examine each of the retrieved URLs thoroughly to locate the information requested.

The lack of on-line thesaurus of controlled vocabulary results in relying on keywords and boolean operators as the methods for searching. When boolean searching is ineffective, however, users will be overloaded with information that is afflicted with a low precision ratio. In addition, the absence of a human intermediary to assist users in identifying their information need prior to searching the engines may contribute to users' frustration and ineffectiveness in finding relevant resources.

Additional studies are needed to examine the effectiveness of the World Wide Web search engines. Studies should incorporate a variety of queries (i.e., broad, specific, complex, etc.) and a higher number of searches. The inclusion of Yahoo in the studies is recommended.

The unrestricted access to the World Wide Web engines and the wealth of resources available via the Internet provide unprecedented opportunities for free global information access. Despite the high volume of URLs searched by these engines, the average turnaround time was very reasonable even during peak hours. Searching the World Wide Web is free and provides information gratification, which may, unfortunately, be plagued with redundancy and low precision.

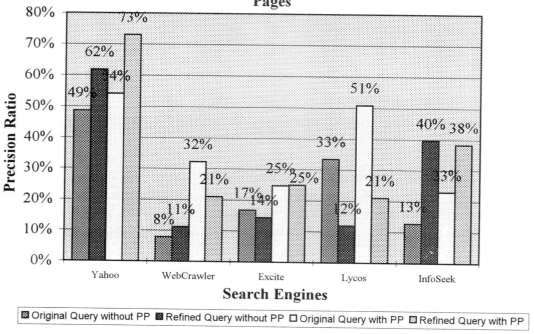

Figure 1. Results of the Five Queries without and with Promising Pages

☒ Original Query without PP ☒ Refined Query without PP ☐ Original Query with PP ☒ Refined Query with PP

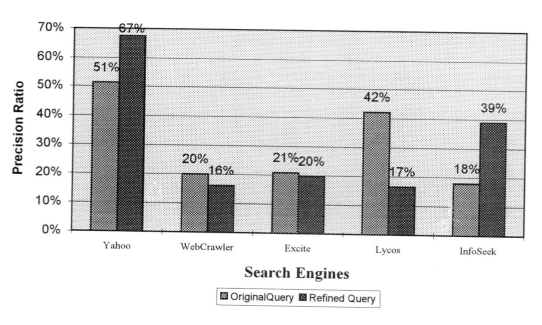

Figure 2. Results of the Five Queries

☒ OriginalQuery ☒ Refined Query

References

Berns, M. (1995). RoboSearch: A critical examination of the family of WWW search engines and how they can be used in education. http://www.oise.on.ca/~mberns/RoboSearch.html

Bertland, L. (1995). Searching the Internet: Subject indexes and search engines. http://www.libertynet.org/~bertland/search.html

December, J. (1994). Challenges for Web information providers. Computer-Mediated Communication Magazine, 1, 8. http://sunsite.unc.edu/cmc/mag/1994/oct/webip.html

Harter, S. (1996). Variations in relevance assessments and the measurements of retrieval effectiveness. Journal of the American Society for Information Science, 47, 37-49.

Leighton, H.V. (1995). Performance of four World Wide Web (WWW) index services: Infoseek, Lycos, Webcrawler and WWWWorm. http://www.winona.msus.edu/services-f/library-f/webind.htm.

Lester, D. (1995). Yahoo: Profile of a Web database. Database, 18, 46-50.

Lycos claims to index 91% of the Web. As of January 20, 1996, Lycos catalog contained 18,923,479 unique URLs. http://Lycos.cs.cmu.edu

MIDS (Matrix Information and Directory Services, Inc.). (1995). Finally, 20 to 30 million users on the Internet. http://www.mids.org/mids/press957.html

Notess, G.R. (1995). Searching the World-Wide Web: Lycos, Webcrawler and more. Online, 19, 48-53.

Notess, G.R. (1995). The InfoSeek databases. Database, 18, 85-87.

Randall, N. (1995). The search engine that could. PC Computing, 8, 165-168.

Scoville, R. (1996). Find it on the Net. PC World, 14, 125-131.

Tennant, R. (1996). The best tools for searching the Internet. Syllabus, 9, 36-38.

Winship, I.R. (1995). World Wide Web searching tools - an evaluation. VINE, 99, 49-54. http://www.bubl.bath.ac.uk/BUBL/IWinship.html

Defining the Undefinable: the Unit of Control for Electronic Resources

Ling H. Jeng
University of Kentucky
Lexington, Kentucky

ABSTRACT

One critical issue in organizing electronic resources is the question of how to define an electronic information object. That is, what exactly is the unit of information that one must organize for the purpose of description and access. This paper reviews the definitions of the unit of control in traditional cataloging and indexing, and discusses the issues involved in attempts to apply the same definitions to electronic resources. Traditional cataloging prescribes that cataloging must only be done with an item in hand. Traditional indexing is done primarily to organize separate parts of an item such as articles in a journal issue, or word strings in the articles. The two principles in determining the unit of control in cataloging and indexing are (a) phyiscal format and constraint, and (b) the naming of an item (traditionally identified as the title). Both traditional principles prescribe that definition of the unit of control be done at the physical level of the information object. The fluid, dynamic nature of most electronic information objects, leads the author to conclude that a logical-level definition of the unit of control must be used to replace the traditional physical-level definition. It is argued that electronic information objects must be defined by the way they are processed and stored at the logical level, with files. A file could be one on a diskette or one on an URL site. An electronic file with a unique file name and its location address constitute a logical unit throughout its life cycle of creation, storage, retrieval, transformation and disposition. Although in many cases, a collection of files with a common link (through usage or content relevancy) must be treated together in the process of organization, individual files still must be maintained separately during its life cycle. A file as the unit of control is a more reasonable basis for considering in the organization of electronic information objects.

Documenting the Revolution: Electronic Recordkeeping and the Internet Public Library

Cory T. Brandt and Christopher Zegers
School of Information and Library Studies, University of Michigan
Ann Arbor, Michigan

Abstract

The preservation of records from contemporary organizations is requisite for the support of future research on the evolution of social structures. In digitally based organizations, recordkeeping practices are generally inadequate to ensure preservation and support present and future organizational analysis. Within the business community, the threats to preservation of electronic records have generally been ignored. Electronically generated records differ in both form and function from documentation arising out of traditional hierarchical bureaucracies. Digital recordkeeping systems are forcing a reevaluation of approaches to documentation. Traditional approaches for the intellectual organization of documentation are inadequate to capture the complex horizontal relationships which exist in networked organizations.

The concept of provenance has been used by archivists for the appraisal of records. Provenance identifies informational and evidential values of records. These values do not encompass the functional or relational values engendered in records. The role of functional values increases as organizations move towards flatter hierarchies and greater participation and boundary permeability. A theoretical and practical approach to recordkeeping is needed which retains the functional values of records. By utilizing a roles-linkage approach to electronic records, functional values of records can be proactively maintained by archivists working in modern organizations. A case study is presented to demonstrate the use of a roles-linkage model for the documentation of an electronically based, informal communications system.

Introduction

The preservation of records from contemporary organizations is requisite for the support of future research on the evolution of social structures. In digitally based organizations, recordkeeping practices are generally inadequate to ensure preservation and support present and future organizational analysis. Electronically generated records differ in both form and function from documentation arising out of traditional hierarchical bureaucracies. Digital recordkeeping systems are forcing a reevaluation of approaches to documentation. Traditional concepts for the intellectual organization of documentation are inadequate to capture the complex relationships which exist in networked organizations. It is rapidly becoming clear that we must look for new theoretical and practical approaches to recordkeeping. This essay examines theoretical approaches to electronic recordkeeping, and presents a practical application derived from archival theory and business computing research.

Recordkeeping in Popular Perspective

The Wall Street Journal is widely read among business executives. It can be used as a barometer for gauging executive interest in a wide range of subjects. Examination of recent Wall Street Journal articles addressing recordkeeping in organizations reveals no relevant discourse on the risks to documentation programs inherent in organizational and technological change. Problems in recordkeeping are most often reported in the press when potential litigation or government regulation is at issue (Salwen, 1992; Salwen and Connor, 1992; Berton, 1992; Zachary, 1994). What is completely lacking in popular business sources is a discussion of the need for recordkeeping systems which are appropriate within evolving organizational contexts.

Non-archival literature on recordkeeping tends to emphasize organizational needs served through records retention programs. Of primary concern is documentation to meet legal requirements (Blotzer, 1994; Skupsky, 1994; Montana, 1995). An emphasis is also placed on recent management trends which are driving better recordkeeping in organizations. The quality movement in particular has focused attention on recordkeeping for accountability and quality improvement (Van Houten, 1994; Butler, 1994; Dmytrenko, 1995; Brum, 1995). Literature on recordkeeping within the business sector also addresses the role of disaster planning in records management (Mueler, 1994). In addition to delineating forces driving records retention, available literature deals extensively with document management technologies such as imaging and bar coding (Davis, 1993; Hoke, 1993; Langemo, 1993; Brown, 1994; Dykeman, 1994; Laplante, 1994; Connelly, 1995). These technologies are primarily used to facilitate records retention in hybrid recordkeeping systems. Hybrid systems incorporate the use of both paper and electronic records as sources of documentation.

While popular literature addresses the need for recordkeeping and new technologies which enable the short term storage of documentation, it does not explore the development of theoretical and practical approaches for the long-term documentation of organizational activity. Changing organizational structures and electronic integration are undermining the ability of records managers and archivists to adequately document economic activity. As is evident in the scope of available literature, this threat to the organization has passed largely unnoticed in corporate circles.

The development of new theoretical constructs and practical approaches to the archival retention of business records is sorely needed. In the absence of greater awareness of the problems for recordkeeping posed by organizational change and electronic integration, a gap in the documentary record will develop. The full impact of inadequate recordkeeping will not be immediately felt. Rather, consequences will become explicit with the passage of time. Organizations will find themselves documentation poor. An oversight which cannot be rectified retrospectively.

Archival Theory and Organizational Change

Organizations and Appraisal in Historical Perspective

Archivists have struggled to define the relationship between organizational context, technology, and recordkeeping systems. These issues are systematically addressed by Francis X. Blouin in a review of Alfred Chandler's, The Visible Hand (Blouin, 1979). Chandler traces change in the organization of economic activity which accompanied industrialization during the latter half of the 19th century (Chandler, 1979). Chandler's work delineates steps in the progression from the owner operated, functionally undifferentiated, merchant house to the vertically integrated, professionally managed, corporation. Through this process, hierarchies were perpetuated for the management of production.

Structural change in organizations does not occur in isolation. Many factors influence transformation in the organization of economic activity. Social and technological variables define the environment for structural change in organizations. In the 19th century, organizational change was accompanied by the introduction of new communications technologies. The historical record, as presented in Chandler's work, suggests that structural and technological change are symbiotically linked. These concomitant forces inevitably create a need for new forms of documentation.

The vertically integrated firm increasingly required records to facilitate internal communications. According to Blouin, "The complexity of the organizational structure led to a complexity in the kinds of records produced." These emerging forms of documentation were not merely additive. They were created to serve fundamentally different organizational needs. The proliferation of hierarchical structures created a need for better means of controlling capital. Blouin concludes that, "Cost accounting was used increasingly as an operational control. Recordkeeping thus shifted from serving a descriptive function to serving as an analytical tool" (Blouin, 1979, p. 318).

Blouin identifies ways in which Chandler's work supports the archival administration of business records. Chandler posits a typology for organizational structures and suggests new directions for the theory of archival appraisal. According to Blouin, "Chandlers thesis presents a basic typology of business structure that will assist in determining the content, use, and relationship of record groups." This typology identifies organizations as progressing from the, "traditional small and/or specialized firm", to, "the more complex firm composed of many sub-units integrated either vertically to control all phases of production and distribution, or horizontally to control a greater share of market dominance" (Blouin, 1979, p. 319).

Transformation in organizational structure is mirrored by fundamental change in records and recordkeeping. As a result, the identification of organizational types assists in establishing archival control of records by placing documents within a conceptual framework. This framework provides context for the comprehensive analysis of recordkeeping systems. Such analysis aids in the identification of records with enduring historical value. This function is referred to by archivists as appraisal. Appraisal is requisite in determining the disposition of records. If appraisal decisions result in the retention of records which reflect structural elements within the organization, the documentary record can be utilized to map change in organizational structure. In the absence of representative documentary materials, organizational change becomes unintelligible with the passage of time.

Archival appraisal theory was pioneered by T. R. Schellenberg who posited evidential and informational values of records (Schellenberg, 1956). Different types of records serve diverse organizational functions and possess these values in varying degrees. Within this theoretical framework, records retention decisions are based upon the identification of evidential and informational value in records which are essentially descriptive in nature. Evidential and informational values are derived from the activity described in records. Blouin extends this theoretical framework by positing a third value of records: "This sort of record would indicate a functional relationship between one branch and another, or the record itself would indicate the requirement for a certain kind of information" (Blouin, 1979, p. 320). Records with functional value allow for the coordination of interdepartmental activity. Such records are both an enabler and a byproduct of the vertically integrated firm.

Sampling is recommended by Blouin as an appraisal tool which maintains information about interdepartmental relationships and information needs. In addition to maximizing the functional value of records, sampling also serves to mitigate problems in the storage of large quantities of paper records. Sampling is not, however, universally applicable. A series of records must exhibit certain prescribed characteristics in order to qualify for sampling (Cook, 1991). Advocacy of sampling for organizational records with functional value assumes that functional relationships remain constant over time. In an organizational environment characterized by flexibility, sampling may result in a distorted view of functional relationships. The identification of functional value in records is not addressed in Blouin's review.

Joanne Yates further contributes to the use of organizational analysis in archival appraisal by defining typical characteristics of communications systems in three organizational types (Yates, 1985). Yates views the functionally departmentalized firm as dependent upon an upward flow of information. This information flow is not evenly distributed. Management requires increasingly aggregated and generalized information as one proceeds up the hierarchy of operational control. As a result, "Certain types of information were pooled at certain levels in the communication flow and progressed upward in very different forms, if at all" (Yates, 1985, p. 143) Yates identifies records created at lower levels of the hierarchy as essentially descriptive, and those generated at higher levels as analytic in nature.

Yates also identifies a trend towards lateral or horizontal communications flows as companies expand. These transactions, "coordinated actions between and within departments." Records generated as a function of lateral communications are referred to by Yates as, "documentary records." These records are held to be distinct in that they, "serve primarily to document issues or facts for future reference." (Yates, 1985, p. 152). The documentary record is created in anticipation of possible future needs and is derived from the need for corporate accountability. In defining documentary records as a function of lateral communications, Yates introduces a record type which is rich in functional values.

Yates draws implications for appraisal from her analysis of communication systems. She contends that, "appraisal strategies should be designed to retain documents that reveal the structure of the communication system" (Yates, 1985, p. 155). She is opposed to the traditional practice of confronting problems in the volume of records by retaining only records generated at high levels in organizational hierarchies. This approach assumes that records of upper management will contain information representative of the institution as a whole. Yates counters that, "The information at the top is only one piece of the organic system of flows that controls and coordinates activities" (Yates, 1985, p. 155). These records do not capture processes fundamental to the function of the organization.

Yates offers alternatives to appraisal methodologies which emphasize high level records retention to the exclusion of all else. For decentralized, multidivisional companies, documentation of one entire division and the central office is recommended. In functionally departmentalized companies, the retention of, "strategic vertical selections" is advocated. Yates contends that adherence to her appraisal criteria will facilitate the illustration of communication flows and organizational processes while minimizing the need for large scale retention of redundant records. The identification of vertical selections assumes that hierarchies are readily identifiable and relatively static. Vertical selection is dependent upon the ability to accurately map organizational structures using uni-dimensional modeling techniques. Within a flexible, networked organizational structure, any attempt to identify vertical selections will necessarily be somewhat arbitrary.

Yates also fails to differentiate between highly formalized and less formal communication systems. Informal communications are more likely to engender horizontal transactions which are not created for "documentary" purposes. Less formalized communications often support functional coordination between departments. The documentary record concept places an artificial limitation on the scope of lateral communications. Any appraisal strategy rooted in this concept is ultimately inadequate for the full retention of functional values in records.

The work of Blouin and Yates has paved the way for closer examination of the relationship between organizational design and the value of documentary records. Despite their contributions to the literature, archival theory has remained constrained by a number of tacit assumptions. Appraisal theorists have traditionally assumed that organizational structure is captured in exclusively vertical representations. Vertical organizations can be easily modeled using flow charts to map reporting relationships, operational controls, and the upward flow of information. Both the practice of retaining only high level records and Yates' alternative technique, vertical selection, are dependent upon a uni-dimensional model for organizational design. Traditional, vertically-oriented modeling techniques utilized by archivists also assume that organizational structure is relatively static.

Traditional models for archival appraisal are rooted in the concept of provenance. Provenance underlies the intellectual and physical organization of records by identifying the location of the records creator within explicit representations of the organizational structure. As a result, records are contextualized through the implicit association of records creators with prescribed roles in the functionally departmentalized organzation. Vertical modelling of organizational design is utilized to facilitate this process. As applied, provenance does not provide adequate contextual information to enable the systematic study of horizontal information flows. Any attempt to map records arising from both vertical and horizontal interactions using modelling techniques which only represent vertical information flows will ultimately fail. The concept of provenance must be exploded to include the full panoply of organizational communications.

Tacit assumptions about the static nature of organizational design have allowed archivists to render appraisal decisions made at the end of the life cycle of records. The application of provenance for records appraisal has generally been retrospective. Archivists eschew active involvement in the process of records creation. Recently, these assumptions about the nature of organizations and the role of the archivist have come under increased scrutiny.

Organizational Trends and Electronic Integration

Organizational trends and the increasing introduction of digital media into the workplace have shaken the foundations of archival appraisal theory. Information technologies are driving organizational change while emerging organizations are creating increased demand for new communications capabilities. These symbiotic processes have undermined many of the assumptions underlying the theoretical context for work with modern organizational records.

Tora K. Bikson has defined the forces driving transformation in records and recordkeeping as resulting from a, "technology push", and a, "demand pull" (Bikson, 1994). Technology drives organizational change which creates a demand for increasing technological capabilities. Bikson identifies five organizational trends resulting from this interplay of forces.

Bikson's Five Organizational Trends

1.   Greater speed and flexibility in information-and-communication intensive tasks.

2.   Denser connectivity.

3.   Flatter hierarchies, greater participation.

4.   Increased utilization of teams.

5.   Greater boundary permeability.

The organizational trends Bikson describes increase the importance of functional values of records in emerging organizations. Functional value is derivative of the relationships made explicit in records. As the number and complexity of cross-functional, horizontal relationships within an organization increases, the importance of mapping these relationships also increases. Flatter hierarchies and team based approaches are dependent upon dense, highly integrated networks for the coordination of activity. These networks are supported through an increase in horizontal communications which do not map to a vertical representation of the organization. Denser connectivity and boundary permeability are also dependent on multi-dimensional information transactions. These trends clearly demonstrate that vertical organizational models are inadequate for organizational analysis and the appraisal of records in a networked environment. Some in the archival community have called for a paradigm shift in archival theory as a response to electronic recordkeeping. What is needed is a conceptual shift towards the use of multi-dimensional, network based models for organizational analysis. The identification of modeling techniques appropriate for networked organizations will empower archivists to define new mechanisms for appraisal.

Electronic Records in Organizational context

Archivists working towards the control of electronic records have begun to challenge many of the tenets of archival theory and practice. Drawing lessons from the electronic environment, Margaret Hedstrom champions a more proactive role for the archivist in managing organizational records (Hedstrom, 1993). This position is rooted in an awareness of the ephemeral nature of electronic records. Metadata capture at the systems level is proposed as an alternative to traditional forms of archival description.

David Bearman believes that metadata retention at the systems level is the key to archival control of electronic records. Bearman defines records as a function of business transactions. These transactions occur within the context of clearly defined business applications designed to support organizational functions. Bearman concludes that, "While the relationship between record-keeping systems and functions is, therefore, always straightforward, the relationship between a record system and organizational units is not" (Bearman, 1993, p. 20).

Bearman's emphasis on business functions is useful where functions are systematically prescribed, but techniques for defining the function of records which are not created systematically are notably absent. Within the confines of systems for the creation of formal, highly structured communications, a provenance rooted in systems is appropriate. When dealing with more loosely structured, informal communications, a different approach is required. Bearman's analysis suggests that archival appraisal must be geared towards mapping operative institutional functions rather than explicitly rendered organizational structures. This approach allows for a more accurate reflection of what has been referred to as "organizational physiology" (Bartlett, 1990). By rendering functional relationships explicit, the archivist can become proactively involved in designing recordkeeping systems which will support the preservation of a more comprehensive historical record.

The Roles-Linkage Model for Archival Appraisal

Ajit Kambil and James Short propose the roles-linkage model for the conceptualization and mapping of multi-dimensional business networks. This model suggests new directions for the appraisal of organizational records. Within this context, roles are, "distinct, technologically separable, value-added activities undertaken by firms or individuals in a given business network" (Kambil and Short, 1994, p. 64). Roles are technologically separable to the extent that they require specific human or material inputs. According to Kambil and Short, "Linkage refers to the different ways that firms or individuals manage economic interdependence across value adding roles in the network" (Kambil and Short, 1994, p. 65). The roles-linkage model facilitates the mapping of complex networked structures by creating a matrix with roles defined along the x and y axes. The point at which roles intersect is assigned value as a linkage. For archival purposes, each linkage can be identified as a record creating transaction between organizational agents.

This approach is not to be confused with matrix management. Matrix management seeks to superimpose a horizontal system of controls over vertical management structures in organizations. In matrix management, vertical controls are functional and horizontal controls are typically organized by project, product, or business area. This attempt to increase the horizontal flow of communications within organizations has been largely abandoned due to the redundancy inherent in a system of dual operational controls (Davis and Lawrence, 1978; Burns and Wholey, 1993; de Laat, 1994). The roles-linkage approach differs from matrix management in that it maps functional relationships while matrix management is used to model reporting relationships.

Roles can be defined by their relational and non-relational elements (Barley, 1990). Records produced through the non-relational elements of a role are more likely to result in the creation of highly systematized records. These can be managed by adopting the tactics of Hedstrom and Bearman and focusing on the retention of systems level metadata. The relational elements of a role are likely to result in the creation of informal communications.

These communications are not systematically generated and as a result, systems level metadata is unavailable. To rectify this paucity of metadata for informal communications, archivists must focus on the relational elements of organizational roles when designing systems for the retention of informal communications.

The roles-linkage approach provides a multi-dimensional representation of role relationships within organizations and empowers archivists to identify and capture functional value in records. Through this process, the constraints of an exclusively vertical model for appraisal are stripped away to reveal underlying complexity. By defining roles, record creating linkages can be identified and appraised. Selection decisions are divorced from vertical criteria rooted in an understanding of the organization as static hierarchy. Selection is reoriented towards a conception of the organization as a network. Through the use of this model, the context for records creation in contemporary organizations becomes intelligible.

The roles-linkage model also portends the need for change in traditional conceptions of provenance. Provenance emphasizes the importance of information about records creators as the keystone for archival appraisal and description. A roles-linkage perspective supports the contention that provenance is fundamentally rooted in organizational functions. These functions can be explicitly rendered through the identification of relational roles.

In uni-dimensional, hierarchical organizations function and department are intentionally correlated. Records generated by a given department correspond to highly specialized roles. In this environment, traditional provenancial information is adequate to identify the creator of records and, by extension, the function those records served. In a networked or team based environment, the relationship between department and function is not intentionally corellated. Resulting structural flexibility is incompatible with conceptual schema that view records as generated by departments with narrowly defined functional responsibilities. By defining provenance as a function of organizational roles, flexibility can be accommodated and systematically documented. From this perspective, the archivist must proactively identify organizational roles. Systems specifications can then be posited which will capture records at significant linkages and allow for a more representative documentary record.

A Roles-Linkage Approach to the Records of the Internet Public Library

E-mail is commonly used as a means of facilitating communications in networked organizations. It functions to coordinate horizontal as well as vertical activities and exhibits few formal characteristics. To date, adequate models for the archival administration of e-mail have not been available. The design of an e-mail based communications management system within the Internet Public Library (IPL) for the capture, retention, and retrieval of messages demonstrates the efficacy of a role based approach to documentation.

The IPL opened to the public at URL http://ipl.sils.umich.edu on March 17,1995, to serve as the first World Wide Web entity to provide traditional library services in electronic form. Public services include organized pointers to valuable sources of information on the web, reference services, multimedia exhibits, and youth activities. The IPL exhibits the characteristics of a virtual organization (Lucas and Barudi, 1994). There is a notable absence of hierarchy in the IPL and information flows in a networked configuration. Few formal records are generated and the predominant mode of coordination is informal e-mail communications. Previous attempts to maintain an archives of IPL records had resulted in what were candidly refered to by the Director as "piles" of unorganized, innaccesible files.

Archival analysis began with an examination of systems level metadata within the IPL. Our initial attempt involved looking at the network system architecture. There was no descriptive overview of system structure or implementation. Software documentation was also generally unavailable. Discussions with server administrators revealed that there were a variety of systems in use, but progress was being made to administer IPL applications using a unified file structure.

It was assumed that organizational records would be physically controlled by the file directory structure created by server administrators. In actuality, the records of the IPL are divided into two very different structural entities. Records which function as the services of the IPL (the web pages) are organized on the server according to functional service department: youth, reference, reading room, MOO, professional development, and exhibits. Records generated by the IPL staff on an ongoing basis (records derived from relational roles) are organized according to departmental mailing lists. These mailing lists consist of youth, reference, technology, library services, MOO, exhibits, staff, class, and administration.

The distribution of an e-mail record depends on an individual staff member's determination of the record's relevance to the function of one or more departments. The server administrator is a member of each mailing list in order to receive all of the records generated by the staff. The server administrator stores records according to their respective mailing lists. Within this system, organization of records is dependent upon the distribution decisions of individual staff members. The identification of records with departmental mailing lists perpetuates a vertical conception of the organization. Cross-functional, horizontal information flows cannot be adequately mapped on the basis of mailing lists alone. This system also does not allow for the capture of messages sent between individuals or cross-functional teams within the IPL.

In formulating a more responsive system for the storage and retrieval of IPL records, a matrix was developed to map roles and linkages within the IPL. Relational roles were defined using "Social Analysis" (Knight, 1978). This technique involves interviews and focus groups with organizational agents. A total of nine distinct roles were derived. Fund raising and collection development were added to the seven explicit departmental roles expressed through mailing lists. A tenth miscellaneous category was included for roles not covered under any of the predefined categories. The number and complexity of roles will vary across organizations.

System design required a mechanism for assigning roles to specific communications. It was determined that any attempt to retroactively appraise communications for role content would prove unmanageable and prohibitively expensive. An alternative is the proactive appraisal of records at the time of creation. Software specifications were posited which would allow system users to select from a range of predefined roles before sending an e-mail message. A two dimensional roles-linkage model was determined to be inadequate to capture the variety of roles subsumed within a single e-mail communication. As an alternative, users are allowed to specify up to three roles for a single transaction.

By combining roles, users are able to broaden or constrain the specific role designation for a given message. As an example, a message might contain information about the youth role and the reference role, or it might alternatively relate to the more specific youth/reference role. Both of these variant role designations are enabled through the use of a multi-dimensional approach. Additional contextual information pertaining to relevant roles can be included on the subject line of an e-mail message. This allows for the system to accomodate structural flexibility and resultant instability in relational roles. Periodic review of role designations will be required to maintain an accurate organizational map. Within a given application environment, a dictionary of roles can be maintained which tracks transformation in roles over time.

Having prescribed relational roles within the IPL, a prototype e-mail management system was postulated which would make limited self-appraisal by records creators seamless yet mandatory. All e-mail communications within the IPL must be created using the communications management system. Fielded routing information is submitted with each message. The user may send messages to individuals or groups. Messages may also be sent to "Minutes" if they contain the structured minutes of a departmental meeting. This feature was included to improve formal conventions for recordkeeping within the IPL. Users proceed to designate three roles for the message being sent. To avoid the possibility of users choosing a single function as a way to save time, three choices must be made. If the record only pertains to one function, the user must also choose two boxes which read "no other functions relevant". The next field which must be addressed is the subject/keyword field. Users are instructed to include descriptive information about the content of the record in this field. Every future response to or use of the record is tracked by transaction logs which are systematically embedded in the message header by the message management system.

A search engine prototype which utilizes the captured roles-linkage values can be viewed at URL http://www.ipl.org/IPLarchives/archives.html. The search engine gives users a structured series of choices which reflect the roles-linkage values within a particular series of organizational records. These series are defined as correspondence, meeting minutes, reference questions, and QRC development. The search engine template for the correspondence and minutes areas allows the user to pick up to three role designations which are of interest. The user is then given a space to search for additional keywords using Boolean operators. When a search request is submitted the system recalls all items which correspond to the desired variables. For example, if a search specifies the keyword "Games" and correlates this with the youth, reference, and technology roles, the user may retrieve records which demonstrate progress towards an interactive reference game for kids.

The implementation of a roles-linkage approach to the retention of organizational records poses a number of problems. The dependence upon self-appraisal by records creators requires that users have a uniform understanding of organizational roles and are able to appropriately identify the relational roles extant in a records creating linkage. This requires a training component for system users to provide guidance in determining roles within a message. Additional training is required for systems adminiatrators, records managers, or archivists who will be responsible for defining and tracking roles within the organization. Universal participation and compliance with system requirements is also problematic. In organizational cultures where policy directives are generally adhered to, policy will be adequate to ensure the full implementation of the system. In looser organizational contexts, technological forcing functions can be built into the message management system to assure compliance.

Conclusion

In the absence of new approaches to the documentation of organizational activity, a portion of the historical record will be lost for future research. Archivists must build upon traditional theoretical approaches in seeking to understand the impact of organizational change and electronic integration on records and recordkeeping. A conceptual shift which recognizes organizations as networked structures is necessary to effectively manage the records of contemporary institutions. New conceptions of the organization require a reevaluation of the nature and role of provenance. Information about the creator of records no longer provides adequate contextual information in determining the function of various records within the organization. In flexible organizations, provenance must be rooted in the definition of roles and resulting records creating linkages. The roles-linkage model provides a concrete mechanism for the determination of roles in a network and the linkages between agents performing various roles. Specifications for recordkeeping systems can be derived from an analysis of value adding roles within the network. This approach requires the proactive involvement of archivists in records creation.

Bibliography

Anderson, Harold P., "Business Archives: A corporate asset." *American Archivist* 45 (Summer 1982): pp. 264-266.

"Avoiding RCRA recordkeeping violations." *Environmental Manager* 6 (Jan. 1995): pp. 6-7.

Bakken, Douglas A., "Corporate archives today." *American Archivist* 45 (Summer 1982): pp. 279-286.

Barley, Stephen R., "The alignment of technology and structure through roles and networks." *Administrative Science Quarterly* 35 (March 1990): pp. 61-104.

Bartlett, Christopher A. and Ghoshal, Sumantra, "Matrix management: Not a structure, a frame of mind." *Harvard Business Review* (Jul.-Aug. 1990): pp. 138+.

Bearman, David, "Record-keeping systems." *Archivaria* (Autumn, 1993): pp. 16-36.

Berton, Lee, "Numbers game: How Miniscribe got it's auditor's blessing on questionable ʾsales." *Wall Street Journal* (May 14, 1992): A1.

Bikson, Tora K., "Organizational trends and and electronic media: work in progress." *American Archivist* (Winter 1994) pp. 49-68.

Blotzer, Michael, "OSHA recordkeeping and worker's compensation." *Occupational Hazards* 56 (Oct. 1994): pp. 67-70.

Blouin, Francis X. Jr., "A new perspective on the appraisal of business records: A review." *American Archivist* 42 (July 1979): pp.312-320.

Brown, Adrian E., "Imaging clears paper jam, helps insurer grow." *National Underwriter* 98 (Jan. 17, 1994): pp. 5, 19.

Brumm, Eugenia K., "Managing records for ISO 9000 compliance." *Quality Progress* 28 (Jan. 1995): pp. 73-77.

Burns, Lawton R., "Matrix management in hospitals: Testing theories of matrix structure and development." *Administrative Science Quarterly* 34 (Sept. 1989): pp. 349-369.

Burns, Lawton R. and Wholey, Douglas R., "Adoption and abandonment of matrix programs: Effects of organizational characteristics and interorganizational networks." *Academy of management Journal* 36 (Feb. 1993): pp. 106-139.

Butler, Tyrone, "A world of opportunity: Records and information management in the global economy." *Managing Office Technology* 39 (Sept. 1994): pp. 69-70.

Carvalho, Joseph III, "Archival application of mathmatical sampling techniques." *Records Management Quarterly* 18 (Jan. 1984): pp. 60-62.

Chandler, Alfred D., Jr., *The Visible Hand: The Managerial Revolution in American Business*. (Cambridge: The Belknap Press, Harvard University Press, 1979).

Clemons, Eric K., et. al., "The impact of information technology on the organization of economic activity: The 'Move to the Middle' hypothesis." *Journal of Management Information Systems* 10 (Fall 1993): pp. 9-35.

Connelly, Jim, "Designing records and document retrieval systems." *Records Management Quarterly* 29 (Apr. 1995): pp. 30-35.

Cook, Terry, "'Many Are Called, But Few Are Chosen': Appraisal guidelines for sampling and selecting case files", *Archivaria* 32 (Winter 1990-1991), pp. 25-43.

Davis, Andrew W., "Tame the office paper tigers with document-imaging systems." *Office Systems* 10 (Mar. 1993): pp. 24-28.

Davis, Stanley M. and Lawrence, Paul R., "Problems of matrix organizations." *Harvard Business Review* (May/June, 1978): p. 131+.

de Laat, Paul B., "Matrix management of projects and power struggles: A case study of an R&D laboratory." *Human Relations* (Sept., 1994) pp. 1089-1110.

"Disaster recovery service saves almost 20,000 rolls of film." *IMC Journal* 30 (Mar.-Apr. 1994): pp. 22-23.

Dmytrenko, April L., "A quality records program is essential for ISO 9000 compliance." *Records Management Quarterly* 29 (Apr. 1995): pp. 60-62.

Dykeman, John, "Is small document imaging ready for prime time." *Managing Office Technology* 39 (Apr. 1994): pp. 14,16.

Edgerly, Linda, "Business Archives Guidelines." *American Archivist* 45 (Summer 1982): pp. 267-272.

Eidelman, James A. and Todd L. Mattson, "Document handling: Document mangement software can manage documents from creation to deletion - part 1." *Law Practice Management* (Mar. 1993): pp. 18-24.

Feretic, Eileen, "At last the paperless office (no kidding)." *Success* 39 (Sept. 1992): pp. 34-35.

Gubernick, Lisa, "Making history pay." *Forbes* 147 (May 13, 1991): p. 132.

Hedstrom, Margaret, "Descriptive practices for electronic records: Deciding what is essential and imagining what is possible." *Archivaria* (Autumn 1993) pp. 53-63.

Hoke, Gordon E. J., "Imaging streamlines operations at Chubb unit." *National Underwriter* 97 (Apr. 12, 1993): pp. 5, 25.

Honkanen, Lorna R., "The role of records and information management in increasing the productivity of business." *Inform* 6 (Nov. 1992): p. 42-44.

Jurney, William F., "Outsourcing non-core functions pays." *National Underwriter* 99 (Apr. 24, 1995): p. 18.

Kambil, Ajit, and James E. Short, "Electronic integration and business network redesign: A roles-linkage perspective." *Journal of Management Information Systems* 10 (Spring 1994): pp. 59-83.

Kipley, David R., "Sampling in archives: A review." *American Archivist* 47 (Summer 1984): pp. 237-242.

Knight, Kenneth, *Matrix Management: A Cross Functional Approach to Organisation* (New York: PBI-Petrocelli Books, 1978).

Langemo, Mark, "Picture this: Imaging is the new buzzword in records handling." *Office Systems* 10 (Oct. 1993): pp. 18-23.

Langner, Mark, "Don't abandon your filing cabinets just yet..." *Network World* 10 (Sept. 13, 1993): pp. 71-74.

Laplante, Alice, "Imaging your sea of data." *Forbes* ASAP Supplement (Aug. 29, 1994): pp. 36-41.

Lucas, Henry C. Jr., and Jack Baroudi, "The role of information technology in organization design". *Journal of Management Information Systems* 10 (Spring 1994): pp. 9-23.

Lutzker, Michael A., "Max weber and the analysis of modern bureacratic organization: Notes toward a theory of appraisal." *American Archivist* (Spring 1982). pp. 119-130.

Maddux, Jim, "OSHA gears up for more streamlined, user friendly recordkeeping standard." *Occupational Health and Safety* 64 (Jan. 1995): pp. 34-36.

McCusker, Tom and Paul Strauss, "Managing the document management explosion." *Datamation* 39 (Jul. 1, 1993): pp. 41-44.

Montana, John C., "It can make you or break you: The importance of records management in litigation." *Records Management Quarterly* 29 (Jan. 1995): pp. 3-8

Mueler, Dick, "Dealing with disaster: The great flood of '93." *IMC Journal* 30 (Mar.-Apr. 1994): pp. 28-29.

Phillips, John T. Jr., "Virtual records and virtual archives." *Records Management Quarterly* 28 (Jan. 1994): pp. 42-45.

Riley, Thomas W., and John G. Adorjan, "Company history a by-product of good records management." *Records Management Quarterly* 15 (Oct. 1981): pp. 5-8.

Salwen, Kevin G., "Bill to stiffen oversight of treasury market clears House panel." *Wall Street Journal* (June 3, 1992): C1.

Salwen, Kevin G. and John Connor, "Probe of Saloman scandal slowed by spotty records." *Wall Street Journal* (May 6, 1992): C1.

Schellenberg, T. R., *Modern Archives* (Chicago: University of Chicago Press, 1956).

Schultz, Charles R., "Archives in business and industry: Identification, preservation, and use." *Records Management Quarterly* 15 (Jan. 1981): pp. 5-8.

Semilof, Margie, "Paperwork faces the digital age." *CommunicationsWeek* (Oct. 17, 1994): pp. 1, 89.

Shaffer, Richard A., "Bury that paper." *Forbes* 154 (Oct. 10, 1994): p. 134.

Smith, David R., "An historical look at business archives." *American Archivist* 45 (Summer 1982): pp. 273-278.

Smith, George David, "Dusting off the cobwebs: Turning the business archives into a managerial tool." *American Archivist* 45 (Summer 1982): pp. 287-290.

Spokes, James Allin, "Records management benefits can (and should) be measured." *Managing Office Technology* 38 (Oct. 1993): pp. 85-87.

Sprague, Ralph H. Jr., "Electronic document management." *MIS Quarterly* (March 1995): pp. 29-49.

Steck, Larry and Francis Blouin, "Hannah Lay & Company: Sampling the records of a century of lumbering in Michigan." *American Archivist* 39 (January 1976): pp.15-20.

Van Houten, Gerry, "ISO 9000 and beyond: A case study of BASF Canada Inc." *Records Management Quarterly* 28 (Oct. 1994): pp. 21-26.

White, Karen, "Establishing a business archives." *Records Management Quarterly* 15 (Oct. 1981): pp. 10-12.

Williams, Robert F., "Document disposition of optically stored records." *Inform* 7(Feb. 1993): pp. 35-45.

Williams, Robert F., "Imaging and the law." *Chief Information Officer Journal* 5 (May-June 1993): pp. 48-51.

Williams, Robert F., "Questions and answers on optical records' legal status." *Journal of Accountancy* 178 (Nov. 1994): p. 75.

Yates, Joanne, "Internal communication systems in American business structures: A framework to aid appraisal." *American Archivist* (Spring 1985) pp. 141-158.

Zachary, G. Pascal, "Technology & health: Red Cross agency in Florida lost track of thousands of listed blood units." *Wall Street Journal* (June 17, 1994): B10.

Impact on Social Structures III: Contexts and Politics

The Politics of Webweaving

Mark Stover
Phillips Graduate Institute
Encino, California

Abstract

Many information professionals today have taken on the new role of "Webweaver," either for their entire organization or for their library. A Webweaver creates and maintains the Web site for his or her organization, but does not necessarily maintain the technical aspects of the Web server (this task normally goes to the "Webmaster"). This paper will deal with the political ramifications of webweaving, and will draw on the personal experiences of the presenter as well as published literature. It will deal with such issues as the choice of the Webweaver, the domain of the Webweaver, the purpose of the Web site, political rules for Webweavers, and collaboration in creating and maintaining the Web site.

Organizational Politics: Some Background

Organizational politics is a fact of life. For some, it is distasteful and should be avoided if possible. For others, it is a game that must be played every day. But for all of us it is a reality that impacts on the quality and the quantity of our work.

One definition of organizational politics that can inform our understanding is as follows: "social influence attempts directed at those who can provide rewards that will help promote or protect the self-interests of the actor" (Cropanzano and Kacmar, 1995, p. 7). This definition recognizes that organizational politics reflects a certain self-centered attitude that may seem pejorative to some. But self-interest need not be without concern for the common good of the organization. Indeed, each member of an organization has his or her own agenda, which in effect serves his or her own self-interest, but some agendas may clearly be more broad-based and organization-oriented than others. These are the agendas that need to be given highest priority, but the politics of the particular organization will dictate where the priorities ultimately lie.

An underlying factor behind most instances of organizational politics is conflict (Cropanzano and Kacmar, 1995). Conflict arises when an organization exhibits certain characteristics, such as lack of rules, limited resources, and a political reward system. Political behavior sometimes rears its head even without the existence of substantial conflict, usually because of individual factors. These include hidden motivation, strong communication skills, and manipulation.

This paper will present organizational politics within the context of webweaving. It will discuss such topics as the choice of the Webweaver, the Domain of the Webweaver, collaboration in designing the Web pages, and the goal of the Web site.

What is a Webweaver

A Webweaver is generally defined as the person who creates and maintains the Web site for his or her organization, but does not necessarily maintain the technical aspects of the Web server. The term "Webmaster" is the preferred title for the person who handles the technical aspects of maintaining the Web site (Cutler and Richard, 1995), although sometimes the two terms are used interchangeably. The Webweaver is more concerned with issues like information content, organization, and design. Sometimes Webweavers are individuals, and other times they are committees, depending on the needs of the organization. A Webweaver may devote his or her entire schedule to creating and maintaining the Web site, or it may be just a small part of his or her job.

Choice of the Webweaver: Who Decides and Why?

The choice of the Webweaver is greatly dependent on who initiates the Web site. Sometimes it is a top-down decision: a senior executive decides that a Web page is a good idea, and simply appoints an employee to do the job (or hires an outside consultant). Other times the decision is made by middle management after a long, thought-out (and usually overly bureaucratic) process. Occasionally, however, an enterprising employee will initiate the process and volunteer for the job. This obviously creates more work for this person, but it also promotes the welfare of the organization as well as producing greater visibility for the new Webweaver.

Domain of the Webweaver

The domain of the Webweaver is a difficult and sometimes highly charged question regardless of how the Webweaver was chosen. In other words, whose job is this anyway? Does webweaving belong to the Library or Information Center? Is it the domain of the Computer Center or MIS department? Or, should webweaving be controlled by the Marketing department?

There are different ways that this question can be answered:

(1) Descriptive

The descriptive approach is the "I got here first" philosophy. Advocates of this viewpoint often claim squatter's rights: "I built the house, so it's my land." This approach has little support in logic, but it does tend to avoid the bureaucratic introspection and political landmines that the next approach seems to engender.

(2) Prescriptive

The domain of the Webweaver can also be viewed from a prescriptive viewpoint. That is, in what department should (with a capital "S") the Webweaver live? A prescriptive or normative argument can take various forms, usually depending on the agenda of the proponent.

First, there is the argument from the Marketing department. Proponents of this perspective argue that the web page is for the purpose of marketing the organization. Also, graphics designers feel comfortable with electronic desktop publishing tools, and are experts in creating and manipulating graphical image files. Thus, there is an argument of mission and purpose ("this is our job") as well as an argument of expertise.

Second, there is the argument from the MIS or Computer Services department. This argument goes something like this: the Internet and computer technology is clearly our domain; thus, creating the Web page should be our job. HTML is simple now, but what about CGI scripting, HotJava, VRML, etc.? Again we find the mission and purpose argument along with the expertise argument.

Third, there is the Library argument. Librarians claim to understand four important aspects of the Web: information technology, information content, organization of information, and endusers. Librarians and information specialists also argue that providing access to information has always been within their domain, and building a Web site is analogous to building an online catalog. Again we discover the two strands of thought: mission and expertise.

Collaboration is the ideal answer to the domain question. The formation of a webweaving team made up of representatives from MIS, marketing, and the library would combine the knowledge and expertise of all three domains. In addition, collaboration would deal a fatal blow to the jealousy and resentment that seems to come with the "winner-take-all" genre of webweaving politics. With each department responsible and accountable for the Web site, finger pointing and backstabbing will diminish considerably.

The WWW Homepage: Marketing Tool, Information Resource, or Communication Conduit?

Yet, even a collaborating team must decide on the purpose of their Web page. Is it a marketing tool? Or is it a blunt, high-powered computer instrument, able to withstand 100 hits per second? Or is it, perhaps, a lean and elegant information guide, highly organized with "see" references and "see also" references and controlled vocabulary? Each organization will have to decide what its Web site will become. One scenario has the Web page glowing with glitz and panache, but leading nowhere in particular. Another scenario has the Web page providing access to the world's information resources, but at the cost of being a dull and lifeless place to visit. The ideal, in the author's opinion, is the Web site that combines the attractiveness and glamour of marketing with the common sense realism of the Computer Center and the organizational consistency and efficiency of the Library.

Criticism of the Web site: Constructive and Destructive Criticism

Through a combination of factors, including coincidence, determination, and possibly bad luck, I was given the task of weaving the Web pages for my organization. Soon after my appointment as

Webweaver, the marketing manager began to advocate her participation in the project. While never having spent even five minutes online, she nevertheless was determined to play a major role in designing and building our Web site. In her mind, a Web site was an important marketing tool, and she wanted to use her skills and expertise to make it work. I was comfortable with this, except for one small problem: her other work responsibilities kept her from collaborating with me. Every time that I would ask to meet with her or request information from her she would respond with the refrain, "I'm too busy right now." After some time it became apparent that her schedule and priorities would keep her away from the Web project indefinitely. I decided to continue alone.

As the word spread that I was designing a Web page for the organization, a certain amount of resentment seemed to spread among a small faction of the staff. This resentment probably stemmed from the feeling among this group that I had usurped the role of the marketing manager in the context of the Web Page. Over a period of several months this group of people "acted out" their resentment in various ways, including withholding of information, refusal to collaborate, sabotage, destructive criticism, and, in general, passive aggressive behavior. Some of the incidents that occurred included the following behavior:

(1) A staff person said to me, "I'm not authorized to give you that piece of information."
(2) Another staff person said to me, "I got into trouble the last time I helped you in this way, so I can't do it this time."
(3) Several people (one in particular) repeatedly refused (in a passive sort of way) to give me information that was to go on the Web Page. Several approaches were taken, including the oft-heard refrain, "I'll give it to you later" (it never came); "So-and-so is the one to talk to about this"; "I'm too busy"; and "It's in Pagemaker, and I can't convert it to WordPerfect."
(4) I heard criticism of my role in developing the Web page "through the grapevine," but these people never came to me directly.
(5) One person made a detailed critique of the Web page, including corrections and suggestions related to style, content, and format. But instead of giving this critique to me, she gave it to the marketing manager, who simply sat on it.

It was unfortunate and ironic that these events happened at the same time that our organization was optimistically talking about a flattening of the organization and collaboration with one another. This experience led me to believe that there was not only the presence of non-collaboration among the members of this particular group, but actually the presence of anti-collaboration. But, to be fair to the organization, there were several other staff members who went out of their way to assist me in the building of the Web site.

Political Rules for a Webweaver

(1) The Webweaver should have a thick skin vis-a-vis destructive criticism, backstabbing, etc.

(2) The Webweaver should be open to constructive criticism

(3) The Webweaver should market the Web inside the organization

(4) The Webweaver should know the mission and purpose of the Web, and stick with it despite political pressure

(5) The Webweaver should be aware of political machinations behind the scenes, and take the appropriate action in response.

Creating and Maintaining the Web site: Collaboration or Stagnation?

The Webweaver will clearly need to rely on others within the organization to create an effective Web site. This will include:

(1) Graphics contact person

No Webweaver is an island; none of us stand alone. Unless the Webweaver comes from the marketing department, he or she will probably not have a great deal of experience in designing, creating, scanning, or manipulating image files. The Webweaver needs to have a connection within the organization who has expertise in this area. This person does not necessarily have to come from the marketing or graphics department. In fact, their willingness to help you is in many ways more important than their role in the organization.

(2) Information providers

Information providers give the Webweaver information content, such as resumes, catalogs, databases, marketing copy, etc. It is obvious that a Web site without information content is just an empty shell. Webweavers need to cultivate information providers across the spectrum of the organization, not just from one or two departments. This will ensure that the Web site is rich, full-orbed, and representative of the entire organization.

(3) Technical support

The Webweaver may need some technical support in creating and maintaining the Web site. This is especially true if CGI scripting and applications like HotJava are to be utilized. A Web site that only uses basic HTML coding is probably underutilizing the power of the Web. Internal or external consultants are sometimes required for more complex programming needs.

Content and Organization: Controversial Choices

(1) Number and size of graphics files

The decision involving the number and size of graphics files may be debated for a variety of reasons. One camp will argue that a Web site should have multiple images that are large and colorful, since this will undoubtedly attract a larger audience on the Web. The other side will counter that Web sites should have as few images as possible to accommodate users with slower Internet connections. This debate could be viewed as the marketing department ("bold and beautiful") versus the information management cadre ("lean and mean"), but it might also be seen as a difference in philosophy between the "haves" (who assume that everyone has a high speed connection) and the "have-nots" (who want as many users as possible to be able to visit the Web site, and thus seek a "lowest common denominator" solution of mostly textual information).

(2) Who or what is emphasized

Each Web site will emphasize one aspect of the organization over another, whether by design or default. Whatever the motivation, this sends a clear message to the neglected department(s): you are less important than the rest of us. The Webweaver should avoid slights like this if possible. If overemphasizing one part of the organization (to the detriment of another part) is unavoidable, the Webweaver should then perform proactive damage control. In any event, hurt feelings and bruised egos are probably inevitable, but even so the Webweaver needs to keep this issue in mind as he or she designs the Web site.

Conclusion

Organizational politics can play an important role in the development of a Web site. Whether one enjoys the political fray or abhors it, organizational politics is a reality in most institutions. The Webweaver must be aware of political realities, on the one hand, but at the same time avoid Machiavellian-like behavior. The politically naive Webweaver will inadvertently hurt the feelings of others, and may ultimately be betrayed by his or her associates. The politically devious Webweaver will be distracted from the task at hand, and may ultimately pay a steep price for his or her devious behavior.

The politics of webweaving can be a dangerous sport, but those who play this game with wisdom and integrity will reap the rewards of a Web site that is attractive, useful, and rich with organizational resources.

Bibliography

Cropanzano, R. S., and Kacmar, K. M. (1995). Organizational Politics, Justice, and Support: Managing the Social Climate of the Workplace. Westport, CT: Quorum Books.

Cutler, M., and Richard, E. (1995). The well-rounded Webmaster. Internet World, 6, 30-32.

Engler, N. (September 1, 1995). The politics of trust: Groupware is only one step toward improved group productivity. Open Computing, 12, 38-44.

Client/Server, Beggarman, Thief: Considering the Relationship Between Academic Libraries and Information Technology Units

Dennis A. Kreps, Jacqueline Johnson and C. Martin Rosen
Library, Indiana University Southeast
New Albany, Indiana

Abstract

The evolution of the contemporary academic library as an independent organism and as a component of the university reflects rational responses to technological infrastructures and to organizational precepts deeply rooted in the industrial era. Like other twentieth century organizations, libraries and universities have sought to optimize the use of capital and human resources through technological centralization and human specialization. As the century draws to a close, however, new infrastructural developments and parallel shifts in organizational paradigms are operating in tandem to alter the internal structure of libraries as well as the relationships between libraries and other arms of the university.

Distributed information processing regimes, such as client/server technology, are supplanting mainframe-based systems at the same time that "flattened" organizationals schemes are replacing the traditional hierarchical organization with a new post-industrial model. These trends operate in tandem to redistribute expertise and decision-making responsibilities across and through organizations in new way that, although unpredictable in the specifics, are certain to result in new interdependencies and inevitably in new organizational conflicts and opportunities. In academic libraries, these technological and organizational changes have a particularly profound effect on the relationship between the library and the university's information technology (or computing services) operations.

In this preliminary version of a paper presented at the ASIS 1996 mid-year meeting, technological, cultural and organizational conditions that influence the relationship between libraries and information technology units and may lead to conflicts between them are described and discussed. Strategies by which librarians and libray managers can avoid and resolve conflicts and achieve good working relationships with their information technology counterparts are offered.

1. INTRODUCTION

Specialization in skills and segmentation of tasks pervade human communities so thoroughly that any reasonable observer is bound to view them as universals that cut across time and technological status, linking the paleolithic era to the information age, and contributing to the mechanisms of social organization in both pre-literate and highly developed societies. Indeed, by the early twentieth century, when management guru Frederick W. Taylor's scientific management principles were placing a capstone of logic atop the labor practices of the industrial era, the inescabability of human specialization had become so clear that imagining a human generalist required reaching back across several centuries and retrieving the notion of the "Renaissance person." We can quibble over whether Renaissance intellectuals were not themselves specialists of a sort, but in today's era, when one could conceivably earn the right to be called a Renaissance person simply by mastering, say, DOS, UNIX, Windows, and the latest Macintosh System, we can hardly dispute that modern aspirations are, in general, highly specific.

If any modern profession can make a plausible claim to a Renaissance-like breadth of interest, it is, of course, library and information science which, like philosophy, appropriates to itself a comprehensive concern with the full range of human learning and activity (Wright, 1977). Even so, the evolution of the contemporary academic library (any library, for that matter) as an independent organism and as a component of the university reflects rational responses to technological infrastructures and organizational precepts deeply rooted in industrial era thought. Mirroring other twentieth century organizations, libraries and universities have sought to optimize the efficient use of capital and human resources through human specialization and technological centralization.

As the century draws to a close, however, new technological developments and parallel shifts in organizational paradigms are operating in tandem to reshape the internal structures of libraries as well as the relationships between libraries and other arms of the university. Distributed information processing regimes, in particular client/server technologies, are supplanting mainframe-based information systems at the same time that "flattened" organizational schemes are replacing the traditional hierarchical organization with a new post-industrial model. Together, these trends lead to the distribution of expertise and decision-making responsibilities across and throughout organizations in new ways that are unpredictable in their specific effects but are certain to result in new interdependencies and inevitably in new organizational opportunities and conflicts. In academic libraries, these technological and infrastructural changes have a particularly powerful influence on the relationship between the library and the university's information technology (or computing services) operations.

In a typical mainframe computing regime, the divisions of responsibilities between libraries and information technology (IT) operations can be sorted along a blurry but defineable border that implies specialized expertise and control of hardware, software and infrastructure on one side, and on the other expertise in the selection, storage, retrieval, and exploitation of information artifacts. Typically, interactions between libraries and information technology operations are governed by conventional formal structures that establish clear, predictable communication, decision-making, and accountability rules that, at least putatively, permit these disparate specializations to complement one another in an efficient, orderly fashion.

In contrast, client/server technologies and distributed computing regimes offer users new freedom and flexibility, but at the same time push complex technical issues and knowledge requirements outward to the desktops of librarians and end-users, where the skills to cope with them are often inchoate and inconsistent. Meanwhile, recent trends toward flattened organizational structures encourage distributed decision-making (or decision-avoidance) but may fail to assure clear communication and accountability processes. As a consequence, functional units that should be cooperating may wind up in conflicts that degrade efficiency and adversely affect service to the scholarly community.

As this confluence of organizational and technological trends proceeds, it is timely to review the technical, cultural, and organizational factors that affect the interaction between libraries and information technology units, and consider strategies by which librarians and library directors can work to achieve an optimal working relationship with their counterparts at the other end of the network.

2. TECHNOLOGIES ARE US

Technological determinism, the notion that technology shapes social organizations, is a widespread commonplace in contemporary thought, but one countered by the argument that technologies are themselves nothing but manifestations of the intentions and desires of humans (Harris, 1994). If life often imitates technology, it is equally true that technology often imitates life. We can prudently sidestep the interesting question of which event is more important by paraphrasing Winston Churchill and agreeing that we first shape our technologies, but then our technologies begin to shape us. When we consider the application of technologies in libraries, for instance, we see that throughout the century, library automation has been intentionally deployed to increase the efficiency and accuracy of manual processes, beginning with the production and distribution of catalog cards, progressing to the implementation of systems that facilitate acquisitions, shared cataloging, circulation, and so forth, and culminating in the implementation of integrated systems that bring functions like acquistions, cataloging, serials control, the printing of labels, the tracking of circulation transactions, management statistics, etc., into a single automation stream. For the most part clear intentions and objectives were the impetus behind each of these developments (at least our predecessors would have us imagine so), and library automation followed in the wake of already existing processes (Molholt, 1985).

Nevertheless, while library systems were undergoing an integrative evolutionary process, librarianship itself was becoming more and more fragmented as organizational structures and individual expertise were increasingly tailored to fit the systems. For example, any number of libraries have undertaken organizational restructuring around the components of an automated system, and even in smaller libraries technical personnel who can claim acceptable competence in a given library system's acquistions, cataloging, and circulation modules are rare indeed. (Rarer still, perhaps, is the technically oriented librarian capable of comfortably taking a shift at the reference desk.) Even well-developed knowledge of a clearly defined sphere of librarianship, say acquisitions, has become only a partially sufficient professional credential at a time when postings for library positions often prefer familiarity with specific modules of specific vendor software. And of course, it is abundantly clear that when librarians talk to other librarians a translation table may be necessary to parse the jargon (even when it isn't compressed in acronyms and initialisms).

Concurrent with the widespread adoption of automated technologies in libraries, the universities as a whole were also exploiting the power of computers to support academic research and to automate administrative functions such as payroll, accounting, and the full range of bursar and registrar activities (tracking grades, enrollment, and the like) (Veaner, 1974). As campus investments in computing technology grew in importance, and especially in cost, universities sought to achieve economies of scale by serving multiple user groups with centralized, large-capacity machinery (Saffady, 1983). It was rare that a library was able to justify ownership of an in-house machine sufficient to meet its needs (De Gennaro, 1971); It was equally rare that a library possessed within itself the expertise to acquire and operate such a system, even if it could afford one.

The implementation of expensive, centralized computing operations serving the needs of the disparate campus constituencies naturally required organizational responses. Most importantly, the machines themselves required a competent staff capable of supplying regular attention and nurturing in order to assure a stable platform on which the growing expectations of the various users could be met. In addition, administrative mechanisms were necessary to balance competing interests of these various groups. Thus, by the early 1970s, the typical campus had created, under one rubric or another, some sort of information technology unit. And, given the technical knowledge required to implement and operate the machines, responsibility for administering these information technology units nearly always fell to specialist technician-managers. This quite reasonable trend had a couple of important consequences.

First, it defined the relationship between information technology personnel and information technology users as one between an expertise-rich, service-providing staff (well, more or less service-providing) and expertise-poor consumers of services. Even when libraries developed internal technical expertise (in the form of systems librarians, for example), there usually remained an arms-length relationship between the library and the management of computing resources. The library could propose, explain, and justify its priorities, needs, and desires, but the disposition of those proposals and the ranking of library priorities among other campus needs rested in other--presumably more knowledgeable--hands. Equally importantly, this division implicitly shielded the library from an obligation to develop the kind of expertise necessary to collaborate as technical equals with information technology personnel in shaping systems specifically designed to meet library needs.

Second, the growth of information technology units managed by technicians created an organizational infrastructure in which the technology itself had a significant influence on decision-making. As early as 1974, Allen Veaner noted that in managing computing operations "the technician tended to promote his own technical interests in software development or hardware utilization" and tended to manage operations "more for the benefit of the staff than for the users." Veaner observed as well that the technician/manager "often looked at the computer as his personal machine" and noted a widespread perception that computing services staff often had greater loyalty to the machines and software with which they worked than to the academic goals of the institution (Veaner, 1974).

Since that time, the technical environment has changed dramatically. The rapid spread of minicomputers and microcomputers across campuses, coupled with reduced costs that enabled many libraries to purchase bundled library systems and hardware are significant developments. Yet, even though networks and servers have replaced mainframes as the focus of technical development, and microcomputers running client software have replaced dumb terminals on librarians' and users' desks, the underlying dynamics of this relationship have hardly changed.

3. DIVERGENT CULTURES

For a time it appeared that universities would attempt to exploit the commonalities between libraries and information technology operations (not least an often remarked upon, though not always clearly overlapping interest in a nebulous commodity called information) through a merged organizational model in which both would be subsumed under a common administrative umbrella. In 1987, Richard Dougherty predicted, correctly it seems, that "because the difference between libraries and computing centers is so great from an organizational standpoint...models that rely on coordination and collaboration are more likely to predominate in the near term than models that subordinate one unit to another" (Dougherty, 1987). Although the interest in merger seems to have waned, few observers would argue that coordination and collaboration have already begun on any large scale. Instead, it appears, anecdotally at least, that public and official statements notwithstanding, tension, competition and distance between libraries and information technology units remain very much the order of the day.

A number of conditions contribute to this state of affairs. Clearly, the allocation of finite funds is always, by its nature, a zero sum game in which one competitor's gain can be construed as another's loss. In addition to fiscal considerations, though , there are significant historical and cultural differences at play that greatly affect communication between these two groups. David Weber concisely identified a far-reaching difference when he observed that a university library operates on a foundation built on centuries of tradition and "a long history of development of standards, philosophies, procedures, connections with the book trade, and as much as a fifty year history of automating operations." By contrast, Weber noted, information technology units on campus are unlikely to have a history exceeding three or four decades (Weber, 1988).

Sheila Creth pinpointed some other factors that contribute to the cultural differentiation between librarians and computing professionals. She noted that although both librarians and computing professionals come to their profession from a variety of fields of study, librarians undergo "a process of acculturation in which they develop a shared philosophy and common values" and thus "are more likely to act within the boundaries of accepted professional beliefs and behavior." In contrast, "there is no socialization process for a computer professional prior to accepting a position in a computer organization" (Creth, 1993, p. 120). Although the latter statement is perhaps a little strong (after all, computer science students must at least exchange tips on how best to arrange their ponytails), it certainly rings true that much more time is spent in library education inculcating in students what it means to be a librarian than one would expect in a computer science curriculum. When Creth examined the professional values of academic librarians and academic computing professionals, she discovered some commonalities (a professional orientation, an interest in the global information community, and a concern with the success of the university), but also revealing differences: computers professionals tend to have a technical orientation and to value entrepreneurial behavior and individual creativity, whereas librarians tend to have a service orientation and prefer consensus decision-making (Creth, 1983).

It is necessary as well to draw attention to an obvious but important fact: the working arrangements under which the two communities operate differ at their very foundations. Academic libraries are typically organized around a faculty model; academic librarians frequently occupy tenure track faculty positions, and even when that is not the case, they typically serve in ranks analogous to those of teaching faculty. It is common that librarians take part in university faculty governance, and when this is the case, the library itself will nearly always organize itself internally according to faculty models. Information technology units are seldom, if ever, organized along these lines. They are most often staffed by a combination of professional and administrative staff and classified staff (though of course the terminology varies from institution to institution).

At most universities, this difference not only affects the organizational status and reporting lines of the two groups, but has significant ramifications in terms of professional development and continung education. It is typical for librarians, like other faculty, to be supported and encouraged (if not required) to participate in professional organizations, attend conferences and workshops, perform research and publication, and so forth. It is rare that similar support and encouragement exists for information technology personnel. The value of professional activity (or service, as it is sometimes called) is often as not subject to cynical questioning, yet it seems likely that in its absence a group of personnel is likely to take on an insularity and narrowness of perspective that is unlikely to have a positive effect on its working relationships in a campus environment.

4. A TRICKLE RUNS THROUGH IT

It may be nothing more than a coincidence that the development of the distributed computing model is emerging at nearly the same time that organizations in the western world are looking critically at the bureaucratic organizational schemes that have so long been the basis for organization and control in complex institutions. If so, it is a remarkable coincidence. Regardless, flattening organizations, removing layers of management, and striving to encourage individual responsibility and exploit individual skill seems to be a lasting management trend (though the names under which it is promoted may change more rapidly than the seasons).

Because the administrative units of universities operate under a strong tradition of autonomy, there appear to be few instances of university-wide organizational flattening. (Although some of the underlying theory doubtless emanated from academic scholars in business, it would be a rare business school indeed that would dispense with its deans and department chairs). In general, most universities continue to operate as traditional bureacratic conglomerations of discreet pyramids. When this is so, the communication stream from unit to unit is well regulated and formalized. Communication between the library and the information technology unit will typically take the form of highly controlled interactions at rigorously defined levels. In the interest of efficiency and accountability, the information technology unit prefers that the library, as one of its largest customers, filter its requests, problem reports, and so forth through some limited number of conduits. If, as is usually the case, the library has identified and articulated needs and priorities that exceed the resources of the information technology unit, library management has a strong interest in insuring that any work done in its behalf be focused on its collective priorities rather than the interests of individuals or individual units in the library. This is a conventional arrangement, but one that works successfully, assuming good management in all the pyramids--and assuming that all the pyramids are using the same internal operating structure.

Interestingly, though, many libraries and information technology units have begun experimenting with new flattened organizational structures (often in the form of a total quality management initiative). The goals and outcomes of these initiatives are often exemplary (though outside the scope of this paper), but the mechanisms they use can create a very murky communication environment. Given the cultural predispositions of information technology units mentioned above, it seems clear that self-managing work groups, non-hierarchical structures, and an emphasis on individual activity can fit neatly into existing paradigms and facilitate quick responses to changing circumstances. In libraries, the same mechanisms can also serve to generate new ideas and foster creativity. The useful flow of interdepartmental information may, however, slow to a trickle when decision-making rests in shared and not readily distinguishable hands.

5. MISSIONARY WORK

Technology, culture, and organizational infrastructures operate in tandem to shape libraries and information technology units as distinct creatures. To a great extent, those differences are conscious and intentional. An unsystematic look at a number of library and information technology mission statements (viewed on websites and solicited from a few internet discussion groups) was suggestive in this regard. Library mission statements, as one would expect, reflect a broad concern with supporting academic work and research goals, a strong emphasis on educating library users in the use of information resources, a commitment to academic freedom, an interest in the preservation of materials, service to the local user community (and typically to a more expansive community of researchers), and often language regarding staff and professional development. In addition, most library mission statements include language about acquiring and utilizing technology in the pursuit of these goals.

Mission statements for computing services and information technology units are, not surprisingly, quite different. Although many (but by no means all) include language regarding the academic goals of the university, the emphasis is very heavily on the technology itself. A particularly striking difference was the manner in which the word "support" was used In these documents. While library mission statments spoke of "supporting" teaching and research, information technology documents frequently spoke of "supporting" software or LANs. Where library documents spoke of educating users, information technology documents often spoke of training users. (In this connection , by the way, this non-rigorous assessment also suggested that an articulated emphasis on training was more likely to emanate from units with names like "Office of Information Technology" than from those with names like "Computing Services."}

Although there was some overlap in the expressed missions of libraries and information technology units, the differences remain great, and are certainly reflected in the allocation of human resources. Consider that any library invests a substantial portion of its professional payroll in direct service to patrons. Indeed, in most libraries, the budgeted cost of reference and bibliographic instruction librarians will greatly exceed the cost of professional technical services and systems staff. In contrast, even when information technology units dedicate some staff to help desks and training, the total outlay for such activities is likely to be a minimal portion of overall personnel costs.

6. PRESCRIPTIONS

Given the technical, cultural, and organizational differences between libraries and information technology units, it seems clear that it behooves librarians to cultivate well thought out strategies for managing these interactions.

Perhaps first and foremost, librarians should strive to develop their own competencies in the technical arena. Replacing a dumb terminal with a smart client does little good if the operator of that terminal declines to accept responsibility for understanding something about its workings. Likewise, although not every librarian needs to master the niceties of network administration, some conceptual grasp of networking principles and implications is now as essential to furnishing competent professional service as an understanding of bibliographic classification or mastery of the reference interview. In the absence of this kind of expertise, librarians will remain in the same position they were in 1974, when Veaner reported that library exploitation of technologies was hindered by the inability of librarians to describe their information needs in a realistic technical context and with precision (Veaner, 1974).

Second, librarians should exploit the full range of formal and informal communication mechanisms at their disposal. In 1974, Veaner described a scenario that remains true today: "The technician-manager represents a highly personalized management style, one in which goodwill, friendship, or personal interest is the key to effective service. Veaner deplored that style, on the grounds that it interfered with rational decision-making, and was an inefficient means of allocating scarce resources (Veaner, 1974). True enough. Still, though the intervening twenty years have led to increased rationality in decision-making, articulated mission statements, and increasingly formal relations across campuses, few observers would claim that all information technology decision-making is rational (nor would most observers claim that all library decision-making is rational). Although we may desire and work toward a rational environment, we are more likely to succeed if we also stay somewhat in contact with the real world.

Third, librarians should collaborate with information technology units in the formulation of strategic initiatives. Creth has observed that "with increased integration of and dependence on information technology, library managers cannot afford to be surprised by decisions about computing support on campus...Equally important, computing center managers should not be caught off guard by decisions that library managers make" (Creth, 1993). Often, for example, there are faculty committees that have input into library planning and policy as well as computing planning and policy. A reciprocal agreement in which the library and the information technology unit have representation on one another's committees seems quite reasonable and simple to implement.

Fourth, libraries should endeavor to ensure that information technology personnel understand how their work contributes to successful outcomes in the library. Although information technology units clearly furnish services, most of the staff have only a veiled understanding of how those services affect educational and research outcomes. Complaints and desires are frequently directed in their direction, but successful transactions are rarely news, and seldom mentioned. If, for example, a reconfiguration of terminals requires rewiring, or a new machine requires configuration by information technology staff, a conscious plan to follow up later with word of how well the new layout or new machine is working may encourage prompt service in the future, at no expense.

Fifth, libraries can initiate and take part in joint training experiences. As mentioned earlier, information technology units are often afflicted by even poorer staff development budgets than those under which libraries suffer. If appropriate training programs, teleconferences, or the like, are undertaken by the library (say, in general service issues, or in information science or library issues), inviting information technology personnel to take part may raise awareness of library values and concerns. Taking part in training opportunities sponsored by information technology may likewise have a beneficial effect. And sharing the costs of such efforts between units may permit increased staff development opportunities.

Second, librarians should exploit the full range of formal and informal communication mechanisms at their disposal. In 1974, Veaner described a scenario that remains true today: "The technician-manager represents a highly personalized management style, one in which goodwill, friendship, or personal interest is the key to effective service. Veaner deplored that style, on the grounds that it interfered with rational decision-making, and was an inefficient means of allocating scarce resources (Veaner, 1974). True enough. Still, though the intervening twenty years have led to increased rationality in decision-making, articulated mission statements, and increasingly formal relations across campuses, few observers would claim that all information technology decision-making is rational (nor would most observers claim that all library decision-making is rational). Although we may desire and work toward a rational environment, we are more likely to succeed if we also stay somewhat in contact with the real world.

Third, librarians should collaborate with information technology units in the formulation of strategic initiatives. Creth has observed that "with increased integration of and dependence on information technology, library managers cannot afford to be surprised by decisions about computing support on campus...Equally important, computing center managers should not be caught off guard by decisions that library managers make" (Creth, 1993). Often, for example, there are faculty committees that have input into library planning and policy as well as computing planning and policy. A reciprocal agreement in which the library and the information technology unit have representation on one another's committees seems quite reasonable and simple to implement.

Fourth, libraries should endeavor to ensure that information technology personnel understand how their work contributes to successful outcomes in the library. Although information technology units clearly furnish services, most of the staff have only a veiled understanding of how those services affect educational and research outcomes. Complaints and desires are frequently directed in their direction, but successful transactions are rarely news, and seldom mentioned. If, for example, a reconfiguration of terminals requires rewiring, or a new machine requires configuration by information technology staff, a conscious plan to follow up later with word of how well the new layout or new machine is working may encourage prompt service in the future, at no expense.

Fifth, libraries can initiate and take part in joint training experiences. As mentioned earlier, information technology units are often afflicted by even poorer staff development budgets than those under which libraries suffer. If appropriate training programs, teleconferences, or the like, are undertaken by the library (say, in general service issues, or in information science or library issues), inviting information technology personnel to take part may raise awareness of library values and concerns. Taking part in training opportunities sponsored by information technology may likewise have a beneficial effect. And sharing the costs of such efforts between units may permit increased staff development opportunities.

7. CONCLUSIONS

The academic library occupies a particularly intricate niche in the university, a spot where the historic tools and attitudes of academic life collide with new devices and lofty expectations that even a few years ago would have been unimaginable. If it is to continue to meet the needs of its users, it must somehow contrive not only to be an exemplary servant to its constituents, but also an intelligent, self-assured client as it engages with its technological counterparts. More than any other part of the university, the academic library, like the Mother Goose rhyme that begins "Rich man, poor man, beggarman, thief," mirrors the broad scope of its parent institution. As the academic and technological conditions in which it operates are transformed, the library must likewise constantly reexamine its internal workings and external connections if it is to continue effectively linking people with the information they seek.

8. REFERENCES

Creth Sheila D. (1993). Creating a virtual information organization: collaborative relationships between libraries and computing centers. Journal of Library Administration, 19,(3/4), 111-132.

De Gennaro, Richard. (1971). The development and administration of automated systems in academic libraries. in Louis Kaplan (Ed.), Reader in library services and the computer (pp. 69-79). Washington, D.C.: Microcard Editions.

Dougherty, Richard M. (1987). Libraries and computing centers: A blueprint for collaboration. College and Research Libraries, 48, 289-296.

Harris, Michael, and Hannah, Stan A. (1994). Into the future: The foundations of library and information services in the post-industrial era. Norwood, N.J.:Ablex.

Molholt, Pat. (1985). On converging paths: The computer center and the library. The Journal of Academic Librarianship, 11 (5). 284-288.

Saffady, William. (1983). Introduction to automation for librarians. Chicago: American Library Association.

Veaner, Allen B. (1974). Institutional, political, and fiscal factors in the development of library automation, 1967-71. Journal of Library Automation, 7 (1), 5-26.

Weber, David C. (1988). University libraries and campus information technology organizations: Who is in charge here? Journal of Library Administration. 9 (4), 5-19.

Wright, H. Curtis. (1977). The Oral antecedents of Greek librarianship. Provo, UT: Brigham Young University.

An Information Needs and Services Taxonomy for Evaluating Computerized Community Information Systems

Ronald D. Doctor and Kalyani Ankem
School of Library and Information Studies, University of Alabama
Tuscaloosa, Alabama

Abstract

Computerized Community Information Systems (CCISs, also known as Public Access Networks, Community Networks, and Free-Nets[1]) are becoming increasingly common in communities across the United States and Canada. In February 1996 there were more than 390 systems either operational or organizing. These systems focus on providing information that people in local communities need in their daily lives. To evaluate how well they accomplish their objectives, we must ask: (1) Who do the systems serve?; (2) What information needs do they try to meet?; and (3) How effectively do they meet those needs? To help answer these questions, we have developed a new taxonomy of information needs and services and have tested the taxonomy in a pilot study of four operational systems. The taxonomy consists of a three dimensional matrix, the axes of which are *Situational (or Subject) Categories*, *Types of Help* provided, and *Socioeconomic Identifiers*. The fourteen *Situational Categories* like education, governmental processes, and social services were further subdivided. Five *Types of Help* were identified: Advocacy, Counseling, Directional, Factual, and Interactive Communication. *Socioeconomic Identifiers* included variables like age group, educational level, gender and income. We tested the taxonomy by examining the several hundred services provided by four CCISs (Victoria Free-Net, Big Sky Telegraph, Blacksburg Electronic Village, and Mobile Free-Net), locating each service within the three-dimensional matrix. We found that : (1) *Directional* and *factual* help dominate the service offerings, but the types of information provided varied considerably from one system to another; (2) Services based on *interactive communications* were significant and growing; (3) *Counseling* services were present but limited; (4) *Advocacy* was almost non-existent; and (5) Information about social services was rare. Services oriented to middle income and upper middle income patrons dominated the four systems. Very few services were specifically targeted to low-income patrons. The pilot study indicated that the taxonomy is useful for evaluating CCIS services. It is particularly useful for identifying areas in which service offerings are weak or non-existent, thus it can be used to help a CCIS improve its services to better meet its objectives.

In the past six years we have witnessed a virtual explosion of information services available through a variety of grass-roots based computerized community information systems (CCISs). Doctor & Ankem (February 1996) have identified more than 390 CCISs either in existence or organizing. These systems provide a wide variety of communication and information services to people in their own homes and in public places in their communities. Through continuing, rapid expansion supported in part by federal development of a National Information Infrastructure (NII), they have the potential for significantly changing traditional power relationships in our society. The questions we must ask are:

- Who do these systems serve?
- What information needs do they try to meet?
- How effective are they in helping people with their day-to-day information needs?
- By what mechanisms and to what extent do they change the distribution of societal power?

This paper describes a taxonomy of information needs and services that we have developed and used to respond to the first two questions. The taxonomy builds upon a considerable body of previous studies about the information needs of ordinary people. (See especially, Childers, 1975; Chen & Hernon, 1982; Dervin & Fraser, 1985; and Dervin & Nilan, 1986.) The literature indicates that people typically seek information and services that fall into fourteen subject, or *situational categories*. In the taxonomy, each category is further subdivided and is classified according to the *type of help* it provides and according to *socioeconomic identifiers* indicating who the information is intended to help. Table 1 shows the three dimensions of the taxonomic schema.

Table 1 - CCIS Information Needs/Services Taxonomy

Type of Help Provided	Situational Category	Socioeconomic Identifiers
Advocacy Counseling) Directional Factual Interactive Communication	Community & Commerce Consumer Affairs Education & Schooling Employment Financial Matters Government & Politics Health & Medical Home & Family Housing Legal Matters Nature & Environment Recreation & Culture Social Services Transportation	Age Group Educational Level Ethnicity Gender Income Level Rural/Urban/ etc.

The resulting three dimensional matrix or profile provides a means for evaluating and comparing the information services offered by various CCISs. We can get an indication of the extent to which each system meets individual and community information needs by identifying whether the system provides information defined by the intersection of each *situational category* with a *type of help* provided by the system and with each *socioeconomic identifier.*

Types of Help

The types of help provided vary considerably across the systems we have examined:

Advocacy involves personally assisting the help-seeking patron solve her/his problem through direct contact with a helping agency or an adversarial agent. There is evidence that people seeking *information* really are seeking help, or *advocacy*. Advocacy may be essential if an information service is to succeed (Bundy, 1972; Voos, 1969). This form of help may involve contacting helping agencies on behalf of, or with, the patron. Such contact may be electronic (e-mail, telephone), print (letters, fax), or in person.

Counseling involves helping the client to understand his/her problematic situation and to understand and use various means available to effectively resolve it. Counseling services usually are provided by professionals. In this taxonomy, counseling stops short of advocacy.

Directional help answers *where* questions like, "where do I get this information?, or "where is information about . . .?" It leads the patron to the information that she/he seeks, but it does not help the patron define what information is needed.

Factual help answers *what* questions such as, "what jobs are available?", "what are my legal rights?", "what entertainment is available tonight?".

Interactive Communications may incorporate any of the other four "helps". It requires at least two parties in direct or indirect communication. It usually takes place via e-mail, or electronic discussion lists, but it also may use the telephone or fax machine. It may involve an exchange of messages between two or more people, or it may involve requests for information or interaction with an organization by filling out and sending an on-line form. Other, more advanced forms of interactive communication also could involve electronic opinion polls or even voting. Interactive communication involving groups tends to foster a sense of community or shared interest. Both *group* and *personal* interactive communication can be effective in providing emotional or other psychological support, a *help* found to be very important to people seeking information (Dervin & Fraser, 1985; Chen & Hernon, 1982). On CCISs, this *help* typically is not professional help, but rather peer self-help or mutual aid.

Testing the Taxonomy

To test the taxonomy, we scanned the services offered by more than 150 operational CCISs and selected four systems (Big Sky Telegraph, Blacksburg Electronic Village, Mobile Free-Net, and Victoria Free-Net) for detailed analysis. Selection criteria included geographical diversity, level of maturity, and type of system.

- Big Sky Telegraph[2] is a mature statewide network funded by Western Montana College and U.S. West. It's emphasis is on education, particularly K-12 education. Big Sky is an affiliate of the National Public Telecomputing Network (NPTN).
- Blacksburg Electronic Village (BEV)[3] is a "cooperative project of Virginia Tech, Bell Atlantic of Virginia, and the town of Blacksburg." (*About the Blacksburg . . .*, February 1996). It became operational in October 1993 following two and a half years of preparation. BEV serves a town of 36,000 citizens. Fifty to 60% of this highly educated, upper income community are members of BEV.
- Mobile Area Free-Net (MAFN)[4] is a relatively young network that opened in early 1995. It serves about 500,000 people in Mobile, Alabama and its surrounding areas. Services available on MAFN are changing rapidly.
- Victoria Free-Net[5] is a free community-based network formed in June 1992. It serves an area with a population of 300,000. It has no paid staff, is run by volunteers, and depends on contracts and individual and corporate donations for funding. It is a mature network. It adheres more closely to the NPTN menu format for Free-Nets than do the other networks examined here.

Although we have assigned each CCIS service to a situational category and type of help, the actual services are not so neatly arranged or identified on the CCISs we have examined. Services typically are scattered across each system's menus, often making it difficult for patrons to locate a particular kind of information. We have *not* addressed issues relating to ease of access or ease of use in this paper. In addition, some services properly fall into more than one category. We have reflected this in our analyses by counting a multi-category service wherever it appears even though this means that the total service counts will be somewhat inflated.

We examined the 600 services provided by the four CCISs, locating each service within the three-dimensional matrix. For this paper, however, we have reported on only two dimensions of the matrix, *situational categories* and *types of help*. Socioeconomic identifiers are discussed in a forthcoming article. Table 2 and Table 3 show the services offered by situational category and by type of help, respectively, for each of the four systems. Tabulations of the results for each system are shown in Table 4 through Table 7.

We found that: (1) Directional and factual help dominate the service offerings but the types of information provided varied considerably from one system to another. Directional help was present in 65% and factual help in 85% of the 600 services offered; (2) Services based on interactive communications were significant and from other work we've done, appear to be growing, but they were highly variable from one system to another. They ranged from 20% to 67% of total service offerings on the four systems, averaging 42% of the 600 services; (3) Counseling services were present but limited, averaging 4.8% over all services; (4) Advocacy was involved in only 1.8% of the 600 services, ranging from zero to 3% of each system's services. One system (Blacksburg) offered no discernible advocacy services at all; (5) Information about housing, legal matters, social services, and transportation was rare; and (6) Services oriented to middle income and upper middle income patrons dominated the four systems. Very few services were specifically targeted to low-income patrons.

Table 2 - Services Offered, by Situational Categories

	Big Sky Telegraph	Blacksburg Electronic Village	Mobile Area Free-Net	Victoria Free-Net
Community & Commerce	14	20	23	31
Consumer Affairs	3	1	2	17
Education & Schooling	28	20	31	31
Employment	5	6	2	10
Financial Matters	1	4	5	6
Government & Politics	2	19	22	26
Health & Medical	5	8	13	29
Home & Family	5	5	5	5
Housing	2	6	1	8
Legal Matters	3	2	2	7
Nature & Environment	4	5	7	20
Recreation & Culture	15	18	39	31
Social Services	3	0	7	2
Transportation	2	4	5	3
TOTALS	92	118	164	226

Table 3 - Services Offered, by Type of Help

	Total	Advocacy	Counseling	Directional	Factual	Interactive Communication
Big Sky Telegraph	92	1	4	60	79	18
Percent of Total		1.1%	4.3%	65.2%	85.9%	19.6%
Blacksburg Electronic Village	118	0	5	85	94	38
Percent of Total		0.0%	4.2%	72.0%	79.7%	32.2%
Mobile Area Free-Net	164	5	10	106	140	110
Percent of Total		3.0%	6.1%	64.6%	85.4%	67.1%
Victoria Free-Net	226	5	10	140	198	89
Percent of Total		2.2%	4.4%	61.9%	87.6%	39.4%

Although it is risky to generalize from examination of only four systems, it does appear that the taxonomy will be useful for evaluating and improving the services offered by CCISs. The pilot project now is being extended to cover systems with greater geographical and socioeconomic diversity. The taxonomy also is being used as an aid in developing the services offered by the West Alabama Free-Net (Tuscaloosa, Alabama).

SUMMARY OF SERVICES

Table 4 - Big Sky Telegraph
June 15, 1995

Number of Services by Situational Category & Type of Help

	Total	Advocacy	Counseling	Directional	Factual	Interactive Communication
Community & Commerce	14	0	2	11	12	3
Consumer Affairs	3	0	0	1	2	0
Education & Schooling	28	0	0	18	25	10
Employment	5	0	0	4	4	1
Financial Matters	1	0	0	1	1	0
Government & Politics	2	0	0	1	2	0
Health & Medical	5	0	1	5	3	1
Home & Family	5	0	0	3	5	0
Housing	2	0	0	2	1	0
Legal Matters	3	0	0	0	3	0
Nature & Environment	4	0	0	1	4	0
Recreation & Culture	15	0	0	10	13	3
Social Services	3	1	1	2	3	0
Transportation	2	0	0	1	1	0
TOTALS	92	1	4	60	79	18
Percent of Total		1.1%	4.3%	65.2%	85.9%	19.6%

Table 5 - Blacksburg Electronic Village
November 5, 1995

Number of Services by Situational Category & Type of Help

	Total	Advocacy	Counseling	Directional	Factual	Interactive Communication
Community & Commerce	20	0	1	11	16	11
Consumer Affairs	1	0	0	1	0	1
Education & Schooling	20	0	0	12	16	11
Employment	6	0	1	4	6	1
Financial Matters	4	0	0	4	4	3
Government & Politics	19	0	0	14	15	2
Health & Medical	8	0	3	7	5	0
Home & Family	5	0	0	5	5	1
Housing	6	0	0	5	5	1
Legal Matters	2	0	0	2	1	0
Nature & Environment	5	0	0	2	4	2
Recreation & Culture	18	0	0	15	13	5
Social Services	0	0	0	0	0	0
Transportation	4	0	0	3	4	0
TOTALS	118	0	5	85	94	38
Percent of Total		0.0%	4.2%	72.0%	79.7%	32.2%

SUMMARY OF SERVICES

Table 6 - Mobile Area Free-Net
July 30, 1995

Number of Services by Situational Category & Type of Help

	Total	Advocacy	Counseling	Directional	Factual	Interactive Communication
Community & Commerce	23	1	2	14	19	17
Consumer Affairs	2	0	0	1	2	1
Education & Schooling	31	0	1	20	29	20
Employment	2	0	0	2	2	1
Financial Matters	5	0	1	2	5	5
Government & Politics	22	0	0	18	17	6
Health & Medical	13	2	2	10	13	7
Home & Family	5	0	0	4	5	5
Housing	1	1	1	1	1	1
Legal Matters	2	0	0	2	2	1
Nature & Environment	7	0	0	2	6	4
Recreation & Culture	39	0	1	23	30	36
Social Services	7	1	2	5	5	5
Transportation	5	0	0	2	4	1
TOTALS	164	5	10	106	140	110
Percent of Total		3.0%	6.1%	64.6%	85.4%	67.1%

Table 7 - Victoria (Canada) Free-Net
August 28, 1995

Number of Services by Situational Category & Type of Help

	Total	Advocacy	Counseling	Directional	Factual	Interactive Communication
Community & Commerce	31	1	0	25	25	16
Consumer Affairs	17	2	0	15	17	3
Education & Schooling	31	0	4	12	24	19
Employment	10	0	1	9	10	1
Financial Matters	6	0	0	2	6	1
Government & Politics	26	1	0	17	25	5
Health & Medical	29	0	3	12	27	9
Home & Family	5	0	0	4	4	4
Housing	8	0	0	8	8	2
Legal Matters	7	1	1	5	6	3
Nature & Environment	20	0	0	9	19	4
Recreation & Culture	31	0	0	18	22	20
Social Services	2	0	1	2	2	1
Transportation	3	0	0	2	3	1
TOTALS	226	5	10	140	198	89
Percent of Total		2.2%	4.4%	61.9%	87.6%	39.4%

REFERENCES

About the Blacksburg Electronic Village (BEV). Available on the WWW at URL: http://crusher.bev.net/project/index.html.

Bundy, M.L. (1972). Urban information in public libraries. *Library Journal*, 97:161-69, 1972.

Chen, C., & Hernon, P. (1982). *Information seeking: Assessing and anticipating user needs.* New York: Neal-Schuman.

Childers, T. (1975). *The information-poor in America.* Metuchen, N.J.: Scarecrow Press.

Dervin, B., & Fraser, B. (1985). *How libraries help.* Sacramento: California State Library.

Dervin, B., & Nilan, M. (1986). Information needs and uses. In M. Williams (Ed.), *Annual Review of Information Science and Technology (ARIST)*, 21, 3-33.

Doctor, R. D., & Ankem, K. (February 1996). A *Directory of computerized community information systems (CCISs).* Unpublished. Available from the authors by sending e-mail to rdoctor@ua1vm.ua.edu.

Voos, H. (1969). *Information needs in urban areas: A summary of research in methodology.* New Brunswick, N.J: Rutgers University Press, 1969.

---

1. The term Free-Net is a registered servicemark of the National Public Telecomputing Network (NPTN).
2. Big Sky Telegraph is available by modem at (406) 683-7680, or on the Internet by telnetting to *bigsky.bigsky.dillon.mt.us* (or 192.231.192.1). Login as *bbs*.
3. Blacksburg Electronic Village is available at the following URLs: *gopher://gopher.bev.net*, and on the WWW at *http://www.bev.net/*.
4. Mobile Area Free-Net is available via modem (334) 405-4636, settings 8N1 and on the Internet at the following URLs: *telnet://ns1.maf.mobile.al.us* (199.78.232.2). Login as *visitor*; *http://www.maf.mobile.al.us/*.
5. Victoria Free-Net is available via modem, (604) 595-2300, and on the Internet at the following URLs: *telnet://freenet.victoria.bc.ca* (134.87.16.100), login as *guest*; *gopher://gopher.freenet.victoria.bc.ca*; and *http://www.freenet.victoria.bc.ca/freenets.html*.

Build It and They Will Come: A Case Study of the Creation, Development and Refinement of an Organized Database of Internet Resources in Science and Technology

Gerry McKiernan
Iowa State University
Ames, Iowa

Abstract

During the summer of 1994, a series of queries were posted to various newsgroups and listservs, requesting information on then current efforts to organize Internet resources.

In a series of subsequent public and individual discussions, the status of existing and planned projects was determined. All identified sites were visited, and subsequently reviewed and evaluated. An assessment of all known efforts indicated that a majority of sites typically organized resources alphabetically, or categorized them in broad or general idiosyncratic categories.

Although each effort provided some value-added organization that assisted users, such efforts would be of limited value with the expected conversion or publication of a substantial volume of information sources on the Net that was widely predicted at the time.

In anticipation of the need to provide better access and organization to an increasing number of significant Internet resources, a prototype collection of selected resources was subsequently created on a personal home page at Iowa State University to test the applicability of using the Library of Congress Classification scheme as an organizational framework. This paper will review the nature of early efforts to organize Internet resources, describe the origin and initial implementation of the demonstration prototype, and discuss the influence of library philosophy and practices, as well as public comment and critique, on its subsequent refinement and development.

Introduction

In Fall 1995, a demonstration prototype database, CyberStacks(sm) <http://www.public.iastate.edu/~CYBERSTACKS/>, was formally established on the home page server at Iowa State University. CyberStacks(sm) is a centralized, integrated, and unified collection of significant World Wide Web (WWW) and other Internet resources categorized using the Library of Congress classification scheme. Using an abridged Library of Congress call number, Cyberstacks(sm) allows users to browse through a virtual library stacks to identify potentially relevant information resources. Resources are categorized first within a broad classification (Fig. 1), then within narrower subclasses (Fig. 2), and then finally listed (Fig. 3) under a specific classification range and associated subject description that best characterize the content and coverage of the resource. The majority of resources incorporated within its collection are monographic or serial works, files, databases or search services. All of the selected resources in CyberStacks(sm) are full-text, hypertext, or, hypermedia, and of a research or scholarly nature.

Origin

CyberStacks(sm) was established in response to perceived deficiencies in early efforts to organize Internet resources and inadequacies in original and current Internet directories and search services. Beginning in the summer 1994, a series of queries requesting information on then current efforts to organize Internet resources were posted to variety of appropriate newsgroups and listservs (e.g. bit.asis.listserv, PACS-L, LIBREF-L, AUTOCAT, STS-L, LITA-L, INDEX-L). In various public and individual discussions, the status and nature of existing projects were determined. Subsequently all identified sites were visited, reviewed and evaluated. At the time, an assessment of all known efforts indicated that a majority of sites typically organized resources alphabetically, or categorized them in broad or general, idiosyncratic categories. Although each effort provided some value-added organization that assisted users in identifying resources, it was recognized that such efforts would be of limited value with the expected conversion or publication of a substantial number of information sources on the Net that was widely predicted at the time. In anticipation of the need to provide better access and organization to an increasing number of significant Internet resources, a prototype collection of selected resources was created to test the applicability of the Library of Congress classification scheme as organizational framework.

Library of Congress Classification

While an increasing number of sites have adapted the Library of Congress classification scheme as a system for organizing WWW and other Internet resources, notably the WWW Virtual Library [1], specific relationships between resources typically are not indicated at such sites. At best selected resources are classified at a *broad* level, and within particular classified groups, listed only *alphabetically*. While a listing within a broad category does offer some assistance in identifying a relevant resource, such arrangements require a user to review an *entire* list to be assured that an appropriate resource on a given or related topic is not overlooked.

In adopting the Library of Congress scheme [2] for CyberStacks(sm), we believed that a more comprehensive application would offer the value-added structure, organization, context, and appropriate level of specificity and description that could assist users in their efforts to identify and use relevant *and* related WWW and other Internet resources. As the Library of Congress system was a well-established system used by research libraries for organizing non-Internet information resources for generations, including other electronic resources, it was considered appropriate for organizing Internet resources as well.

'Library-Organized'

During the early phases of the implementation of CyberStacks(sm), it became obvious that in order to manage a collection of relevant resources, it was essential to define the nature of the collection that would be organized and to establish criteria for considering potential resources for inclusion. After reviewing a number of existing efforts, it was decided that the creation of a collection of significant resources in science and technology would not only serve the needs of specialists within the Science and Technology Section of the Reference and Instructional Services Department at Iowa State University, but the needs of its clientele as well. As the Section provided reference, as well as instructional service, it was decided to establish CyberStacks(sm) initially as a collection of significant World Wide Web (WWW) and other Internet reference resources in selected fields of science and technology

Initially, only resources that were the equivalent, or an analog, to a print or other electronic reference work were considered for inclusion with the CyberStacks(sm) collection. Although this approach limited the breath of the collection, it also provided for a manageable and definable number of resources suitable for an experimental prototype. These included, abstracting and indexing services, bibliographies, biographical sources, dictionaries, directories, handbooks, guides to the literature, maps, and standards [3]. As we wished to create a true 'virtual' library – an electronic parallel to our physical Reference Collection, this approach was considered necessary and appropriate. Based upon an assessment of their content and structure, we have since expanded our definition of candidate resources to include those that may be considered as one of these defined conventional Reference works .

Notable examples of this expanded definition are entire Web sites. To be selected for inclusion, a site must be well-organized, comprehensive in its coverage, authoritative, and significant. For categorization, these sites are treated as encyclopedias or directories depending on their structure and content.

Underlying our selection of resources for the CyberStacks(sm) collection is a general collection development philosophy that considers discrete Internet resources as the units to be identified and described with a virtual collection, a view finely articulated by Demas, McDonald and Lawrence in a seminal article on collection development and the Internet:

> "... [T]itle by title selection of high quality resources is one of the most important values librarians can add in providing access to information resources, including those accessible via the Internet. A careful selection of resources is the touchstone of the electronic library" [4].

Although CyberStacks(sm) does include a significant percentage of discrete resources, as well as selected Web sites, the selected discrete resources need not be independent to be included. The hypertext nature of the WWW makes it possible to include only a selected part of a site within its collection, as well as an entire site if it is deemed relevant and significant. It is our view that a 'library-organized' collection such as CyberStacks(sm) should seek to identify significant resources for the user, by differentiating between significant sites and significant resources within sites.

As guiding principles for the selection of World Wide Web (WWW) and other Internet resources for CyberStacks(sm), we have adopted the same philosophy and general criteria used in the selection of non-Internet resources. Among the features considered in the selection of items for the CyberStacks(sm) collection are authority of the source, accuracy of information, clarity of presentation, uniqueness within the context of the total collection, recency or timeliness, favorable reviews and community needs [5].

Other library traditions, conventions and approaches also influenced the development of CyberStacks(sm) in its early stages. Many of these were coincidentally considered by Britten in an excellent review paper on building and organizing Internet collection prepared for the 1994 Charleston Conference. Of note is his clear articulation of the role that libraries and the library profession have played in organizing information throughout history, and his call for the creation of a central Virtual Library Collection, in place of dozens of similar, yet separate collections [6], an approach adopted within CyberStacks(sm).

During the development of CyberStacks(sm), we learned of other projects to organize Internet resources. These were later reviewed and analyzed and selected features from the more innovative efforts were subsequently incorporated within its scheme.

The Engineering Electronic Library, Sweden (EELS) [7] service, a cooperative project of the Swedish University of Technology Libraries consortium, offered an excellent model of the use of cooperative collection development within defined subject areas in a wide range of engineering disciplines. In addition to providing a model for developing a virtual collection, the EELS project was the first service to be identified that made use of a standard classification scheme to organize Internet resources [Fig. 4]. Although the project made use of the Engineering Information (Ei) numeric Classification Codes, it provided an excellent example of organizing Net resources at the level of specificity subsequently articulated within CyberStacks(sm).

The OCLC Internet Cataloging Project [8] and its associated FirstSearch service database NetFirst(tm) [9] also influenced the development of CyberStacks(sm). Each are outstanding examples of efforts that have applied a well-established cooperative cataloging model to managing and describing a variety of significant WWW and other Internet resources. This effort is complemented by the NISS Information Gateway [10], which makes use of Subject Area Leaders and Subject group participants in a more focused cooperative Internet cataloging and collection development effort. Other Internet projects based in the United Kingdom, most notably the Edinburgh Engineering Virtual Library (EEVL) [11], OMNI (Organising Medical Networked Information) [12] and the Social Sciences Information Gateway (SOSIG) [13], have also provided excellent examples of Web-based functions and features that could be applied to the development of a Web-based collection of science and technology Internet resources with Reference value. The concept of the Virtual Advisory Board [14] established within CyberStacks(sm) embodies several of the more innovative features and functions available within these projects.

As a result of a call to critique the CyberStacks(sm) posted to a number of relevant listservs and newsgroups in November 1995 [15], a number of enhancements were developed which complemented or strengthened the original organizational approach within CyberStacks(sm) and played a key role in refining the service.

The most fundamental change influenced by public comment was the conversion of the entire CyberStacks(sm) infrastructure to the Tables function available for use within the Netscape browser. Initially, CyberStacks(sm) sought to facilitate access to broad and specific categories and classifications with similar structures created with line-by-line and page-by-page HTML coding. After receiving comment on the legibility and usability

288

of such structures, and after visiting several dozen Web sites, we decided to formalize the CyberStacks(sm) presentation using this function. Concurrently, we also increased the font size of headings, and incorporated appropriate icons at primary and secondary levels, within selected tables.

During the initial review period in late November and December 1995, many users commented on the lack of resources within the CyberStacks(sm) collection. While we had explicitly noted that CyberStacks(sm) was a demonstration prototype with only a handful of incorporated resources, many users expected a more comprehensive collection. In a subsequent modification of the CyberStacks(sm) outline before adopting the Tables function, we decided to clearly indicate the availability of a resource by hotlinking the broad category and subcategory, as well as the general and specific associated classification. A similar enhancement was subsequently transferred into a reconfigured table-based CyberStacks(sm) outline.

In the late Fall review period and during the preliminary research phase of CyberStacks(sm) in summer 1994, a number of users criticized the use of the Library of Congress Classification system as an appropriate strategy for organizing Internet resources. Others noted the widely-acknowledged inconsistencies of the Library of Congress classification or proposed Dewey as a more appropriate classification system [16].

While we believe that browsing is a valid and effective information seeking strategy for locating, identifying and locating information sources that can overcome the inherent inconsistencies to be found in any classification system, and have structured the CyberStacks(sm) collection accordingly (**Fig. 1, Fig. 2, Fig 3**), we realize the limitations of a single approach for all users. From the onset we intended to incorporate direct subject searching an as integral part of the CyberStacks(sm) collection. The need for direct searching was subsequently noted by some users during the Fall review period.

To enhance subject access to incorporated resources within CyberStacks(sm), we plan to assign appropriate standard Library of Congress Subject Headings (LCSH) to each profile, and to concurrently create a browsable 'hyper-thesaurus' of their subject headings, as well as an alphabetical listing. These terms, or phrases, in turn then would be linked to a list of titles assigned the selected subject heading. In this list, users would have the option of connecting directly to the resource, or linking to the classification range where the resource is incorporated within CyberStacks(sm) [17]. The creation of a Cross-Classification Index [18] of all subcategories with incorporated resources was developed to enhance access to resources within the CyberStacks(sm) collection and as a preliminary form of the envisioned 'hyper-thesaurus'.

With research funds made available in December 1995, we were able to systematically review dozens of Web sites with resources suitable for the CyberStacks(sm) collection. As a result of this review over 500 candidate titles were identified for future incorporation. While we had previously fully incorporated individual resources within the CyberStacks(sm) collection, before providing additional means of access, we decided to establish a separate Title Index [19] of all identified candidate resources, before full incorporation. Although only a fraction of these titles have been fully described, categorized and classified within the CyberStacks(sm) scheme, in response to user expectations and desires, we considered it more important to provide some level of access to identified and relevant resources than to wait until funding and time permitted the preparation of a complete profile. This list not only provides users with some level of access to appropriate resources, but also offers them the opportunity to select resources they consider most appropriate for full incorporation.

In a series of listserv and newsgroup postings planned for Spring 1996, users will be invited to review this Title Index and rank resources for priority incorporation within the CyberStacks(sm) collection.

User participation in the development of CyberStacks(sm) has not been limited to periodic calls for comment. From its inception, we decided that users should be provided with a direct opportunity to develop its collection, and a variety of features have been integrated within CyberStacks(sm) to facilitate user involvement. Interested individuals, institutions, organizations, agencies and publishers are encouraged to participate in its development by nominating relevant URLs and their associated names or titles. To facilitate incorporation of nominated resources, users are encouraged to suggest a Library of Congress classification category with the nominated title. A separate Nomination Form [20], as well as an e-mail link have been integrated within CyberStacks(sm) to facilitate nominations.

Through a separate Suggestion Form [21], users are encouraged to communicate their desire for incorporation of yet identified but appropriate resources for the CyberStacks(sm) collection. For resource types that are not currently available, CyberStacks(sm) plans to contact appropriate Internet publishers, and to recommend that a desired work be published in an Internet format.

Conclusion

CyberStacks(sm) was established as a demonstration prototype to enhance access to the Internet through the application of a well-established library classification scheme. Through the course of its development, potential users have been invited to comment and critique the philosophy, theory and approach adopted by CyberStacks(sm) to organize selected Net resources. User comment has proved to be instrumental in improving its overall structure and organization and was directly responsible for the creation of enhanced access functions. In subsequent phases of its development, users will again be invited to comment on the CyberStacks(sm) approach. As with its initial implementation, we expect that they will provide equally significant and valuable insight which no doubt will further enhance its general usefulness.

NOTES

[1] "LoC WWW Virtual Library." Internet WWW Page, at URL: <http://www.w3.org/vl/LibraryOfCongress.html> (version current at 12 February 1996).

[2] *LC Classification Outline* (Washington, D.C: Library of Congress, 1990)

[3] "List of Reference Resource Types." Internet WWW Page, at URL: <http://www.public.iastate.edu/~CYBERSTACKS/ref_book.htm> (version current at 13 February 1996).

[4] Demas, Samuel G., Peter McDonald, and Gregory Lawrence, "The Internet and Collection Development: Mainstreaming Selection of Internet Resources," *Library Resources and Technical Services* 39, no. 3 (July 1995): 280.

[5] American Library Association. Reference and Collection Development and Evaluation Committee, *Reference Collection Development: A Manual* (Chicago: American Library Association, Reference and Adult Services, 1992)

[6] Britten, William A., "Building and Organizing Internet Collections," *Library Acquisitions: Practice and Theory* 19, no. 2 (Summer 1995): 247.

[7] "Engineering Electronic Library, Sweden (EELS)." Internet WWW Page, at URL: <http://www.ub2.lu.se/eel/eelhome.html>(version current at 13 February 1996).

[8] "InterCat." Internet WWW Page, at URL: <http://www.oclc.org:6990/>(version current at 13 February 1996).

[9] "NetFirst." Internet WWW Page, at URL: <http://www.oclc.org/oclc/netfirst/netfirst.htm>(version current at 13 February 1996).

[10] "NISS Information Gateway." Internet WWW Page, at URL: <http://www.niss.ac.uk>(version current at 13 February 1996).

[11] "Edinburgh Engineering Virtual Library (EEVL)." Internet WWW Page, at URL: <http://eevl.icbl.hw.ac.uk/>(version current at 13 February 1996).

[12] "OMNI, Organising Medical Networked Information." Internet WWW Page, at URL: <http://omni.ac.uk>(version current at 13 February 1996)

[13] "Social Sciences Information Gateway (SOSIG)." Internet WWW Page, at URL: <http://www.esrc.bris.ac.uk/>(version current at 13 February 1996)

[14] "Virtual Advisory Board." Internet WWW Page, at URL:
<http://www.public.iastate.edu/~CYBERSTACKS/advisory.htm>
(version current at 13 February 1996).

[15] McKiernan, Gerry, "Announcing CyberStacks(sm),"
bit.listserv.pacs-l (27 November 1995).

[16] Mundie, David, "CyberDewey." Internet WWW Page, at URL:
<http:ivory.lm.com/~mundie/DDHC/CyberDewey.html>(version current
at 13 February 1996)

[17] McKiernan, Gerry, "two-dimensional limitations / 3-D
Possibilities - CyberStacks(sm): An Alternative Model for
Selecting | Organizing | Presenting | Accessing WWW Resources:
A Position Paper Prepared for the OCLC Internet Cataloging
Project Colloquium," Internet WWW Page, at URL:
<http://www.public.iastate.edu/~CYBERSTACKS/OCLC-P.htm>(version
current at 2 February 1996).

[18] "Cross-Classification Index." Internet WWW Page, at URL:
<http://www.public.iastate.edu/~CYBERSTACKS/cross.htm>
(version current at 13 February 1996).

[19] "Title Index." Internet WWW Page, at URL:
<http://www.public.iastate.edu/~CYBERSTACKS/title_1st.htm>
(version current at 13 February 1996).

[20] "Nomination Form." Internet WWW Page, at URL:
<http://www.public.iastate.edu/~CYBERSTACKS/nom_form.htm>
(version current at 13 February 1996).

[21] "Suggestion Form." Internet WWW Page, at URL:
<http://www.public.iastate.edu/~CYBERSTACKS/suggest.htm>
(version current at 13 February 1996).

Science and Technology Main Menu

CyberStacks(sm)

Select a General Classification Category

 Q	 R	 S	 T
Science	Medicine	Agriculture	Technology

 U	 V
Military Science	Naval Science

Browse TITLE Listing

Search CROSS-CLASSIFICATION Index

Browse COMBINED CLASSIFICATION Index

CyberStacks(sm)

Fig. 1

Science (Q)

| Q-Science | R-Medicine | S-Agriculture | T-Technology | U-Military | V-Naval |

	Science (General)	**Q**
	Mathematics	**QA**
	Astronomy	**QB**
	Physics	**QC**
	Chemistry	**QD**
	Geology	**QE**
	Natural History & Biology	**QH**
	Botany	**QK**
	Zoology	**QL**
	Human Anatomy	**QM**
	Physiology	**QP**
	Microbiology	**QR**

CyberStacks(sm)

Fig. 2

Science -- Natural History & Biology
(QH)

| Q-Science | R-Medicine | S-Agriculture | T-Technology | U-Military | V-Naval |

SELECT	QH
Natural History (General)	1-74
Nature Conservation. Landscape Protection	75-77
Microscopy	201-278.5
Biology (General)	301-425
Genetics	426-470
Reproduction	471-489
Life	501-531
Ecology	540-559
Cytology	573-671
Economic Biology	705
CyberStacks(sm)	QH

| Q | QA | QB | QC | QD | QE | QH | QK | QL | QM | QP | QR |

Fig. 3

EELS

ENGINEERING ELECTRONIC LIBRARY

The Swedish Univ. of Technology Libraries

Welcome to the Engineering Electronic Library, Sweden (EELS), an information system, presented under World Wide Web, for quality assessed information sources on the Internet mainly intended for technical universities.

CONTENTS:

1. About EELS

2. About EELS subject tree

3. The Swedish Univ. of Technology Libraries

4. Browse EELS

.5. Search EELS

Browse EELS:

1. ENGINEERING (using Engineering Information Inc's EI classification)

- ☐ 400 Civil Engineering

- ☐ 500 Mining Engineering

- ☐ 600 Mechanical Engineering

- ☐ 700 Electrical Engineering

- ☐ 800 Chemical Engineering

- ☐ 900 Engineering, General

Fig. 4

Impact on Social Structures IV: Information Transfer

Electronic Journals and Scholarly Communication: A Citation and Reference Study[1]

Stephen P. Harter and Hak Joon Kim[2]
School of Library and Information Science, Indiana University
Bloomington, Indiana

Abstract

The journal is fundamental to formal scholarly communication. This research reports highlights and preliminary findings from an empirical study of scholarly electronic journals. The purpose of the research is to assess the impact of electronic journals (ejournals) on scholarly communication, by measuring the extent to which they are being cited in the literature, both print and electronic. The intent is to provide a snapshot of the impact ejournals were having on scholarly communication at a given point in time, roughly the end of 1995. This study provides one measure of that impact, specifically on the formal, as opposed to informal, communication process. The study also examines the forms in which scholars cite ejournals, the accuracy and completeness of citations to ejournals, and practical difficulties faced by scholars and researchers who wish to retrieve ejournals through the networks.

Introduction

The first scholarly journal, *Journal des Sçavans*, was published as a new medium of communication in 1665, and was soon followed by the *Philosophical Transactions of the Royal Society* (Osburn, 1984). For more than three centuries the journal has played a pivotal role in the creation and transmission of knowledge by serving as the primary medium of scholarly communication, and has remained essentially unchanged in form and function over its lifetime. Science as we know it is scarcely imaginable without the scholarly journal.

Despite its benefits to science and scholarship, the paper journal system has been subject to much criticism. Deficiencies noted by some authors include perceived problems with the peer review process (that it suppresses new ideas, favors authors from prestigious institutions, and causes undue delays in the publication process), high costs that are escalating faster than the rate of inflation, and lack of selectivity. Spiraling costs and long publication delays are perhaps the most serious of these criticisms.

At the same time that the costs of producing the paper journal have increased sharply, developments in computer and communications technology have accelerated. And of course we now have the dramatic explosion of the World Wide Web. Technology increasingly offers the possibility of using computers and communication networks to create alternative electronic forms of the conventional paper journal. It is possible that these new forms of computer-based communication will transform the scholarly communication system. There is much debate and

---

[1]We are grateful to the Online Computer Library Center (OCLC), Inc. for partial funding of this research.

[2]Email addresses are harter@indiana.edu and hajkim@indiana.edu, respectively.

discussion concerning how the roles of the various participants in the scholarly communication process, including libraries, may be redefined in the process (Meyer, 1993).

Although electronic journals (or <u>ejournals</u>) have been under development since 1976 (Turoff and Hiltz, 1982), ejournals in their non-experimental phase did not begin until the 1990s, with a few exceptions. The first peer-reviewed electronic, full-text ejournal including graphics was *Online Journal of Current Clinical Trials* (*OJCCT*) (Keyhani, 1993). In the most recently published list, and one of the few research projects involving ejournals, Hitchcock, Carr, & Hall (1996) identified 115 scholarly, peer-reviewed ejournals in science and technology, and there are many more in the social science and humanities. These constitute the first wave of what are likely to be many more scholarly ejournals to come.

Ann Okerson wrote, "One can fantasize endlessly about electronic 'journals,' but without active authorship and readership there is nothing" (quoted in Collins and Berge (1994)). We would add "use" to authorship and readership. If ejournals are not *used,* they cannot play an important role in scholarly communication. There has been much discussion and speculation in the literature about perceived advantages and disadvantages of ejournals, and about problems and issues related to their development and use. Such speculation is necessary and important. The present study is aimed at gathering hard data regarding the readership, use, and impact of ejournals. What kinds of ejournals are being published, and how often? What impact are ejournals having on the scholarly communities they are serving? To what extent are scholars and researchers aware of, influenced by, using, and building their own work on research published in ejournals?

The present study assesses the impact of scholarly ejournals by examining the <u>artifacts</u> of scholarly communication--the journal article and its references. In bibliometric studies, citation analysis is a well-known technique that has a long history in studies of scholarly communication (Borgman, 1990). As an artifact of scholarly communication, citations reveal formal communication patterns and scholarly impact. The major advantages of citation analysis are its high reliability and unobtrusiveness. Several standards for citing electronic publications have been promulgated (Li & Crane, 1993; Walker, 1995; Brown, 1995).

This research provides hard citation data concerning the impact of ejournals on the conduct of research and scholarship. At another level, publishers of ejournals can gain some information regarding use by recording the number of subscriptions to an ejournal or the number of times articles are accessed or downloaded from host servers. While these kinds of data provide useful indicators of one type of use, they do not measure the extent to which ejournal articles are playing a role in the scholarly and research process, that is, in the advancement of knowledge. While the meaning of citations can certainly be debated, what is clear is that they reflect an influence or impact of some kind on the author of the citing article.

The purposes of this study are to:

1. assess the accuracy and completeness of citations to ejournals
2. identify the extent to which scholars publishing in both print and electronic journals cite ejournals and other epublications
3. identify fields in which researchers actively use scholarly ejournals
4. identify highly cited ejournals and articles in ejournals in these fields
5. record and analyze interesting demographic characteristics and access problems of ejournals

The last stated purpose deserves further comment. Although it was not originally part of our study to investigate demographic data, we found as the research progressed that we were learning information of great interest to us that had little to do with the referencing of ejournals. As part of our original research plan, in order to investigate the references of articles in ejournals it was necessary that each ejournal in the population be accessed and articles and other information about the journal to be downloaded and printed for analysis. A useful byproduct of the study has resulted from a study of these data, which revealed several interesting demographic characteristics and access problems associated with the population of ejournals. Because of space limitations, only a few of these can be discussed here.

Summary of Methods

The method followed in the first part of this study is one of defining and drawing appropriate samples of ejournals, obtaining data from printed documentation and ejournal articles, conducting descriptive analyses, and reporting the findings in tables and prose. In the second part of the study, tools published by the Institute for Scientific Information (ISI) are used to conduct cited reference searches and other citation analyses. The following section describes how the ejournal samples were drawn for study.

Our interest in this research was on scholarly electronic journals that publish articles reporting scholarship or research that are refereed or peer-reviewed. Other types of publications-- newsletters, zines, and the like, were not subjects of study. We chose to use two published directories that include data on electronic journals: Mecklermedia's *Internet World's on Internet 94* (Mecklermedia, 1994)[3], and the Association of Research Libraries' *Directory of electronic journals, newsletters and academic discussion lists* (Okerson, 1995).

Ejournals selected from the ARL directory were taken from the section entitled "Electronic journals, magazines, and zines" and identified there as "peer-reviewed." Ejournals selected from the Mecklermedia directory were taken from the section entitled "Electronic journals and newsletters" and identified there as "refereed." All ejournals meeting these criteria became members of the sample. The two lists were combined and duplicates were removed. There were 134 ejournals in the final list. Four titles were eliminated from the sample for various reasons, and one title was added, for a refined initial sample of 131 ejournals.

Next, recent articles and other documentation (journal description, instructions for potential authors, statement of scope, etc.) from each of the ejournals were downloaded or otherwise obtained and printed for examination. The access and demographic study was conducted on all 131 ejournals in the refined initial sample.

For the reference study, we had two criteria for selecting the journals to be studied from the 131 ejournals in the refined sample. First, the ejournal must have published one or more articles that reported the results of research or scholarship. Second, the ejournal be peer-reviewed or refereed articles, as described in the ejournal documentation. Many ejournals were eliminated because they failed to meet the first criterion. A few were removed because of the absence of any statement in the ejournal documentation indicating that it was peer-reviewed or refereed. This characteristic, as well as all the other demographic information related to the ejournals, was taken directly from the ejournals. There were several instances where the data in the two

---

[3]As of June, 1995, the 1995 edition of this directory was not available.

directories (both providing self-reported survey data) did not agree with the information provided in the ejournals themselves.

To be included in the reference study, an article must, in our judgment, have reported the results of research or scholarship and must have cited at least one reference. Our sample of articles for the reference study was defined as the last four available scholarly, peer-reviewed articles of each of the 77 scholarly ejournals. If one or more issues or articles of the year 1995 were not available, one or more issues from 1994 and, if necessary, 1993, were used.

For the cited work study, the population of seventy-seven ejournals used in the reference study defined the initial sample. However, in order for an ejournal article to be cited, especially in a print publication, the lag time in conventional print publishing must be considered. One must provide some time for articles to be read, to influence a researcher or scholar in some way and thus become part of a study in progress, and eventually to be cited in the published article reporting the results of that study. For this reason, the cited work study was done only on scholarly electronic journals that commenced publication in 1993 or earlier. There were thirty-nine such journals. Table 1 summarizes the characteristics of the three ejournal samples used in the study.

Table 1. Ejournal Sample Sizes for the Three Studies		
Purpose of Sample	Origin of Sample Members	Sample Size
Access and Demographic Study	ARL directory and Mecklermedia directory	131 epublications
Reference Study	Peer-reviewed or refereed scholarly journals in the initial sample	77 scholarly ejournals
Cited Work Study	Ejournals in the reference study that began publication in 1993 or earlier	39 scholarly ejournals

Demographic Characteristics of Ejournals

Subjects Covered

We assigned the 131 ejournals in the sample (consisting of all known ejournals at the time the sample was selected) to broad subject categories that coincided in most cases with university departments or professional schools. Subject categories could not be determined for seven ejournals. Although we were fortunate to have access to some fee-based journals, thanks to temporary passwords supplied by OCLC, Inc., we did not have access to three other fee-based ejournals in the sample. Also, three ejournals could not be accessed at all, either by using the information in the two directories or by using other means, such as Internet search tools. Finally, the language of one ejournal was Polish, and we did not attempt to obtain a translation. Since we required all of our demographic data to come from the ejournals themselves, rather than secondary sources, these seven journals were eliminated from the sample. Save for a very few exceptions, then, the remaining demographic data are for the 124 ejournals to which we were able to gain access.

Table 2 shows the subject categories with highest frequencies. Education, literature, and mathematics were the top three categories, with library and information science a somewhat surprising fourth, with seven ejournals. There were five ejournals under the heading of religious studies. We were also somewhat surprised at some of the subject categories with relatively low frequencies -- for example, physics, biology, engineering, and sociology with only one or two representatives each. Of course, since the publication of the ARL and Mecklermedia directories we used to select our sample, many more ejournals in these subject areas have appeared, coinciding with the explosion of the World Wide Web. Our demographic data represent the state of affairs as of June, 1995, and can be taken as a benchmark, against which subsequent studies of electronic journals can be compared.

Many new ejournals have evidently arisen from an introspective consideration of the new communication media themselves, and with a concern with how they will affect society and traditional disciplines and communication patterns. Computer science, communication, and the broad subject we called "information technology, media, and society" are examples.

A final way to characterize the subjects of the ejournals in the sample is to classify them into the traditional four broad areas of scholarship and research in the university: sciences, social sciences, humanities, and professional. Table 3 summarizes a breakdown of subjects into these four main categories. While we might have guessed that the sciences and possibly the professions would be most heavily represented, this was not the case. The four categories are essentially equal in size. Whatever the motivation may be for launching an ejournal, it is apparently held by scientists, social scientists, humanist scholars, and professionals alike.

Scholarly, Peer-Reviewed Ejournals

The major purpose of this research was to study the effects of scholarly, peer-reviewed ejournals on formal scholarly and scientific communication, as measured by cited references. For the reference study and cited work study it was necessary to obtain and examine individual issues of the ejournals in the sample to identify which met our selection criteria. These criteria were that the ejournal must have published at least one article reporting the results of research or scholarship must be refereed or peer-reviewed, as stated in the documentation provided by the ejournal (corresponding to what is usually the front-matter in a print journal).

Table 2. Subject Categories with the Highest Number of Ejournals	
Subject	Number of Ejournals
Education	13
Literature	12
Mathematics	10
Library and Information Science	7
Computer Science	6
Communication	5
Information Technology, Media, and Society	5
Medicine	5
Religious Studies	5

Table 3. Distribution of Ejournals in the Sample in the Sciences, Social Sciences, and Humanities.	
Broad Subject Category	Number of Ejournals in Sample
Sciences	28
Social Sciences	34
Humanities	31
Professional	31
Could not determine	7
Total	131

Table 4 reports the results of our analysis of the scholarly nature of the 131 ejournals in the initial sample. Only 77 ejournals were judged to be scholarly and peer-reviewed. Twenty-five ejournals in the initial sample were in our judgment neither scholarly nor peer-reviewed. These were zines and newsletters for the most part. Six other ejournals did not meet our selection criteria for various other reasons.

Table 4. Scholarly, Peer-Reviewed Ejournals in the Sample	
Journal is:	Number of Journals
Scholarly, Peer-reviewed	77
Scholarly, Not Peer-reviewed	16
Neither Peer-reviewed nor Scholarly	25
Eliminated for Other Reasons*	13
*Not a journal, publishes data only, publishes reviews only, or could not determine	

Media of Publication

Scientific and scholarly journals are today being published in many media: CD-ROM, floppy disk, on computer networks such as the Internet, and of course, print. The literature has tended to use the term ejournal -- short for electronic journal -- to refer to networked journals but not other forms of electronic journals (on floppy disk, etc.). We have used the same terminology in this report, though technically it is at best potentially misleading and at worst incorrect.

Most (nearly three quarters) of the ejournals in the sample started as an original publication -- they began their lives in electronic form. Exactly one-fourth of the sample began and continue as print journals. That is, they exist in two parallel forms, print and electronic. And in three known cases -- *Modal Analysis, Essays in History*, and *Journal of Extension*, the print version has been replaced by an electronic version. Table 5 summarizes these findings.

Table 5. Media of Publication*		
Media of Publication	Number of Ejournals	Percentage (%)
Electronic version only	86	69.4
Print and electronic versions	31	25.0
Print version replaced by electronic version	3	2.4
Not clear whether print version continues	4	3.2
*Media of publication could not be determined for 7 ejournals. Other media such as CD-ROM are not considered in this table.		

Several models have been developed for the relationship between print journals and their electronic counterpart. (See Table 6.) The *Chicago Journal of Theoretical Computer Science* and other ejournals will provide individual articles in paper form, though the journals themselves are not published in a paper version. The *Journal of Financial and Strategic Decisions* calls its ejournal "secondary to" the print journal, by which is meant that the electronic version is the ASCII format and does not accurately represent the print version. *Slavic Review* publishes its electronic version a few months after the print version has appeared (called a "postprint edition"). *Public-Access Computer Systems Review (PACS Review)* has published at least two volumes in book form, many months after the appearance of the electronic version. Several journals publish some but not all of the print journal electronically. Finally, both an electronic and a print version of a journal may exist, but with different pricing arrangement.

Table 6. Models for the Relationship between Print Journals and their Electronic Counterparts
Ejournal replaces print journal
Ejournal coexists with print journal
Journal is in electronic form only, but individual articles can be ordered in paper form
Ejournal is "secondary to" the print journal
Electronic version is published several months after the print version
Print version is published several months after the electronic version
The full print version is not available electronically
Both versions exist but with different pricing arrangements

Pricing Arrangements

Whether there exists a charge for a given ejournal is not as simple a question as it may first appear. Questions and distinctions not always made for print journals become important for an interpretation of the meaning of cost figures. For example:

- Is there a cost distinction between providing access to current issues versus archival issues?

- Is there a print counterpart of the ejournal?
- Is the ejournal included with membership in a society?

Clearly the answers to these questions will be important information needed to interpret the cost, if any, of an ejournal, as well as the meaning of pricing trends. We identified eight different categories of ejournals in the sample, depending on the answers to these questions. Table 7 condenses the eight categories into just two: ejournals in which all issues are free, and ejournals for which some form of fee exists. For nearly nine out of ten ejournals in the sample, all issues are free. And in some of the remaining ejournals, there is no fee for some kinds of access. For example, *JAC Online*, a journal of composition theory supported by the Association of Teachers of Advanced Composition and the University of South Florida, charges a fee to view the current issue, but there is no charge to examine archival issues. A chi-square test of the hypothesis that there is no relationship between pricing arrangement and whether the ejournal is peer-reviewed could not be rejected ($p=.487$).

Table 7. Gross View of Pricing Arrangements for Peer-Reviewed Ejournals in the Sample		
Pricing Arrangement	Number of Ejournals	Percentage (%) of Ejournals
All issues of electronic version are free *	67	88.2
Fee for some or all issues of electronic journal	9	11.8
*Membership in a society is required for three ejournals.		

Reference Study

The purpose of the reference study was to analyze the references from a sample of articles in scholarly ejournals, to measure the extent to which authors of ejournal articles are currently citing ejournals and other online sources. Such authors can be assumed to be more knowledgeable about and sympathetic to the electronic media than typical authors. Thus the results of the reference study should provide a kind of upper bound on the current influence of ejournals and other electronic publications on scholarly communication.

Among the 77 scholarly and peer-reviewed ejournals in the sample, two were fee-based ejournals for which we had no subscription.[4] These ejournals were eliminated from the sample. In addition, *Radioscientist ON-LINE,* published by the New Zealand National Committee for the International Union of Radio Science, included only one article, which had no reference, so it was also eliminated from the sample. Therefore, the final sample size for the reference study was reduced to 74.

To examine their references, we retrieved and printed the last four available scholarly, peer-reviewed articles published by each of the 74 ejournals. Because the ejournals in the sample were distributed in different ways, a variety of means had to be employed to do this, ranging from email, listserv, and ftp commands to using Web browsers. This part of the study was quite illuminating as to the difficulties involved in accessing and using ejournals. Six of the 74 ejournals had published fewer than four articles as of September, 1995, when the data collection took place. In these cases we studied the articles that were available.

Table 8. Samples in the reference study.	
Entities	Sample Size
Available electronic journals -- scholarly and peer-reviewed	74 ejournals
Articles -- the most recently published four, or in six cases, fewer, articles appearing in the ejournals	279 articles

---

[4]We thank OCLC, Inc. for providing temporary access to the following fee-based ejournals so that we could conduct the reference study on them: *Applied Physics Letters Online, Current Opinions in Medicine, Current Opinions in Biology, Immunology Today Online, Online Journal of Current Clinical Trials,* and *Online Journal of Knowledge Synthesis for Nursing.*

Table 8. Samples in the reference study.	
Entities	Sample Size
References -- the first twenty, or sometimes fewer, references appearing in the articles	4317 references

Table 8 summarizes the data relating to the samples in the reference study. We took the first twenty references in each ejournal article to build our set of references. If an article had fewer than twenty references, we studied all the references in that article. For this portion of the study there were a total of 4,317 references from the most recent 279 articles published in 74 scholarly and peer-reviewed ejournals.

Each of the 4317 references was classified as to its format (book, serial, book chapter, online source, etc.). Online sources were further subclassified (web page, email, ejournal article, etc.). Finally, the accessibility of the references to online sources was tested by actually trying to retrieve the cited item.

Table 9 shows the formats and frequencies of the most frequent reference sources cited by the 279 ejournal articles. Print serial (43.3%) was the format most frequently cited, with books (26.9%) and book chapters and other parts (16.0%) occupying the second and third ranks respectively. This distribution is roughly what is found in reference studies conducted using print journals in various fields, e.g., library and information science (Harter, Nisonger, & Weng, 1993).

References were classified as "online sources" in Table 9 if they were of a variety of electronic subtypes: web pages, electronic personal papers, email messages, ejournal articles, news group postings, listserv postings, and others. Only 83 online sources (1.9% of the total number of references) were cited by the 74 ejournals (279 articles). Among the 74 ejournals, only twelve had one or more reference to an online source and the other 62 ejournals had none at all.

The distribution of online and ejournal references in the twelve ejournals that have at least one reference to an online source is highly skewed. The ejournal *Public-Access Computer Systems Review* had 34 online references (40.9%) and *Electronic Journal of Virtual Culture* and *Ejournal* accounted for a further 25 (30.1%) and 9 (10.8%) respectively from among the total number of 83 online references to online sources. Thus online references are distributed among only a few ejournals; 68 (81.8%) of the total come from these three.

Table 9. Format and Number of Cited References		
Formats	Number of References	Percentage of Total (%)
Serial	1,871	43.3
Book	1,160	26.9
Book chapter and other parts	689	16.0
Proceedings	140	3.2

Table 9. Format and Number of Cited References		
Online source	83	1.9
Report	80	1.9
Presented paper	52	1.2
Other*	230	5.3
Subtotal	4,305	99.7
Could not determine	12	0.3
Total	4,317	100.0

> * Others include legislation, mimeograph, provision, unpublished raw data, film, fax, computer file, hearing, offprint, law, treaty, international covenant, video, committee decision, and many others.

Table 10 shows the distribution of the online references of each four reviewed articles in the top three ejournals with online references. This distribution is also skewed, with most references to online sources appearing in only three articles. Thus the number of online references also depends on the characteristics of individual articles within the same ejournal, although the degree of skewness is not so large as for the overall population of ejournals.

Table 10. Distribution of Online References Among the Twelve Articles in the Sample for the Ejournals with Most Online References (*PACS-R, EJVC,* and *Ejournal*).	
Number of References to Online Sources	Number of Articles
0	3
1-5	5
6-10	1
11-15	3

Table 11 shows the types and frequencies of references to online sources. "Web Page" was the most frequently cited document type, with "Electronic Personal Paper" ranking second and "Email Messages" and "Ejournals" jointly occupying the third rank. We could not determine the types of twelve of the 83 online references because they contained incomplete bibliographic information and the online sources were not accessible.

One of the important findings of the reference study is that the citation styles of online references are frequently inconsistent, incomplete, and/or are inaccessible -- that is, they do not lead to the wanted online resource, in contrast to the citation styles of print references.

Table 11. Types, Number, and Accessibility of Cited Online Resources		
Type of Online Resource	Number of References	Number and Percentage (%) of Accessible References
Web Page	12	10 (83.3)
Electronic Personal Paper	10	7 (70.0)
Email Message	9	2 (22.2)
Ejournal Article	9	6 (66.7)
Newsgroup Posting	7	0 (0.0)
Listserv Posting	5	2 (40.0)
Electronic Directory	5	5 (100.0)
SGML Encoded Document	5	5 (100.0)
Electronic Preprint	3	1 (33.3)
Computer Software	2	2 (100.0)
Electronic Newspaper	2	2 (100.0)
Online Catalog	1	1 (100.0)
Local File	1	0 (0.0)
Type Could Not be Determined	12	0 (0.0)
Total	83	43 (51.8)

Each of the 83 references to online sources was examined and attempts were made to access the material cited. Obviously one of the potential advantages of citations to online resources is that if the reader can retrieve such resources quickly, the communication process has obviously been enhanced. The third column of Table 11 shows the results of the accessibility tests of the 83 references to online resources. Email messages and newsgroup postings were especially inaccessible, and none of the twelve resources that could not be classified could be accessed. Overall, only about half of the online resources were accessible online.

Table 12. Access Protocols and Accessibility for the 83 Online References		
Access Protocol	Number of Online References	Number and Percentage (%) of Accessible References
URL	47	31 (66.0)
Email	13	4 (30.8)
Listserv	9	6 (66.7)
Usenet newsgroup	7	0 (0.0)
Electronic newspaper	2	2 (100.0)
Incomplete access information provided	5	0 (0.0)
Total	83	43 (51.8)

Table 12 reports accessibility findings in another way, by type of access protocol. Online information resources are accessible in several ways, and the 83 online references we found are analyzed according to these. Over half of the cited references included a Uniform Resource Locator (URL). We tried to access the online resources using a Web browser. However, only two-thirds of these led to the desired resource (see Table 12). Instead, we obtained the browser message "The server does not have a DNS entry" or the infamous server error message "404 URL Not Found". Several types of online references, such as Web pages, electronic personal papers, SGML encoded documents, software programs, and local file references, were mainly cited through URLs, often only with a URL.

Only four of the thirteen references including email addresses led to the desired online source. In seven cases, we received the message "User Unknown" in response to our email message. In two other cases, no error message was received, but there was no response and the online resource could not be obtained.

Nine of the online references were to listserv postings, with six (66.7%) being accessible. Accessible in this case meant that we could, through the given listserv access information such as name and discussion date, we could retrieve the original sources using listserv commands. However, three out of nine listserv references were not accessible. For instance, one listserv reference cited the 1994 file of *CYBERIA-L*. Although we could access the *CYBERIA-L* archive, we could not find the original source because the archive of *CYBERIA-L* did not include archives for 1994.

Seven Newsgroup postings were cited, from two different Newsgroups. We could access the archives of one of them but not the other, obtaining the message, "No such group." The Newsgroup that we could access maintained postings only from 1996. Finally, two newspaper articles that can be accessed through commercial online providers such as Nexis/Lexis were cited, and we were able to access these articles through the same providers.

We labeled five online references as "incomplete access information provided." These were cases in which no information was provided about how to access the source, or the information that was provided was insufficient for us to gain access to the resource.

In summary, except for commercially-provided electronic newspapers (to which not all Internet users will have access), none of the access methods led to perfect retrieval. The overall rate of 51.8% must be considered to be extremely low, considering that the online resources cited were apparently important enough for an author to cite them and yet in just one or two years, nearly half were no longer accessible, given the information provided in the citation.

Recall that the reference study was conducted to fix a kind of upper bound on the current influence of ejournals on scholarly communication. We argued that authors of ejournal articles would probably be more inclined than other authors to cite ejournals and other electronic sources. This still seems like a reasonable assumption to us.

We examined 4317 references in 279 scholarly, peer-reviewed articles appearing in 74 ejournals. Among these, only 83, or 1.9%, were to online sources, and only nine, or 0.2%, were to ejournals. Only twelve of the 74 ejournals in the sample cited one or more online sources. Only eight of the 74 ejournals cited another ejournal even once, and only one ejournal (not surprisingly, it was the ejournal *Ejournal*) made two or more references to other ejournals. References to online sources are concentrated in a few ejournals, with *PACS-R, Electronic Journal on Virtual Culture,* and *Ejournal* accounting for more than 80% of all online references. And among this group, most are concentrated in just a few articles.

It is worth noting the identity of the ejournals in which the great majority of the references to online sources are made. The top three have as their central subjects of interest topics related to electronic communication. Among the twelve ejournals citing at least one online reference, the five ejournals dealing with online topics (*PACS-R, Electronic Journal on Virtual Culture (EJVC), Ejournal, Interpersonal Computing and Technology, Journal of Computer-Mediated Communication*) account for 71, or 85.5 % of the references to online sources. This suggests that referencing online sources, and ejournals in particular, is a function mostly of academic discipline. One would expect a journal with a name like *Electronic Journal on Virtual Culture* to cite electronic sources, by virtue of the subject matter treated in the journal. Indeed, as subjects of academic treatment, the ejournals listed above focus on new topical areas that have arisen as a result of the new electronic environment.

On the other hand, the seven ejournals that have as their subject matter traditional academic specializations (sociology, education, library and information science, psychology, cognitive science, and mathematics), cite only twelve online sources between them, and five ejournal articles.

All of this taken together seems clear evidence that ejournals presently play almost no role in scholarly communication, as measured by references cited. Of course there are other ways of measuring impact; we do not claim that counting references and citations should be relied on exclusively. Interviews with scholars, for example, might well lead to a different conclusion -- but we doubt it. Certainly informal communication is being changed in a major way by the Internet -- especially by listservs, email, and web pages -- even if such communications are not being cited in large numbers. But the reference study suggests that a significant effect on the formal communication system is yet to happen. Obviously, this conclusion may well be very different in two or three year's time.

Tables 11 and 12 show that a high percentage (almost 50%) of online resources are not directly accessible from the information provided in references. Direct online accessibility to such resources is obviously potentially very convenient to readers, much more so than for print references. However, if readers cannot gain access to the original sources of the cited material, the references that link the citing and cited works are much less useful than references to print sources. Note that the references we studied appeared in recently published ejournal articles. One might reasonably expect such references to be largely correct and complete and to lead to the full online information source. This was not the case. It is worth contemplating what percentage of these same references will lead to the original information source in two or three years additional time -- say in the spring of 1998 -- it will very likely be much lower than 50%. Clearly, the accessibility of cited online resources is potentially a very serious problem in the conduct of research and scholarship, especially if the percentage of references to such sources increases beyond its current very small size.

Cited Work Study

The reference study reported in the previous section examined the cited references of 74 scholarly, peer-reviewed ejournals. In the cited work study, it is the references of thousands of print (and a very few electronic) journals that are of interest. The Institute of Scientific Information (ISI) publishes three citation indexes -- *Science Citation Index (SCI), Social Sciences Citation Index (SSCI),* and *Arts and Humanities Citation Index (AHCI)* -- that allow searches of journal names as cited works. When a cited work search on an ejournal such as *PACS Review* is conducted on *SSCI*, one retrieves bibliographic citations to all the articles in journals indexed by *SSCI* that have cited *PACS Review* in one or more reference.

Since ISI indexes thousands of scholarly journals, which it represents as the most significant journals in the various fields of scholarship, a cited reference search should retrieve the majority of all citations made in scholarly journals to the cited work. Such a search will not reveal citations to a work made in less significant journals or in books and other materials. In the context of the World Wide Web, a cited work search will not reveal the hypertext links (analogous to citations) to works made in Web pages. However, these limitations notwithstanding, the ISI indexes are widely recognized as providing a valuable measure of the scholarly impact of articles, journals, and authors -- that is, the formal impact. Not the only, or even necessarily the best, measure, but valuable nonetheless.

Eugene Garfield, the founder of the Institute for Scientific Information, addressed the issue of the meaning of citation for individuals in a section of his book entitled "What Do Citation Counts Measure":

The only responsible claim made for citation counts as an aid in evaluating individuals is that they provide a measure of the utility or impact of scientific work. They say nothing about the nature of the work, nothing about the reason for its utility or impact. Those factors can be dealt with only by content analysis of the cited material and the exercise of knowledgeable peer judgment. Citation analysis is not meant to replace such judgment, but to make it more objective and astute. (Garfield, 1979, p. 246).

Much the same comment applies to the application of citation-based measures to the evaluation of journals. A number of studies have examined the meaning of citation as an evaluation tool for journals (McAllister, Anderson, & Narin, F., 1980) and research performance (Narin, 1976; Lawani, 1986). Bibliometric measures have also been used as methods for the evaluation of departments, universities, and published works.

This portion of the research reports the results of cited work searches of all three ISI citation indexes for the scholarly, peer-reviewed ejournals in the sample that have had a reasonable chance of being cited. Since the time lag in the publication schedules of print journals is substantial, we reasoned that a minimum of two years should be necessary to provide time for an ejournal article to be read, become part of an author's research, and eventually be cited in a print journal. For this reason, we limited the cited work searches to those scholarly, peer-reviewed ejournals that began publishing in 1993 or earlier. There were thirty-nine such ejournals in the sample.

The cited work study is in progress. Results from this portion of the research will be presented at the conference.

REFERENCES

Borgman, C. L. (Ed.). (1990). *Scholarly communication and bibliometrics*. Newbury Park, California: Sage Publications.

Brown, H. (1995). *Citing Computer Documents*. Last revised on July 16, 1995. URL http://neal.ctstateu.edu/history/cite.html.

Collins, M. P., & Berge, Z. L. (1994). IPCT Journal: A Case Study of an Electronic Journal on the Internet. *Journal of the American Society for Information Science, 45*, 771-776.

Garfield, E. E. (1979). *Citation indexing: its theory and application in science, technology, and humanities*. New York: Wiley.

Harter, S. P., Nisonger, T. E., & Weng, A. (1993). Semantic relationships between cited and citing articles in library and information science journals. *Journal of the American Society for Information Science, 44*, 543-552.

Hitchcock, S., Carr, L., & Hall, W. (1996). *A survey of STM online journals 1990-95: The calm before the storm*. January 15, 1996 (Updated February 14, 1996). Available at URL http://journals.ecs.soton.ac.uk/survey/survey.html.

Keyhani, A. (1993). The Online Journal of Current Clinical Trials: An innovation in electronic journal publishing. *Database, 16*, 14-23.

Li, X., & Crane, N. B. (1993). *Electronic style: A guide to citing electronic information.* Westport, CT: Meckler.

McAllister, P. R., Anderson, R. C., & Narin, F. (1980). Comparison of peer and citation assessment of the influence of scientific journals. *Journal of the American Society for Information Science, 31,* 147-152.

Mecklermedia. (1994). *Internet World's on Internet 94: An international guide to electronic journals, newsletters, texts, discussion lists, and other resources on the Internet.* Westport: Mecklermedia.

Meyer, R. W. (1993). *Roles in scholarly communication under an electronic model.* [email to Steve Harter], [Online]. Available email: RMEYER@VM1.TUCC.TRINITY.EDU.

Narin, F. (1976). *Evaluative bibliometrics: The use of publication and citation analysis in the evaluation of scientific activity.* Cherry Hill, New Jersey: Computer Horizons, Inc.

Okerson, A. (Ed.). (1994). *Directory of electronic journals, newsletters and academic discussion lists* (4th ed.). Washington, D.C.: Association of Research Libraries.

Osburn, C. B. (1984). The place of the journal in the scholarly communications system. *Library Resources and Technical Services,* 315-324.

Schauder, D. (1994). Electronic publishing of professional articles: Attitudes of academics and implications for the scholarly communication industry. *Journal of the American Society for Information Science, 45,* 73-100.

Smith, L. C. (1981). Citation analysis. *Library Trends, 30,* 83-106.

Turoff, M., & Hiltz, S. R. (1982). The electronic journal: A progress report. *Journal of the American Society for Information Science, 33,* 195-202.

Walker, J. R. (1995). *MLA-Style Citations of Electronic Sources.* January 1995 (Rev. 4/95). URL http://www.cas.usf.edu/english/walker/mla.html.

An Electronic WWW Archive for Conference Information in Library and Information Science

Mark Rorvig
University of North Texas
Denton, Texas

The age of the electronic conference is upon us. Conferences are now announced on the WWW; abstracts and papers are submitted and peer reviewed on the WWW; and individuals even register online. The conference proceedings, however, are still subject to the old fashion process of printing, binding, and sale (often at outrageous prices) to libraries and conference sponsors and participants. This paper describes the structure of a permanent electronic archive for WWW Conferences in Library and Information Science, sponsored by the University of North Texas and Scarecrow Press. Existing services and plans for future alternative archival services are reviewed and discussed.

ILL: New Models, New Ways

Bill Ruane
Network Support Incorporated
Ottawa, Ontario

The following is the summary of the attached presentation/paper that looks at how public access to current collections may be improved and the cost of ILL transactions be reduced by applying "digital technology" and business techniques to the ILL process. It will also look at the business impacts on costs and revenue collection in this electronic model for both copyright protection and royalty fee collection. It will also explore how the public may now view information retrieval based on both traditional media (paper) and the emerging digital storage and retrieval methods.

1   Outline

The Canada Institute of Scientific and Technical Information has recently implemented an automated intelligent document delivery system, IntelliDoc. This implementation has given CISTI the opportunity to make improvements to the CISTI Document Delivery service, reducing service response time frames, manpower requirements, and simultaneously accommodate growth of the services. It has also allowed CISTI to market new services and apply value based pricing to the current services. These results were not only achieved by the application of technology but principally by implementing electronic workflow process that took advantage of the technology capabilities and rethinking their service delivery paradigm.

The lessons learned in the implementation of IntelliDoc are now being incorporated into a product called Relais by Network Support Inc. (the developers of IntelliDoc). The University of Alberta will be the first client of Relais. The product will incorporate public access interfaces, patron and financial record validation and a full statistical reporting capability. More importantly the automated intelligent document delivery capability has been extended to provide an electronic warehouse capability. This warehouse could contain many items including the library catalogue. These could be electronic publications, information in the form of both physical and electronic archive items, public records, maps industrial widgets etc. This warehouse will have a full electronic access capability based on the Relais public access module and a EDI transaction set. This electronic warehouse approach would allow users of Relais better access to local collections and reduce the cost of the Borrowing and Lending transactions to the community, by reducing mediation needed to support the current services.

Using an EDI transaction set based on the ILL protocol will also allow electronic mediation of ILL requests between institutions and within Relais, that is the forwarding or onward transmission of requests to preferred suppliers or institutions without manual intervention. As the ILL protocol implementation matures it is not unreasonable for communities to electronically mediate requests between themselves without any manual intervention. Relais has been designed with this capability in mind.

The impact on the traditional ILL procedures will be significant. The workflow processing will be electronic, the inter institutional mediation process will be electronic and the consumer will be able to shop for the best buy and service level. The library will be now be able to place value added packing to their collections by exploiting it's strengths, by packing information "information" bundles that meet market demands. The library staff will now have to reorient its focus away from process to adding value to the information that they are the custodians of. The "network" will also bring a new audience to the Research Libraries that have never had the capability to easily access their holdings till now. This opens up new revenue opportunities for hard pressed institutional coffers.

The publishers will have security in protecting their property as the transactions will have a complete audit capability, thus generating revenue that may enable "electronic publishing" to become more of a reality.

2 Introduction

2.1 The Library Today

Traditional, service oriented, labour intensive in some of the operations, underestimates it's future value and role staff tend to play a subordinate role within the organizational structure.

Strengths

- earlier adopters of standards and technology
- one of the few repositories of information that has been codified and generally publicly accessible. Compare to Records Management World the other Great repository of information
- service tradition, well organized to find and exchange information within the library community
- Professional staff, open access philosophy vv the Records Management World which is closed and operates on a "need to know" basis

Weaknesses

- Conservative culture, not attuned to rapid change in many cases, and resistant to the innovative use of technology, tends to dissipate effort on process not creating value for their service portfolio
- Does not place a market value on the service that it provides to the point when it acquiesces to collect fees, the cost in many cases exceeds the revenue
- To ready to play a subordinate role in the organization and the result in many cases is a poor return on the professional skills required within a good library

Opportunities

- To become a part of the mainstream corporate management as the preferred supplier of content as a part of the corporate product portfolio. The IT departments have always had difficulty delivering content with technology.
- To establish value for their services and become the preferred distributors for electronic products that have copyright, royalty protection requirements
- Establish themselves as the provider of all records based information within a corporation and use their professional skills and traditional service culture as the means of establishing that position.

2.2 The Digital Library Vision

The vision is in the eye of the beholder. What is articulated and what is reality has a wide divergence.

The IBM definition is one of a wide array of information storage, management, search, retrieval and distribution technologies, much of which is available today, all available in a single architecture.

The objective in this case when the information is digitized, is that information can be shared on public networks like the Internet or private networks like the IBM Global Network.

2.2.1 How far down the road are we?

Examining the reality is a little different. In the classic IBM digital library reference one digital collection referred to consists of 20,000 manuscripts.

Reality is that 80% of the worlds information is still paper and still growing. The major databases are still predominantly structured databases and are not in relational form. For every 20 structured databases there is only one fully searchable text database.

As IBM has stated the technologies that we are need to achieve the digital library are generally available but we are confronted by many technical procedural techniques that we have not mastered yet to get to the digital data world. A large part of these techniques to implement require agreement on the standards that everybody will adopt to make the technology work within a common architecture.

2.3 What are the problems?

The obvious is one is data preparation and data conversion to create the information content for the digital repository. Ultimately where we want to be is the creation of all data at source in digital form. This has been the holy grail of the computer industry since day one and how far have we advanced?

Lets look at some examples of how we are proceeding to reach this objective. We have the promise of SGML as the portable open format for text and multimedia databases. However the data preparation is still complex, error prone and expensive. Everybody likes the idea but are terrified by the implementation effort and costs.

Other concerns from the potential creators and owners of these databases are their protection in terms of intellectual property, copyright and royalties. If they are going to invest in setting up these processes and buy into the digital and network access vision then they have to be very comfortable with the mechanism that are going to address these concerns and provide the revenue to create and sustain these information sources.

These problems are not going to be resolved in the immediate future. We will need to define the key the technical capabilities and concentrate on the development of the legal framework that protects the digital data creators.

Other technical issues include the standards. Good examples are no standards in the CD ROM world; Text retrieval systems, no portable index's; circulation systems, all product proprietary implementation standards. We even see differences in the Z39.50 implementations, sometimes divergence from the standards and in some cases just sloppy product. I am sure everybody can give good examples. We have many more emerging problems arising from the lack of a common interface standard for the WWW for a user interface that allows all the services to be accessed in a common environment and the reuse of data between applications.

Back to reality, the world is still paper, a smattering of electronic text and a few GIFF and TIFF files and the major providers of this information are having their funding curtailed or reduced as demand increases. Although the digital library may be largely a vision, the networks have become a reality and the network users have discovered that there are very few real sources of information outside the library community.

We are seeing demand growing at a rate of 20% per annum in large institutions, and in some cases, for specialized collections and new services, a growth of 20% per month. A good example of new services is Patron initiated services

The problem now is funding, vertical collections that create more inter institutional borrowing, high request growth rates, paper based collections, and today's culture that demands information "NOW".

2.3.1   The ILL and Document Delivery Process

The current methods to accept an information request is based on the Inter Library Loan and Document Delivery process. This requests is generally the result of a a search of an electronic catalogue that reveals the local institution not having the item, a request is then sent to a alternate institution that is believed to carry the item. It generally means a a form being generated by the patron that is either hand carried or mailed to a central ILL office, then forwarded as an electronic request (fax or E mail) to the potential supplier institution. If the potential supplier does not have the item then a response is sent in some form to the requesting ILL office and the process is repeated.

If the respondent institution has the item or article, it is prioritized based on local rules, copied or loaned as per policy and sent to the requesting ILL office, generally by mail. In some cases a fax may be provided as a premium service. There are significant variations in service levels from institution to institution. At best the patron gets something back in several weeks that they then have to pick up at the ILL office. There are cases where the process cab take several months. Even if they want to pay for a premium service they can't, as it is a "free" service and the ILL staff, in some cases as a measurement of their performance are evaluated on how many free copies they get, not on the cost of obtaining the "free" copy and the service level provided to the patron.

The document suppliers fill some of the void for premium service. They however as the demand increases are finding it difficult to maintain their service levels as specialisation increases and fragments the manual processing into more sub processes that then requires more staff to manage the process and maintain the service levels.

So the institutions and the alternate suppliers are running into a service wall and are constrained by funding, manpower and resource escalation if traditional methods are used to meet the increasing demand. The increasing fragmentation in demand for different types of service in turn creates additional costs that erode the premium service revenue that is generated by the service.

What hopes do the ILL and document suppliers have to manage these problems. The obvious answer is technology. Why has it not been applied in these areas? The ISO ILL protocol has been available for many years and defines the methods and messages for enabling automated ILL processes between institutions and document suppliers. Why has it not been fully implemented. All we see are some simplistic implementations that have implemented the basic Messaging formats for exchanging requests that are immediately transformed into paper by the recipient and then follow all of all the old manual processes. To put this into perspective we have counted 18 processes for the average ILL Borrowing and its subsequent Lending process at the supplier institution (see Exhibit A). Except for the action of picking the item and sending it the patron no value is added by any of those processes to the information requested by the patron. In the simplistic Messaging implementations of the ILL protocol does not reduce the number of processes, it only reduces the time to pass the requests between institutions and record keeping. In the above scenario we are allowing searches of two alternate locations to find the required item and the market price requested for the item paid is as is by the requester. When the "free" copy mentality takes over the process effort takes off, as does the real cost.

If we are to provide the incremental leap needed to deal within the constraints that the ILL processes are facing and meet the increasing demand, then we have to aim to reduce the manual processing effort significantly, remove the paper transaction mentality and aim to eliminate all of the no value added manual tasks. What I am suggesting is an implementation of the ILL protocol, in the same manner, with the same impact as EDI has had on manufacturing industries, where ordering, vendor selection, purchasing, inventory management and financial reconciliation became automated processes. I am proposing an extension of the auction model concept that Clifford Lynch espouses in his "System Architecture and Networking Issues in implementing the North America ILL and Document Delivery (NAILLDD) Imitative paper. Similar concepts are articulated by Joe Zeeman in the "Interlending in the Emerging Networked Environment" paper.

3 Opportunities for Improvement

The opportunities offered by technology in the ILL area and Document Delivery are:

1. To increase increase the user options and the number of value added services without increasing manpower/costs

2. Reduce turnaround times for service from days to hours

3. Tracing of requests copyright, royalty and financial information for each request

4. Automating the requesting and delivery process between institutions and allowing patrons unmediated access to the ILL and Document Delivery services.

5. Redirecting the clerical and professional skills available to add value to the information services provided by the institution instead of performing non value added ILL manual tasks and processes.

3.1 Automating the ILL process

To take advantage of these opportunities the reduction of manual effort in the ILL service delivery methods is a primary concern. We quoted 18 processes for a typical ILL request processing. We believe that this can be reduced to two processes, three if it is felt that the Ill requester organization wishes to validate the ILL transaction before it is released to a responding institution (see exhibit B). I will describe the significant impact of this reduction later in the presentation. To date using the techniques and technology described the number of manual processes were reduced at CISTI for the Document Delivery Operation from twelve to two These tasks were all associated with supporting the Pick, Copy, and Re-shelve process on the stacks.

The key technology that was employed to achieve these results was a workflow system with automated processing and document management system capabilities and series of common interfaces that were required to link the workflow processes to the document management life cycle that managed the use of the information requested (see exhibits C and D).

3.2 Standards and Standardization

The key to integrating these three complex system elements and allowing the transfer of requests from and between patrons, institutions, and the electronic delivery of the requested information is standards. These may be based on defacto or internationally recognized standards such as CCITT or ISO.

In CISTI this allowed us to take the core system products and provide an open architecture that we believe will allow us to produce systems that will permit network access to a multitude of information types from a single interface. The standards based approach that we espouse is not to try and make all information to conform to one type but link it in a subject based array that may link many information types, both physical and electronic, at many locations in a logical manner that is retrievable based on registered standards. This would be achieved by using a requester mechanism to that deals with the information as an object that will be delivered to a point as defined by the requester and then viewed or recreated by the reusing the information based on its standards based creation method. In it's simplest form this is an electronic warehouse with defined entry and exit points and a variety of objects that can be retrieved from the electronic or physical shelves and sent to the loading dock for onward delivery by surface or electronic means. All events are recorded electronically including the accounting and stock reconciliation for all of the events that occur around the order process, the information retrieval and the delivery or the forwarding of the request to an alternate location.

This has been achieved in manufacturing, the leading example of which is the automotive industry with physical movement of goods and orders electronically monitored, and the electronic management of the accounting and stock reconciliation functions. It is called EDI and based on well defined standards that have developed over the years. These standards are developed by industry based interest groups that set the EDI standards for their industry transaction sets but within the overall ANSI and ISO EDI standards.

The Library world has had an ILL protocol standard for five years but has had at best a limited and uneven implementation. Hence the NAILDD project group and its recently formed implementation group. I believe that the lessons that the manufacturing world learnt with it's implementation of EDI, can be applied to the ILL transaction world.

3.3 Two implementation models for consideration

I am sure that there are many thoughts, positions and on implementing the ILL protocol. Some even have experience, as at the National Library in Canada, and the Research Triangle Park Consortia. I would like to concentrate on two examples that have been articulated by two leading industry figures in recent articles. Both present similar conclusions and concentrate on the Service Delivery Aspects of the ILL protocol. The articles are from:

- Joe Zeeman
- Clifford Lynch

Joe Zeeman describes 6 scenarios and Clifford lynch describes 3. Both describe scenarios that range from a simple transaction where the requesters and receivers are the ILL offices or sections and the patron is just an appendage, to the scenario where the patron completes the searches an the requester system is an intermediary system such as OCLC that completes the transaction with the respondent system and only statistics are reported to the patron and respondent ILL sections.

In the Joe Zeeman paper there is one model that advances the patron Initiated ILL model using an ILL Utility to search for the potential suppliers and receive the item at the patron desktop. This scenario is however prefaced with the caveat that the development effort would be substantial and could only be implemented in a client server environment. Clifford Lynch advances a radical model that he calls the dynamic auction model that may be "potentially feasible". In this model the borrower requests bids from the lenders across the network and depending on the responses selects the preferred lender based on criteria that may include price, delivery time and previous service record. The lending institution would set its's price dynamically on a request by request basis as their demand increases or decreases or the uniqueness of the item requested. These two models tend to be a de-centralized models and cut out the centralized intermediary systems. The benefits are that consortia can be formed that can supply 80% of its needs and retain the revenue that would flow to an outside centralized intermediary system provider.

We believe that the principles espoused by Lynch and Zeeman which are well defined within the ILL Service Definition, can be implemented now using the techniques developed at CISTI and expanded on at the University of Alberta. We believe that we have already implemented about 80% of the functionality and the processes defined in the standards and the task is to standardize the current electronic processes to conform to the ILL Protocol Service Definition

4   The Technology Enablers

Why do we think that we can do it all now? What is it that makes us able to do what the industry experts consider technically obtuse? We are not library system vendors. Our background is automating process and integration of process into a system solution that meets a set of business objectives. What we see in the ILL transaction are a series of repetitive processes that have strict guidelines and rules on the steps that are to be followed. How they are implemented is at the discretion of the requester and responder. The implementation should reflect the institutional needs and policies and reflect the institutions business objectives.

For us, the obvious answer was electronic workflow to manage the process and integrated with electronic document management to manage the information life cycle. This was the approach taken at CISTI and Alberta and the key to how we plan to implement the ILL protocol Service Delivery Model based primarily on the modified auction model, aimed at ILL Document Delivery consortia by 1997.

4.1   The CISTI Experience Cost Benefits

In the CISTI Implementation we automated 10 of the 12 tasks associated with copying (Lending functions) and delivery to the patron location. This is the electronic delivery model.

The CISTI cost benefits were as follows:

1.   Reduction in photocopier positions from 17 to 13

2.   Reduced document Delivery times by 75%. Turnaround time is the now same working day for over 92% of requests supplied as documents. The remainder are orders that require special handling i.e in depth searches etc.

3.   Delivery costs are reduced by a $1 a page for fax and international deliveries. Paper and media costs are eliminated for electronic delivery.

4.   Volumes have increased from an average of 1200 a day to 1500 a day with no increase in staff and or reduction of service levels.

5.   Allowed a flexible pricing model to be introduced that allows CISTI to match market needs to value pricing and maximize revenue opportunities.

6.   Statistics that allow tracking of orders at all stages of processing and service levels achieved.

4.2   Expanding the CISTI model at the University of Alberta

The CISTI implementation was expanded to cover all of the 18 tasks identified in the ILL borrowing and Lending Cycle. Of the 18 tasks 16 have been included in the Relais implementation (Relais is the product developed from the CISTI IntelliDoc implementation). The key additions are the patron search for an item in the catalogue is now turned into an electronic order that is sent to one of 14 campus locations, copied electronically and delivered if requested directly to the patrons desktop. Incoming orders without call numbers from other institutions will be automatically call numbered and directed to the appropriate location without any manual intervention. Orders that cannot be satisfied at the local Campus locations but are identified in the search as being held by other locations in Edmonton will be forwarded to these locations for fulfilment. Messages confirming supply will be returned to the Requester notifying them of the supply point.

When the second (multiple search capability) is instituted this will allow second searches for items that are not identified in the local catalogue to be searched for at alternate holdings and the order to be automatically generated and sent to the alternate holding.

If a patron cannot find an item a Borrowing Requests can be generated that is fed to an ILL mediation work queue, where the preferred lending location will be added to the request which will then be forwarded automatically to that location. Of course all of these transactions are being tracked. The patron database will maintain order profiles for the patron and a financial validation mechanism that will allow addition of EFTPOS capabilities in the future.

The benefits to the University of Alberta of this capability in addition to the benefits that accrued at the CISTI implementation will be as follows:

1.   Reduction in ILL staff effort. This will be accomplished by the following:

-      40% of requests received will be automatically call numbered and require no manual intervention
-      45% of the remaining requests will require only 50% of the traditional effort required to complete the call numbering
-      25% of orders to the NEOS consortia will be delivered electronically
-      The WWW interface will supply formatted Borrowing requests for processing. This combined with the reduction in paper handling will save at least one person for these activities.
-      Order processing will be in one stream eliminating special handling teams for priority orders

The reduced manpower requirements have now allowed the University of Alberta to plan to implement an on campus delivery service in 1996.

4.3   Next steps; applying the Zeeman/Lynch models

The current application is built around the premise of searching the catalogue and a connection based transport for the transfer of the order information to the ILL system. Currently we can also accept orders and deliver documents in a connection less environment. We can forward unfilled requests to alternate institutions and will shortly be able to conduct multiple searches and forward the request to a supplier with the required item.

To achieve the goals articulated by Zeeman and Lynch and give the patron choice requires more than a search capability. The Manufacturing world solved this with EDI transactions. We propose to modify our current workflow to incorporate a EDI request sequence using the ILL Protocol Service Definitions to manage the process. The basic sequence between the Requester and Responders would have the following sequence (see exhibit E):

Requester	-	issue a price and availability request to responders that requester has supply agreements with. These agreements define response times, pricing and payment rules etc
Responder	-	responds with availability information and at what price and delivery information. This response could be based on current load., item value (vertical/specialized collection) and method of delivery. This electronic response is generated based on workflow rules and requires no manual intervention
Requester	-	receives all responses. Based on local policies evaluates responses based on workflow rules database and issues a electronic supply order to the selected responder. The workflow selection rules could include supply history, price parameters and urgency of supply as input parameters.
Responder	-	receives order confirmation, picks and copies required item, ships item to patron directly or delivery point selected by the patron based on delivery information in the ILL service message. The system generates financial information that becomes part of an EDI/EFTPOS transaction between the institutions. No paper is passed or manual effort expended on the financial reconciliation.

The Messaging for this supply request/auction would follow the ILL Protocol Service Definition for State Transitions. The sequences would be completed in minutes and a message then passed to the patron on the supply status. These ILL sequences would only be initiated when a local supply is not available to the patron.

Responsibility for searching the catalogue for availability in this model would always be with the responder. In a limited or preferred supplier environment searching may be done by the requester prior to issuing the supply requests to the preferred suppliers. At this time it is difficult to predict what the correct mix of searching and EDI requests will provide the optimum solution. A well structured trial will help to develop that algorithm.

Based on our current implementation we believe that this all possible and are committed to developing the workflow and conducting a trial starting in Fall 1996.

4.4   The Information Warehouse

This now opens up some interesting possibilities. We have used standards based searching methods for immediate identification and with EDI standards based message transactions we can describe many types of item and processes to be performed within the message envelope.

4.4.1 What's in the Warehouse and how to access it

Now we can add information types into the Warehouse that moves beyond the traditional library world. We have a means that can identify and retrieve both physical and electronic objects at multiple locations. We have a virtual warehouse that can has electronic access and delivery methods. A "CyberInformation Warehouse".

How to access it in a uniform manner. Although we can access information in a uniform manner with MS Windows that has well defined standards, allows interchange of data in "object" format and its reuse to generate new transactions.

This has not yet extended to the Web world. We see the "Browser" mode alive and well and little consideration for reuse of the information. Any data manipulation is at the element level and not concerned with "object" manipulation. The preferred tools PERL and CGI scripts are straight from the Unix world and always unique to the application.

The result for the library world is that every application has its set of Web forms, all asking for the same information and as the user moves from function to function the information from the catalogue cannot be reused for a ILL request, the patron information used for accessing the catalogue cannot be used to re-enter the Reserve system, the citation database uses a different Marc format from the catalogue record. This makes it hard to use the same data or object capture modules for displaying the returned information from a query.

What is needed is a standards based interface. Maybe Java and Netscape may provide it as the problem is recognized, and we get past the initial Web Hype.

5 Impacts

What are the impacts and the spin offs from these impacts in terms of money and people. The ILL model that we discussed earlier is dramatic. The table in exhibit F describes the current ILL tasks and Time frames and compares it with a model that is based on our Relais implementation and a ILL protocol service in place.

The table shows a ILL request when it goes through a complete Borrowing and Lending Cycle. In the this scenario the ILL staff processing time in the reduces from 55 minutes to 7 minutes. This does not included the Patron travel time to the ILL office or the search facilities, or ILL staff travel time on a multi site campus, which is eliminated in the automated electronic delivery model.

Using a cost base of $30,000 per annum ($125 per day) as an ILL staff cost and an average of 100 borrowing requests a day for 240 days a year, the current methods would cost $343,750 per annum compared to $43,750 for the automated electronic delivery model.

Service time for a patron request is reduced to one working day from five days at best and delivery is to the patron desktop.

5.1   Broadening the market for ILL services

Besides the network generated demand the system now allows the information supplier to go and solicit new clients as now they have resources freed up to provide additional capacity as at the University of Alberta. This enhances revenue without increasing costs. This could be in the form of extended delivery services or in depth searches for patron projects.

At the University of Alberta they will now offer campus delivery. A service that was not feasible before because of the level of effort required and the incremental revenue was offset by incremental costs.

5.2   The modified auction model using EDI and workflow techniques applied to the Zeeman/Lynch implementation models

The impacts here are more speculative and subjective at this time. We believe in a consortia that the fill rate for requests would move up substantially. The fill rate appears to be a bout 50% at this time and level of effort required to move this up with current manual search methods is counterproductive in terms of cost. If this fill rate is increased it will mean more revenue remaining within the consortia. It will also mean that consortia does not have to turn to a single supplier when a requests cannot be filled within the consortia. The end of monopoly or the oligopoly for ILL support.

5.3   Information Access methods for the end user

Not withstanding the data re-use issues and need for common standards the public now has unprecedented access to information using the Web and Internet access. If we adopt the Warehouse concept the patron at a single point of access can retrieve and use many information types and not be constrained by its form. This opens up archives that were previously unreachable because of their locations and methods of storage. The barrier in this example is the culture that Archivists have, which is not one of public access.

5.4   Impacts on the ILL staff and retraining/reorientation to meet the impacts of the new service delivery models

As we see in the ILL example the reduction in clerical level from current methods is potentially between 40% and 80%. Alberta has chosen to increase services and revenue. The impact could also be applied to staff reductions.

5.5 Protection of Intellectual property

With all events within the transaction being tracked and the Patron information being validated, access to the available intellectual property is now monitored. The option becomes to either restrict the use of the information or allow access based on a payment scheme This could be subscription driven and kept as patron information, or payment made on a page by page basis.

5.6 Revenue generation and protection

The same revenue and tracking mechanisms can also generate and calculate the required billing information and can include delivery cost on a variable basis that includes delivery method, changes or prioritization of the delivery methods. This would be done electronically and passed in a format that fits into an institutional model that uses an EFTPOS means of reconciliation. This eliminates the syndrome in many ILL offices where the cost of producing the invoice exceeds the revenue produced. With a fully featured system for occasional patrons, payment could also be requested prior to transaction acceptance via a POS payment method. This removes that high handling costs associated with minimal revenue associated with occasional ILL users.

5.7 Summary

The proposed scenario plays to the strengths of the Library community, that we discussed at the start of the presentation. It uses

- their capabilities as early adopters of standards and technology
- technology to expand public access to the great repositories of codified information. This is coupled with the service tradition and organizations that are attuned to the finding and exchange of information between a variety of sources
- the available Professional staff and skills to provide further public access, using technology, to what were previously physically inaccessible collections for the general public.

For the Library staff, using their strengths with the proposed technology and methods, allows them to become :

- An integral part of the mainstream corporate management as the corporate content and information supplier of choice
- adds value to their services, provides revenue opportunities by allowing their

institutions to become the preferred distributors for electronic products that have copyright, and royalty protection requirements

Innovative service providers, with significantly reduced costs and improved service levels for the patron community.

Exhibit B

ILL BORROWING AND LENDING CYCLE
USING RELAIS

Borrowing Institution

Patron Search

Optional Validation of ILL
Request

TO

FROM

Pick, Copy and Reshelve
Requested Item

Lending Institution

Exhibit D

Relais System

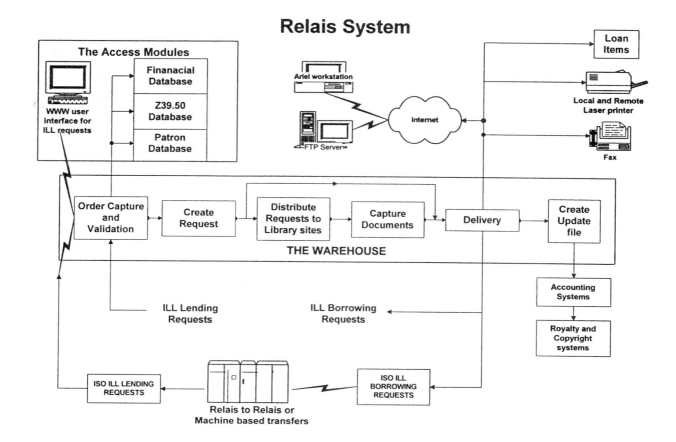

Exhibit E

The EDI Warehouse

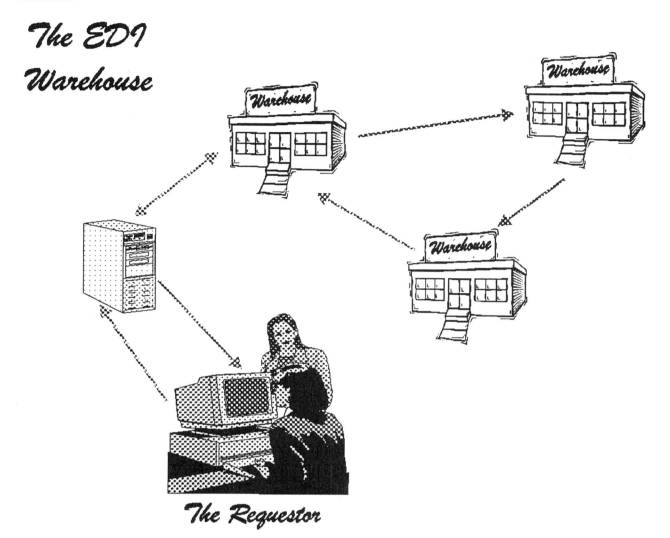

The Requestor

Exhibit F

Task and Level of Effort for a ILL Borrowing/Lending Cycle							
Task #	TASKS	Elapsed Time (Days)	Task Time (Minutes)	Relais Elapsed Time (Hours)	Relais Task Time (Minutes)	CISTI Implemen-tation	University of Alberta Implemen-tation
	Borrowing Institution						
1	Patron Search	Day 1	10	1	10		X
2	Patron Request at ILL Office		5				X
3	ILL Entry into System		2				X
4	Search 1 for item requested		3				X
5	Search 2 for item requested		3				
6	Item details entered into system		2		2 (optional validation)		X
	Sub Total	1 Day	25	1 Hour	12		
	Lending Institution						
7	Retrieval and printing of requests	Day 2	1			X	
8	Sort/ Reject Requests		1			X	
9	Search Catalogue		1			X	
10	Pick, Copy and Re-shelve Requested Item		5	4	5		
11	Return item to ILL Office		5			X	
12	Post or Fax item	Day 3	10			X	
13	Enter status into system		2			X	
	Sub Total	2 Days	25	4 Hours	5		
	Borrowing Institution						
14	Item received and stored	Day 4	1			X	
15	Message to Patron		2	1 Item to Patron			X
16	Patron to ILL office		5			X	
17	System closed	Day 5	2			X	
18	Invoicing		5			X	
	Sub Total	2 Days	15	1 hour	0		
	Total	5 days	65 Minutes	6 hours	7 Minutes		

This table reflects the time taken to process a copy request by the Patron and ILL staff either using a manual system with an electronic Messaging system such as AVISO compared to an Automated Document Delivery System with Electronic Delivery such as Relais.

336

The ILL staff processing time in the first scenario is 55 minutes and with the automated system 7 minutes. In the table no time is included for Patron travel time to the ILL office or the search facilities, or ILL staff travel time on a multi site campus, which is eliminated in the automated electronic delivery model.

Using a cost base of $30,000 per annum ($125 per day) as an ILL staff cost and an average of 100 borrowing requests a day for 240 days a year, the current methods would cost $343,750 per annum compared to $43,750 for the automated electronic delivery model.

Service time for a patron request is reduced to one working day from five days at best and delivery is to the patron desktop.

A BIBLIOMETRIC STUDY OF THE REMOTE HYPERTEXT LINKS IN PUBLIC LIBRARY WORLD WIDE WEB SITES

Richard J. Kuster
School of Library and Information Science, Indiana University
Bloomington, Indiana

ABSTRACT

This paper introduces the bibliometric technique of citation analysis as a method for the evaluation of public library home pages. By identifying the remote hypertext links contained in the World Wide Web sites maintained by public libraries in the United States and the relative frequencies of the occurrences of these remote links, a core list of Internet resources is identified. This study will be of interest not only for theoretical reasons, but also because of the practical application of the methods and findings to a public library whose librarians might be interested in creating a World Wide Web home page or in updating or improving an existing home page.

INTRODUCTION

The digital revolution is having a profound impact on the means by which public libraries are providing information services to their patrons. One significant impact of this digital revolution has been caused by the recent proliferation of information sources available through the Internet. Public libraries are utilizing these online resources for a variety of purposes such as answering reference questions, doing research, and for educating and entertaining library patrons.

There have been many books and articles published recently which provide guidance to the public library in establishing, managing, and utilizing Internet resources for the benefit of their patrons.[1] These publications, although helpful in such endeavors, do not adequately address the question of which Internet resources should be made available to the library's patrons and other potential users.

It has been observed that the growth of the Internet has reached epidemic proportions and it is estimated that a count of the Web sites worldwide would number in the millions. This growth has been attributed to the success of the World Wide Web (the "Web") and the development of user-friendly Web browsers such as Mosaic and Netscape.[2]

According to its head librarian, the St. Joseph County Public Library in South Bend, Indiana, became the first public library in the United States to establish a Web home page on March 14, 1994. A public library "home page" is the opening screen to which a user with a Web browser connects when accessing the library's resources via the Internet. The home page usually includes an introductory message containing a description of the library, its collection, and its services, along with hypertext links to other Web resources that the creators and designers of the home page consider to be of potential use or interest to the library's patrons or to librarians in performing their duties.

These links are of two types: (1) local links which provide access to information sources residing on the library's server which are maintained by persons affiliated with the library; and, (2) remote links which provide access to information sources residing on the servers of other Internet participants maintained by persons who are not affiliated with the library. The physical location of the digitized information accessible through a remote or external link may be as close as the next room or as far away as the other side of the world. The physical location of the digitized information accessible through a local or internal link is located on the same computer as the library's home page. A hypertext link, whether local or remote, consists of a unique address know as a "uniform resource locator" which is commonly referred to as a "URL."

Currently there are approximately 150 public libraries in the United States which maintain Web sites.[3] Each of these Web sites contains its own unique collection of information resources accessible through a combination of remote and local hypertext links. The primary objective of this study is to identify the common remote links to which the public libraries in the United States are connected. Knowledge of the resources which have been determined to be useful and of interest by the 150 Web pioneers will be of interest to not only these pioneers as they endeavor to update and improve their existing Web sites, but also to the thousands of other public libraries in the United States in the establishment of their own individual home pages.

CONTEXT

Lancaster indicates that the consensus among library professionals and scholars is that in the digital environment, libraries and librarians will continue to provide many of the same important functions with regard to the organization and dissemination of information as they have provided in the past.[4] Therefore, libraries and librarians will be active participants in the development, accessing, and maintenance of digital information resources. The large volume of literature being generated by scholars in the field of library and information science would seem to indicate that the library community has

not just been involved, but that they have become the pioneers of the digital age.

An example of this pioneering is the work being done by Demas. He has organized an "electronic resources council" at his library to assess and coordinate the electronic resources to be selected for use at the library. He considers the identification and selection of remote Internet sites to be within the scope of the professional responsibilities of the collection development librarians in his library.[5]

Demas reports that his library has appointed a group of "Internet Prospectors" who are charged with the task of assisting collection development in "sifting" through the "nuggets" of scholarly materials on the Internet and recommending remote sites which would be of potential interest and use to the other librarians and to the patrons of the library. The stated goal of this project was "to expand the dimensions of the collection development efforts to incorporate networked resources." Based upon the results of this project, the library integrated Internet site selection into an "ongoing collection development activity," concluding that "title selection of high quality resources is one of the most important values librarians can add in providing access to information resources, including those accessible via the Internet, and that although the electronic retrieval and network delivery of Internet resources changes the way information is stored and manipulated, traditional collection development concepts, principles, and practices apply equally to Internet selection."[6]

Miksa and Doty suggest some problems with the comparison of the traditional library with the digital library. They point out that a traditional library is a collection of information sources in a physical place. In the case of a digital library, the meanings of these concepts of "collection," "information sources," and "physical place," must be redefined. They conclude that a digital library is a collection of information sources in a place which is not necessarily a physical location, "but rather a place as an intellectual construct--a logical or intellectual space where location implies a rationalized set of relationships imposed on the members of a collection." They suggest that the concept of a "logical space" is very closely related to the concept of physical space.[7]

If the traditional library and the digital library are logically related, then it is appropriate to apply traditional collection development concepts, principles, and practices to Internet selection as Demas has suggested.

Small points out that there is an obvious relationship between the network of hypertext links embedded in hypertext documents and the network of citation links embedded in the printed scholarly literature. He suggests that hypertext links and citation links both define communication paths which, when viewed holistically, form vast communication networks or webs.[8]

Small gives credit to Jorgensen and Jorgensen for pointing out the relationship between links in hypertext documents and citation links in printed documents. According to Jorgensen and Jorgensen, the library community should assume the primary responsibility for organizing and maintaining the integrity of the digital communications networks created by links in hypertext documents.[9]

There are several assumptions with regard to the present study which seem to be supported by the literature. The first assumption is that there is a sufficient logical relationship between the digital library and the traditional library to support the use of traditional collection development and collection evaluation methods in the digital environment.

The second assumption is that there is a sufficient logical relationship between a cited reference in a printed scholarly article and a hypertext link in a hypertext document

to support the use of collection development and collection evaluation methods involving the bibliometric method of citation analysis.

The earliest know collection evaluation study involving the method of citation analysis is that conducted by Jewett in 1848. He compiled a list of the documents cited as references in several respected treatises and compared the list with the holdings of the Smithsonian Library.[10]

But a subsequent and more thorough study by Gross and Gross is considered to be the seminal work for the design of an evaluative study of a library's resources using the method of citation analysis. These researchers tabulated the cited references in the articles contained in the 1926 volume of a prominent chemistry journal. They were able to identify a core collection of journals consisting of those journals on their list with the highest citation frequencies.[11]

The method used in the present study is the same as that used by Gross and Gross except that instead of tabulating cited references from a printed journal, we are tabulating remote links in hypertext documents, identified by URL's rather than cited references. This is the first known application of the bibliometric method of citation analysis in the evaluation of hypertext documents. However, the wide-spread use of the method in the evaluation of print resources is evidence of the general acceptance of validity of such an analysis.[12]

Another method of evaluation related to the present study and having wide-spread acceptance in the literature, is that of the overlap study. In an overlap study, the collections of two or more libraries are compared in an attempt to identify those information sources that are unique to each library and those that overlap, or that all of the libraries have in common. One use of such a study is to identify collective collecting patterns.[13]

Thus, the objectives of the present study are to identify the core Internet resources being used by public libraries and to identify any collective collecting patterns of these libraries with regard to these resources. Also, it will be interesting from a theoretical standpoint to determine whether or not the distributions of URL's correspond to the classic bibliometric distributions as identified by Pareto, Bradford, and others.

There are lists of sites being maintained by various organizations which purport to identify the best Internet sites. The determination of the "best" sites to be included on these lists is determined in a variety of ways. For example, the "Webcrawler Top 25" is a list of the most frequently linked URL's on the Web which is based upon documents that have been searched by the Webcrawler search engine.[14] It is expressly stated that the list is "only an estimate of the real truth." Although the compilation of this list is for all users of Web resources who may not be exactly the same group as those being serviced by public libraries, it is expected that the results of the present study will correspond to the entries on this list.

"The Best of the Web" contains a list of cites determined to be the best as a result of their popularity based upon the votes of participating Internet users.[15] Awards are given in a number of different categories reminiscent of the "Oscars." Although many of the awards focus on aesthetics, it is anticipated that the results of the present study will also correspond with the list of award winners.

A study was also done by PC Magazine to determine the "Web's 100 most informative and technically adept sites" by the magazine's editorial staff.[16] Although the determination of the sites to be included in the resulting list were determined subjectively, it is also expected that the results of the present study will contain many of the cites included on this list.

An advantage of citation analysis which has been noted when used in studies done in other areas, such as journal ranking and academic program ranking, is that of objectivity. This advantage carries over to the present study involving the assessment of Web sites. Since most other published lists of Web sites involve a subjective assessment, the present study may produce a somewhat different result.

The result may also be somewhat different due to the difference in perspective. The present study focuses on public libraries. The most popular sites overall may not be appropriate for inclusion in the resources of public libraries because of their commercial or otherwise objectionable content.

Dillon, Jul, Burge, and Hickey have developed a classification system for Internet resources.[17] Once a core list of Internet resources is developed, the resources can be classified according to this system. This will provide some evidence of the types of Internet resources that libraries are using and provide some guidance to libraries considering the development of new resources on their local server.

METHOD

The starting point of this study was the determination of those public libraries in the United States who have created and are currently maintaining a Web home page. One method of identifying these libraries would be to conduct a search using one or more of the available Web search engines. However, the St. Joseph County Public Library in South Bend, Indiana, has been conducting periodic searches for such sites since November of 1994 and maintains a list of the results of these searches.[18] Also, libraries creating new home pages are requested to "register" their home page for inclusion on this list. This resource seems to be the most comprehensive listing of public libraries with Web home pages available. Because of the registration aspect of the list and the fact that it has been in existence for a substantial period of time, the list was considered to be superior to anything that could be produced by an independent search and therefore selected for use in this study. Thus, it is assumed that this list accurately identifies those public libraries in the United States with Web home pages that were in existence at the time of this study.

The St. Joseph County Public Library's list contains a listing of not only those public libraries with Web home pages in the United States, but also public libraries around the world maintaining a presence on the Web. Since many of these sites were in languages other than English, the study focused only on public libraries in the United States.

In order to determine the feasibility of the study, twenty-five libraries were randomly selected from the list. Then the home page of each of the public libraries in the sample, and all of the pages linked to the home page which resided on the local server, were copied using a program called "Grab-a-Site."[19] Then all of the URL's representing hypertext links to resources residing on remote servers were extracted from the pages obtained from each local library site.

After the extraction process, all of the URL's from the library sites were combined and the resulting data was loaded into "Bibliometrics Toolbox"[20] for analysis. The output from this software program consists of a list of the URL's ranked by frequency and a comparison of the distribution of these frequencies with recognized bibliometric distributions.

CONCLUSION

At the time of the submission of this paper, the research on the population of public library Web sites was still in progress. However, the results of the preliminary study, conducted on the sample, confirmed that the methods and techniques used in this study were feasible. Therefore, similar studies will be possible for the

analysis and evaluation of other types of information centers maintaining a presence on the Web.

This study is of significance not only because it illustrates the use of traditional bibliometric methods of analysis in evaluating Internet resources, but also because the resulting list of Web sites with the highest frequencies will be of practical use to those individuals charged with the design and maintenance of public library Web home pages.

ACKNOWLEDGMENTS

The guidance of Stephen P. Harter and Thomas E. Nisonger, and the assistance of Geoff McKim and Carrie Goodrum are hereby acknowledged with gratitude.

NOTES

1. Valauskas, Edward J. & John, Nancy R. (1995). The Internet Initiative: Libraries Providing Internet Services & How They Plan, Pay, and Manage. Chicago: American Library Assn.

2. Internet Statistics [Internet Site: http://lcweb.loc.gov/global/internet/net-stats.html] (1996). Washington, DC: Library of Congress.

3. Public Libraries on WWW Servers [Internet Site: http://sjcpl.lib.in.us/homepage/PublicLibraries/PubLibSrvsGpherWWW.html#wwwsrv] (1996). South Bend, IN: St. Joseph County Public Library.

4. Lancaster, F.W. (1994). Collection Development in the Year 2025. In Recruiting, Educating, and Training Librarians for Collection Development, ed. Peggy Johnson & Sheila S. Intner (pp. 215-229). Westport, CT: Greenwood Press.

5. Demas, Samuel (1994). Collection Development for the Electronic Library: A Conceptual and Organizational Model. Library Hi Tech, 12(3), 71-80.

6. Demas, Samuel; Peter McDonald, & Gregory Lawrence (1995). The Internet and Collection Development: Mainstreaming Selection of Internet Resources. Library Resources & Technical Services, 39(3), 275-290.

7. Miksa, Francis L. & Philip Doty (1994). Intellectual Realities and the Digital Library. Digital Libraries '94 Proceedings, 1-5.

8. Small, Henry (1995). Navigating the Citation Network. Proceedings of the 1995 Annual Meeting of the American Society for Information Science, 118-123.

9. Jorgensen, Corinne & Peter Jorgensen (1991). Citations in Hypermedia: Maintaining Critical Links. College & Research Libraries, 52, 528-535.

10. Jewett, C.C. (1848). Report of the Assistant Secretary Relative to the Library, Presented Dec. 13, 1848. In Third Annual Report of the Board of Regents of the Smithsonian Institution to the Senate and House of Representatives, 39-47.

11. Gross, P.L.K. & E.M. Gross (1927). College Libraries and Chemical Education. Science, 66, 385-389.

12. Nisonger, Thomas E. (1992). Citation Studies. Chapter 8, in Collection Evaluation in Academic Libraries: A Literature Guide and Annotated Bibliography, Englewood, CO: Libraries Unlimited.

13. Nisonger, Thomas E. (1992). Overlap Studies. Chapter 6, in Collection Evaluation in Academic Libraries: A Literature Guide and Annotated Bibliography. Englewood, CO: Libraries Unlimited.

14. Webcrawler Top 25 [Internet Site: http://webcrawler.com/WebCrawler/Top25.html]. America Online.

15. The Best of the Web [Internet Site: http://wings.buffalo.edu/contest/]

16. Metz, Cade (1996). The 100 Top Web Sites. PC Magazine, 15(3), 100-118.

17. Dillon, Martin, Erik Jul, Mark Burge, & Carol Hickey (1993). Assessing Information on the Internet: Toward Providing Library Services for Computer-Mediated Communication. Dublin, OH: Online Computer Library Center.

18. Public Libraries on WWW Servers (1996). [Internet Site: http://sjcpl.lib.in.us/homepage/PublicLibraries/PubLibSrvsGpherWWW.html#wwwsrv] South Bend, IN: St. Joseph County Public Library.

19. Grab-a-Site [Computer Software, Beta Version] (1995). Salt Lake City, UT: Blue Squirrel.

20. Brooks, T.A. (1987). Bibliometrics Toolbox [Computer Software, Version 2.8]. Seattle, WA: North City Bibliometrics.

SIG Sessions

Electronic Scientific Publications: Role of the Gatekeepers

Sponsoring Organization: SIG-STI

Session Abstract

The exponential growth of scientific publications over the last several decades presents a formidable information management challenge for scientists and information professionals alike. Scientists need to locate and assimilate current information for their research, while information managers seek to provide access to this information. Until recently, this problem has been confined to print sources; however, the digital revolution promises to provide a mechanism for creating, retrieving and storing scientific publications online. Electronic discussion groups, pre- prints, and journals are becoming increasingly available. A critical feature of the scientific publication process for printed materials has been the gatekeeper function performed by the peer- review process. As the new medium is developed, it is apparent that the gatekeeper function must be addressed. This session will provide a forum for presentation and discussion of electronic publications currently utilized by scientists and the gatekeeper functions needed in the electronic environment.

Session Organizer:

Natalie Schoch, Ph.D.
Assistant Professor
University of Maryland at College Park
College of Library and Information Services, 4121E Hornbake Building,
University of Maryland, College Park, MD 20742-4345
301/405-2052
nk28@umail.umd.edu

Presenters:

Paul Ginsparg, Ph.D.
Research Scientist
Los Alamos National Labs, Los Alamos, NM
ginsparg@qfwfq.lanl.gov
"The High Energy Physics Electronic Pre-Print Archive"

Julie Hurd, Ph.D.
Science Librarian
University of Illinois at Chicago
Science Library, (M/S 234) Box 8198, Chicago, IL 60680
(312) 413-3060
jhurd@uic.edu
"New Roles for Gatekeepers after the Digital Revolution"

Ann C. Weller
Deputy Director
Library of the Health Sciences (M/C 763) Universoty of Illinois at Chicago,

1750 W. Polk Street, Chicago, IL
312/996-8974
312/996-9584
ACW@UIC.EDU
"The changing role of peer review in an electronic environment."

Moderator:

Natalie Schoch, Ph.D.
Assistant Professor
University of Maryland at College Park
College of Library and Information Services, 4121E Hornbake Building,
University of Maryland, College Park, MD 20742-4345
301/405-2052
nk28@umail.umd.edu

Digital Library Trends and Issues:
An NSF Perspective

Sponsoring Organization: SIG-CR (Classification Research)

Session Abstract

PURPOSE

The purpose of this panel presentation will be to present the key trends and issues that emerged from the NSF-sponsored Allerton Institute and the UCLA/NSF Workshop on the Social Aspects of Digital Libraries. We hope to provide attendees of ASIS MidYear '96 with an overview of current developments in user-centered digital library research and the issues that interdisciplinary DL researchers are considering concerning users' information needs and end user searching and filtering. The panel will also help attendees see the research directions that federal sponsors, NSF in particular, feel are important for understanding the use and implications of digital information infrastructure, as our research methods, systems, and expectations of systems continually evolve.

RATIONALE

The panel format is straightforward: the panelists will each give 15-minute reviews of their respective NSF-sponsored events and give the ASIS MidYear '96 audience an indication of the attendees and their disciplinary affiliations. For The final half-hour, the moderator will use the panelist presentations to engage the audience in a lively discussion of DL research. The perspectives of the researchers, practitioners, etc. in the audience will be of significant value to the panelists as this is their opportunity to get some feedback on the conclusions and issues raised in the Allerton Institute and the UCLA Workshop.

OVERVIEW OF THE ALLERTON INSTITUTE

The Allerton Institute brought together an interdisciplinary group of researchers and practitioners involved in the design and study of information systems, in user-centered research in traditional libraries, and in a wide range of digital library projects. The purpose of the forum was to present both the range of user-centered methods available for studying digital libraries and rationales for choosing amongst them; it also looked ahead to new methods and developments and mapped out the challenges they entail. Some of the issues discussed were:

> What are appropriate measures for gauging digital library outcomes at the individual, group, institutional, and global levels?

> How can we best incorporate knowledge of user needs and behavior in designing digital library interactions and interfaces?

> What do we need to know about how people use electronic texts and how can we gain this knowledge and apply it to the development of digital libraries?

> What can we learn from studies of traditional library use?

How can we develop an understanding of the computerization of library work that will help as digital systems are incorporated into current institutional practices?

How can we deal with the ethical, practical, and conceptual issues that arise in the remote observation of online (and off-line) behavior on a very large scale?

How do we foster effective communication among digital library designers, users, and social science researchers?

Each Institute participant submitted a brief discussion document outlining their work and the issues they were most anxious to explore. These were used to develop the five major Institute sessions, which focused on co-design approaches, understanding work practice and institutional change, migrating foundational approaches to virtual library environment, studying electronic information seeking behavior, and understanding diversity and change associated with a large, heterogeneous user population. Participants included researchers from the fields of Computer Science, Sociology, Library and Information Science, Education, and Psychology who are involved in digital library projects in a wide range of settings.

OVERVIEW OF THE UCLA WORKSHOP

The UCLA Workshop is also a response to the Digital Libraries National Challenge Application designated by the Information Infrastructure Technology and Applications Task Group under the High Performance Computing and Communications Initiative. National Challenge projects are intended to focus on large societal problems and bring human and technological resources to bear on their solution. Digital Libraries are a prime example of such problems, for they cross all disciplines and all sectors of society.

Many social aspects of digital libraries need to be addressed, as we come to understand the full range of issues they encompass. The workshop will focus on two social problems that are urgent in developing the National and Global Information Infrastructures: information needs and end user searching and filtering. These two problems were selected because they are urgent, enough research exists to frame them but not enough to solve them, and the work on these problems is scattered across multiple disciplines that need to be brought together to form a research community. The workshop will identify the following research questions to be addressed in the social aspects of digital libraries:

Information needs

Social context and culture

To what extent can digital library interfaces, information retrieval algorithms, intelligent agents, and other system components be generalized across application domains and to what extent must they be tailored to each environment?

Information needs and information seeking

To what extent are information needs and uses generalizable across user and learner groups and to what extent do they need to be tailored?

What is the relationship between information seeking and learning in digital libraries?

Linking user-learner needs and behavior to digital library design.

What systems design techniques are appropriate in applying user needs research to digital library design?

End user searching and filtering

Organization, description and representation of information

Which methods of organization can be generalized for digital libraries applications? Which cannot? How can methods developed for single database, single system applications be adapted to multiple database distributed applications?

How well do current standards and structures work, such as the Anglo-American Cataloging Rules (AACR), Machine Readable Cataloging (MARC), SGML, TEI, UNICODE, etc.? How do these standards interact and conflict? What new standards are needed? How useful will these and other standards be in facilitating multi-lingual, multi-media, multi-level information retrieval in the Global Information Infrastructure?

Search capabilities for users

What search capabilities are specific to individual problem domains and which are generic? How should problem domain areas be divided? By subject area (e.g., science, medicine, arts), by age group (children, adults), by problem goal (e.g., fundamental research, business application), by form of content (text, numeric, graphics, moving images, sound), etc.

Interface design for information retrieval

What human-computer interaction principles can be applied to the information retrieval environment and which are unique to IR? How can we extend interface design to encompass a broader definition of the information process cycle? How can we facilitate interaction among the various digital libraries communities, and the related communities providing the technical computing and communications infrastructure on which digital libraries rely?

MODERATOR:

Efthimis N. Efthimiadis
Assistant Professor
Department of Library and Information Science
Graduate School of Education & Information Studies
University of California at Los Angeles
241 GSE&IS Building,
Mailbox 951520
405 Hilgard Avenue,
Los Angeles, CA 90095-1520
tel: 310-825-8975;
fax: 310-206-4460;

efthimis@ucla.edu

PANELISTS: TBA

National Information Policy Caught in the Digital Revolution

Sponsoring Organization: SIG IFP (Information Policy)

Session Abstract

The Digital Revolution is challenging the ability of policy makers, information providers, and users to adapt to new information management requirements. We see approaches like the application of export and security laws to software and information. The frenzy of corporations to conduct business in the electronic era and publish electronically may drive significant changes in our current rather haphazard national information policy. Legislation has already been introduced to implement parts of the "White Paper" on copyright and intellectual property, making changes which could affect the rights of both users and publishers in ways yet to be seen. This panel will discuss the current status of copyright and intellectual property reform, the Freedom of Information Act including electronic FOIA, A-130, Paperwork Reduction Act (PRA) and other aspects of national information policy as they are affected by the digital revolution.

Laws as apparently unconnected as munitions export laws are being applied to software and information.

Bonnie Cooper Carroll, Information International, Moderator

Daniel C. Duncan, Vice President, Government Relations, Information
        Industry Association
Donald Johnson, Director, National Technical Information Service
TBA, the user perspective

Finding Information on the Net

Sponsoring Organization: SIG PUB (Information Generation and Publishing)

Session Abstract

The net is a vast database of valuable information, but only now is the knowledge of information science being applied to making that information more accessible through indexes, searchers, and feedback. Three experts in search and retrieval will discuss the current state of Internet/Web indexing and search engines and what will soon be coming. This will include Yahoo, Net First, Lycos, Alta Vista, WAIS, Web Crawlers and other such systems.

Marjorie M.K. Hlava, Access Innovations, Moderator

John Sullivan, OCLC, Net First
Brewster Kahle, Founder of WAIS, Inc.

The CommuniStation Project at Rutgers: An Exploration of Democracy in Learning

A Panel

Session Abstract

This panel is intended to explore the relationship of technology in the classroom through the case of the CommuniStation project at Rutgers University. CommuniStation is an interactive multimedia undergraduate research tutorial The program is media-rich, incorporating sound, images, animation, movies, and text in its repertoire. Its real benefit to the classroom is that it provides a variety of navigational opportunities utilizing the hypertextual capabilities of the Netscape software application which provides its interface. The philosophical underpinnings which guided the design of CommuniStation place high value on personalized, interactive, and engaged learning.

The development of CommuniStation is a collaborative effort between Kathleen Burnett, a Rutgers professor whose research and teaching involves the design, production and evaluation of new information technologies, Nancy Roth, a Rutgers professor who teaches the required undergraduate course in communication research for which CommuniStation was designed, and David Petroski, a doctoral student at the School of Communication, Information and Library Studies. Multimedia examples are created by students enrolled in the MLS and MCIS programs at the School of Communication, Information and Library Studies in partial satisfaction of course requirements.

The panel is particularly applicable to the convention theme, "The Digital Revolution: Assessing the Impact on Business, Education and Social Structures." because it addresses the issues of collaborative ("democratic") learning and the ways that technology may affect learning processes. The overall view of the panel is that technology provides an opportunity to break the bounds of the "traditional classroom" as we know it, enhancing the richness of learning experiences for both educators and students alike. The panel, consisting of three paper presentations , will examine various issues that are relevant to how technology can make the learning experience more collaborative and rewarding for students . The first presentation will be a discussion of how the project was conceived and the basic theoretical issues that served as the impetus for starting the project, as well as the current status of the project. The second presentation will discuss the collaborative community of faculty, doctoral students, and masters level students involved in a multimedia design and use course, and their contributions to the production of the undergraduate hypertext project. The third paper will discuss the overall implications of a technology that allows learning to occur in a community outside the bounds of the physical classroom. A demonstration of the program will conclude the panel.

Participants:

Kathleen Burnett
Assistant Professor
School of Communication, Information and Library Studies
Rutgers University
Phone: 908/932-9760
Fax: 908/932-6916
Email:kburnett@scils.rutgers.edu

Graham McKinley
Department of Communication
Rider University
2083 Lawrenceville Rd.
Lawrenceville, NJ 08648
Phone: 609/895-5472
Email: mckinley@zodiac.rutgers.edu

David John Petroski
Doctoral Student
School of Communication, Information and
Library Studies
Rutgers University
Phone: (908) 932-7304
Fax: 908/932-6916
Email:dpetroski@scils.rutgers.edu

Nancy Roth
Assistant Professor
Dept. of Communication
School of Communication, Information and
Library Studies
Rutgers University
Phone: 908/932-1727
Fax: 908/932-6916
Email: nroth@scils.rutgers.edu

Internal Web Pages:
How Corporate and Academic Research Environments are Managing Information Access and Flow Internally Using World Wide Web Technology

Sponsoring Organization: SIG-MGT (Management)

Session Abstract

Companies and academic departments/divisions have begun to use Web servers to facilitate communications and manage data among their researchers, without any connection to the outside world. Such systems provide a high level of security and take advantage of the easy-to-use graphical user interface and management features of web servers. Proprietary software and custom applications can be loaded on the server and clients to facilitate these goals. It has been estimated that about 80 percent of Netscape's revenue comes from selling software that supports corporate intranets.

This panel will highlight three such servers, two from corporate research, and one from academic research. Each speaker will discuss use of the servers by researchers and staff, focusing on how this new technology is facilitating research and communication; how the technology is being managed; the roles of information professionals; and what new challenges have arisen from the server implementation.

Session Organizer:

Michael R. Leach
Chair-Elect, SIG-MGT
Head Librarian
Physics Research Library
Harvard University
17 Oxford St., Cambridge, MA 02138
(617) 495-2878 (phone)
(617) 495-0416 (fax)
leach@phys2.harvard.edu
library@huhepl.harvard.edu

Presenters:

J. Michael Kenyon
Systems Analyst
Texas Instruments Semiconductor Group
Texas Instruments
SC Group Library
P.O. Box 655303 MS 8240
Dallas, TX 75265
Phone: 214-997-2138
Fax: 214-997-2139
kenyon@ti.com

Lisa Mitchell

Information Specialist
The Charles Stark Draper Laboratory, Inc.
Technical Information Center - MS 74
555 Technology Sq.
Cambridge, MA 02139
Phone: (617) 258-3555
FAX: (617) 258-1919
emitchell@draper.com

Michael R. Leach
Director
Harvard University, Physics Research
Harvard University, Physics Research Library
17 Oxford St., Cambridge, MA 02138
Phone: (617) 495-2878
Fax: (617) 495-0416
leach@phys2.harvard.edu

Moderator:

Helen M. Manning
Technical Information Manager
Texas Instruments Incorporated
P.O. Box 655303, MS 8222
Dallas, TX 75265
Phone: (214)997-2523
fax: (214)997-2504
hmanning@ti.com

Health Care Information Technology: Changing the Way Society Seeks Health Care

Sponsoring Organization: SIG-MED (Medical Information systems)

Session Abstract

Nowhere will the Digital Revolution have greater personal impact than in the delivery of health care. SIGMED presents a panel of experts who explore the efforts now underway to leverage digital technologies to improve the quality of health care, improve access, and enable patients to be more involved in maintaining their own health status.

Health care consumers generally find the only evidence of computer use is the bill they receive at the end of the process. Health care providers in primary care practice find few computer based tools to assist them in caring for their patients. Only health care administrators, who heavily utilize data processing tools to manage health care delivery, readily perceive the indispensable benefits that information gathering and analysis bring their enterprises. The Digital Revolution will see medical care move from making only partial use of computer capabilities to making aggressive use of information analysis and communications to meet the nations health care needs and expectations.

Panelists will discuss major efforts being undertaken in health care delivery, including issues involving provider education, information capture and analysis, and information delivery. Future health care information systems will be important everywere that people seek care: in clinicians' offices, in wellness centers, or in their homes. These systems will underline the economic nature of medical information itself. Once collected reliably and aggregated across significant populations, health care information will be an essential asset for planning and delivering care. Acquiring and selling health care information will be an important industry, and one that will make information security and confidentiality a major issue. The society will benefit, however, from a narrowing of the care quality gap that exists between those served at major medical centers and those seeking care at small, remote locations. By delivering needed information directly to the place where people go for their care, systems will ensure that everyone gets the best care available every time.

The forum will draw on academic, industry and clinical resources to review why there is growing investment in medical information management. Our panelists will discuss how these systems will work, and the important role that information science specialists must play in extending the present efforts in the business, educational and social spheres to the population in general.

Session Organizer:

Douglas M. Stetson, MD
Principal Scientist
J. D. Stetson Associates, Inc.
1276 Eleventh Avenue, Suite 201
San Francisco, CA 94122-2203
voice/fax 415/681-5566
dstetson@jdsa.com

Business viewpoint: Clinical Information Systems: The Clinical and Business Case for Significant Investment.

Presenter:
TBA. Kaiser point of contact for member's use after presentation:

Kirsten Cherry
Communications Manager
The Permanente Medical Care Program Clinical Information Systems Group
1800 Harrison St
Oakland, CA 94612-2998
510-267-5670 voice
510-267-5378 fax
ciskmc@ncal.kaiperm.org

Abstract:

Kaiser Permanante is agressively developing a new and comprehensive Clinical Infomation System (CIS) to directly support the practicing physician and other caregivers who provide health care services to members. Automated, easily accessible clinical infomation that supports decision making between caregivers and members is the main feature of the effort.

The new system will improvement management, administration and reporting of the care delivery process. Achieving the Kaiser Permanante vision requires world class technology solutions that will ultimately deliver the largest, most sophisticated private sector system of its kind.

The Kaiser Permanente Clinical Information System speaker will address the strategic and tactical implications of delivering a comprehensive CIS and how the organization expects to realize dramffic improvement in every aspect of the care delivery process.

Education Viewpoint: New Media: The Revolutionary Vehicle for Healthcare Delivery.

Presenter:

Donna Hill Howes, RN, MS
President and Executive Producer 98.6 Productions and
Executive Producer
LMA Film and Video, Inc and Times Mirror/Mosby Publishing
2125 Oak Grove Road, Suite 200
Walnut Creek, CA 94598
510-944 5337 voice
510-947-5341 fax
103706.2702@compuserve.com

Abstract:

The new media promise revolutionary changes for health care. The impact of the new media on consumer information and patient education is key to driving change. We are poised to provide better preventive measures, better health, more targeted sales of pharmaceuticals and managed care.

Today pioneering efforts are spreading; they presage tomorrow's reality: Virtual Medicine, delivering capabilities such as Telepresence Surgery allowing a surgeon in one site to perform surgery on a patient at a remote site; Distance Learning, redefined as doctors and nurses in Singapore, the Middle East and Idaho all become classmates in the same three year graduate course, "The Business of Medicine" offered electronically by the Johns Hopkins University, Schools of Medicine and Continuing Medical Education; and 3-D virtual reality consumer shopping were customers select their health care supplies interactively through television.

Ultimately, the new media will result in reucing the high cost of health care in the country while empowering the consumers by providing them with desease management and prevention strategies. Information science will lead the way.

Development Viewpoint: Impact of Clinician Oriented Computer-based Tools on Outpatient Care

Presenter:
Dr. Daniel Essin Associate Director, Information
Systems Department University of Southern California
Los Angeles, CA 213/226-3188
essin@usc.edu

Dr. Essin has developed a user-friendly documentation system for clinicians. He has a fundamental understanding of where information search and delivery has impact on medical care at the point of care.

Societal Viewpoint: Value Creation in Health Care: Extending Patient Participation in Health Care Management

Presenter:
Art Schiller
President
Value Creation Strategies
PO Box 42
Lincoln, MA 01773
617/259-9201 voice
617-259-8950 fax
ASchiller@aol.com

Mr. Schiller is a consultant in medical information systems and a board member of a new enterprise involving retirement communities relying on computer based systems for communication and enhanced access to health care. His clients are large government and commercial organizations that deal with telemedicine and rural health care, among others. His broad based, real world experience will serve as a valuable anchor to other more topical speakers.

Legacy Data: Conversion and Retention

Sponsoring Organization: SIG PUB (Information Generation and Publishing)

Session Abstract

Electronic retention of an organization's "legacy data" can increase accessibility while diminishing cost and space requirements. What items from paper records beyond text need to be retained; are bit mapped images more acceptable than SGML encoded text in establishing authenticity? What is the status of electronic signatures? What are the pitfalls of a conversion and once converted, what do you do with the Data? DTD evolvement and the conversion progresses is a moving target. These and other issues in converting legacy data to electronic form will be explored by leaders in recent corporate conversions.

Buzzy Basch, Basch Associates, Moderator

Craig Booher, Kimberly Clark
Jay Ven Eman, Access Innovations
Joe Knudson, U. S. Pharmacopeial

Teaching During the Revolution:
The Implications of Digital Curricula

Sponsoring Organization: SIG-LAN

Session Abstract

The structure and presentation of information becomes more fluid in a digital environment, and those who develop those structures greatly influence the curriculum. As information professionals move from coordinating access to information to creating and structuring that access, they also move from a support role to active collaboration with teachers and researchers. This revolution changes the way educators and information professionals work and the way students learn.

This session will compare three innovative projects at the University of Southern California. Each exemplifies a different approach to digital curricula and research.

The first project, Fine Arts 121, was a prototype which used the World Wide Web to deliver locally-mounted digital materials for a course on western art since 1500. The faculty member wanted to change the way she taught her class, and move from lecturer to interactive facilitator. While this project was initiated by the faculty member, she sought the help of the Library and the Center for Scholarly Technology to construct her Web site. The instructor used the Web site to encourage students to interact with the material and each other independent of class sessions or location. URL: http://www.usc.edu/dept/finearts/fa121/

Because of the success of Fine Arts 121, the Library decided to expand this approach through the Jumpstart Program for Curricular Technology. This program takes the USC Library into new areas of direct involvement in curricular design and multimedia technology implementation. Every semester, the Library reviews faculty proposals and selects three new projects for development. Each project features an interdisciplinary project team of librarians, computer professionals, and academics to develop leading edge curricular technology projects. In this way, technology is applied to real-world teaching needs and disseminated across the campus through Web pages. URL: http://www.usc.edu/Library/CST/jumpstart.html

The first two projects focus on specific courses. The third project, the Information System for Los Angeles (ISLA), strives to create a research tool that can be used by a variety of groups both within and outside the University. ISLA will be a digital research archive of materials about Los Angeles in multiple information formats accessed through a unified interface. Its scope includes a variety of information types from many historical periods, linked by spatial and temporal coordinates. The project will combine library retrieval methods with geographic information systems (GIS). URL: http://www.usc.edu/Library/ISLA/

Session Organizer:

Karen Howell
Head, Networked Information Development, Center for Scholarly Technology
University of Southern California

University Library, Los Angeles, CA 90089-0182
Phone: 213 740-2933
Fax: 213 740-7713
khowell@usc.edu

Presenters:

Karen M. G. Howell
Head, Networked Information Development, Center for Scholarly Techology
University Library, University of Southern California
Los Angeles, CA 90089-0182
Phone: 213-740-2933
Fax: 213-740-7713
khowell@usc.edu

Lucy Siefert Wegner
Director, Center for Scholarly Technology
University Library, University of Southern California
Los Angeles, CA 90089-0182
Phone: 213 740-8819
Fax: 213 740-7713
lwegner@usc.edu

Marianne Afifi
Systems Development Librarian, Center for Scholarly Technology
University Library, University of Southern California
Los Angeles, CA 90089-0182
Phone: 213-740-8817
Fax: 213-740-7713
afifi@usc.edu

SGML Authoring Tools

Sponsoring Organization: SIG PUB (Information Generation and Publishing)

Session Abstract

There is much written and presented on the theories involved in the SGML, CALS, and DTD standard and creation. There is, however, precious little done on who has implemented, how is it implemented, descriptions of running systems using SGML or associated software. This workshop will cover the actual logistics of implementing SGML in a production environment and a review of the pros and cons of individual authoring tools.

Marjorie M.K. Hlava, Access Innovations
Patrick Sauer, Access Innovations

Evolving Information Economics:
Responses to the Digital Revolution

Session Sponsor: SIG CRS (Computerized Retrieval Services)

Session Organizer:
M. J. Norton, Ph.D.
Assistant Professor
School of Library and Information Science
University of Southern Mississipi
Southern Station Bx 5146
Hattiesburg, MS 39406-5146
601-266-4228
fax 601-266-5774
mjnorton@whale.st.usm.edu

Session Abstract

The session will present three papers related to the evolution of issues and policies brought about by the digital revolution. Management communications and structures have been significantly impacted by the digital revolution. How is information value affected by these new hierarchies? How do some of these structures affect the provision of resources? A report on the issues and concerns generated by the increased digitization of records will be presented by a traditional database vendor service representative. Discussion of changes in the business climate and conduct will be presented. Information economics has to develop new theories for evaluating value in a digitial world. The value of short term information trends as reflected in curriculum development will be examined as an example of issues and problems inherent to the digitial revolution. Methods for evolving better mechanisms for anticpating marketability will be suggested based on information economics theory.

Digital Accessibility: Information Value in Changing Hierarchies

June Lester, DLS
Professor and Director
School of Library and Information Studies
University of Oklahoma
401 West Brooks, Room 120
Norman, OK 73019-0528
Jlester@uoknor.edu

With access to authority levels merely a few keystrokes away the rigid managerial hierarchy has experienced contractions of layers. Increased and nearly instant access as well as heightened expectations for responses create demands for attention which may impact management itself. Planning to provide more resources in the digitial age requires new forms of resource control techniques, including better time managment and evaluation of information value. So many voices can now be heard that new structures and economies must be considered. Addressing all the needs of all the players on the digital information field will require some creativity. Will the modified management structures be able to address the digitial revolution?

Practical Economics: Digital Impacts on the Database Vendors

Anne Caputo, Director of Academic and Library Programs
KNIGHT-RIDDER INFORMATION, Inc.
1525 Wilson Blvd. Suite 650
Arlington, VA 22209
703-908-2388
Anne_Caputo@corp.dialog.com

Descriptive and practical discussion about the issues and concerns that impact the evolving pricing models currently in use and likely to be in use in the short term future. A presentation about changes in the way traditional vendors think about pricing/charging models in the new age of,

- ☐ Internet availability of data.
- ☐ Changing technical capabilities for storage and communication of data.
- ☐ Changing contractual arrangements with the data holders/owners.
- ☐ Changes in the customer/user base and the impact of the end-user on pricing.
- ☐ What is the meaning of 'value-added service' in the new paradigm?

Short Takes in the Digitial Revolution

M. J. Norton, Ph.D.
Assistant Professor, School of Library and Information Science
University of Southern Mississippi
Hattiesburg, MS 39406-5146
601-266-4228
mjnorton@whale.st.usm.edu

In accelerating motion the digital revolution is transforming the fundamental compentencies expected of a number of professions. Striving to keep ahead of the digital edge forces short term curricular decisions that may have less than desireable impacts. Additional measures for identifying long term market positions need to be developed. Risk taking and reduction of uncertainty will be re-examined in the context of the digital revolution. Where will the future employment markets be for information professionals -- can we better predict areas of demand?

The Digital Revolution in Education: Approaches to Evaluation

Sponsoring Organization: SIG-LAN

Session Abstract

One can scarcely open a newspaper or professional journal these days without seeing an article on the use of technology in education. Many of these articles begin and end with sweeping statements about the effects technology is having and will have on educational processes and outcomes. However, few of them present any concrete evidence on which to base these claims. This situation is reflective of the current state of evaluation of the use of technology in education. We are only at the beginning of the evaluation process.

The focus of this presentation is on the effects that the Digital Revolution is having, or will have, on academic institutions. These effects, as well as issues surrounding them and methodologies to investigate them, will be explored by panel members, each of whom is currently conducting research in this area. Panel members will discuss their pioneering efforts to begin to understand: what we should be measuring, how we should go about measuring it, and whether there currently is any early evidence to support claims that technology is changing the face of education.

Session Organizer:

Cynthia L. Lopata
Assistant Professor
Syracuse University
School of Information Studies
4-193 Center for Science & Technology
Syracuse, NY 13244
315-443-4157
FAX 315-443-5806
cllopata@mailbox.syr.edu

Presenters:

Rob Kling
Professor
Dept. of Information & Computer Science
University of California, Irvine
14 Angell St.
Irvine, CA 92717
714-856-5955
FAX 714-824-4056
kling@ics.uci.edu
"Scholarly Communication & Information Technology Use in Context"
Rob Kling is currently working on a study, funded by the U.S. Dept. of Education, to examine how much faculty and students use digital library resources and to identify institutional practices that enhance their effective use.

Stephen Ehrmann
Manager, Educational Strategies Program
Annenberg/CPB Project
Corporation for Public Broadcasting
Washington, DC
sehrmann@linknet.com
"The Flashlight Project to Develop & Share Evaluation Procedures"
Stephen Ehrmann is currently working on the Flashlight Project, a three-year
program, started last January, to develop measures which universities and their
departments can use to study their educational strategies for using technologies.

Cynthia L. Lopata
Assistant Professor
Syracuse University
School of Information Studies
4-193 Center for Science & Technology
Syracuse, NY 13244
315-443-4157
FAX 315-443-5806
cllopata@mailbox.syr.edu
"Barriers to the Development & Use of IT Performance Networks in the Academic
Environment"
Cynthia Lopata is currently working on a project, funded by the U.S. Dept. of
Education, to develop measures for assessing the performance and impacts of
networking in the academic environment.

Suggested Moderator:

Michael Stallings
Systems Analyst
Microsoft Library
Microsoft Corporation
One Microsoft Way, 13/1259
Redmond, WA 98052
206-703-2114
FAX 206-936-7329
mstall@microsoft.com

Planning GII: Implications for Education and Training
SIG ED

Ching-Chih Chen
Simmons College
Moderator

Manuscript not received at time of publication.

Network-Centered Computing: Web-Based Interfaces for Organizational Databases

Sponsoring Organization: SIG-HCI (Human-Computer Interaction)

Session Abstract

The digital revolution has entered a new phase which is exemplified by the focus of Comdex 1995. That focus is the Internet and the World Wide Web. Comdex, which annually draws over 200,000 exhibitors and attendees, is the largest computer show in the world. The last time Comdex had an overall unifying theme was in the late 80's when the focus was on CD-ROMs and multimedia. The exhibitors and attendees at that conference envisioned wide-spread use of CD-ROMs and multimedia which would extend even to the consumer market. This vision has largely become reality, with both Dataquest and IDC, computer marketing research firms, confirming that most PCs sold in the last year have included multimedia capabilities.

Given the enormous resources, in terms of creativity, marketing and capital, that the participants at Comdex control, their predictions that we are moving into a computing world that is centered on a global information net should be taken seriously. IBM CEO, Louis Gerstner, in his Comdex 1995 speech, called this phase of the digital revolution "Network-centered computing." As corporations, organizations, and educational institutions move to enlist in this revolution, there is a growing awareness that the very basic hypertext capabilities of current World Wide Web applications are not powerful enough to satisfy end-users' need for information.

Software firms in all areas are moving to add value to the standard Web page. One aspect of this trend is the use of Web page interfaces to provide access an organization's information.

The use of the Web for a front-end provides organizations a relatively inexpensive way to offer distributed network services to its employees and customers.

This presentation will focus on the design aspects of Web-based interfaces to databases where the networking capability of the organization is provided by the Internet and the interface and database is built around Web-based authoring and programming tools.

Working prototypes of these types of applications will be shown.

Session Organizers:

Janette B. Bradley
System Developer
Intelligent Information Group
2100 Courtland Cr.
Carrollton, TX 75007
(voice) 214/492-6517
(fax) 214/492-3999
jbradley@sol.acs.unt.edu

Guillermo A. Oyarce
The Internet Store
MIS, Manager
P.O. Box 331565,
Fort Worth, TX 76163
(voice) 817/545-1625
(voice) 817/267-3155
(fax) 817/545-4883
goyarce@unt.edu

The Museum Education Site License Project: Networked Delivery of High Quality Images and Accompanying Text

Sponsoring Organization: SIG VIS

Session Abstract

This presentation will discuss the technical and logistical issues involved in the delivery and exchange of museum images and textual data as part of a large multi-site collaborative project.

The Museum Education Site License Project (MESL) is a major demonstration project designed to identify and resolve the problems of licensing and delivery of images and accompanying text from content providers to groups of content users.

The project is serving as a laboratory for developing and testing the legal, administrative and technical mechanisms needed to enable the full educational use of museum collections through routine delivery of high-quality museum images and information to educational institutions.

University participants include: the Universities of Illinois, Maryland, Virginia, and Michigan, as well as Columbia, Cornell, and American Universities. Content providers include: the Library of Congress, the National Gallery of Art, the National Museum of American Art, the Harvard University Art Museums, the Houston Museum of Fine Arts, the George Eastman House, and the Fowler Museum of Cultural History.

During the two-year project period, the participants are exploring standards and mechanisms for exchanging images and data between institutions, mounting and delivering this information to university users, development of tools for incorporating images and data into the instructional process, and develop parameters for licensing of this type of content.

The speakers will discuss their experiences in the exchange of image and text data between museums and universities, and the issues faced in mounting and delivering this information to their end users through the first full year of the MESL project. They will focus on the necessity of standards for multi-institution distribution of image and text data, and will also discuss the infrastructure needed for delivering multimedia information. Finally, they will talk about the experience of collaboration between different institutions, as well as the collaboration between different units at their own institution (library, computer center, academic departments).

Howard Besser
University of Michigan School of Information and Library Studies
Ann Arbor, Michigan

Jennier Trant
Getty Art History Information Program
Santa Monica, California

David Milman
Columbia University
New York, New York

Role of the Science and Technology Information Professional in Meeting the Needs of Scientists in the Digital Environment

Sponsoring Organization: SIG-ED (Education)

Session Organizer:

Samantha K. Hastings
Assistant Professor
University of North Texas
POB 13796
Denton, TX 76203-6796
817/565-2445
Fax: 817/565-3101
hastings@lis.unt.edu

Presenters:

Ed Kownslar
"An Evaluation of Digital Resources for Meeting the Information Needs of Chemists."

Gary Littlefield
"Tele-Medicine to Meet the Medical Information Needs of Native Americans."

Kenneth G. Madden
"Flight Safety Information: Format, Production, and Distribution in a Digital Environment."

Marie S. Nuchols
"Effect of Digital Information Formats in Meeting the Needs of an AIDS Resource Center."

Suggested Moderator:

Samantha K. Hastings
Assistant Professor
University of North Texas
POB 13796
Denton, TX 76203-6796
817/565-2445
Fax: 817/565-3101
hastings@lis.unt.edu

Expanding the Classroom:
The Role of Electronic Media in Science Education

Session Sponsor: SIG STI (Scientific and Technical Information Systems)

Moderator:
Natalie A. Schoch
College of Library and Information Services
University of Maryland, College Park, MD

Session Abstract:

Innovations in electronic technologies offer exciting new modes for delivering scientific information in educational settings ranging from graduate science education to K-12. No longer confined to flat diagrams, data and text on a two-dimensional printed page, electronic resources are able to convey complex scientific information such as three dimensional images, models, movement and sounds. Using electronic media, students can examine and manipulate complex images, data sets, and other information. In addition to products such as CD-ROMs and software on diskette, many sources of electronic teaching materials are being developed and distributed via the Internet. This session will provide a forum for discussion of innovative electronic materials which are being developed and used by science educators.

UNDERSTANDING SCIENCE: VISUALIZING THE MOLECULAR WORLD AND SIMULATING THE EQUIPMENT

Gabriele Wienhausen, Department of Biology and Barbara Sawrey, Department of Chemistry & Biochemistry, University of California, San Diego, La Jolla, CA

We have developed an interactive lab manual for the wet-lab, Biochemical Techniques, to improve student preparation and cognition. The software makes lab time more efficient, it aids understanding of the processes that take place in the lab, and acts as a self-paced tutorial and as reference material.

Students can review an experiment, learn more about the main technique being used, or can practice math skills they must apply in the lab. On-screen information, screen features, and overall layout were carefully designed taking into account pedagogical and cognitive implications of the learning process. On-screen information is presented to the students in a non-linear fashion. Numerous branching points, layers and "food-for-thought questions" force the students to become actively involved in the learning process. Photos, movies, illustrations, and animation help students visualize the experimental steps and the equipment set-up, as well as the events happening on the molecular level. Simulations allow students to practice the use or set-up of equipment. Built into the modules is a system that allows electronic communication between instructor and students, as well as on-line library research.

INTEGRATING THE WORLD WIDE WEB INTO CHEMICAL INSTRUCTION

Kathy Whitley,
Science & Engineering Library,
University of California,
San Diego, La Jolla, CA

Chemical information lends itself particularly well to the visual nature of the World Wide Web. Numerical and bibliographic databases, electronic journals, and tutorials abound on the net. Through the UCSD Science & Engineering Library's Internet Faculty Partnership Program, librarians have teamed with academic faculty members to compile course specific web pages and to train students in methods of Web access. The author will show examples of chemistry course pages and an online Netscape tutorial as well as discuss ways of encouraging academic faculty to "get on the Net."

Author Index

Subject Index

Surveillance technologies, 206

WWW, see also Internet

ASIS Mid-Year 1996 Conference Committees

Technical Program Committee

José-Marie Griffiths, Chair

Anne Bishop
Phil Doty
Carol Hert
Paul Kantor
Cecilia Preston
David Rodgers

Local Arrangements Committee

Pat Earnest, Chair

Referees for Contributed Papers

The papers contributed to this volume were selected from abstracts of manuscripts reviewed by two referees. Papers judged appropriate to the conference by both referees were accepted, contingent on revisions suggested by the referees.

The Contributed Papers Chair gratefully acknowledges the time and effort given to the reviewing process by the following people:

Claire Beghtol
Anne Bishop
Heting Chu
Rowan Fairgrove
Martha Henderson
Carol Hert
Joe Janes
Ling Hwey Jeng
Don King
Don Kraft
Michael Leach
Geoffrey Liu
Beth Logan
Gregory McClellan
James R. Mullins
Nester Osorio
David L. Rodgers
Howard Rosenbaum
Gail Thornberg
Peiling Wang

Preparation of the Proceedings

The Proceedings of this Conference were assembled in a variety of ways.

Approximately half of the Contributed Papers were received in printed format the other half were received in a wide variety of electronic formats. The Editor gratefully acknowledges the assistance of Ms. Traci Yavas, masters student at The University of Tennessee School of Information Sciences, who spent countless hours working with these documents.

She was ably assisted by Ms. Kimbra Wilder, also a student in the program.

The SIG sessions were prepared by printing out the Session Descriptions from the conference Web page. HTML coding by Ms. Catherine E. Ingram at Indiana University is gratefully acknowledged. The production process was managed by Ms. Yavas of Tennessee and by Ms. Priscilla Seaman, also a student in the SIS program at Tennessee.

Production of the 1996 Mid-Year Conference Web Site

The production of the proceedings and the development of the conference web site went hand-in-hand: the web site served as a collaborative tool for authors and conference committees to keep current on what had been received, corrections to titles and the schedule, and similar management tasks.

Several papers were provided in html format, and these papers were linked to the program itself. It was intended that the conference proceedings would reflect the state of research at the time the papers were physically due (1 March 1996) for the printed proceedings; authors were encouraged to prepare more current versions of findings to be added to the program at the web site, closer to the date of the actual conference. At least one author took advantage of this opportunity, and solicited comments via the ASIS listserv (ASIS-L@asis.org) on his paper as available on the web site. Additional information, based on these comments, would be added into his paper presentation at the conference itself.

At this writing (3 April 1996), plans are to keep the web site intact and accessible from the ASIS page at http://www.asis.org. Further updates to the program, papers, and other conference matters will be available there.

The editor gratefully acknowledges the contributions of the following people in the construction of the Web site:

University of Tennessee
>   Alice Kirby (initial design and maintenance)
>   George Hoemann (graphics and forms)
>   William Rosener (forms and support in the review process)
>   Chris Hodge (author index)
>   Priscilla Seaman (html preparation)

Indiana University
>   Catherine E. Ingram (html preparation)

Jeanette Bradley (imagemaps and graphics)

And,

>   --the authors (Steve Harter, Howard Rosenbaum, Michael Stallings, William Rosener) who prepared full versions of their papers for the site,

--the authors and session organizers who checked in on their own entries to be sure they were up to date.

AMERICAN SOCIETY for INFORMATION SCIENCE

1996 Mid-Year Meeting

Marriot Mission Valley Hotel, San Diego, CA
18-22 May 1996

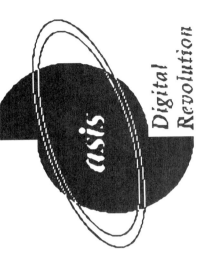

Final Program (as of 3 April 1996)
Best viewed with Netscape 2.0

Digital libraries   Internet topics

Author Index	Conference Page

Date	Event
Saturday, May 18, 1996	**Professional Development, 9:00 a.m - 5:00 p.m.** **Copyright in an Electronic World**, with Mickie Voges, Director of the Legal Information Center and Associate Professor of Law, Chicago-Kent College of Law **Javascript / Java Programming**, with Kemer Thomson. 1:00 p.m. - 5:00 p.m. **Practical HTML: A Hands-on Workshop**, with Roy Tennant, Manager, Information Systems Instruction and Support, University of California - Berkeley Tours: Behind the Scenes at the San Diego Zoo, 9:30 a.m. Tijuana, Mexico - Shopping with Lunch, 9:00 a.m. **Governance** Budget and Finance / Executive Committee, 6:00 p.m.

391

Professional Development, 9:00 a.m. - 5:00 p.m.

Managing Web Servers: The Technical, Fiscal, and Personnel Issues, with Michael Leach, Head Librarian, Physics Research Library, Harvard University ❦ **Developing a Quality Presence on the Net**, with Howard McQueen, President, McQueen and Associates, Inc. ❦ **Advanced HTML Workshop**, with Roy Tennant, Manager, Information Systems Instruction and Support, University of California - Berkeley ❦ **From Boolean/Thesaurus to Non-Boolean/Free Text Searching: An Information Survey in Historical Perspective**, with Everett Brenner, Consultant ❦ **Technology Based Information Management Using Lotus Notes**, with Kris Liberman, Manager, Market Intelligence Tools and Technologies, Market Intelligence Group, Lotus, and Walter Stine, Director of Information Management, Giga Information Group

Tours:
A Day at the San Diego Wild Animal Park, 10:00 a.m.

Governance
9:00 a.m. - 12:00 noon: ASIS Board of Directors
12:00 noon - 3:13 p.m. Leadership Development Program
3:30 p.m. - 4:15 p.m. Chapter/SIG Workshop Discussion
4:30 p.m. - 5:15 p.m. SIG Cabinet Meeting
5:15 p.m. - 6:00 p.m. Chapter Assembly Meeting

6:00 p.m. - 7:30 p.m.: Welcome Reception, around the pool at the Marriott Mission Valley

Sunday May 19, 1996

MONDAY, 20 MAY 1996

9:00 a.m. - 10:30 a.m. Monday

Plenary Session:

Sherry Turkle. Massachusetts Institute of Technology.

Professor Turkle's most recent research is on the psychology of computer-mediated communication which is reported in her latest book, **Life on the Screen: Identity in the Age of the Internet**. Among her other writings are: "Project Athena at MIT" and "Growing up in an Age of Intelligent Machines: Reconstruction of the Psychological and Reconsiderations of the Human."

Herb Brody's Interview with Professor Turkle.

The cover of the April 1996 issue of Wired which features her; the page from HotWired on Pamela McCorduck's interview with her.

393

10:45 a.m. - 12:15 p.m. Monday

Social Impact I: Information Policies

Alexandria Declaration of Principles and GII, Ching-chih Chen, Simmons College

Big Brother is Watching you: The Panopticon in the Information Age, Julie Albright, University of Southern California

Assessing Impact from the Outset: Establishing a Strategic Research Program and Cooperative Research Policy for a New Community Network, Linda Schamber, University of North Texas

Educational Impact I: Digital Libraries I: Building and Modeling ✎

Understanding Digital Library Use: From Information Retrieval to Communications Support, Lisa Covi, University of California

Digital Library Models and Prospects, Gregory Newby, University of Illinois at Urbana-Champaign

Electronic Scientific Publications: The Role of the Gatekeepers, SIG STI Natalie Schoch, University of Maryland, Moderator

Business I: Changes in Directions

An Integrated Approach to Creating the Information-Enabled Organization: Actions in Support of Change, Michael O. Luke, Whiteshell Laboratories

Web Usage by American Fortune 500 Business Organizations, Yin Zhang and Hong Xu, Graduate School of Library and Information Science University of Illinois at Urbana-Champaign ✎

"Information Markets and the Information Highway; Building New Bridges, not New Roads," Rosalie Liccardo Pacula and Gary Schneider, University of San Diego

394

1:30 p.m. - 3:00 p.m. Monday

Social Impact 2: Access and Control ☚
The WebSCOUT Resource Discovery and Presentation System for the World-Wide Web, William Rosener, University of Tennessee

Information Retrieval in Cyberspace, Dania Bilal Meghabghab and George V. Meghabghab, Valdosta State University

Defining the Undefinable: The Unit of Control for Electronic Resources, Ling H. Jeng, University of Kentucky

Documenting the Revolution: Electronic Recordkeeping and the Internet Public Library, Cory T. Brandt and Christopher Zegers, University of Michigan

Educational Impact 2: Challenges to Traditional Libraries
Electronic Indexes and the End User, Michael G. Bernier and Enid L. Zafran, The Bureau of National Affairs

Extending The Kantor-Saracevic Derived Taxonomy of Value in Using Library Services: Three Definitions from the Microsoft Library Use-Statistics Database, Michael Stallings, Microsoft Corporation

The Mann Library Gateway - A Cataloger's Tale, Gregory A. McClellan, Cornell University

Business Impact 2: Impact Assessment
Assessing The Impact of Information on Small Business: A Lisrel Model Approach, Jean Tague-Sutcliffe and Liwen Q. Vaughan, University of Western Ontario

"Hispanic Managers Communicating Electronically in Anglo Businesses: Potential Interactions Between Culture and Technology," Gary P. Schneider and Carmen M. Barcena, University of San Diego

"Events-Based Financial Reporting: The Potential of the Internet," Gary P. Schneider and Carol M. Bruton, University of San Diego ☚

The Digital Revolution and the Cattle Ranching Community, Amanda Spink, University of North Texas

Digital Library Trends and Issues: An NSF Perspective, SIG CR Efthimis N. Efthimiadis, University of California at Los Angeles, Moderator ☚

395

3:15 p.m. - 4:45 p.m. Monday

Social Impact 3: Contexts and Politics

The Politics of Webweaving, Mark Stover, Phillips Graduate Institute ☙

Client, Server, Beggarman, Thief: Can Academic Libraries and Computing Services Operations Just Get Along? Martin Rosen, Dennis Kreps, and Jacqueline F. Johnson, Indiana University Southeast

An Information Needs And Services Taxonomy for Evaluating Computerized Community Information Systems, Ronald D. Doctor and Kalyani Ankem, University of Alabama

Build it and They Will Come: A Case Study of the Creation, Development, and Refinement of an Organized Database of Internet Resources in Science and Technology, Gerry McKiernan, Iowa State University ☙

National Information Policy Caught in the Digital Revolution, **SIG IFP** Bonnie Carroll, Moderator

Finding Information on the Net, **SIG PUB** Marge Hlava, Moderator ☙

3:15 p.m. - 4:15 p.m.: The CommuniStation Project at Rutgers: An Exploration of Democracy in Learning, Kathleen Burnett, Rutgers University

4:30 p.m. - 6:00 p.m. Monday

Governance: Constitution and Bylaws, Education, and Membership Comittees

6:00 p.m. Monday

Tours: Harbor Cruise

TUESDAY, 21 MAY 1996

9:00 a.m. - 10:30 a.m. Tuesday

Plenary Session: Everett Rogers (invited)
The Homeless and their Home on the Net

10:45 a.m. - 12:15 p.m. Tuesday

Educational Impact 3: Digital Libraries II
A Hybridized Hypertext and Boolean Retrieval Model for Bibliographic Databases Dietmar Wolfram, University of Wisconsin-Milwaukee

"Fuzzy Matching as a Retrieval-Enabling Technique for Digital Libraries," T.R. Girill and Clement Luk, National Energy Research Supercomputer Center ☾

Selective Feedback for Optimal Search Nick I. Kamenoff, Monmouth University

"Approaches to Facilitating Query Formulation and Interpretation in Database Searching," Peter Jacso, University of Hawaii

Internal Web Pages: How Corporate and Academic Research Environments are Managing Access to and Flow of Information, SIG MGT Michael R. Leach, Harvard University Physics Research Library ☾

Health Care Information Technology: Changing the Way Society Sees Health Care, **SIG MED** Stetson, Douglas M., J. D. Stetson Associates, Inc.

Legacy Data: Conversion and Retention, **SIG PUB** Buzzy Basch, Basch Associates, Moderator

---

12:30 p.m. - 1:30 p.m. Tuesday

Governance: Standards, Nominations, and Proceedings Evaluation Comittees

12:30 p.m. - 3:00 p.m. Tuesday

Tours: San Diego State University Electronic Course Reserves Room

1:30 p.m. - 3:00 p.m. Tuesday

Teaching During the Revolution: The Implications of Digital Curricula, **SIG LAN** Karen M.G. Howell, University of Southern California, Moderator

SGML Authoring Tools, **SIG PUB** Marge Hlava, Moderator

Evolving Information Economics: Responses to the Digital Revolution, SIG CRS x, Moderator

Educational Impact 4: Digital Libraries III
Integration of Model-Based Interfaces and Intelligent Systems to Digital Libraries S. Narayanan, Nagesh Reddy, and Scott Walchli, Wright State University

In the Trenches of the Digital Revolution: Intellectual Freedom and the "Public" Digital Library Howard Rosenbaum, Indiana University

Measures for the Academic Networked Environment: Strategies, Guidelines and Options Cynthia L. Lopata and Charles R. McClure, Syracuse University

3:15 p.m. - 4:45 p.m. Tuesday

Social Impact 4: Information Transfer
The Impact of Electronic Journals on Scholarly Communication: A Citation and Reference Study Stephen Harter and Hak Joon Kim, Indiana University

An Electronic WWW Archive for Conference Information in Library and Information Science Mark Rorvig, University of North Texas ✪

ILL: New Models, New Ways Bill Ruane, Network Support Inc.

"A Bibliometric Analysis of Public Library World Wide Web Homepages," Richard J. Kuster, Indiana University ✪

Educational Impact 5: Teachers and Learners
Information Seeking Behavior of Science Faculty: The Impact of New Information Technologies Julie Hurd and Ann C. Weller, University of Illinios at Chicago

Some Thoughts About the Relationship Between Information and Understanding Michael O. Luke, Whiteshell Laboratories

Issues and Challenges for the Educational Environment Howard Besser, University of Michigan

The Digital Revolution in Education: Approaches to Evaluation, SIG LAN Cynthia Lopata, Syracuse University

3:15 p.m. -4:15 p.m. "Planning GII: Implications for Education and Training, SIG ED Ching-Chih Chen, Simmons College, Moderator

6:00 p.m. Tuesday

Dine-Around Dinners

WEDNESDAY, 22 May 1996

9:00 a.m. - 10:30 a.m. Wednesday

Network-centered Computing: Web-based Interfaces for Organizational Databases, **SIG HCI** Patricia Vanderburg, University of California, Moderator

The Museum Education Site License Project: Networked Delivery of High Quality Images and Accompanying Text, **SIG VIS** Howard Besser, University of Michigan, Moderator

9:00 a.m. - 10:00 a.m.: Role of the Science and Technology Information Professionals in Meeting the Needs of Scientists in the Digital Environment, **SIG-ED** Samantha K. Hastings, University of North Texas, Moderator

9:00 a.m. - 10:00 a.m.: Expanding the Classroom: The Role of Electronic Media in Science Education, **SIG STI** Natalie Schoch, University of Maryland, Moderator

10:45 a.m. - 12:15 p.m. Wednesday

Plenary Session: Arno Penzias,
Vice President for Research, AT&T Bell Labs (invited)

400

1:00 p.m. Wednesday

<u>Tours</u>: San Diego Supercomputer Center, 12:30 p.m. - 3:00 p.m.

1:00 p.m. Wednesday

Governance: ASIS Board of Directors

Questions, problems to: <u>Gretchen Whitney</u>
SIS University of Tennessee, gwhitney@utkux.utcc.utk.edu
423-974-7919, FAX 423-974-4967

The American Society for Information Science

Since 1937 ASIS has been the society for information professionals leading the search for new and better theories, techniques, and technologies to improve access to information.

ASIS brings together diverse streams of knowledge, focusing what might be disparate approaches into novel solutions to common problems. ASIS bridges the gaps not only between disciplines but also between the research that drives and the practices that sustain new developments.

For further information about ASIS, its structure, officers, programs, and other activities, please see its World Wide Web site at:

http://www.asis.org

The site is best viewed with Netscape, however it is Lynx-friendly.

Other Books of Interest from Information Today, Inc.

The Evolving Virtual Library: Visions and Case Studies
   Edited by Laverna M. Saunders ($39.50/168pp/ISBN 1-57387-013-7)

ProCite in Libraries: Applications in Bibliographic Database Management
   Edited by Deb Renee Biggs ($39.50/221pp/ISBN 0-938734-90-3)

CD-ROM Finder, 6th Edition 1995
   Kathleen Hogan and James Shelton, Editors ($69.50/520pp/ISBN 0-938734-86-5)

The Electronic Classroom: A Handbook for Education in the Electronic Environment
   Edited by Erwin Boschmann ($42.50/240pp/ISBN 0-938734-89-X)

Document Delivery Services: Issues and Answers
   By Eleanor Mitchell and Sheila Walters ($42.50/333pp/ISBN 1-57387-003-X)

Multimedia in Higher Education
   By Helen Carlson and Dennis R. Falk ($42.50/176pp/ISBN 1-57387-002-1)

CD-ROM for Library Users: A Guide to Managing and Maintaining User Access
   Paul Nicholls and Pat Ensor, Editors ($39.50/138 pp/ISBN 0-938734-95-4)

Electronic Image Communications: A Guide to Networking Image Files
   By Richard J. Nees ($39.50/95pp/ISBN 0-938734-87-3)

Navigating the Networks
   Deborah Lines Anderson, Thomas J. Galvin, & Mark D. Giguere, Editors
   ($29.95/255pp/ISBN 0-938734-85-7)

Challenges in Indexing Electronic Text and Images
   Raya Fidel, Trudi Bellardo Hahn, Edie Rasmussen, and Philip Smith, Editors
   ($39.50/316pp/ISBN 0-938734-76-8)

ASIS Thesaurus of Information Science and Librarianship
   By Jessica L. Milstead ($34.95/150pp/ISBN 0-938734-80-6)

Key Guide to Electronic Resources: Health Sciences
   Edited by Lee Hancock ($39.50/494pp/ISBN 1-57387-001-3)

Key Guide to Electronic Resources: Engineering
   Edited by Melissa McBurney ($39.50/162pp/ISBN 1-57387-008-0)

Key Guide to Electronic Resources: Agriculture
   Edited by Wilfred Drew ($39.50/124pp/ISBN 1-57387-000-5)

Key Guide to Electronic Resources: Language and Literature
   Edited by Diane Kovacs ($39.50/120pp/ISBN 1-57387-020-X)

Directory of Library Automation Software, Systems, and Servicesl
   Edited by Pamela Cibbarelli ($79.00/450pp/ISBN 1-57387-021-8)

Library Technology Consortia: Case Studies in Design and Cooperation
   Edited by Jerry Kuntz ($42.50/165pp/ISBN 0-88736-886-7)

Entertainment Technology and Tomorrow's Information Services
   Edited by Thomas E. Kinney ($34.95/128pp/ISBN 1-57387-006-4)

Information Management for the Intelligent Organization
   By Chun Wei Choo ($39.50/250pp/ISBN 1-57387-018-8)

Small Project Automation for Libraries and Information Centers
   By Jane Mandelbaum ($35.00/350pp/ISBN 0-88736-731-3)

CD-ROM Book Index
   Edited by Ann Niles ($39.50/207pp/ISBN 0-938734-98-9)

Proceedings of the 16th National Online Meeting, May 2-4, 1995
   ($55.00/448pp/ISBN 1-57387-004-8)

Annual Review of Information Science and Technology, Volume 30
   Edited by Martha Williams ($98.50/525pp/ISBN 1-57387-019-6)

To order directly from the publisher, include $3.95 postage and handling for the first book ordered and $3.25 for each additional book. Catalogs also available upon request.

Information Today, Inc., 143 Old Marlton Pike, Medford, NJ 08055, (609) 654-6266